THE MONOLOGIC IMAGINATION

THE MONOLOGIC IMAGINATION

Edited by Matt Tomlinson and Julian Millie

OXFORD
UNIVERSITY PRESS

Oxford University Press is a department of the University of Oxford. It furthers
the University's objective of excellence in research, scholarship, and education
by publishing worldwide. Oxford is a registered trade mark of Oxford University
Press in the UK and certain other countries.

Published in the United States of America by Oxford University Press
198 Madison Avenue, New York, NY 10016, United States of America.

Library of Congress Cataloging-in-Publication Data
Names: Tomlinson, Matt, 1970– editor. | Millie, Julian, 1967– editor.
Title: The monologic imagination / Matt Tomlinson and Julian Millie, eds.
Description: Oxford ; New York, NY : Oxford University Press, [2017] |
Series: Oxford Studies in Anthropology of Language | Includes bibliographical references and index.
Identifiers: LCCN 2016045075 (print) | LCCN 2017012737 (ebook) |
ISBN 9780190652821 (pdf) | ISBN 9780190652838 (ebook) |
ISBN 9780190652845 (online course) | ISBN 9780190652814 (pbk. : alk. paper) |
ISBN 9780190652807 (cloth : alk. paper) Subjects: LCSH: Dialogue analysis—Political aspects. |
Monologues. | Discourse analysis—Political aspects. | Communication—Political aspects. |
Anthropological linguistics. Classification: LCC P95.455 (ebook) |
LCC P95.455 .M66 2017 (print) | DDC 401/.41—dc23
LC record available at https://lccn.loc.gov/2016045075

9 8 7 6 5 4 3 2 1

Paperback printed by WebCom, Inc., Canada
Hardback printed by Bridgeport National Bindery, Inc., United States of America

CONTENTS

ACKNOWLEDGMENTS

The chapters in this volume have emerged from several years of discussion at and across various sites, including a conference panel at the American Anthropological Association meetings in Chicago in 2013 and a workshop on monologism held in Melbourne, Australia, in August 2014. In assembling this set of dialogues on the topic of monologue, we have been encouraged, assisted, and inspired by many people. We especially thank Laura Ahearn, Mark Ashley, Dick Bauman, Anders Sybrandt Hansen, Kathy Lothian, Howie Manns, Chaim Noy, Sherman Tan, and the generous and insightful manuscript reviewers for Oxford University Press. The Melbourne workshop was sponsored by a Monash Research Accelerator Grant awarded to Julian Millie, which is gratefully acknowledged.

An earlier version of Jane E. Goodman's chapter was published as "Acting with One Voice: Producing Unanimism in Algerian Reformist Theater," *Comparative Studies in Society and History* 55(1) (2013): 167-197. We thank the publishers for permission to use this material.

MT and JM
September 2016

CONTRIBUTORS

James Barry is an Associate Research Fellow at the Alfred Deakin Institute for Citizenship and Globalisation, Deakin University, Melbourne, Australia. He conducts research on the intersections of religious, linguistic, and national conceptions of identity in the Middle East, especially Iran.

Jon Bialecki is a fellow in the School of Social and Political Science at the University of Edinburgh. He is the author of *A Diagram for Fire: Miracles and Variation in an American Charismatic Movement* (California, 2017).

Philip Fountain is Teaching Fellow in Religious Studies at Victoria University of Wellington. He is coeditor of "Salvage and Salvation: Religion and Disaster Relief in Asia" (*Asian Ethnology*, 2016), *Religion and the Politics of Development* (Palgrave Macmillan, 2015), and "Anthropological Theologies: Engagements and Encounters" (*Australian Journal of Anthropology*, 2013).

Zane Goebel is Associate Professor in the Department of Languages and Linguistics at La Trobe University, Melbourne, Australia, and author of *Language, Migration, and Identity: Neighborhood Talk in Indonesia* (Cambridge, 2010) and *Language and Superdiversity: Indonesians Knowledging at Home and Abroad* (Oxford Studies in Sociolinguistics, 2015).

Jane E. Goodman is Associate Professor in the Department of Anthropology at Indiana University, author of *Berber Culture on the World Stage: From Village to Video* (Indiana, 2005), and coeditor of *Bourdieu in Algeria: Colonial Politics, Ethnographic Practices, Theoretical Developments* (Nebraska, 2009).

Courtney Handman is Assistant Professor of Anthropology at the University of Texas at Austin. Her work focuses on the linguistic mediation of Christian sociality. Her book *Critical Christianity: Translation and Denominational Conflict in Papua New Guinea* was published by the University of California Press in 2015.

Don Kulick is Distinguished University Professor of Anthropology at Uppsala University, Sweden, where he directs the Engaging Vulnerability research program. His books include *Language and Sexuality* (with Deborah Cameron, Cambridge, 2003) and *Loneliness and its Opposite: Sex, Disability and the Ethics of Engagement* (with Jens Rydström, Duke, 2015).

Julian Millie is an Australian Research Council Future Fellow in Anthropology at Monash University in Melbourne, Australia, and author of *Bidasari: Jewel of Malay Muslim Culture* (KITLV/Brill, 2004) and *Splashed by the Saint: Ritual Reading and Islamic Sanctity in West Java* (KITLV/Brill, 2010).

Alan Rumsey is Professor of Anthropology at the Australian National University in Canberra, coauthor of *Ku Waru: Language and Segmentary Politics in the Western Nebilyer Valley, Papua New Guinea* (Cambridge, 1991), and coeditor of several volumes including *Sung Tales from the Papua New Guinea Highlands: Studies in Form, Meaning, and Sociocultural Context* (ANU Press, 2011).

Matt Tomlinson is Associate Professor of Anthropology at the Australian National University in Canberra, and author of *In God's Image: The Metaculture of Fijian Christianity* (California, 2009) and *Ritual Textuality: Pattern and Motion in Performance* (Oxford, 2014).

Greg Urban is the Arthur Hobson Quinn Professor of Anthropology at the University of Pennsylvania, author of several volumes including *Metaculture: How Culture Moves through the World* (Minnesota, 2001), and coeditor of several volumes including *Natural Histories of Discourse* (Chicago, 1996).

Krista E. Van Vleet is Associate Professor of Anthropology at Bowdoin College in Brunswick, Maine. She has conducted ethnographic research in Bolivia and, more recently, Peru. She is the author of *Performing Kinship: Narrative, Gender, and the Intimacies of Power in the Andes* (Texas, 2008) and *Making Families through Adoption* (with Nancy E. Riley, Sage, 2011).

Kristina Wirtz is Professor of Spanish at Western Michigan University, and author of *Ritual, Discourse, and Community in Cuban Santería: Speaking a Sacred World* (Florida, 2007) and *Performing Afro-Cuba: Image, Voice, Spectacle in the Making of Race and History* (Chicago, 2014), winner of the Edward Sapir Book Prize from the Society for Linguistic Anthropology.

THE MONOLOGIC IMAGINATION

INTRODUCTION

IMAGINING THE MONOLOGIC

Matt Tomlinson

In late 2008 and early 2009, talk of dialogue was everywhere in Fiji's political sphere. Fiji's military leader, Voreqe ("Frank") Bainimarama, had executed a coup in December 2006 and was going through the standard international protocol for postcoup leaders: attempting to legitimize his actions in terms of popular will, both appealing to and threatening foreigners who wanted to have a say in the nation's future, and hand-picking military officials who would slowly take over the civil service. In this context, what everyone agreed upon—Bainimarama, his opponents, ostensibly neutral observers—was that dialogue was now extremely important.

The actual dynamics of dialogue, however—how conversations would unfold reciprocally, how speakers would respond to each other—were not clear. At times, the dialogues proposed seemed nondialogical, if one adopts the colloquial sense of "dialogue" as an open-ended process of engagement and response. At the very least, getting dialogues started in Fiji seemed to involve coercion and resistance. Bainimarama was willing to engage in formal meetings for dialogue as long as his major political opponents were excluded from participating. A series of "dialogue sessions" among various political leaders, intended to lead to a President's Political Dialogue Forum, had its "meetings . . . regularly canceled or delayed" under pressure from the prime minister (Fraenkel 2010: 417). In December 2008, a delegation from the European Union visited Fiji and its spokesperson, Gabrielle Zimmer, said that the European Union should "maintain the pressure" for democratic elections in Fiji, adding, "what is important is that dialogue should start. . . . I think if actors in Fiji are strong and put strong pressure on the Government, it is possible for the election to be held."[1]

---

1. Mary Rauto, "More Pressure Applied for Polls," *Fiji Times*, December 2, 2008, 3. Democratic elections were eventually held in September 2014, and Bainimarama won.

The dialogue that could lead to free elections, Zimmer implied, would not begin automatically: it needed a push, and the European Union was ready to give it by, for example, refusing to subsidize Fiji's sugar industry.

I was conducting research in Suva, Fiji's capital city, during this period and was continually struck by the insistence upon dialogue. I even participated in a formalized dialogue myself: I conducted short-term research with an NGO named the Ecumenical Centre for Research, Education and Advocacy, and as part of that work, helped coordinate a three-day workshop on "Sustained Dialogue on Bible and Culture" at a church in Suva. (My most vivid memory of the event is of a pair of men from an extremely conservative evangelical church who were trying to come to grips with the fact that other congregations allowed women to speak in church.) In Bainimarama's Fiji, with his enemies intimidated, the press censored, and the national constitution soon to be abrogated, many people agreed that dialogue needed to take place. But some of the proposed dialogues, besides being designed with a degree of exclusion and coercion, seemed foreclosed, their outcomes already declared. For the European Union's Zimmer, dialogue would necessarily lead to democratic elections, and quickly. For Bainimarama, dialogue would clearly result in everyone agreeing with whatever he said. Such dialogues seemed to be imagined monologically.

Monologue, as a topic, is decidedly out of fashion in contemporary anthropology. And, it might seem, it is out of fashion for good reason: Mikhail Bakhtin emphasized the dialogic nature of all discourse, as speakers respond to past utterances and anticipate future ones. As he famously put it, "The word in language is half someone else's. . . . In all areas of life and ideological activity, our speech is filled to overflowing with other people's words" (Bakhtin 1981a: 293, 337). Within a single utterance, there are always multiple voices. Hence any anthropological project—whether it aims to understand how power works in the world, how ethics contour everyday action, how rituals succeed or fail, how gender is performed, or almost any other topic—can be insightful and analytically effective only by attending to the dialogic interplay of voices. Because "the orientation of the now-said to the already-said and the to-be-said, is ubiquitous and foundational," dialogue is a starting point for anthropologists (Bauman 2004: 5; see also Mannheim and Tedlock 1995; Besnier 2009: 109). There is no truly singular voice and no truly one-way communication: there is only interaction, suffused as it is with multiple voices and accents.

For Bakhtin, monologic discourse was theoretically impossible for any speaker other than Adam, the first human, who faced the "virginal and as yet verbally unqualified world with the first word" (1981a: 279). But Bakhtin (1981b) also observed that the creators of epics, as opposed to novels, made worlds closed in their pastness, their reverence for tradition, their unchangeability, and their fixedness of meaning and value—monologic tendencies all. He also identified as monological those nationalist projects that aim to unify meanings in "one consciousness" with "a unified accent" (1984: 82). Monologues might never be fully realized, then, but people can and do try to speak monologically. This is apparent when people claim to represent a nation's *Geist*, speak in the voice of "we, the people," and speak in the voice of God. As Michael Holquist puts it, discussing 1930s Nazi Germany, "Totalitarian government always seeks the (utopian) condition of absolute monologue" (1990: 34); as another speaker, the New Zealand evangelical minister Brian Tamaki, puts it, "I will always and only give voice to what God says." The idea that monologue can exist in intention, if not in outcome, is well described by Bruce Mannheim and Dennis Tedlock when they write that the speaker of monologue "expects no answer" (Mannheim and Tedlock 1995: 1–2).

How speakers try to speak monologically is a question that runs through the following chapters. A key point that emerges is that monologue depends on both erasure—the flattening of language to make people, their actions, and their voices disappear (Irvine and Gal 2009)—and creative performance that attempts to unify speakers in a way that might be called the "repeat after me" phenomenon. Shutting people up and refusing to recognize their voices may be a precondition of monologue but it is never sufficient; monologue also requires a creative act of discursive displacement or overwriting, an insistence that the voice you are about to hear is the only one—with the implication that the only possible forms of uptake are either perfect assent or faithful repetition. I will now discuss these two interrelated processes in turn.

Erasure, as defined by Judith Irvine and Susan Gal, "is the process in which ideology, in simplifying the sociolinguistic field, renders some persons or activities (or sociolinguistic phenomena) invisible. Facts that are inconsistent with the ideological scheme either go unnoticed or get explained away" (Irvine and Gal 2009: 404). Erasure is monological in the sense that monologues are often meant to replace other utterances, other texts—to silence their pronunciation and stop their circulation.

In an obvious Bakhtinian sense, projects of erasure are dialogical because they are responding to those previous utterances and texts they are designed to replace. But the monologic imagination often takes the form of denial or dismissal, refusing to take up the other expression in a meaningful way. Michael Lempert and Michael Silverstein observe: "In a trivial sense, all speech is 'interdiscursive' in the sense that it has ties to other contexts. . . . The question is, how does an utterance 'formulate . . . its own connection to other events'?" (2012: 150; their quotation is from Agha 2007: 72). In erasure, understood as a strategy of monologism, the connection to other events or discourses is deliberately not recognized.

For example, during the Cultural Revolution in China, Chairman Mao's famous "Little Red Book" was used in "a movement to 'revolutionize daily life' . . . [which] consisted of replacing daily talk with quotations from Chairman Mao. When you got out of bed in the morning, instead of saying, 'Let's get up,' you said, 'Carry the revolution through to the end.' When you went to bed, you said, 'Never forget class struggle'" (Gao 1987: 318–319). This is a kind of overwriting in which the original text—regular daily talk—was (meant to be) gone, disappeared, not remaining as a resource or point of engagement. The novelist Vikram Seth, riding in a truck through western China in the early 1980s, reports being told by the driver that young people were "disturbed and selfish" due to the Cultural Revolution. "And as for their skills," Seth recounts, "even their literacy [was lost]—no-one really studied anything in school, that is if they went to school at all. All day they had to recite and discuss the quotations of the Chairman, as if that was the totality of all knowledge" (Seth 1983: 76). Daily talk and "all knowledge" were portrayed as necessarily the production of the Chairman, its true author and principal (in Erving Goffman's [1981] sense).

Another kind of erasure is prospective: it anticipates criticism and rules it out. This is, of course, also dialogic in the Bakhtinian sense, as it responds to a future voice—and yet, such a reading is too simple, because prospective erasure does not rule out a particular response, but any meaningfully engaged response at all. The charismatic church leader in New Zealand, Brian Tamaki, declared in his infamous sermon on homosexuality:

> You have got to understand my role and my call. I want to tell you what I am not. I am not a politician. So I don't have to be politically correct. That is true. I am not a religious voice. So I do not have to be religiously correct. . . . It is very important that you understand my role so you don't misunderstand what I am saying. . . . This is what I have been called. This is my role. . . . This is what I am. I have been called to represent the voice of God in the earth today. No! That is true. You can say, who is he? . . . He represents the voice of God. What God is saying about things. What God thinks about all sorts of things. You might have an opinion from a certain group, you can have an opinion from a minority or majority or all sorts of opinions, but I will always and only give voice to what God says about that certain thing. . . . Therefore something that I am saying, is called truth. In the middle of people's opinions, truth will come. Because that is all God is. . . . I will only bring and communicate by a revelation what God has said or is saying about something. Do you understand that? It is not an opinion. . . . These are not my opinions. (Quoted in Lineham 2013: 117; ellipses in original)

In this remarkable statement, Tamaki does several things that scholars of language will recognize as claims to authority, including denying his authorship and identifying the genre in which his words are to be classified. What is most interesting, for an analysis of monologue and dialogue, is how Tamaki refers to other people's opinions in general and dismisses them all in a double displacement: his own speech is taken over by God ("I will only bring and communicate by a revelation") and God's speech should replace other people's opinions with the pure truth.

In an example of finer prospective targeting in monologic practice, Donald Brenneis describes an Indo-Fijian dispute-resolution event (*pancayat*) where the original complainant was excluded lest her testimony get in the way of a harmonious resolution. Brenneis explains that *pancayat* are considered by Indo-Fijians to be "the definitive Indian occasion for the amicable settlement of conflict" (Brenneis 1990: 214). This amicability is managed in several ways. One is the setting: "The *pancayat* . . . is held on neutral ground" (227). Another is the rules for speaking: the *pancayat* follows a question-and-answer format, but the questioning is not confrontational. A third way the amicability is managed is through the selection of participants. Before the event takes place, the committee that will convene it has already gathered the information it needs, and respondents' answers are known in advance. "The orchestration of *pancayats* as events is a delicate job," Brenneis observes: "The appropriate witnesses must be located and their accounts compared and checked. . . . Witnesses and audience alike must be carefully controlled" (228). In the example Brenneis offers, a woman identified as "Jeshwan's wife" claimed that a man named Amka had sworn at her and another woman, Rina Devi, as they worked in a field whose ownership he disputed. Later, a story circulated that on another occasion Amka had sworn at a third woman. Because swearing at women is insulting, a *pancayat* was planned to resolve the matter. Jeshwan's wife was not notified that the *pancayat* would take place because "the *pancayat* does not provide the opportunity to judge between competing accounts" (219); instead, Rina Devi said that she had not been sworn at, and, as Brenneis puts it, "everyone seemed satisfied that Amka had probably not sworn at Jeshwan's wife either" (220). The point of the committee's careful strategy, in which participants and their potential accounts were maneuvered into position, was so that the *pancayat* could result in "an official and definitive account" of what happened; a successful *pancayat* "becomes the basis for later discussion and a new baseline against which the subsequent behavior of the disputants can be measured" (227). This is a dialogic process in which the multiplicity of voices is intentionally muted.

As the examples from Maoist China, Brian Tamaki's sermon, and the Indo-Fijian *pancayat* help illustrate, monologue is often a kind of performance, an interaction between speakers or writers and their audiences in which genuine interchange is denied. Indeed, the colloquial English-language understanding of "monologue" is often as a dramatic or comic speech in which the actor simply "holds the floor" at length without significant interruption. If dialogue in its broadest sense is described metaphorically as a kind of conversation, then monologue features a "recipient design" (per Sacks, Schegloff, and Jefferson 1974: 727) in which speech is crafted to minimize the possibility that it will be transformed in uptake.[2] A speaker's others are not meant to revoice utterances but to accept them silently or replicate them accurately. This understanding of monologue is diverging from that of Bakhtin, but a full understanding of the politics of monologic practice cannot do without it. In this volume, authors attend to both faces of monologue: the erasure of multiple voices within speakers' utterances, and controlled verbal performances in which, whatever the number of participants, there is meant to be only a single voice representing a single opinion.

Monologic performance is considered an ideal in particular speech contexts in indigenous Fiji, where I have conducted much of my fieldwork. Methodist ministers usually deliver sermons without much feedback from the congregation beyond an occasional "*vinaka, vinaka*" ("good, thanks"). When Fijian chiefs speak on formal occasions, they speak not to persuade, but to impress; their impressiveness comes partly from "slow, even halting" speech with long pauses (Arno 1990: 254; see also Arno 1985, 1993), and no attempts by other speakers to cut in.[3] In Samoa, according to Alessandro Duranti, Christian sermons "are based on a more extreme monologic model of communication" than are other formal speech genres, and "During a sermon . . . no appreciation of the pastor's delivery is signified by the audience" (Duranti 1994: 88). In the opening speeches of a Samoan chiefs' council meeting (*fono*), there is usually no commentary on the performance, and "interruptions are rare and confrontative" (104); speakers hold the floor at such length that their conversation proceeds by what Duranti calls "macro turn" dynamics, with a "macro turn" being "a turn [at speaking] that coincides with what could be thought of as an entire speech" (78).

The written texts on which some of these performances partly depend (e.g., sermons based on biblical passages) have features suggestive of monologism. The Book of Revelation (22:18–19) famously declares that if anyone adds to it, "God shall add unto him the plagues that are written in this book," and if anyone removes words from it, "God shall take away his part out of the book of

---

2. Sacks, Schegloff, and Jefferson define "recipient design" as "a multitude of respects in which the talk by a party in a conversation is constructed or designed in ways which display an orientation and sensitivity to the particular other(s) who are the co-participants" (1974: 727).

3. See also Nabobo-Baba (2006), who writes of the pedagogical use of monologues by indigenous Fijians.

life," a strong argument for leaving the text alone in its singular, sealed fixedness. Ideologies of texts' sacredness can further predispose people not to change anything. As the theologian Nāsili Vaka'uta writes, many Tongan Methodists "do not welcome a new translation of the Bible that uses vocabularies that are meaningful to the present generation of Tongans. [It is] the 'Word of God,' [and] no one is good enough to re-translate it. . . . The Bible offers the first and final word; there is no space for *an–other* word" (Vaka'uta 2011: 11; emphasis in original).[4] Consider also Felix Keesing's memorable description for Samoa: "the Bible, together with the interpretations placed upon it, appears to have an all but magical finality" (Keesing 1934: 409).

In considering monological performances, a key question arises: How, per Greg Urban, does "a form of linguistic interaction . . . itself function . . . as a sign vehicle" (Urban 1986: 384)? That is, monologues and dialogues signal something in their form, whether that "something" is an understanding that "we" share a tradition, or that individuals need to exchange "distinctive contributions" to generate social solidarity, or even that social balance is achieved through managed competition that occasionally requires the display of aggression (382). Urban compares six distinct traditions of ceremonial dialogue in South America, of which, for the purposes of this volume, the examples of the Kuna and the Shokleng are the most intriguing. For Kuna and Shokleng who perform ceremonial dialogues, "the overt communicative purpose of the dialogues is semantically monologic" (381). In other words, myths are recited in narrative performances where one speaker tells the story and a respondent moves the speaker along by affirming what he has just said. The story is a monologue, but the performance takes an explicitly dialogic form which, Urban argues, models a state of social solidarity when that solidarity might be in question.

Urban's work usefully calls attention to the push-and-pull of monologue and dialogue, a dynamic that becomes evident when one analyzes text and performance in the same frame. In his examples, Kuna and Shokleng performers dialogically craft a monologue. I suggested above that the *pancayat* described by Brenneis can be thought of in a similar way. In a counterposed example that I have discussed at length elsewhere (Tomlinson 2014: 104–113), Fiji's government, led by Bainimarama, attempted to create a dialogical document called the "Peoples Charter for Change, Peace, and Progress," but did so through monological strategies. The text claimed to represent "We, the People of Fiji," and it featured voices distinctly articulated with particular groups—the military, Catholic social justice advocates, jargon-besotted bureaucrats—but displays of public support for the Charter were engineered through duplicity and coercion. The

4. "An–other" is Vaka'uta's spelling.

document was able to stand for "We, the People" only by silencing a good number of those people. "Speaking in a singular or monologic 'voice'—and thus, with a singular social identity relative to a clear and distinct project," as Webb Keane (2003: 235) observes, "is the highly marked outcome of political effort rather than a natural or neutral condition."[5]

A fruitful way to think of the push and pull of monologue and dialogue is in terms of centripetal and centrifugal forces acting upon discourse. For Bakhtin, all utterances are acted upon by a metaphorically centripetal pull with "unifying [and] centralizing" tendencies counterbalanced by a metaphorically centrifugal push with "decentralizing," "stratifying" tendencies (Bakhtin 1981a: 272–273). The conjunction of these forces is what generates heteroglossia—the multiplicity of voices and relations within utterances, which anthropologists have found such a fruitful field of study. As Holquist (1990: 70) observes, "The idea of heteroglossia comes as close as possible to conceptualizing a locus where the great centripetal and centrifugal forces that shape discourse can meaningfully come together."

The metaphorical model of centripetal and centrifugal force is especially useful when analyzing monologic strategies of creating a "we," whether that "we" is an ethnic group, a nation, a church, or another kind of social body (see Urban 1996: chs. 1–2; Urban 2001; see also Bialecki 2011). The dynamics of "we"-making can be called unification: a design for presenting a single voice meant to represent a collectivity as a single speaking, acting entity. Centripetal force is maximized. A prime example is national constitutions. "We, the people" cannot exist until we declare ourselves into existence, and this declaration must be monological to the extent that no voice within the text can say, "but not me" (even if they are excluded in practice). Indeed, a state's legitimacy can depend on the sleight of hand by which mutuality becomes unanimity. As Benjamin Lee puts it, when the authors of the US Declaration of Independence wrote that "we hold these truths to be self-evident," they configured "the mutual subjectivity and agency of a 'we' [that] the Constitution will

---

5. Don Kulick (1993) describes a genre of dispute in Gapun, Papua New Guinea, in which attempting to engage in dialogue is considered extremely disrespectful and provocative. A *kros* is a public event in which a speaker, often a woman, begins a loud monologic denunciation of someone who has offended her. Those who are denounced can attempt to respond, but doing so escalates the conflict, because "kroses are primarily occasions of self-display"; attempting to turn the monologue into a dialogue therefore calls into question the agitated speaker's worthiness, her "status and right to self-assertion" (Kulick 1993: 515). Analyzing a ferocious *kros* between a woman and her husband which draws in the woman's father—who takes his son-in-law's side in the dispute—Kulick observes that each person who speaks "structures the greater part of her or his contributions to the ongoing talk as monologic litanies. The speakers do not talk *to* one another; they shout *at* one another" (Kulick 1993: 520). As Kulick observes, this kind of competitive self-assertion is strongly gendered; indeed *kros*es can be seen as crucibles in which competing gender expectations and characterizations are forged.

enshrine as the source of its legitimacy" (Lee 1997: 326). This "we" expands from its authors to encompass its audience, but not dialogically. Rather, dialogue is a model invoked after the fact to legitimize what has happened. (The Declaration of Independence itself does, of course, have a "they": the King of England and "our British brethren"; but the Constitution does not generate its "we" by opposing a "they.") In understanding monologue as an extreme centripetal pull toward an imagined center of gravity which is often conceptualized as a social collective, one can see how "We, the people" can never exist in the unified form we take on the page, and critical engagement with the established text is limited by the fact that declaring that "we" might not exist is considered either absurd or treasonous.

In analyzing monological aspects of performance, then, anthropologists need to attend to a wide range of phenomena: texts and processes of entextualization, genre norms and expectations of performers' and audiences' conduct, language ideologies of correct, authoritative, or effective usage, and so forth. Although this is a detailed and demanding task, the elements are all ethnographically apprehensible. Close attention to them can illuminate the ways in which people work at monologue—performers and audiences alike. After all, monological performances often compel silence but not agreement, or compel formal agreement that masks audience members' personal disagreement. Even if audiences do not respond in the moment of performance, they often do so later, although they may need to do so indirectly—not in the village meeting, say, but through back channels of gossip and genres such as parody. Even Samoan preachers' sermons, after all, can be responded to "in separate, often more private, contexts" (Duranti 1984: 184n2).

A final point: ethnographically grounded studies of the co-presence of monological and dialogical tendencies can serve as a useful corrective to overstatements of dialogism's total configuration of discourse and persons. As Holquist, a sensitive and sympathetic interpreter of Bakhtin, acknowledges, "extrapersonal social force is accorded so much weight in [Bakhtinian] dialogism that it almost (but not quite) begins to verge on determinism" (1990: 38). Moreover, when dialogue is treated unproblematically as discourse's natural state, it becomes easy to pathologize monologue: "There is no sender without a receiver," Roman Jakobson wrote, and then interrupted himself, "oh, yes, there is, only if the sender is drunk or pathological" (Jakobson 1953: 15). The monological genre of "official discourse" is described as a kind of autism, "autism for the masses," in which otherness is not recognized (Holquist 1990: 52).

This volume will serve, hopefully, to show that whatever one thinks of monologuists—their political stances, their religious authority, and so forth— treating dialogue as natural trivializes it and treating monologue as pathological misses the point. Both dialogue and monologue are projects, and they implicate each other. We stick with Bakhtin in saying that only dialogue is ultimately possible; but we do not dismiss the political force of monologue. Rather, we see it as a lure, a hoped-for possibility that many speakers try to craft and use in efforts that have political and religious consequences. Indeed, many of the authors in this volume tend in the direction taken by Mukarovsky, who wrote, "The relation between monologue and dialogue can be characterized . . . as a dynamic polarity in which sometimes dialogue, sometimes monologue gains the upper hand according to the milieu and the time" (quoted in Holquist 1990: 58; see especially Wirtz's discussion, this volume). This position contrasts starkly with the version of Bakhtinian orthodoxy that holds that "dialogue is real; monologue is not" (Holquist 1990: 59).[6]

Greg Urban begins the volume by examining how replication—the reproduction of an element or aspect of culture—involves processes of both copying and response. He observes how these processes have shaped different anthropological understandings of culture. Older models of culture as a process of acquisition are, he notes, monological to the extent that they describe a group consensus being passed down through the generations. Newer models, in contrast, emphasize dialogism, where culture is configured as something that people respond to "polyphonically," per Bakhtin. From this starting point, Urban explores the relationship between copying and response in replication, arguing that whereas "response always involves some measure of copying"—whether, for example, in the explicit repetition of form (as in direct reported speech) or in anaphoric copying (in which sources are indicated but not explicitly repeated)—not all copying is necessarily response. In the final part of his chapter he returns to the question of replication and culture theory in the light of monologic and dialogic models. Modern economic practices, he argues, often attempt to create metacultural heterogeneity out of relative cultural homogeneity. Conversely, modern political forms, exemplified by nations and their Constitutions, emphasize metacultural homogeneity ("we the people," portrayed as a single and single-voiced being) in contexts of relative cultural heterogeneity. Urban concludes by urging anthropologists to rethink culture as something with both monologic and dialogic aspects, replicated in both copies and responses, with replication occurring "with

6. Or as Yakubinsky put it in the 1920s, "Dialogue . . . appears to be a more 'natural' phenomenon than monologue" (quoted in Holquist 1990: 57). Compare Vološinov (1986: 72) on how "the monologic utterance is . . . an abstraction, though, to be sure, an abstraction of a 'natural' kind. Any monologic utterance . . . is an inseverable element of verbal communication. Any utterance . . . is but one link in a continuous chain of speech performances"—bearing in mind that some scholars, including Holquist (1990: 8), hold Bakhtin to be the real author of Vološinov's works.

different degrees of awareness on the part of the actors involved" and metacultural evaluations simultaneously constituting, reflecting, and reshaping culture.

Alan Rumsey examines three genres of sung narrative from the highlands of Papua New Guinea, analyzing relationships between monologism and dialogism in their construction and performance. In doing so, he questions Bakhtin's characterization of the epic—the paradigmatic monological genre—in terms of separation from an "absolute past." Rumsey describes the *tom yaya kange* genre of the Ku Waru as fully dialogical in Bakhtin's sense, as singers can take liberties to adapt and reshape stories, even including themselves as characters, but monological in performance, with no audible audience interaction. *Tom yaya kange* can thus be seen as a genre which is epic-like but in which separation from the past is expressly overcome. Conversely, *pikono* sung tales of the Duna are dialogical performances of Bakhtinian monologues. They follow a pattern in which a stretch of text with gradually descending pitch and little textual repetition is followed by a stretch of melody based firmly on a grounding pitch and much textual repetition. The formulaic pattern is considered traditional and unchangeable, and adaptations in form or content are not allowed. However, audience members are expected to contribute to the narrative's development by interjecting words meant to represent the perspectives of characters in the story or those of audience members as if they were conversing with the characters. Rumsey also considers the Huli genre of *bi té* as an intermediary case, with audience response limited to formulaic affirmation and limited adaptation of the songs allowed, for example, for inclusion in the Catholic liturgy. Contrary to simplistic views of "epic" as the canonical narrative genre in "oral cultures," Rumsey shows how widely their genres can differ with respect to the canonical forms of dialogism and monologism that one finds in them.

Jon Bialecki, like Urban and Rumsey, brings monologue and dialogue into the same analytical frame to ask how these apparently opposed tendencies can in practice be co-present and even co-constitutive. He examines the work of political scientist Ruth Marshall and anthropologist Thomas Csordas, and observes in both a seemingly contradictory emphasis on Pentecostal/charismatic Christianity's autocratic and democratic impulses—which is to say, its monological and dialogical tendencies. Marshall, writing about Nigeria, argues that Pentecostalism conflates spiritual and social power but also prevents the development of theocracy; Csordas, focused on Catholic charismatics, describes projects of turning prophecies into fixed, newly sacred texts whose human authorship is erased but also notes a countervailing "open intersubjectivity during charismatic events, where subjects encounter each other as 'another myself.'" Turning to his own field experience with members of the Vineyard church movement based in southern California, Bialecki analyzes a prophetic vision of the movement's founder in which a heavenly honeycomb dripped onto people beneath it. This prophecy was monologic, Bialecki writes, insofar as it presented a scenario with only two figures: the saved and the unsaved, "those who accept God's grace . . . and those who are repelled by it," with no response possible except to figure out which category one fits into. But this monologic prophecy "is simultaneously a *democratic* claim," Bialecki argues, opening the possibility to all followers of individually validated divine experience and prophecy. In the cases described by Marshall, Csordas, and himself, then, Bialecki perceives a dynamic where, counterintuitively, the monologic enables the dialogic; "there are times when the monological, which is supposed to be a denatured and perverted form of the dialogic, can give rise to and sustain dialogical speech acts of its own."

Kristina Wirtz, investigating the relationship between monologue and dialogue in Cuban Revolutionary discourse, proposes that scholars attend to the "mono-logic"—the semiotic and ideological forces designed to compel alignments toward unity, coherence, and continuity. The mono-logic operates at multiple levels: diffuse inner selves moving toward singular, stable ones; citizens moving from endorsement of the Revolution to existential constitution of its essence. Wirtz characterizes the mono-logic in terms of drives toward coherence and continuity that are never quite reached. In Cuba, political leaders have for decades insisted that citizens undergo a continual process of "conscientization" in which inner selves and outer displays jointly cultivate faith in Revolutionary principles. Wirtz identifies two semiotic "calibrations" of such discourse. One is the charismatic, in which heroic figures like José Martí and Fidel Castro embody such overwhelming authority that they are portrayed as "absolute" speakers, "addressing an audience that receives the speaker's utterance in perfect agreement." Another is the nomic, in which voices with no credited author, seen and heard in slogans on banners and in graffiti, for example, present "universalized Truths voiced by no one and therefore, potentially, by everyone." Inevitably, heteroglossic criticism of the mono-logic surfaces: in irony, parody, wry jokes, and, in an especially vivid ethnographic moment, in an audience's utter silence in the face of increasingly desperate political exhortation at a public meeting, an event that leads Wirtz to observe that "Heteroglossia . . . does not always require voices." Ultimately, she argues that the implications of attending to the mono-logic are anthropologically profound for the way they reframe dialogism and heteroglossia as always co-constituted by drives toward unity at and across the levels of psyche, self, society, and history. "Monologicality," she observes, "is as deeply historical a social fact as dialogicality."

In the next chapter, Zane Goebel shows how monological forms provide semiotic resources to actors in emerging dialogical environments where conventional structures for communication have a weak presence. He begins by describing the developmentalist aspirations of the Suharto regime (1966–1998). Suharto's government heavy-handedly implemented uniform national development policies for a highly diverse populace. Anxious that tendencies toward social fragmentation would harm the nation's progress, the government promoted a single national language (Bahasa Indonesia), a single national philosophy (*pancasila*, the five principles), massification of schooling, and the regulation of media infrastructures. The national philosophy emphasized harmonious relations, promoting concepts such as "unity in diversity," "getting on," and "working together to achieve goals." But the urban residential areas being constructed in Indonesia during Suharto's reign were dialogical spaces that did not automatically reproduce state agendas. Goebel closely analyzes a conversation within one such space, the meeting of a neighborhood women's committee. The committee's membership was made up of women from diverse ethnic backgrounds, which brought an indeterminacy to the meeting's communicative forms. Goebel observes that the state ideology provided semiotic resources for participants to dialogically construct a monological model of good neighborliness, which emerged when the women discussed one neighbor's refusal to join with and support the committee's activities. Participants repeated others' invocations of principles that resonated with the national philosophy, replicating not only content but also the sonic qualities and codeswitching patterns of their neighbors; "the copying of talk and the responses to these copies," Goebel writes, created "an emergent monologic voice about good neighborship by providing an example of what one shouldn't do." He emphasizes that dialogical sites of emergent culture can facilitate monological replications, including the traditionally monologic model of "culture" itself.

James Barry analyzes political discourse among Iranians in Iran and California and argues that community- and national-level discourses can be seen as competing unitary languages—counterposed monologues—that allow for heteroglossia only in limited ways. Beginning at the national level, he observes how official language about commitment to the Revolution, and Iran's status as an Islamic republic, attempts to generate the centripetal force that will pull the nation together. Such discourse is taken up in several ways, including enthusiastic endorsement by political leaders, qualified commentary by observers who ask why Iranians are failing to live up to their ideals (Barry notes that one popular book, now in its twenty-second edition, is titled *Why Are We Helpless?*), and, quite simply, being ignored as "background noise" by people who know it is fruitless to challenge what the government says. At the community level, Barry describes how leaders of the Armenian community craft unitary language to depict Armenians as people who speak a certain way, worship in a certain way (they are Christians within a nation that defines itself as Islamic), yet have displayed notable loyalty to the Iranian national ideal. The subject of ethnic groups is nettlesome for the country's

Persian leaders; the Ayatollah Khomeini claimed that the division of Islam's global ʾummah into separate nations was a colonial divide-and-rule strategy, and this idea inflects the understanding of ethnicity as a potential problem within the Islamic Republic. Nonetheless, Barry observes, the government attempts to enfold Armenians as loyal subjects by acknowledging their contributions to the Revolution and sacrifices during the 1980s war with Iraq. Ultimately, a limited space of heteroglossic identity discourse, sharply demarcated by the "red lines" of national taboo, emerges for Armenian Iranians.

In her chapter on Algerian theater troupes, Jane E. Goodman critiques the well-worn claim that voluntary civic associations are inherently democratizing, modernizing forces. In 1930s-1950s urban Algeria, unanimism—monological expression of unanimous group consensus in public rituals such as voting—was both what theater companies portrayed on stage and how they operated off stage. Contrary to theorists from Tocqueville to Habermas to Huntington, Goodman writes, civic associations can have monological tendencies in which dialogism and plurality are downplayed. Observing that "Algerians began performing unanimity well before the revolution," she identifies three possible sources of Algerian interest in public displays of unanimity. One is the Islamic reformist doctrine of tawḥīd, which holds that Muslims must unite, overcoming their social divisions in an emphatic return to principles of monotheism as mediated by the Qur'an, Hadith, and Sunna. Another is forms of practice found in traditional Berber village assemblies, in which unanimous male consent is required for decisions to be taken. The third is the machinations of the colonial state, which grouped all Algerians together as Muslims, "thus making Islam emerge as the single factor around which the indigenous population could unite." By analyzing monological displays of unanimism against the difficult "back-stage" work that must take place for a singular voice to be expressible in public, Goodman argues that scholars can rethink the relationship between civil society and the state in newly nuanced ways.

Philip Fountain turns to seemingly monologic aspects of theology, focusing on the practice of theological articulation in creeds—official statements of religious bodies' positions on doctrine, belief, and practice. He observes that creeds, which might seem monological due to their single-voiced presentation of standardized, non-debatable claims, are always inherently dialogical because they "are only ever articulated in the midst of multiple competing alternatives." Yet their rigidly unified and declarative mode of expression does raise the specter of monologism for religious groups who, in trying to declare what they stand for, seek either inclusiveness or flexible practicality. Fountain analyzes the case of the Mennonite Central Committee (MCC), an Anabaptist service organization, whose director of overseas services encouraged the writing of a formal missiological statement in the early 1990s. He wanted a creed of sorts, something to define the group's principles and guide its actions. The person charged with drafting the document admitted, in its final stages, that she was "less and less convinced" that such a statement was needed, and the process of creating a creed sputtered to a halt as all involved grew wary of seeming prescriptive or doctrinaire. In articulating a theology, Fountain argues, the MCC actually disarticulated theology, actively creating "a proactive avoidance of a systematic, concise theological statement; an evasion of creedal clarity." He compares two other cases of creedal articulation. In a second example from the MCC, he describes a recent successful effort to draw up a statement of "convictions," noting that the document was widely (although not universally) accepted because it was usefully ambiguous and provided no practical guidance. In a contrasting example from a more conservative Anabaptist service group, the Christian Aid Ministries, he shows how their monologically oriented Statement of Faith did many things the MCC could not bring itself to do—it gave straightforward assertions to which one was required to assent—and yet it, too, could not give practical guidance to the organization's fieldworkers, and it could only engineer its cohesive theology by turning its back on a wide section of the global Mennonite community.

Julian Millie revisits the themes of Greg Urban's opening chapter in order to analyze the interplay between cultural and metacultural expression in Islamic preaching. Millie focuses on the relationship between the style of Islamic preaching enjoyed by West Javanese Muslims and the images of preaching they construct in public representations. Millie notes that Islamic oratory invariably includes elements that are repetitive and solemn, especially the citation and translation of Qur'an and Hadith, which have canonical authority. Yet these repetitive, solemn elements do not, by themselves, make for a sermon that audiences want to hear. Preachers also rely on their abilities to move listeners with their skillful multivocality, drawing on many genres and ways of speaking within listeners' competency, not just religious ones. "Preaching is a pious speech genre," Millie observes, "full of impious speech." Public representations of preaching (e.g., in preaching manuals) do not mention this dynamic, however. Occasionally they deny it explicitly. When speaking and writing normatively about oratory, Indonesians construct a monologic image that characterizes preaching as the circulation of religious knowledge. The multivocality and generic variation that preachers mobilize so skillfully are absent from these representations and are even proscribed on religious grounds. Millie locates the clash between preaching's multivocally textured performance and its monologic metaculture in the context of Islam's broad support in West Java. Ninety-eight percent of West Javanese are Muslims, and the conviction that Islam should have a high presence in public life runs deep; many Muslims agree that Islamic knowledge should be constantly restated. The public reverence for Islam disallows overt recognition of the ways in which successful religious oratory depends on the skillful verbal acrobatics of clever preachers, even as the multivocality of real preaching ensures that the circulation of Islamic knowledge continues without interruption. Millie argues that the monologic construction of preaching does, however, sustain the public aspiration that Islam be maintained as a sphere separated from worldly matters.

Each set of three chapters is followed by a discussion, with Don Kulick engaging with the contributions of Urban, Bialecki, and Rumsey; Krista E. Van Vleet with those of Kristina Wirtz, Zane Goebel, and James Barry; and Courtney Handman with those of Jane E. Goodman, Philip Fountain, and Julian Millie. Taken together, the chapters and commentaries show how understanding dialogue and dialogism depends on attending to the monologic imagination. Bakhtin was right: monologue is artificial, partial, and never fully successful. But as the following case studies demonstrate, working at monologue is a project that many speakers find compelling. A focus on monologism gives us new insights into languages' political design and deepens our understandings of the necessary interplay between monological and dialogical tendencies.

References

Agha, Asif. 2007. *Language and Social Relations*. Cambridge: Cambridge University Press.

Arno, Andrew. 1985. "Impressive Speeches and Persuasive Talk: Traditional Patterns of Political Communication in Fiji's Lau Group from the Perspective of Pacific Ideal Types." *Oceania* 56(2): 124–137.

Arno, Andrew. 1990. "Disentangling Indirectly: The Joking Debate in Fijian Social Control." In *Disentangling: Conflict Discourse in Pacific Societies*, ed. K. A. Watson-Gegeo and G. M. White, 241–289. Stanford, CA: Stanford University Press.

Arno, Andrew. 1993. *The World of Talk on a Fijian Island: An Ethnography of Law and Communicative Causation*. Norwood, NJ: Ablex.

Bakhtin, M. M. 1981a. "Discourse in the Novel." In *The Dialogic Imagination: Four Essays*, ed. M. Holquist, trans. C. Emerson and M. Holquist, 259–422. Austin: University of Texas Press.

Bakhtin, M. M. 1981b. "Epic and Novel: Toward a Methodology for the Study of the Novel." In *The Dialogic Imagination: Four Essays*, ed. M. Holquist, trans. C. Emerson and M. Holquist, 3–40. Austin: University of Texas Press.

Bakhtin, M. M. 1984. *Problems of Dostoevsky's Poetics*. Ed. and trans. C. Emerson. Minneapolis: University of Minnesota Press.

Bauman, Richard. 2004. *A World of Others' Words: Cross-Cultural Perspectives on Intertextuality*. Malden, MA: Blackwell.

Besnier, Niko. 2009. *Gossip and the Everyday Production of Politics*. Honolulu: University of Hawai'i Press.

Bialecki, Jon. 2011. "No Caller ID for the Soul: Demonization, Charisms, and the Unstable Subject of Protestant Language Ideology." *Anthropological Quarterly* 84(3): 679–704.

Brenneis, Donald. 1990. "Dramatic Gestures: The Fiji Indian *Pancayat* as Therapeutic Event." In *Disentangling: Conflict Discourse in Pacific Societies*, ed. K. A. Watson-Gegeo and G. M. White, 214–238. Stanford, CA: Stanford University Press.

Duranti, Alessandro. 1994. *From Grammar to Politics: Linguistic Anthropology in a Western Samoan Village*. Berkeley: University of California Press.

Fraenkel, Jon. 2010. "Melanesia in Review: Issues and Events, 2009—Fiji." *The Contemporary Pacific* 22(2): 416–431.

Gao, Yuan. 1987. *Born Red: A Chronicle of the Cultural Revolution*. Stanford, CA: Stanford University Press.

Goffman, Erving. 1981. *Forms of Talk*. Philadelphia: University of Pennsylvania Press.

Holquist, Michael. 1990. *Dialogism: Bakhtin and His World*. London: Routledge.

Irvine, Judith T., and Susan Gal. 2009. "Language Ideology and Linguistic Differentiation." In *Linguistic Anthropology: A Reader*, 2d ed., ed. A. Duranti, 402–434. Malden, MA: Blackwell.

Jakobson, Roman. 1953. "Chapter Two." In *Results of the Conference of Anthropologists and Linguists*, Memoir 8, ed. Claude Lévi-Strauss, 11–21. Baltimore: Waverly Press.

Keane, Webb. 2003. "Self-Interpretation, Agency, and the Objects of Anthropology: Reflections on a Genealogy." *Comparative Studies in Society and History* 45(2): 222–248.

Keesing, Felix M. 1934. *Modern Samoa: Its Government and Changing Life*. London: Allen & Unwin.

Kulick, Don. 1993. "Speaking as a Woman: Structure and Gender in Domestic Arguments in a New Guinea Village." *Cultural Anthropology* 8(4): 510–541.

Lee, Benjamin. 1997. *Talking Heads: Language, Metalanguage, and the Semiotics of Subjectivity*. Durham, NC: Duke University Press.

Lempert, Michael, and Michael Silverstein. 2012. *Creatures of Politics: Media, Message, and the American Presidency*. Bloomington: Indiana University Press.

Lineham, Peter. 2013. *Destiny: The Life and Times of a Self-Made Apostle*. Auckland: Penguin.

Mannheim, Bruce, and Dennis Tedlock. 1995. "Introduction." In *The Dialogic Emergence of Culture*, ed. D. Tedlock and B. Mannheim, 1–32. Urbana: University of Illinois Press.

Nabobo-Baba, Unaisi. 2006. "A Place to Sit (and Stand), Vugalei Fijian Epistemology: An Exploration into Teaching and Learning and Ways of Knowing of a Particular Cultural Group." In *Dreadlocks Vaka Vuku*, ed. M. Prasad, 48–59. Suva, Fiji: Pacific Writing Forum, University of the South Pacific.

Sacks, Harvey, Emanuel A. Schegloff, and Gail Jefferson. 1974. "A Simplest Systematics for the Organization of Turn-Taking for Conversation." *Language* 50(4): 696–735.

Seth, Vikram. 1983. *From Heaven Lake: Travels through Sinkiang and Tibet*. London: Chatto & Windus/The Hogarth Press.

Tomlinson, Matt. 2014. *Ritual Textuality: Pattern and Motion in Performance*. New York: Oxford University Press.

Urban, Greg. 1986. "Ceremonial Dialogues in South America." *American Anthropologist* 88(2): 371–386.

Urban, Greg. 1996. *Metaphysical Community: The Interplay of the Senses and the Intellect*. Austin: University of Texas Press.

Urban, Greg. 2001. *Metaculture: How Culture Moves through the World*. Minneapolis: University of Minnesota Press.

Vaka'uta, Nāsili. 2011. *Reading Ezra 9–10 Tu'a-Wise: Rethinking Biblical Interpretation in Oceania*. Atlanta, GA: Society of Biblical Literature.

Vološinov, V. N. 1986. *Marxism and the Philosophy of Language*. Trans. L. Matejka and I. R. Titunik. Cambridge, MA: Harvard University Press.

1

CULTURAL REPLICATION

THE SOURCE OF MONOLOGICAL AND DIALOGICAL MODELS OF CULTURE

Greg Urban

Imagining the group as speaking with one voice—the "monologic imagination" of this volume's title—had been at the heart of anthropological theorizing about culture since the publication of *Primitive Culture* in 1871. Edward Burnett Tylor ([1871] 1889: 1) concluded his oft-cited definition of culture with the catchall: "and any other capabilities and habits acquired by man as a member of society," where the word "society" conveyed a sense of singularity, of oneness. Everyone shared the same culture; culture was a group property. What the individual acquired was what the collectivity already possessed.

Singularity is a characteristic of other dominant theories in the history of anthropology. A prime example is Émile Durkheim's ([1912] 1969) conception of society, with its "collective representations." Not reducible to intra-individual processes, the latter were, for him, the work of a group, which imprinted itself upon individuals. A similarly monologic imagination inspired Clifford Geertz (1973: 89), who defined culture as "an historically transmitted pattern of meanings embodied in symbols, a system of inherited conceptions expressed in symbolic forms by means of which men communicate, perpetuate, and develop their knowledge about and attitudes toward life." Again, telltale oneness: "an historically transmitted pattern," "a system."

Given the salience of the monologic imagination in anthropology's history, why did the discipline venture away, in recent decades, from monologism into the land of dialogism? Today we find ourselves required to clear even a small space for single-voicedness. One factor: beginning in the 1980s, a unitary conception of culture no longer appeared adequate to ethnographic realities. Perhaps this had to do with the growing prominence of research in complex societies, where unity seemed less plausible than in small-scale societies. Perhaps the growing body of research conducted by insiders on their own societies was foregrounding differences that were effectively invisible to outsiders. Whatever the reasons, an ironic[1] consensus was emerging that monological conceptions "essentialized" the group, overplayed the whole as against the parts, underplayed differences. If not obvious before, it came to seem now that culture was not uniformly shared within groups, that people acquired it in differing degrees, that culture—to use another key word—"circulated." Parts of it were acquired by some people and not by others; and the parcels themselves were unstable, undergoing change as they circulated.

Another factor contributed: during this period the English translations of writings by Bakhtin and Valentin Voloshinov began to appear, including the 1981 Emerson and Holquist translation of *The Dialogic Imagination*. The latter work introduced readers to a range of concepts, including dialogism, heteroglossia, and polyphony. Fourteen years later, Dennis Tedlock and Bruce Mannheim (1995: 15) published an anthropological manifesto of sorts on the dialogical character of culture: "Whenever we speak or write, and whether or not we do so in direct response to another speaker or writer, our discourse occurs in the context of previous (or alternative) utterances or texts and is in dialogue with them, whether explicitly or implicitly." Theirs was an edited volume entitled *The Dialogic Emergence of Culture*. They sprinkled their introduction with references to Bakhtin.

Around this time, for some anthropologists, culture itself came to be seen as responded to rather than acquired. It no longer imposed itself on individuals, as if spoken with a single voice, *pace* Tylor, Durkheim, Geertz, and many others. Now it appeared to be by its very nature dialogical. The word so frequently bandied about in the latter 1990s was "polyphony," an idea of multi-voicedness that summed up this new way of viewing culture and social relations.

Some work, to be sure, recognized dialogue as a socially transmitted interactional style, a piece of acquired culture, but not an approach to culture. Indeed, Bakhtin's principal insight concerned dialogism as style. His work focused on the stylistic differences between the older epic tradition in Europe and the newer dialogism of the novel as discursive form. However, as the idea of dialogism spread, it came to represent more than a modern discursive style. It reshaped anthropological thinking about the culture concept. Culture came to be viewed less and less as acquired, in Tylor's sense, and more and more as responded to.

---

1. Ironic, that is to say, if it is, indeed, a consensus—that is, if anthropologists have been speaking with one voice.

Without rolling back the clock to an earlier single-voiced conception of culture, I propose in this chapter, nevertheless, to question the concept of response. What exactly is it? What is the difference between acquiring culture and responding to it? Where does response come from? I will argue that the contrasting notions of culture as acquired and as responded to spring from a common font. They derive from the realities of culture as something that makes its way, via social transmission, through space and time. More specifically, these approaches to culture both spring from the processes of *replication*. The latter are, I suggest, the basis for all culture.

Replication involves copying some aspect of culture (a behavioral routine, a word, a way of speaking, a belief, a story, a pattern, an idea, etc.) by an individual or group from other individuals or groups. However, the replica and its model need not be—indeed, probably rarely are—identical. "Acquisition," as an anthropological concept in Tylor's sense, emphasizes the extent to which model and replica are similar. "Response," in the recent literature on dialogism, emphasizes the extent to which the two are different. Similarity and differences are matters of degree.

A further observation: replication processes are themselves potential objects of reflection. Similarity and difference between original and copy can be cognized, talked about, signaled to others. Moreover, the similarity or difference lends itself to judgment as good or bad, giving the talk and signaling an evaluative dimension: "you're not doing it correctly; do it this way"; or "there's nothing new here." Such reflective talk and signaling can in turn itself undergo replication, becoming part of reflective culture—metaculture. This kind of culture in turn influences how individuals cognize instances of replication, as well as what they strive to accomplish in replicating. For example, do they want to make the replica as precise a copy of the model as possible (as in the case of a ballet pupil or music student); or, conversely, do they want to render the replica sufficiently different from its model as to be proclaimed an innovation (as when a composer composes a new song; or a mystery writer writes a new mystery)? The different questions focus attention on different aspects of the replication process. Something like a shift in metacultural questions underlies the movement from monological to dialogical conceptions of culture. As I hope to show, however, the focus of questioning in each case is ultimately the same: processes of replication.

Differential Awareness of Replication

The acquisition of grammatical and phonological patterns based on models around one, especially as a child, is an obvious example of replication with relatively low or no awareness on the part of the acquirer. The same is true of the phonetic patterns and paralinguistic features associated with accents. To these, we could add innumerable non-linguistic cultural phenomena, such as the comfortable spatial distances between interlocutors studied by Hall (1966), styles of walking, body postures, patterns of eye contact, and so forth. All of these things most of the time most of us never think about. We might, indeed, be inclined to suppose that the vast majority of cultural replication processes proceed beneath the level of normal reflective awareness. They fly under the radar, so to speak.

At the same time, prescriptive grammar education in school—as part of meta-cultural signaling about the replication of linguistic forms—heightens awareness of the replication process involved in grammar. Here the metasigns foreground sameness rather than difference, conformity to normative patterns, and, hence, a kind of monologicality. Sociolinguistic studies (Labov 1972: 70–109; 2001) demonstrate the role of relatively more formal contexts in triggering normative orientations to the replication of standard pronunciation practices; again sameness and faithfulness in copying.

The oral narration of stories, such as myths, provides in abundance examples of replication processes, though here there is typically a greater awareness of the processes. In the case of myths, in the indigenous Brazilian communities in which I have conducted field research, awareness focuses on telling a story that has already been told before—as in: "tell us the one about . . ." The request itself calls forth the replication process, with the emphasis on sameness—"the one about . . ." I have been able to show that the replication of myths involves some measure of formal replication as regards word choice.

In one community—known in the literature as Shokleng or Xokleng or Laklãnõ—there was, in fact, a ritualized telling of the origin myth in relationship to which considerable emphasis was placed on precision in replication. The ritual form of telling, as described elsewhere (Urban 1986, 1994), was dialogic in the pragmatic sense, albeit not the semantic sense, involving two interlocutors. Typically, one of the two was older and the other younger, so that something reminiscent of the teacher-student relationship was operative, though the two could also be equals. The explicitly stated aim was to reproduce the myth of origin with syllable-by-syllable fidelity. The first speaker uttered the first syllable; the second speaker repeated it. The first speaker then uttered the second syllable, which the second speaker repeated, and so on in rapid-fire back and forth fashion, the acoustic effect of which was stunning. The ritual foregrounded the ideal of exact copying of the original, under penalty of spiritual sanction.

As I have mentioned, Bakhtin viewed dialogism as a style emerging with the novel as a literary form, where the novelist strives to construct a new piece of written discourse, one not a close copy of any that have come before. Even in this arena of maximally reflected upon discourse—prose artfully crafted for publication—replication outside of awareness creeps in, as Mark Twain so astutely observed of his own writing in his 1879 speech "Unconscious Plagiarism" (Twain 1910: 56–57). Commenting on his 1869 book, *Innocents Abroad, or The New Pilgrims' Progress*, he wrote:

> When my first book was new, a friend of mine said to me, "The dedication is very neat." Yes, I said, I thought it was. My friend said, "I always admired it, even before I saw it in *The Innocents Abroad*." I naturally said: "What do you mean? Where did you ever see it before?" "Well, I saw it first some years ago as Doctor Holmes's dedication to his *Songs in Many Keys*." Of course, my first impulse was to prepare this man's remains for burial, but upon reflection I said I would reprieve him for a moment or two and give him a chance to prove his assertion if he could. We stepped into a bookstore, and he did prove it. I had really stolen that dedication, almost word for word.

Here are the two dedications:

> Holmes (1862): To the most indulgent of readers, the kindest of critics, my beloved mother, all that is least unworthy of her in this volume is dedicated by her affectionate son.

> Twain (1869): To my most patient reader and most charitable critic, my aged Mother, this volume is affectionately inscribed.

As I intend to show subsequently, the degree of similarity in this instance is comparable to that found in oral replication processes, where speakers strive to reproduce a passage exactly the way they heard it. Of course, Twain thought he had written something original, totally new, and so he was offended by the suggestion that he might have lifted the dedication from Holmes. His first thought was to prepare his friend's "remains for burial." However, in retrospect he recalled that just two years earlier he had "read and re-read" the Holmes book. "The dedication lay on the top, and handy," he explains, and "so, by-and-by, I unconsciously stole it," quipping: "Perhaps I unconsciously stole the rest of the volume, too . . ." (Twain 1910: 57).

In novelistic and other modern prose writing, the reflective cultural emphasis is on difference, on creating something distinct from what has come before, on producing the new, just as Twain mistakenly thought he had done. At the same time, what makes these modern discursive forms dialogical, according to Bakhtin, is that the writing appears as a response to earlier works. Here, arguably, Bakhtin was pointing out the continuities in discourse, not only the dissimilarities, despite the reflective emphasis on difference. However, response is not simply a continuation or copy of earlier words and ideas. It adds to or modifies or contradicts or even affirms what has already been said.

Types of Replication Employed in Response

In face-to-face dialogical interactions, a hearer's response need not take the form of overt word-for-word copying of the speaker, although it sometimes does so. Most typically response involves the creation by the hearer of an internal copy of the speaker's words. Evidence of that internal copy can be found in what I will call "anaphorized replication," where the replica appears as an overt mark ("uh-huh," "right," "yeah") that indexically points to the prior words for which an internal copy has been created. I have found it also possible, in quasi-experimental situations, to elicit a nearly word-for-word copy from a hearer who has produced an anaphorized replicator, confirming the internal copying process.

Anaphorized copying by the hearer of the speaker's prior statement can be distinguished from ordinary anaphora, which brings into the response part of the speaker's words—as in "do it," where the "it" refers to the action described in the speaker's turn. The limiting case of anaphoric replication is presupposition or "zero anaphora" (Saeboe 1996). In the latter, the response utterance makes sense only if some of the speaker's words are imagined as present. I will give examples of this phenomenon in the next section.

Yet another form of copying as response is dialogical reported speech, either direct ("you said: 'x'") or indirect ("you said that"). Reported speech provokes awareness of difference between the speaker's utterance and the response. In direct discourse, the actual words are copied. In indirect discourse, the meaning is copied. However, the framing clause ("you said") in each case distinguishes the responder from the speaker in a way that the simple copying of words does not. It makes maximally salient to consciousness that the hearer is not the speaker, even when the responder is in agreement.

Not always realized with perfection, though nonetheless a key form of copying, is paraphrase. The ideal paraphrase is one that puts the same meaning in different words, rendering any iconicity between the surface forms of the two utterances undetectable. The similarity gets noticed through the semantic meaning. In empirical examples from actual dialogues, paraphrastic copies typically carry over some words from the original, or, minimally, use devices like the partial anaphora mentioned earlier. Apparently, it is often easier to poach words from the original stimulus, than to forge all of the phrasing anew.

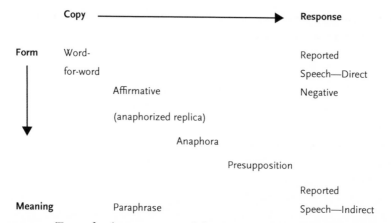

Copy ————————————————▶ **Response**

Form   Word-   Reported
           for-word   Speech—Direct
                        Affirmative   Negative

                        (anaphorized replica)

                             Anaphora

                        Presupposition

                                                      Reported
Meaning   Paraphrase   Speech—Indirect

FIGURE 1.1 Types of replication organized along two continua, whether the replication involves primarily word forms or meanings and whether the replica counts more as copy or as response.

Figure 1.1 represents an attempt to diagram the relationships among these various types of replication. The horizontal axis represents the continuum from types that appear more as copies to those that more readily seem to be responses. The vertical axis represents the continuum from replication of surface forms (as in word-for-word copies) to replication of the meanings associated with those forms.

Does All Response Contain Copy?

Deliberate copying as response occurs in ritualized discursive interactions, for example, the dialogical origin-myth telling of the Shokleng discussed in the "Differential Awareness of Replication" section. The responder rearticulates each syllable uttered by the lead speaker, with the myth unfolding in duplicate. Such dyadic telling may be likened to the replication of a stretch of DNA, and, indeed, in the Shokleng case the symbolic message encoded in the ritual form seems to be: "create as precise a copy as possible of what you hear"; "transmit with fidelity the material form of this story."

Such overt copying as response is a feature of at least some collective deliberations as well. Laura Graham ([1995] 2003: 137–174), for example, in her account of the men's council or *wará* among the Xavante of central Brazil, documented a striking example. During a 1985 meeting she recorded and photographed, the men lie about on the ground in a circle. They are on their backs, looking up at the sky, with their heads pointed toward the center of the circle, or on their sides (see photo on p. 153). Here is the English translation of one of her examples (Example 3, p. 157):

SIBUPA: [the Xavante] before us always lay together
    when they always ate larvae
    it was like that
WARODI: before they had food
SIBUPA: yes, before they had food
WARODI: before they had food
SIBUPA: before they had game

Graham notes: "The pattern of repetition in mature men's speech is so prevalent that even members of the audience repeat their own aside affirmations in exchanges among themselves" (157). The words seem to become detached from their moorings in specific individuals, emerging instead as productions of the group, an archetypal example of the collective production of a single voice.

In the snippet, Warodi responds to the stimulus utterance from Sibupa with a paraphrase. For Sibupa's utterance "when they always ate larvae," he offers: "before they had food," that is, before their ancestors had other types of food, they would eat larvae. Sibupa then affirms Warodi's paraphrase by precisely replicating Warodi's words with the addition of the affirmative marker, "yes," which, as I have suggested, can itself be construed as an anaphorized replicator. Warodi follows this with a repetition of his own prior statement, to which Sibupa responds with yet another replica, this time changing one of the words.

In Western figurations, the political arena is maximally dialogical or even polylogical, a space of contestation and difference. In the Xavante case, the analog to the political arena is the *warã*. Here the emergence of a single voice—a form of consensual monologism—arises out of processes of dialogic response as explicit replication.

Such replication, albeit in modified form, also takes place in typical conversations between two adults. Here is an example from the concluding scene of Alfred Hitchcock's 1955 romantic thriller, *To Catch a Thief*:[2]

FRANCIE:[3] Were you afraid I'd make you admit that without me you couldn't have saved yourself? That you needed the help of a good woman? That you're not the lone wolf you think you are?

---

2. Script available at http://www.scribd.com/doc/17716412/To-Catch-a-Thief-Screenplay.

3. Francine is played by Grace Kelly and Robie by Cary Grant.

ROBIE: All right—without you I couldn't have done it. I needed the help of a woman. I guess I'm not the lone wolf I thought I was, Francie.

FRANCIE: I just wanted to hear you say it.

Note that Robie might have responded simply "yes, you're right." However, he instead copies her words:

FRANCIE: . . . without me you couldn't have saved yourself

ROBIE: . . . without you I couldn't have done it

The copy includes replication of word forms ("without," "couldn't," "have"). "Done it" creates an anaphoric stand-in for "saved yourself/myself," while the shifter "you" (referring to the addressee of the stimulus utterance) gets transformed into "I" (referring to the speaker of the response utterance). The next two paired stimulus and response utterances show more complete replication, perhaps as a pragmatic suggestion of playful assent:

FRANCIE: . . . you needed the help of a good woman

ROBIE: . . . I needed the help of a woman

FRANCIE: . . . you're not the lone wolf you think you are

ROBIE: . . . I'm not the lone wolf I thought I was.

The pronominal transformations, along with tense shifts, occur here as well, marking the replicas as responses, a point to which I will return, as the awareness of response as distinct from copying or acquiring hinges upon such transformations. They are analogous to those found in reported speech.

In the *To Catch a Thief* example, "done it" is a stand in for "saved myself." It creates a copy or replica of the stimulus utterance *in absentia*, so to speak, by virtue of anaphoric reference. It points back to a previously uttered phrase, therefore obviating the need for copying the phrase itself. Evidently, Robie could have uttered: "without you I couldn't have saved myself." There might well be poetic reasons for why the anaphoric reference makes more sense here. The paraphrastic quality, for example, creates a greater degree of difference between the stimulus and response utterances, which parallels the social distance between the two individuals at the start of the interchange. As Robie's utterances become more obvious paraphrases of Francie's, he in turn warms to her, giving himself over to her words and so to her. Indeed, as one might anticipate in a romantic thriller, this final scene ends in an extended kiss.

In paraphrase, a gap opens between stimulus and response utterance, but anaphora in some measure bridges that gap, pulling the stimulus utterance via reference into the response utterance. This is true also where the response utterance, rather than repeating the stimulus or drawing it in via anaphora, presupposes it, as in the following example adapted from Silverstein (2014):

A: and you went to [undergraduate] school here or
B: in Chicago at, uh, Loyola
A: oh oh oh oh oh! I'm an old Jesuit boy myself, unfortunately
B: oh are ya? Where'd ya go?
A: Georgetown, down in Washington
B: oh yeah yeah

B's responses to A's questions, followed by A's response to B's question in each case, bring a portion of the stimulus utterance into the response utterance via presupposition or zero anaphora (Saeboe 1996; Oh 2005, 2006; see also Shopen 1973). Looked at from the perspective of response as replication, therefore, the utterances unfold as follows, exhibiting a kind of covert replication process:

A: and you went to [undergraduate] school here or
B: [I went to [undergraduate] school] in Chicago at, uh, Loyola
A: oh oh oh oh oh! I'm an old Jesuit boy myself, unfortunately
B1: oh are ya [an old Jesuit boy yourself]?
B2: Where'd ya go [to [undergraduate] school]?
A: [I went to [undergraduate] school at] Georgetown, down in Washington
B: oh yeah yeah [you went to [undergraduate] school at] Georgetown

Insertion of the anaphorically referenced material makes clear the extent to which replication underlies the stimulus-response pattern characteristic of dialogism.

Indeed, we might say that a purely pragmatic dialogue—one in which the respondent gives an acknowledging response, such as "uh-huh," but not a semantic contribution to what the speaker has said—always involves a repetition of the original speaker's words with no modification at all—that is, anaphorized replication. The reproduction takes place via the anaphoric pulling in of the stimulus utterance into the response. This accords with the kind of dialogical interaction pattern reported by Rumsey (2014) for eastern highland Papua New Guinea area storytelling, though he describes the response, quoting Pugh-Kitingan, as one indicating to the "performer that the story is not being wasted on a sleeping audience in the dark." In the view I am proposing here, the "yes" is an anaphorized stand-in for the replication of words that have just been spoken. Actual replication of words, of course, is the surest way of indicating that the respondent is not asleep and has heard what the speaker has said.

All of the examples suggest that response involves some measure of copying. Replication can, indeed, be described in terms of the "original" utterance and the "copy." The examples of response I have given, however, show that although the original (that is, the stimulus utterance) gets to some extent copied in the response, the response adds something to the original. This is true even in the Shokleng dyadic origin-myth telling. The second speaker's response, although a perfect copy of the lead speaker's syllable, also adds something to that first syllable. It adds the affirmation that the second speaker has heard what the first speaker said—and it makes that affirmation publicly accessible to the original speaker as well as to an audience or overhearers.

Is All Copying Response?

I have just proposed that all response involves some kind of copying of the original that is responded to. What about the reverse? If a copy takes place, is it a response? Here I return to the example of Mark Twain's dedication in his first book. Twain's friend proposed that he, Twain, had copied the dedication from an earlier book, one by Oliver Wendell Holmes. What are we to make of that copying? Had it been a response?

The Shokleng dyadic origin-myth telling involves copying, but it might be said to count as a minimal response. This is because the copy is publicly acknowledged as a copy. Consequently, the added acknowledgment makes it more than a copy. It makes it a copy that, owing to the co-presence of the original, signals its existence as a copy. Indeed, many ritual instances of copying could count as responses in this sense, for example, swearing into office ceremonies, as in President Obama's second inauguration in 2013, which, unlike the first, came off relatively without a hitch, containing only one slight stumble:

ROBERTS: Please raise your right hand and repeat after me:
      I Barack Hussein Obama do solemnly swear
OBAMA: I Barack Hussein Obama do solemnly swear
ROBERTS: that I will faithfully execute
OBAMA: that I will faithfully execute
ROBERTS: the office of President of the United States
OBAMA: the office of President of the United State[s]
ROBERTS: and will to the best of my ability
OBAMA: and will to the best of my ability
ROBERTS: preserve, protect, and defend
OBAMA: preserve, protect, and defend
ROBERTS: the Constitution of the United States

OBAMA: the Constitution of the United States
ROBERTS: so help you God?
OBAMA: so help me God.[4]

Notice that in the opening phrase Chief Justice Roberts says: "I Barack Hussein Obama" even though the first person singular pronoun is assumed to refer to Obama. This is in keeping with Roberts's initial command: "repeat after me." The copying indicates that Obama acknowledges that he has repeated after Roberts. His copy is an expression of compliance. There is public recognition of the copying process. The relationship between original and copy is that of command (stimulus) and response (compliance).

In the final couplet of this swearing-in, something different happens. A question gets asked and an answer given. This difference is signaled both by the interrogative form of Roberts's utterance, and also by the pronominal shift. Roberts refers to Obama as "you," and Obama replies with "me." The couplet is thus a full and genuine response, in the dialogical sense discussed earlier, even though it follows from a series of Shokleng-style replications. It is worth observing that the Presidential Oath, like the myth, is a piece of traditional discourse to be spoken verbatim. The form of the oath is specified in the US Constitution, Article II, section 1:

> "I do solemnly swear (or affirm) that I will faithfully execute the Office of President of the United States, and will to the best of my Ability, preserve, protect and defend the Constitution of the United States."

Interestingly, the final couplet in the Obama inauguration is not part of the Constitution, and, indeed, there has been some controversy over whether George Washington or other early presidents actually uttered the words "so help me God."[5] Still, the question and response is undeniably part of traditional discourse.

In the Shokleng origin-myth telling, as in the US presidential swearing-in ritual, the copying process is publicly obvious both to the interlocutors themselves and to any audience or overhearers. In the case of Twain's dedication, the copying was anything but obvious to Twain, who expresses horror at the thought

---

4. Transcribed from video of the United States presidential inauguration, January 2013, http://abcnews.go.com/Politics/video/inauguration-2013-president-obama-takes-oath-office-18273470 on June 10, 2014. The slight stumble occurs when Obama repeats the words "United States," the final "s" being either absent or unclearly articulated.

5. See, for example, the online piece: http://www.nonbeliever.org/commentary/inaugural_shmG.html.

that copying (read "plagiarism") has taken place. We don't know whether it was obvious to Oliver Wendell Holmes. However, it was apparent to Twain's friend, who was familiar with both works. From the point of view of publicity, no signal of the status of the copy as copy seems to have been readily accessible to a broader public. Hence, at least from the perspective of socially recognizable discourse processes, this would not count as an instance of response, even if it is an instance of copying.

One could argue that the "copy," in this case, is not identical to the original, as indicated in this phrase-by-phrase comparison:

HOLMES: To the most indulgent of readers,
TWAIN: To my most patient reader
HOLMES: the kindest of critics,
TWAIN: and most charitable critic,
HOLMES: my beloved mother,
TWAIN: my aged Mother,
HOLMES: all that is least unworthy of her in this volume is dedicated by her affectionate son.
TWAIN: this volume is affectionately inscribed.

The similarity is striking, especially in the first three phrases, though the fourth is divergent. Still, the divergence between original and copy might suggest response.

Here, however, I note that, in other instances, divergence shows up between original and copy even when the signals of copying are present. They result from entropic processes. In one set of experiments I conducted on the replication of discourse, I asked individuals to listen to a short recorded narrative, and then try to say it back as exactly as possible, word for word. They were instructed to then listen to the original again and try again to repeat it, and so forth. Here is an example of one sentence and a second attempt at replication by one individual:

ORIGINAL: In the sixteenth century, a dramatic series of religious, social, and political protests produced a new and influential form of Christianity.
COPY: In the sixteenth century, a series of dramatic social and political changes led to a new form of Christianity.

The changes we see in Twain's dedication are similar to those found in attempts to copy verbatim stretches of discourse that were heard and (partially) remembered. Such differences do not signal the kind of adding on characteristic of response, as discussed earlier, though they may come to look that way to one not familiar with the contexts. They rather signal the operation of entropic forces on the copying process.[6]

The same kind of entropic process can be seen in Obama's first swearing-in during January 2009:

ROBERTS: Are you prepared to take the oath, Senator?
OBAMA: I am.
ROBERTS: I Barack Hussein Obama do solemnly swear
OBAMA: *I Barack*
OBAMA: I Barack Hussein Obama do solemnly swear
ROBERTS: that I will execute the office of President to the United States faithfully
OBAMA: that I will execute [nods]
ROBERTS: the off ... faithfully the pres ... the office of President of the United States
OBAMA: *the office of*
    President of the United States faithfully
ROBERTS: and will to the best of my ability
OBAMA: and will to the best of my ability
ROBERTS: preserve, protect, and defend the Constitution of the United States
OBAMA: preserve, protect, and defend the Constitution of the United States
ROBERTS: So help you God?
OBAMA: So help me God.

Relative to the 2013 version, Obama's timing on the first copy appears here to have caused problems. He begins to repeat Roberts's words before Roberts has finished. I have indicated the overlap by putting this response in italics. This in turn throws Roberts off, so that he incorrectly replicates the next clause:

2009: that I will execute the office of President to the United States faithfully
2013: that I will faithfully execute the office of President of the United States

This causes Obama to ask Roberts to repeat—he does this by nodding. Roberts then stumbles over the line he has already misquoted.

In swearing-in ceremonies, the Shokleng origin-myth telling, and other ritualized forms of copying, there is awareness of copying but not of response. The

---

6. Tomlinson (2010) documents the changes a biblical verse (Genesis 1:26) undergoes as it moves from written text into oral circulation in Fiji. The changes are of the same order as those encountered in these experiments, but the reason for the changes is not entropy but rather the turning of "the stilted original version into a memorable poetic paraphrase" (744).

copiers see themselves as reproducing an original series of utterances that had previously been produced by someone else. They are trying to replicate the same discursive forms. They are not explicitly attempting to change those forms, to produce something different. If response is involved, it is of the most minimal type. The copiers signal that they are copying.

The Mark Twain case takes this one step further. He was, apparently, blissfully unaware of having produced a dedication strikingly reminiscent of one published earlier by Oliver Wendell Holmes. Not only was he unaware; he was horrified by the thought that he might have copied someone else. In his awareness, he had written something new and different, something catchy, interesting. He was not at all trying to be—or so he thought—Oliver Wendell Holmes. It is this lack of awareness that led him to dub this instance of replication "unconscious plagiarism."

Worth reflecting upon for a moment are the differences between plagiarism and unconscious plagiarism. In the former, there is awareness of copying, in the latter no awareness. In the former, there is also some effort made to conceal the copying from public scrutiny. There is no publicly accessible signal contained within the copy indicating that it is a copy other than the fact of its iconicity with some earlier form. In unconscious plagiarism, there is also no publicly accessible sign marking the copy as a copy. However, there is also no evidence of an effort at concealment.

This would suggest that awareness of the copy qua copy, and public marking or signaling of it as such, are characteristic of response. But I hesitate on this matter, since the relationship between copying and response likely has deep roots in psychological development, during which the boundaries between self and other are erected, a topic that has been of special interest in the psychoanalytic literature (Winnicott 1971; Kohut 1978; Wolf 1988). This is witnessed in the literature on discourse interactions between adults and children around age two, the stage when what Bloom (1970: 151ff.) called the "anaphoric no" develops. The latter is the negative form of what I called earlier "anaphorized replication." The "no" is a stand-in for what the interlocutor has said in the previous turn. Wode (1977: 88) gives an example of such anaphoric negation:

(4A) ADULT: Do you want salt?
(4B) CHILD: No, sugar.

Following the idea that the "no," like affirmative markers ("uh-huh," "right," "yeah"), is an indication of internal replication, the "no" may be seen as an overt mark of the child's internal copy of the adult utterance. However, it does more than that. It "rejects" (Cameron-Faulkner and Lieven 2007) the adult's suggestion that the child wants salt. Here we are evidently in the realm of response, with the word "sugar" indicating an alternative the child does want.

In any case, it may be that, in early developmental phases, before the acquisition of recognizable linguistic ability, the copy is not a "copy" at all because the self is not fully differentiated from the other. Conceivably, response only arises in conjunction with the differentiation of self and other, and simultaneously the differentiation of copy from response, with lack of distinction persisting in "unconscious plagiarism" of the Twain sort, where the copying results from a sort of taking into the self of the other—in Twain's case the taking in of Holmes's dedication.

Whatever the matter in psychoanalytic terms, from the point of view of culture and public circulation, it is possible to reach a conclusion. Copying counts as at least a minimal kind of response when the copied discourse includes some kind of marker of its status as copy. This may be the simple fact of iconicity in cases where the original is so well known that the copier can presume the discourse will be understood as a replica. The public mark may be space-time contiguity between copy and original, as in the Shokleng ritualized origin-myth telling or the US presidential swearing-in ceremony. It may also be an anaphoric or fully referential segment attached to the copy.

This last, of course, includes the phenomena known as reported speech, upon which I have already touched. Reported speech was central in Bakhtin's formulation of dialogism. So-called "direct quotation" ("You said: 'x'"), where the quotative explicitly declares the "x" a word-for-word replica, appears similar to the swearing in or the origin-myth-telling copying. Correspondingly, "indirect quotation" ("You said that 'x'") appears closer to the paraphrastic form of copying, since the "x" in this case purports to contain a copy of the original speaker's meaning albeit not its words. However, both are distinct from the other types of copying insofar they bring the difference between original speaker and responder into referential focus.

To return to the question with which this section began: Is all copying response? While unconscious plagiarism, as described by Twain, may count as response in some deep psychological sense, it does not from the point of view of culture and publicly interpretable signs. I would go further and suggest that much of culture passes to individuals who do not respond to it but rather assimilate it, as in the case of first language acquisition by a child. Perhaps we need to rethink the extent to which dialogism ought rightly to supplant monologism in cultural theory. At the same time, response as an orientation to culture clearly plays a role, not least in contemporary social life. We cannot simply return to earlier models.

From Cryptomnesia to Metaculture

Cryptomnesia: "the appearance in consciousness of memory images which are not recognized as such but which appear as original creations."[7] The term resonates with what Twain called "unconscious plagiarism." However, it focuses attention on the "appearance within consciousness" rather than, as in Twain's case, the production of actual discourse. Once the words are made public, in Twain's instance through writing and publication, they become part of an external world, a world that can then be cognized. They are not only memory images.[8]

To press the matter further, we might ask: What internal reflection processes led Twain to dub his experience "unconscious plagiarism?" The internal reflection turns out also to be of external origin—the remark by his friend about the dedication. It was the friend who observed what he regarded as an instance of replication, suggesting that Twain borrowed the words from Holmes. Twain did not come to his revelation exclusively through his own rumination. The reported incident suggests that Twain took his friend's suggestion as an insult. We might well ask: Why?

The answer is perhaps obvious to readers: regarding a piece of creative writing as derivative—as a "copy"—devalues it, diminishes its literary value. But again we can ask: Why? The answer here too is obvious: Twain must have held a value regarding literary works, or a standard against which such works, including his own, should be measured: they should be original and new. The value is also widely shared, most likely by Twain's friend, among others. The interaction between Twain and his friend became an instantiation of that widely circulating value.

The value of originality is a part of culture, to be sure, but it also reflects back on other culture, that is, on the relationship among literary works. It is therefore a piece of metaculture—culture that is about culture. So the Twain example appears, from this perspective, not simply as intrapsychic process, as in the definition of "cryptomnesia"; it appears instead as cultural process—the clash between an ideal to which Twain subscribed and the reality of the book he produced. The metaculture (the ideal of originality) was out of accord with the culture (the book

---

7. http://www.merriam-webster.com/medical/cryptomnesia.

8. As Matt Tomlinson pointed out to me, Twain himself continued to find fascination in the phenomenon of unconscious assimilation of literary discourse. In his book, *Following the Equator*, published nearly two decades after his unconscious plagiarism speech, Twain (1897: 107–108), reflecting on the poetry of an Englishman living in New Zealand whom he had met, wrote:

Perhaps no poet is a conscious plagiarist; but there seems to be warrant for suspecting that there is no poet who is not at one time or another an unconscious one. The above

dedication). Culture, in its meta form, weighs in when it comes to evaluating culture, in its object form, as transmitted through replication. How common is this clash?

Metacultural Heterogenization/Cultural Similarity

Nowadays, we find assertions of novelty in the economic realm: in the touting of automobiles, computers, cell phones, movies, music, and, of course, novels. We also find them in universities with the emphasis on producing new research, new knowledge; and we find them in the arts. Such assertions are metacultural. They move through space and time; they circulate like other aspects of culture, passing from individual to individual and group to group via processes of social transmission and social learning. At the same time, they reflect back on culture, and even influence the movement of culture.

It is hardly coincidental that dialogism, in Bakhtin's sense, arose with the modern novel. A characteristic of that literary genre is that any given novel must be different from others that have come before it. The novel must be new. But it cannot be totally new, totally different, since, if it were, it would be unrecognizable. Rather, the novel must embody a response to other novels, other discourse that has come before it. It must in some measure look like them. The encounter between voices internal to the novel is analogous to the encounter externally between any given authored novel and its predecessors.

Bakhtin was, of course, acutely aware of the connection between dialogism, the novel, and modernity. He treated the novel as arising with the Renaissance and the consciousness of a "new beginning" (Bakhtin 1981:7), what might be thought of as a metaculture of newness or differentiation. The present appears not just as a continuation of the past but also as a break from it. It exhibits in some measure the property of novelty. Correspondingly, the subjectivity of the individual comes into focus. The individual is represented as experiencing the world and responding to it. Of course, that world includes the words of others. Correspondingly, for Bakhtin the novel is a quintessentially modern form

---

verses are indeed beautiful, and, in a way, touching; but there is a haunting something about them which unavoidably suggests the Sweet Singer of Michigan [Julia A. Moore]. It can hardly be doubted that the author had read the works of that poet and been impressed by them. It is not apparent that he has borrowed from them any word or yet any phrase, but the style and swing and mastery and melody of the Sweet Singer all are there. Compare this Invocation with 'Frank Dutton'—particularly stanzas first and seventeenth—and I think the reader will feel convinced that he who wrote the one had read the other.

because it foregrounds the narrator, who responds to the words of the narrated characters through the framing of reported speech.

Reported speech in the novelistic genre is not yet truly "polyphonic," a phenomenon Bakhtin saw as developing with the writings of Dostoevsky. The characteristic of polyphony in Dostoevsky, according to Bakhtin, is that the narrator's voice no longer furnishes the dominant ground of unification of the narrative. Rather, distinct voices emerge in their own right as equally valid, creating a relativistic field or arena of discourse. The novel becomes, so to speak, a colloidal suspension of voices, each capable of commenting on and interpreting the other.

Perhaps it is obvious by this point that the idea of culture as responded to, rather than acquired, as in Tylor's definition, can be viewed as an essentially modern invention, or, at least, as an outgrowth of a metaculture of newness or differentiation, in much the way Bakhtin viewed the novel as an essentially modern literary form. If the narrator responds to the words of others, so too, in effect, can anyone exposed to culture—thought of in this context as the prior words and deeds of others. Hence, when filtered through the lens of metacultural newness, culture no longer appears as if it were acquired from the past; it appears rather as responded to.

Without fully developing the point here, I want to suggest the possibility that a metaculture of newness or differentiation may (perhaps even usually does) co-occur with homogeneity at the cultural plane, with minimal actual differentiation. A metaculture of newness encourages differentiation, and especially so where true differentiation is difficult to achieve. This possibility provides an answer to the question: Why should assertions of newness circulate?

If people spontaneously differentiate themselves culturally—adopting distinctive styles in the consumer realm, responding to others in the discursive realm—why should they continually tell themselves how good differentiation is, how valuable newness is? From the perspective I am proposing, a metaculture of differentiation arises where there is a felt need to produce greater difference, or perhaps to make differences appear greater than they actually are, as in the economic realm in order to sell goods or in the area of research in order to tout new findings.

In the language of replication I have been using throughout this paper, a metaculture of difference celebrates the gap between original and copy. With even minimal difference, it conjures an interpretation of copying as response or as creation of the new. It focuses attention on distinctiveness to the exclusion of sameness. It makes the monological appear dialogical, perhaps even polylogical.

Some evidence of how the ideal of difference causes people to assert their individuality is the mockery of that very ideal in Monty Python's *Life of Brian*. The central character in the film, Brian, an ordinary fellow, just happens to be born on what will later be known as "Christmas Day" in a stable next to the true Messiah, Jesus Christ. As the plot unfolds, Brian gets mistaken for Christ, and he develops a following. He denies that he is the Messiah, but his following continues to grow. One morning, while still naked, Brian throws open the shutters and to his horror the throngs have already assembled outside. He closes the shutters, gets dressed, opens them again, and attempts to reason with the crowd. A "dialogue" of sorts ensues. Brian tells them: "Go away. You are all individuals." They respond in unison: "We are all individuals."

What renders this sequence a rich parody is that the semantics of the response involves an assertion of the individuality of the responders. However, in fact, the responders merely parrot—that is, copy—what has been told to them by Brian. Moreover, that the crowd does so in chant-like unison foregrounds the pragmatically monological character of the interaction: they speak with one voice.

An added ironic twist is the meek assertion by one individual in the crowd: "I'm not." By semantically denying that he is an individual, he pragmatically demonstrates that he is. Indeed, he is the only one willing to engage both Brian and the crowd "dialogically," in Bakhtin's sense. His response represents a rejection of Brian's original assertion, and therefore an assertion of his own distinctiveness as an individual with respect to Brian.

Metacultural Homogenization/Cultural Difference

Having considered the possibility that a metacultural ideal of difference or dialogism or newness, however we wish to call it, might co-occur with a culture of similarity or homogeneity, let me now turn to the opposite possibility, namely, that a metaculture of similarity or monologism or tradition might overlay a culture of difference or heterogeneity. The latter phenomenon is actually well-known, albeit not one usually thought of in connection with replication, copying, and response. Widely known, in particular, is the length to which modern collectivities, especially nations, go to try to produce discursive agreements, to speak with a single voice.

In constitution-making, the goal is a constitution or set of statements on which the constitution-makers can agree. In the case of the US Constitution, the work was done in closed-door meetings. On May 29, 1787, the committee of the whole adopted supplementary standing rules of the House, of which the following three seem especially noteworthy in connection with the circulation of discourse during the convention (Farrand 1911: 15):

That no copy be taken of any entry on the journal during the sitting of the House without the leave of the House.

That members only be permitted to inspect the journal.

That nothing spoken in the House be printed, or otherwise published, or communicated without leave.

The rules are metacultural, pertaining to the problem of copying and response as part of the deliberation process. The first of these explicitly prohibits copying of journal entries. Why? Evidently, the point of this rule and the others is to make sure that Congress speaks to the public with a single voice—that is, in the terms of the theme of this volume, that monologism prevails. If delegates to the Convention spoke as one, this would in turn, arguably at least, encourage the population outside the closed doors to receive the constitution with less questioning of it. In the language of replication, the American people would copy the constitutional words rather than respond to them.

The same can be said of allowing only members of the Convention to inspect the journal, and of restricting the further circulation of anything said within the Convention, although a note on the last of these points indicates that the rule was not always followed. Still, the metacultural directive seems clear: speak with one voice.

The journal entries of the proceedings, indeed, mention no disagreements or arguments, other than one or another motion proposed by a specific representative being objected to by another or turned down. For example, the journal entry for May 31, 1787, included the following (Farrand 1911: 46):

It was then moved & seconded to proceed to the consideration of the following clause of the fourth resolution (submitted by Mr Randolph) namely

"Resolved that the members of the first branch of the national legislature ought to be elected by the people of the several States."

and on the question to agree to the said clause of the fourth resolution it passed in the affirmative [Ayes—6; noes—2; divided—2]

The wordings gradually accumulated through voting. The entire document was then turned over to a sub-committee to do the drafting, followed by more discussions of wordings, and another go at the document by the "style committee," which produced another draft.

In retrospect, all of the closed-door proceedings, as recorded in the journal, are so stripped down that it is difficult to understand today, more than two centuries later, why they were kept secret. Yet kept secret they were. According to historian Max Farrand (1911: xi-xii): George Washington, who had kept the journal in his possession, "deposited these papers with the Department of State in 1796, where they remained untouched until Congress by a joint resolution in

1818 ordered them to be printed." Even these minimally descriptive entries did not see the light of day for nearly three decades.

Farrand, along with many subsequent historians (see, e.g., Beeman 2009), attempted to reconstruct the proceedings not just from the journal, but from notes taken by a number of the delegates, most notably James Madison. Madison and others recorded, for their own purposes, the controversies that took place. Madison too, however, felt that his notes should not be published until after his death. He died in 1836, with the notes seeing the light of print in 1840 under the title *The Papers of James Madison*. Madison's jottings reveal contestation; the resolutions were, in fact, responded to, and often vigorously. Regarding the May 31, 1787, resolution, concerning popular election of members to the first branch of the legislature (that is, what became known as the House of Representatives), Madison's notes include the following (Farrand 1911: 48):

> Mr. Sherman opposed the election by the people, insisting that it ought to be by the (State) Legislatures. The people he said, (immediately) should have as little to do as may be about the Government. They want information and are constantly liable to be misled.
>
> Mr. Gerry. The evils we experience flow from the excess of democracy. The people do not want virtue; but are the dupes of pretended patriots. In Massts. it has been fully confirmed by experience that they are daily misled into the most baneful measures and opinions by the false reports circulated by designing men, and which no one on the spot can refute.

Responses such as these were, undoubtedly, what the Founding Fathers wished to keep out of the public eye, at least, that is, until the single-voiced constitution had had a chance to settle in. Madison's notes did not appear in print until fifty-three years after they were written.

The point here is that single-voicedness—monologism, in the terms of this book—was a metacultural ideal implemented through the regulation of discourse processes. Moreover, the metaculture of similarity or monologism overlaid a culture of differentiation and rampant dialogism. The constitution came into existence by the repeated insistence upon limiting copying to the final official wording. Responses, at least the Convention-internal responses to the wording, were reined in by metaculture. Metacultural homogeneity thus goes along with its opposite: cultural heterogeneity. Culture and metaculture here stand in a contradictory relationship, just as they do in the economic realm discussed earlier, though there the terms are reversed: a metaculture of heterogeneity and difference overlays a culture of homogeneity and sameness.

It is worth noting that the closed constitution-making of the American variety is not fashionable today. Nowadays, experiments are underway with open or "inclusive" forms (Hart 2003; Landemore 2015). However, these inclusive forms do not involve a simple metaculture of dialogism, even though they appear to stress consultation with the broader public. The idea remains to create a monological discourse out of the dialogical processes leading up to it, which Elster (2012) conceptualized as hour-glass shaped—a period of broad public consultation narrowing to a small group of constitution-writers, whose results then circulate further outward. In reality, the difference with the US procedure, looked at in terms of discourse processes, is not as great as it might at first seem. Rather than concealing the dialogism from the national public, inclusive forms allow the dialogism to drown out the responses, enabling the monological discourse to surface.

Conclusion

Perhaps I have by now sufficiently complicated the initial question regarding dialogical and monological views of culture—whether culture is acquired (that is, copied) or responded to. I have been at pains to show that response involves (if it is genuinely response) copying. This places both copying and responding in the arena of replication. Indeed, how could it be otherwise? Even the received terminology of the Hegelian dialectic suggests this relationship, with "*thesis*" giving rise to "anti*thesis*" and, in turn, to "syn*thesis*." However, not all replication is necessarily response, unless, of course, we want to reserve copying for the self-aware, publicly acknowledged process of replication, with "replica" taken as the unmarked term.[9]

In actual dialogue, copying as response takes any of a range of forms, from word-for-word replicas, on the one extreme, to paraphrase, on the other. The range extends, in other words, from copying forms to copying meanings. Affirmative responses—like "uh-huh" in English or the eastern highland New Guinea markers described by Rumsey, anaphorized replicators—represent substitutes for a word-for-word copy, which, however, could, in the informal experiments I have done, be elicited from a responder who utters it, albeit with varying degrees of faithfulness. From such complete anaphoric copying we move on to

---

9. While I have not been consistent in this chapter, I believe there is merit in taking "replica" to be the general or unmarked term, with "copy" referring more specifically to occurrences in which there is at least minimal self-awareness of similarity between model and replica. In this terminology, "response" would involve some degree of self-awareness of the difference between replica and model, with minimal or even no awareness of similarity.

partial anaphora, and then zero anaphora. Reported speech represents a special case along this continuum, perhaps parallel to it, in which responders consciously create a distinction between their own words and those of the speaker, though they may duplicate the actual word forms, as in direct reported speech, or the meanings, as in indirect reported speech.

To constitute a response, something must be added to the copy to make it distinct, and some kind of public acknowledgment of the original on which the copy is based must take place. In Shokleng origin-myth telling, where the purpose is to copy as precisely as possible, the original is acknowledged by virtue of spatio-temporal contiguity between the speaker's and responder's syllables. Contiguity makes plain that copying is a response to the original.

Not all copying need be response, however. The copy may be based on many distinct models, in relation to which no particular original stands out. For example, in Twain's case, to include a dedication in a book would not itself constitute unconscious plagiarism. Such dedications are part of the general culture of authorship, which Twain replicated via instantiation. Nor for that matter are dedications to one's mother. Again, no unconscious plagiarism in that; no cryptomnesia. What suggests that Twain had unconsciously adopted Holmes's dedication as a model, or at least what suggested as much to Twain's friend, is the similarity in wording. But even here we may question whether it is appropriate to call such "copying" response.

Response seems to require not only acknowledgment of the original—absent in Twain's case—but also of the separateness of originator and responder. Indeed, in true plagiarism, the writer endeavors to conceal from the public eye the original on which the writing is based. There is no true response. From the perspective of external cultural processes, there is no distinction between original and copy. The two are merged as one. Though the replicator has an awareness of the replica as copy, that awareness is concealed from the public. In Twain's case—cryptomnesia or unconscious plagiarism—it is as if he had assimilated the Holmes original the way a child assimilates a mother tongue, probably through seeing it many times. Replication as assimilation is not so much response as it is an expression of merger, lack of differentiation, participation, so to speak, in a common substance.

The distinction between copy as response and copy as merger takes us into a depth psychological realm, one that can be only touched upon tangentially here. What does it mean to be a distinctive self in the world? The question has been explored in psychoanalysis (e.g., Winnicott 1971; Kohut 1978; Wolf 1988: 56ff.), where the sense of difference ("self/object differentiation") is posited as emerging over the course of child development. The process is, moreover, one that may never be fully complete, with the self-other boundary remaining for certain purposes less than sharply etched. If something is unconsciously assimilated, it is not as if one is aware of a difference between self and others from whom the culture was assimilated. On the contrary, one may more have a sense of similarity between self and other. The process is more akin to the monological model of culture prominent in the earlier history of anthropology.

At the same time, in Twain's case, the replica was not identical with the alleged model. However, as I hope to have shown, the difference between model and replica alone is not prima facie evidence of response. Even in cases of minimal response where "response" consists in public acknowledgment of the copy as copy, as in the 2009 US presidential swearing-in or the experimental evidence I referred to, difference emerges. As anthropologists have long observed (Sapir 1921; Herskovits 1949, 1955), entropic forces resulting in "cultural drift" gnaw away at language and culture, reshaping replicas over time.

To be publicly acknowledged as response, the replica must include some kind of semiotic mark. The signal could be as elementary as spatiotemporal contiguity, as in back-and-forth conversation. It could be as fully referential as reported speech. In the case of novels, the generic framing of the written form as a novel—where the emphasis is on producing something new—acknowledges the existence of other novels that have come before it. Specific aspects of plot or setting or character development may also serve to acknowledge more specific genealogies for a given novel. These too are public signals, at least for those who are able to read them.

The public signals of copying or response can become organized and abstracted as developed metaculture; and they can include evaluative and normative components. Furthermore, metaculture can be not simply a reflection of culture, but a way to encourage the ideals it promotes in a world out of sync with those ideals. It can focus attention and stimulate response rather than copying, as in the contemporary economic realm and also in the creative arenas of arts and sciences, even though it overlays apparent homogeneity at the cultural plane, with individuals seemingly copying one another. Alternatively, it can, as in the political realm of constitution-making, focus attention on homogeneity and stimulate copying, even though it overlays dissent and response at the cultural plane.

This brings me to a final conclusion: that dialogism and monologism are both manifestations of cultural replication, of the broader motion of culture through space and time. Dialogism foregrounds response; monologism copying. As metacultural ideas and ideals, both can be linked in seemingly paradoxical ways to their opposite at the cultural level. For anthropological theory, the sanest conclusion is that we need to nuance, rather than abandon, the formulation of culture as acquired, training our analytical gaze on the replicative processes through which "acquisition" occurs, and circulation develops. These processes involve both copying and response, and they take place with different degrees of awareness on the part of the actors involved. And, finally, awareness itself—as a community-level characteristic—can be circulated through metaculture, whose relationship to culture we must problematize.

References

Bakhtin, Mikhail. 1981. *The Dialogic Imagination*. Trans. C. Emerson and M. Holquist. Austin: University of Texas Press.

Beeman, Richard R. 2009. *Plain, Honest Men: The Making of the American Constitution*. New York: Random House.

Bloom, Lois. 1970. *Language Development: Form and Function in Emerging Grammars*. Research Monograph No. 59. Cambridge, MA: MIT Press.

Cameron-Faulkner, Thea, and Elena Lieven. 2007. "What Part of No Do Children Not Understand? A Usage-Based Account of Multiword Negation." *Journal of Child Language* 33:251–282.

Durkheim, Émile. (1912) 1969. *The Elementary Forms of the Religious Life*. Trans. J. W. Swain. New York: Free Press.

Elster, Jon. 2012. "The Optimal Design of a Constituent Assembly." In *Collective Wisdom: Principles and Mechanisms*, ed. H. Landemore and J. Elster, 148–172. Cambridge: Cambridge University Press.

Farrand, Max. 1911. *The Records of the Federal Convention of 1787*. Vol. 1. Ed. Max Farrand. New Haven, CT: Yale University Press.

Geertz, Clifford. 1973. *The Interpretation of Cultures*. New York: Basic Books.

Graham, Laura. (1995) 2003. *Performing Dreams: Discourses of Immortality among the Xavante of Central Brazil*. Austin: University of Texas Press.

Hall, Edward T. 1966. *The Hidden Dimension*. Garden City, NY: Doubleday.

Hart, Vivien. 2003. "Democratic Constitution Making." United States Institute of Peace Special Report 107 (July).

Herskovits, Melville J. 1949. *Man and His Works: The Science of Cultural Anthropology*. New York: Knopf.

Herskovits, Melville J. 1955. *Cultural Anthropology*. New York: Knopf.

Holmes, Oliver Wendell. 1862. *Songs in Many Keys*. Boston: Ticknor and Fields.

Kohut, Heinz. 1978. "Remarks about the Formation of the Self: Letter to a Student Regarding Some Principles of Psychoanalytic Research." In *The Search for the Self: Selected Writings of Heinz Kohut: 1950–1978*, vol. 2, ed. Paul H. Ornstein, 737–782. New York: International Universities Press.

Labov, William. 1972. *Sociolinguistic Patterns*. Philadelphia: University of Pennsylvania Press.

Labov, William. 2001. "The Anatomy of Style Shifting." In *Style and Sociolinguistic Variation*, ed. Penelope Eckert and John Rickford, 85–108. Cambridge: Cambridge University Press.

Landemore, Hélène. 2015. "Inclusive Constitution-Making: The Icelandic Experiment." *Journal of Political Philosophy* 23(2): 166-191. doi: 10.1111/jopp.12032.

Oh, Sun-Young. 2005. "English Zero Anaphora as an Interactional Resource." *Research on Language and Social Interaction* 38(3): 267–302.

Oh, Sun-Young. 2006. "English Zero Anaphora as an Interactional Resource II." *Discourse Studies* 8(6): 817–846.

Rumsey, Alan. 2014. "Monologue and Dialogism in Highland New Guinea Verbal Art." Revised version of talk given at 2013 AAA panel on "The Monologic Imagination," Washington, DC.

Saeboe, Kjell Johan. 1996. "Anaphoric Presuppositions and Zero Anaphora." *Linguistics and Philosophy* 19:187–209.

Sapir, Edward. 1921. *Language: An Introduction to the Study of Speech*. New York: Harcourt, Brace.

Shopen, T. 1973. "Ellipsis as Grammatical Indeterminacy." *Foundations of Language* 10:65–77.

Silverstein, Michael. 2014. "Discourse and the No-thingness of Culture." *Signs and Society* 1(2): 327–366.

Tedlock, Dennis, and Bruce Mannheim, eds. 1995. *The Dialogic Emergence of Culture*. Urbana: University of Illinois Press.

Tomlinson, Matt. 2010. "Compelling Replication: Genesis 1:26, John 3:16, and Biblical Politics in Fiji." *Journal of the Royal Anthropological Institute*, n.s., 16:743–760.

Twain, Mark. 1869. *The Innocents Abroad: Or the New Pilgrim's Progress*. Hartford, CT: American Publishing Company. Project Gutenberg http://www.gutenberg.org/files/3176/3176-h/3176-h.htm.

Twain, Mark. 1897. *Following the Equator: A Journey around the World*. Hartford, CT: American Publishing Company.

Twain, Mark. 1910. "Unconscious Plagiarism." In *Mark Twain's Speeches*, by Mark Twain, 56–58. New York: Harper and Brothers.

Tylor, Edward Burnett. (1871) 1889. *Primitive Culture: Researches into the Development of Mythology, Philosophy, Religion, Art, and Custom*. New York: Henry Holt.

Urban, Greg. 1986. "Ceremonial Dialogues in South America." *American Anthropologist* 88(2): 371–386.

Urban, Greg. 1994. "Repetition and Cultural Replication: Three Examples from Shokleng." In *Repetition in Discourse: Interdisciplinary Perspectives*, vol. 2, ed. Barbara Johnstone, 145-161. Norwood, NJ: Ablex.

Winnicott, D.W. 1971. *Playing and Reality*. New York: Basic Books.

Wode, Henning. 1977. "Four Early Stages in the Development of Li Negation." *Journal of Child Language* 4(1): 87–102.

Wolf, Ernest S. 1988 *Treating the Self: Elements of Clinical Self Psychology*. New York: Guilford Press.

2 DIALOGIC PROPHECIES AND MONOLOGIC VISION

Jon Bialecki

"The Highest Voice" and the "Inquisitors' Kiss"

A chapter, let alone an edited volume, about Bakhtin and monologue may strike some as being purposefully perverse. Its man-bites-dog edge comes from the way that it appears to be a purposeful inversion of the usual Bakhtinian concerns with heteroglossia. One might further imagine that writing a monologic Bakhtinian account of social life would be theoretically rather hard sledding; or to be more exact, one might think that it might be a challenge for those academics who do not focus their studies on populations that understand themselves to be monotheists. After all, it would seem to be a fair supposition that the one area where identifying and articulating monologue should be easy is in the anthropology of Christianity, a religion that claims that Jesus is both the Truth and the Word.

This is in short a baseline claim that the cacophony of voices implicit in heteroglossia seems to be the inverse of the monotheistic presumption. This also seems to be the implicit logic behind Bakhtin's statement made in *Dostoevsky's Creative Work*, where he stated that Christ is "the highest voice," the one who "must crown the world of voices, must organize and subdue it" (Coates 1998: 95). Counterpoised against this, though, must be Bakhtin's emphasis on the kenotic nature of Christ, the vision of Jesus as someone who emptied himself out completely through his immersion into the material world. This would be a vision of Christ not as monological, but as the author who must erase himself to make space for the heteroglot voices of others. Under this reading, the Bakhtinian Jesus is also the one that appeared in *The Brothers Karamazov*, as written by Bakhtin's inspiration, Dostoevsky: the completely silent figure that only responds to the Great Inquisitor's complete rejection of him with a wordless kiss.

Putting these two actualizations of Jesus alongside each other, there appears to be a contradiction in Bakhtin, where Christianity is at once the clearest instance of monologue and at the same time the empty grounding of heteroglossia. This deadlock in Bakhtin's thinking should be taken seriously, especially because of its religious overtones. It was, after all, Bakhtin's Christian associations and belief that got him sent into his half-century long exile; to view Bakhtin's thoughts regarding the monologic, the heterologic, and Christianity as a mere secondary issue seems to be in poor taste. Even worse, it threatens to undermine our understanding of Bakhtin's argument.

I will leave the question of what Bakhtin personally believed to scholars of Bakhtin; here, instead, I will take up the question of what this contradictory doubling in Bakhtin's thought means for an anthropology of religion in general and an anthropology of Christianity in particular. Does this tell us anything about how Christianity's own organization and possibilities are structured? The problem will be thought through by way of a specific ethnographic case: that of the Vineyard, a Southern California-originated but now worldwide church movement. The Vineyard is notable for two things. First, it tends to skew more middle class, and with more highly educated members, than other American charismatic groups. The second is that the Vineyard engages in an intense range of religious practices commonly associated with Pentecostalism—healing, deliverance from demons, speaking in tongues, and so on (see Bialecki 2011a, b; Luhrmann 2012). This means that by way of the miraculous in general and prophecy in particular Vineyard believers appear to have privileged access to divine truth. This is a promising constellation of capacities and understandings if one is looking for a pure sample of the monological speaker.

So how does prophecy work in the Vineyard, and can it be thought of in terms of monologue? The first thing to understand about prophecy is that in most instances of it, its import seems to be profoundly underdetermined; in fact, this occurs to a degree that seems to foreclose an understanding of prophecy as monological. When Vineyard believers describe the phenomenological aspects of prophecy, they state it mostly comes in the form of a passing, but sometimes intense, sensual impression, or uncharacteristic urge or desire; even more frequent is prophecy being received in the form of a mental picture that appears in a flash. A brief image of a sword cutting through darkness, a flower opening up, or a vision of a person running through a field, may constitute the phenomenological nub that a prophetic utterance by a believer is built around.

Not only does the message come in a form that seems to leave its interpretation open, but there is also a sense that, to the degree that it is capable of being glossed as an imperative, the action that the sensation is understood as symbolizing or indexing is understood to be voluntaristic in nature. While people will sometimes make major life changes based on what they believe to be divine promptings—on anything from careers to marriages—there are also those who do not take up the message. This is either because they feel there is a lack of certainty as to what the call is that the sensation is supposed to be heralding (the imagistic nature of these events can sometimes make them quite difficult to decode) or because prophetic messages are placed into a sort of suspension by having recipients or interpreters classify them as in effect commissive speech acts, a foretaste of an opportunity or turn that will come to the believer . . . in due season, and under the right circumstances. Not all prophetic events are capable of being presented as contingent or indeterminate, of course: there is nothing subtle about a vision of the word "seminary" flashing before one's eyes in letters made of fire. But because of the poetic and imagistic nature of so much of Vineyard prophecy, much of it can be treated as voluntaristic and underdetermined.

This voluntaristic and underdetermined aspect works not only during prophecy personally experienced but also affects the form prophecy takes as reported speech. It is common not to have a prophetic experience directly oneself, but for someone else to share a prophecy that they have received and believe is intended for you. This is because while many people experience the kind of visions and sensations that are understood as prophetic, many others do not; those who lack a prophetic gifting or who have a weak or unreliable capacity for prophecy must get their prophecy second-hand. There are also times when someone gets a message for someone who has their own prophetic capacity as well; this sometimes takes the form of a sudden and often insistent sense that one must communicate a specific image to someone, even though the recipient of the prophetic sensation may not understand the import of that which he or she is supposed to impart to the ultimate intended recipient of the prophetic message.

Understandably, these messages have undergone a sort of typification, forming a protocol or speech genre. The most common form of sharing a prophetic word in the Vineyard is to describe the vision and then gloss it with a reading ("I saw a sword / I think God is saying that you are a warrior for him"). There is also another form, more often used with people who have no context for prophecy, which takes the form of a question ("Do you have a bad relationship with your father?"). This question will often be followed by a description of a vision and by a gloss, which is often a message of hope or healing related to the original question. What is important to note in these cases is that the gloss is not (usually) understood as a part of the original prophetic message, as indicated by the qualifiers that frequently accompany the statement; recipients are often asked to provide their own gloss, or are asked if either the gloss, or the description of the prophetic experience, "sounds right" or is "getting at something." This refers not only to whether the message "conforms to God's character," that is, matches Vineyard members' conception of what God is like (which is for the most part a therapeutic, positive vision; see Rakow 2013); it also means whether it speaks to the person's current concerns or hits an emotional chord. If it fails this latter test, then the recipient is free to discard the message, an act which usually does not cast aspersions on the person who offered the prophecy. Unlike the Deuteronomic code, in the Vineyard false prophets are not put to death.[1]

Finally, it is important to understand that prophetic utterances cannot collectively be looked at as a corpus, forming a singular authoritative meta-text. In addition to the uncertain validity of any specific prophetic utterance, there is the sense that one would not necessarily envision a wider pattern among prophecy as a totality. God is often described as "messy," as not reducible to human expectations or desires, and thus his intentions are beyond any human totalization.[2] Now, people do believe that God has a plan for their lives; many Vineyard believers also think of their relationship with God as having different temporalized periods characterized by closeness or distance, intimacy or estrangement.

This odd, tentative, and open character of prophecy, which invites a dialogic response instead of forestalling it, makes sense. It is consonant with other ethnographic accounts of this movement; the title alone of Tanya Luhrmann's book on the Vineyard, *When God Talks Back*, starts off with God in a dialogic relationship with the believer. This also makes theoretical sense within the Bakhtinian paradigm that informs this chapter and this volume. Given the constitutive alterity of all language for Bakhtin, it is no surprise that even if it is not the full embrace of multiplicity that constitutes the Bakhtinian novel, in prophecy the ever-present seams of language show.

The more interesting question perhaps is not whether we can identify heteroglossia in the prophetic admixture taken from the imagistic divine voice of God, the reported speech and interpretive gloss given by the prophetic medium, and the final response given by the ultimate recipient of the prophecy. A more striking question is what the political effects of this are, either at the level of politics as a self-conscious object of discourse (Spencer 2007; Candea 2011) or at the level of a micro-politics, the latent shifts in sensibilities and potential in quotidian interactions and imagination that open up the way to new political formations (Deleuze

---

1. Deuteronomy 18:20: "But any prophet who speaks in the name of other gods, or who presumes to speak in my name a word that I have not commanded the prophet to speak—that prophet shall die" (New Revised Standard Version).

2. Although retroactive accounts are sometimes capable of being put forward with a semblance of confidence.

and Guattari 1999; Bialecki 2009, 2010, 2015). There are reasons to believe that this is the case, at least when one looks at the wider discussion of what constitutes a Pentecostal and charismatic politics.

At this point, I would like to briefly consider the works of Ruth Marshall and Thomas Csordas in this regard. Ruth Marshall, a political scientist who writes on African Pentecostalism with an ethnographer's sensibility, sees the Pentecostal miraculous as a force that precludes theocracy, which for our purposes we can take to be an architecture of governance as perhaps the ultimate in monological social forms. Within Pentecostalism, "the people decide," Marshall writes. Since "prophetic power is accessible by all . . . Pentecostal temporality and its framing of miracles" is

> dependent on an openness to interpellation and the fragile and fallible power of individual discernment. God has promised, but it is up to every individual to interpret the exhortation and prescriptions of the Word and its revelation through miracles and signs as particular manifestations of this providence. (Marshall 2009: 215)

This is a system of religiosity that is by no means democratic, but it is impossible for it to become authoritarian, either; and this impossibility is an effect of the dialogic and heteroglossic open dialectic between the divine and the human.

I quote Ruth Marshall at length because this reading of Pentecostalism, the miraculous, and prophecy is not the only understanding of Pentecostal-charismatic politics that has been put forward. I think that it is instructive to contrast Marshall's opinion with another political science account; this other account draws its evidence from the same ethnographic West African Pentecostal scene that we saw Marshall addressing. Unlike the previous vision of Pentecostal openness, this account sees in Pentecostal sovereignty a failure to "institute the distinction between power and right," where the economy of the miraculous encourages "the conflation of personal spiritual power and the power over others, giving rise to a politics of conviction and vengeance." In this account, there is a "stalling of a dialectical relation between powers" and a "conflation of spiritual and temporal authority in religion." For this author, "divine power is not a means, but pure manifestation, pure violence." Here, the Pentecostal structure of the miraculous, and hence of prophecy, is a re-theologized but otherwise faithful iteration of the political-theological state of the exception, originally theorized by the Nazi political scientist Carl Schmitt (1985); an authoritarian, and hence monological, vision. This contrasting view comes from none other than . . . Ruth Marshall (2009: 211–213).

This contradiction in Marshall's work can be seen in the work of other scholars who have grappled with charismatic-Pentecostal politics. Thomas Csordas
has thought through charismatic phenomena in ways that are very similar to the
dialogical model that we have here, albeit couched in the technical terms of a
cultural phenomenology; for him, Pentecostal-style religious practice entails a
necessary moment of open intersubjectivity during charismatic events, where
subjects encounter each other as "another myself" who cannot be rendered as a
mere object in that moment (Csordas 1994: 13).

However, Csordas has also documented instances of public prophecy becoming entextualized and autocratic. He recounts "bulwark prophecies," so named
because during the 1970s a series of these prophecies commanded the Catholic
charismatic movement to unify so that it could serve as "a bulwark against the
enemy." These prophecies were given at large quasi-public spaces, such as Saint
Peter's Basilica in Rome, and at significance-laden times (such as a 1975 Catholic-
charismatic world conference). However, it was their formal features that did as
much work as the locales in which they occurred. Read synoptically, what is striking about these bulwark prophecies was that they were speech acts structured to
occlude their status as reported speech, being presented in a way that tended to
erase the prophetic human intermediary. Furthermore, the deictic work of the
pronouns was to produce both the idea of crisis, and the unity of the Catholic
charismatic movement, as a *fait accompli*, with God presented as unilaterally,
directly, and effectively announcing a global and unavoidable state of affairs, using
the first-person singular, speaking to a single second-person plural. Together, this
prophecy was a series of prophetic commissives that worked to "minimize the
intertextual gap between prophecy and sacred scripture," creating a sense of unified biblical and prophetic authority (Csordas 1997a). Unsurprisingly, Csordas
saw these prophecies as instrumental in the increasingly authoritarian and isola-
tionist turn that much of the Catholic charismatic movement would take in the
next decade (see also Csordas 1997b).

The contradictory stances in Marshall's and Csordas's accounts do not mean
they are theoretically deficient. If there is any error here, it is in essence the same
"error" we see in Bakhtin, which suggests something more along the lines of per-
spicaciousness than failure. But this also hints at something more broad-ranging,
suggesting a regularity or relation between religious monologue and dialogue.
Once may be an accident, but three times is a pattern.

There seem to be at least two ways of thinking through a relation between
the monological and dialogical here. The first hypothesis is that there may be
moments in which the dialogic nature of prophecy becomes abused, where the
prophet uses his authority to tip the social scale so as to be overweening. It is true
that in Vineyard-like churches, it is not uncommon to hear of prophecies which

are supplemented by power differentials between the person giving prophecy and the person receiving it; the classic example of this sort of prophecy is when a male pastor receives a "word" about a teenage female church member, suggesting that she has engaged in some kind of immoral thought or action. While this is not always overtly sexualized, the social awkwardness of dismissing or challenging this kind of prophecy should be obvious, especially if it is presented in a semi-public or public space. To a large degree, much of the Vineyard's practices regarding prophecy, such as the marked gap between imagistic content and interpretation and the emphasis on the final recipient of prophecy being the judge as to the proper reading, fit, and even the validity of prophecy, is designed to vitiate in advance these kinds of abuses of prophetic authority.

A similar narrative of prophecy as an authoritative form capable of being abused can be read into Marshall's (2010) account. In an article-length work published after her book, she presents a different vision of the Pentecostal prophetic. Here, the Schmittian institution of the state of exception justified by divine force is associated not with Pentecostal pastors but with the Nigerian state; by way of contrast, drawing on Giorgio Agamben's (2005) discussion of Paul's epistles to the Romans, Marshall presents Pentecostals as not instituting a new order. Rather, Pentecostalism produces immanent ties with an eschatological horizon that expresses an ahierarchical, auto-subjectifying, providential, and miraculous body of Christ, continually manifest. This manifestation of Pentecostalism works to arrest the forces of lawlessness associated with the corrupt Nigerian state and does not act as something arriving from a divine outside to arrest the natural order. In this formulation, pastoral attempts to "monopolize charisma, harnessing supernatural power for the performance of miracles . . . mirrors in many ways the exercise of power on the part of the political elite," forming what is in essence a Schmittian monological perversion of the original pluriform and universally available divine Pentecostal power (Marshall 2010: 216).

There are problems with this vision of the monological as merely an abuse, however. First, the prophetic statement assumes a preexisting social relationship, but that social relationship is predicated on a power to be understood as speaking on behalf of God. This problem can be sidestepped by saying that this is in some ways a matter of performativity—that monological "abuses" of prophecy are self-establishing—although the felicity conditions for such bootstrapping are not quite clear. Furthermore, this explanation would not help us understand our third case, the Catholic charismatic bulwark prophecy presented by Csordas. In all the circulated recordings, transcriptions, and narratives of the prophecy, the human reporters of these speech acts are unknown; it seems self-evident that if they were spoken or reported by a movement leader, this would have been commemorated or at least recorded. This cannot be thought of as a moment of the abuse of the form. This is not to say that because we cannot identify an abuse in the Csordas case that the Vineyard and Nigerian cases cannot be thought of as abuses; these other instances seem to be self-evidentially the usurpation of divine power for strategic goals which are "pathological" in the Kantian sense of the word. This merely suggests that the monological prophetic as an abuse of the dialogic prophetic may simply be one mode of monological prophecy; it also opens up the possibility that the pathological self-interested monological prophetic may even be a derivation of either dialogic prophecy, or of some differently constituted form of monological prophecy.

Honeycombs in the Sky

This brings us to the second hypothesis: that there is some other through-line transversing all of these cases, the formal feature of which is hinted at in the semipublic nature of these statements—pastors speaking to audiences in the Nigerian case, public proclamations for Catholic charismatics in Rome. What I want to suggest is that these monological speech acts serve to create a field where prophetic heteroglossia can occur; in short, I am arguing that while the dialogic may be the natural condition of speech, at least here it is monologue that serves as its warrant.

This is best demonstrated through example. There are several disparate origin stories of the Vineyard, but one that has received a great deal of attention involved not miracles, but their absence. John Wimber was a middle-aged, overweight, and overworked church growth consultant affiliated with the Fuller School of World Missions; his supervisor suggested that Wimber run a church "so he would have something to do on weekends." Wimber felt moved to preach on healing, and after every service he and the church members would pray over the sick—without success. Sometimes they would catch the very colds they were trying to heal.

As Wimber tells it, one morning he received a call from a church member whose wife had the flu. Wimber comes over and is disheartened by what he sees—the woman he is expected to heal is an absolute mess. Wimber prays a perfunctory prayer and turns around to explain how healing does not always work; meanwhile, the wife gets up, apparently cured, to make them all coffee. Wimber is shocked. He recalls himself silently mouthing "we got one" and pumping his fist in victory on the way out.

Once in the car, Wimber has a vision:

> Suddenly in my mind's eye there appeared to be a cloud bank superimposed across the sky. But I had never seen a cloud bank like this one, so I pulled my car over to the side of the road to take a closer look. Then

I realized it was not a cloud bank, it was a honeycomb with honey drip-ping out on to people below. The people were in a variety of postures. Some were reverent; they were weeping and holding their hands out to catch the honey and taste it, even inviting others to take some of their honey. Others acted irritated, wiping the honey off themselves, complain-ing about the mess. I was awestruck. Not knowing what to think, I prayed, "Lord, what is it?"

He said, "It's my mercy, John. For some people it's a blessing, but for others it's a hindrance. There is plenty for everyone. Don't ever beg me for healing again. The problem isn't on my end, John. It's down there." (Wimber and Springer 1991: 52)

Wimber states that this experience "revolutionized" his life "more than any other experience." Its effects, I would add, went beyond Wimber's life.

We know of this prophecy because Wimber recalled it both in his writings and from the podium, and furthermore did so more than once; there are several instances where he narrated this honeycomb vision, either as part of a speech or sermon or in print. The question is why he should turn to this striking but some-what idiosyncratic vision so many times. The answer to this lies in part with how a Bakhtinian analysis would code this narrative. This vision, I suggest, is at its core a monological utterance. What this statement does is create a complete landscape where there are only two sorts of figures: those who accept God's grace (which includes healing and other charismatic gifts by implication) and those who are repelled by it. There is no opportunity for a transvaluation of these categories, or for the proliferation of new ones; the only real response left for anyone heralded by this vision is to elect one's positing in the prophetic scheme. It is a statement that "expects no answer" and does the same work by fiat as is done by Schmitt's sovereign.

But this totalizing statement also does something else. This monological speech act is simultaneously a democratic claim. Unlike many other Pentecostals and charismatic movements which limit the scope of prophetic authority and miraculous powers to a certain restricted set of leaders, the Vineyard has been dedicated to the concept that Pentecostal-style religious experiences, including prophecy, are universally available to all believers; as Wimber often put it, in the Vineyard "everyone gets to play." This approach was combined with another sensi-bility that valued experimentation and discovery over any preemptive regulation. Again quoting John Wimber, the Vineyard's stance was to "let the bush grow" before "cutting it back." This was not a risk-free stance; several times during the 1980s and 1990s, the Vineyard was plunged into controversy in the evangelical world by the presence of unusual phenomena that were supposedly expressions of the presence of the Holy Spirit. This included behaviors such as getting "drunk in the spirit," a name for seemingly hours' long periods of intoxication after being affected by the Holy Spirit during a church meeting, and also included "Holy laughter," the term used for prolonged peals of laughter as a result of experiential contact with the Holy Spirit. There were even reports of people making animal sounds or pantomiming animal motions as a result of what was understood as contact with the Holy Spirit; while these moments of animal mimesis were often explained as being the Holy Spirit imparting a message by the iconic representations of certain animals tied to important biblical hermeneutics, such as lions or lambs, this activity was far too unusual for many of the more stolid evangelicals that the Vineyard was attempting to reach out toward.

However, all of these later unusual pneumatological expressions, and the negative reactions that they provoked, could be seen as being intimated in the original honeycomb vision. The honeycomb vision cannot be challenged on its own terms, but it does allow for the recipient to engage in or receive prophetic speech that is ultimately authoritative and from God, but at the same time is also negotiable speech from immanent interlocutors; and those who reject such "messy" expressions are presented as rejecting the Holy Spirit as well. So perhaps this explains the relation between the monologic and the dialogic in Csordas and Marshall—both instances of monologism are doing the work of creating or recreating communities, while the dialogical is the speech that those communities engender. This may even be a way for us to understand Bakhtin's own religious sentiments, but that may be going too far. At the very least, this exercise has gotten us to the promised man-bites-dog moment: not only is the monological worth thinking through in Bakhtinian terms, but there are times where the monological, which is supposed to be a denatured and perverted form of the dialogic, can give rise to and sustain dialogical speech acts of its own.

We should also note, though, that whatever the relationship is between prophecy as dialogical speech and prophecy as a monological act, we cannot see the interactions between them as occurring in any sort of well-ordered causal sequence where a grounding monologic temporally precedes a later dialogic freedom. While Wimber presents his honeycomb vision as occurring early in the history of the Vineyard, we should also note that for most believers this was a retroactive projection, something heard about well after the fact. Most Vineyard believers, rather than encountering the honeycomb narrative as part of an inaugural grounding introduction to Vineyard practice, would encounter it long after having started to experiment with the kind of Pentecostal spirituality that the vision supposedly heralded; and now that Wimber has passed on in 1997, it is my suspicion that most casual new church members do not hear about this instance of prophetic speech at all.

This is not to say that this monological statement is now void, however—the sensibilities behind the vision remain an important part of what the Vineyard is today. Rather, we should see the monological and the dialogical as co-constitutive; that just as the polyvocal prophetic interactions are "grounded" by the universalist sensibilities in the monological honeycomb vision, the typological distinctions inherent in the monological binary codification of human responses to the Spirit only makes sense when held up against the complex pluralizations engendered by actual acts of Pentecostal-oriented practice. This co-constitutive nature is hinted at in the nested virtual causative sequences implicit in the retelling of the honeycomb narrative itself. Recall that the vision of the honeycomb in some ways marks the inaugural moment of the Vineyard, but the inaugural moment of the Vineyard can only occur in the immediate wake of a specific act of the kind of Pentecostal miraculous that is characteristic of the Vineyard—a healing where there are multiple parties with discordant initial expectations and reactions (recall the husband's concern, the wife's calm reaction, and Wimber's initial skepticism and subsequent surprise). It may be that both monologue and dialogue here are actually variants of one another, or alternately expressions of some other generative problematic, some crisis of authority that at some moments wears the mask of a permissive welter of different voices, and at other moments wears the mask of a universal coding, extending to the furthest horizons.

References

Agamben, Giorgio. 2005. *The Time That Remains: A Commentary on the Letter to the Romans*. Stanford, CA: Stanford University Press.

Bialecki, Jon. 2009. "Disjuncture, Continental Philosophy's New 'Political Paul,' and the Question of Progressive Christianity in a Southern Californian Third Wave Church." *American Ethnologist* 36(1): 110–123.

Bialecki, Jon. 2010. "Angels and Grass: Church, Revival, and the Neo-Pauline Turn." *South Atlantic Quarterly* 109(4): 695–717.

Bialecki, Jon. 2011a. "No Caller I.D. for the Soul: Demonization, Charisms, and the Unstable Subject of Protestant Language Ideology." *Anthropological Quarterly* 84(3): 679–703.

Bialecki, Jon. 2011b. "Quiet Deliverances." In *Practicing the Faith: The Ritual Life of Pentecostal-Charismatic Christians*, ed. M. Lindhardt, 249–276. New York: Berghahn.

Bialecki, Jon. 2016. "Diagramming the Will: Ethics and Prayer, Text and Politics." *Ethnos* 81(4): 712–734.

Candea, Matei. 2011. "'Our Division of the Universe': Making a Space for the Non-Political in the Anthropology of Politics." *Current Anthropology* 52(3): 309–334.

Coates, Ruth. 1998. *Christianity in Bakhtin: God and the Exiled Author*. Cambridge: Cambridge University Press.

Csordas, Thomas. 1994. *The Sacred Self: A Cultural Phenomenology of Charismatic Healing*. Berkeley: University of California Press.

Csordas, Thomas. 1997a. "Prophecy and the Performance of Metaphor." *American Anthropologist* 99(2): 321–332.

Csordas, Thomas. 1997b. *Language, Charisma, and Creativity: The Ritual Life of a Religious Movement*. Berkeley: University of California Press.

Deleuze, Gilles, and Félix Guattari. 1999. *A Thousand Plateaus: Capitalism and Schizophrenia*. Minneapolis: University of Minnesota Press.

Luhrmann, T. M. 2012. *When God Talks Back: Understanding the American Evangelical Relationship with God*. New York: Alfred A. Knopf.

Marshall, Ruth. 2009. *Political Spiritualities: The Pentecostal Revolution in Nigeria*. Chicago: University of Chicago Press.

Marshall, Ruth. 2010. "The Sovereignty of Miracles: Pentecostal Political Theology in Nigeria." *Constellations* 17(2): 197–223.

Rakow, Katja. 2013. "Therapeutic Culture and Religion in America." *Religion Compass* 7(11): 485–497.

Schmitt, Carl. 1985. *Political Theology: Four Chapters on the Concept of Sovereignty*. Cambridge, MA: MIT Press.

Spencer, Jonathan. 2007. *Anthropology, Politics and the State: Democracy and Violence in South Asia*. Cambridge: Cambridge University Press.

Wimber, John, and Kevin Springer. 1991. *Power Healing*. San Francisco: HarperSanFrancisco.

3 MONOLOGUE AND DIALOGISM IN HIGHLAND NEW GUINEA VERBAL ART

Alan Rumsey

Introduction

In this chapter, I will be discussing issues of dialogism and monologism in relation to genres of epic-like sung narrative in the Highlands of Papua New Guinea. The term "dialogism" in its Bakhtinian sense, of course, refers not to dialogue per se but to the intermingling of distinct social "voices" in given stretches of discourse. Likewise, "monologism" as used by the contributors to this volume refers not to monologue per se but to the construction of an apparently unitary, transcendent voice. Examples of literal dialogue that I would take to be monological in this sense are:

- many of the various genres of "ceremonial dialogue" found all over Native South America, in which a pair of speakers recites a set text incrementally across interactional turns, as described in Urban (1986);
- certain forms of Vedic recitation that are practiced in India, in which two or more pupils recite a given text incrementally, dividing it into words or small groups of them and taking turns with each other according to various set patterns of alternation;[1]
- catechism, in which a set text of questions and answers are spoken by the catechist and catechumens in turn.

---

1. For discussion and video examples, see http://www.namboothiri.com/articles/anyonyam. htm.

Greg Urban (1991) has made some useful distinctions for understanding the features of discourse that are relevant here, based on the extent to which it:

- involves back and forth alternation between speakers ("form-defined dialogicality");
- involves semantically responsive turn-taking ("content-defined dialogicality");
- is formulaic versus substantive.

The Vedic recitation is an example of form-defined dialogue which is semantically monologic. Catechism is an example of form-defined dialogue which is semantically dialogic, but totally formulaic in that the words to be uttered are entirely fixed, for example:

Q. What is the chief end of man?
A. To glorify God and enjoy Him forever!
Q. What rule hath God given to direct us how we may glorify and enjoy Him?
A. The word of God as heard by all people directly. (Westminster Shorter Catechism [1647])

A kind of discourse that is complex in this regard, but ubiquitous across languages and speech communities, is the phenomenon of reported speech, which can be used to place any given speech event into a kind of dialogical relationship with another one (whether real or imagined). The brilliant work of Mikhail Bakhtin (1981) and Valentin Voloshinov (1973) has shown how pervasive a role is played by reported speech in the creation of evaluative stances in discourse and placed it in relation to the wider range of discursive phenomena that have been studied under the rubric of "voicing."

These include not only explicit attributions of speech or thought by one speaker to another, as in ordinary quotation, but also implicit ones, such as the one by Charles Dickens in his novel of *Little Dorrit*—when he says about one of his characters "Mr. Tite Barnacle was a buttoned-up man, and consequently a weighty one."[2] Although Dickens does not frame this statement explicitly as reported speech, other more subtle aspects of the framing make it clear, at least to readers familiar with the mores of Victorian England, that this statement is being voiced from the point of view of a particular element of Victorian society whom

---

2. This example is taken from Bakhtin (1981: 305), who treats it as an instance of "*pseudo-objective motivation*, one of the forms for concealing another's speech—in this example, the speech of 'current opinion.'"

the author is holding up to ridicule for, among other things, the assumption he imputes to them that "clothes make the man."

This is a prime example of what Bakhtin meant by "dialogism," the interplay of distinct social voices in what from the formal point of view looks like an utterance by one person. It is also "heteroglossic" in that the voices are conflicting ones, related to distinct positions and interests within a given social field. For Bakhtin, the novel of course represented the pinnacle of development of such dialogism.

For him, the genre that is the complete antithesis of the novel in this respect is epic, which he characterized according to three "constitutive features":

1. epic takes as its subject "the absolute past"
2. "national tradition (not personal experience and the free thought that grows out of it) serves as the source for the epic"
3. "an absolute epic distance separates the epic world from contemporary reality, that is, from the time in which the singer (the author and his audience) lives" (Bakhtin 1981: 13)

In the rest of this chapter, I will be comparing what Bakhtin had to say in this respect with genres of verbal art from the Papua New Guinea Highlands which were the object of study of a comparative project I led at Australian National University during 2003–2006. The main focus of the project was a range of genres of sung narrative that are found within a contiguous region as shown on map 3.1. Among the relevant features that all the genres have in common, all have semi-improvised sung narrative texts performed by a single singer. Among the relevant differences, there are considerable regional differences in tempo and in the role that is expected to be played by the audience.[3] As we shall see, this ranges from silence in the Hagen-Nebilyer-Kaugel area (shown at the east end of map 3.1), to regularly required one-syllable interjections in Huli (further to the west), to more lengthy questions or comments in Duna (to the west-northwest of Huli). Where interjections or longer interventions occur, they do not interrupt the flow of the story, but may be used by the performer to shape expressions or events in a certain way. There are also differences regarding the framing of the narrated events in relation to the here and now, and corresponding differences in the varieties of dialogue and monologue that are found within them.

---

3. For a fuller introduction to Highlands sung tales, see Niles and Rumsey (2011) and Niles (2014).

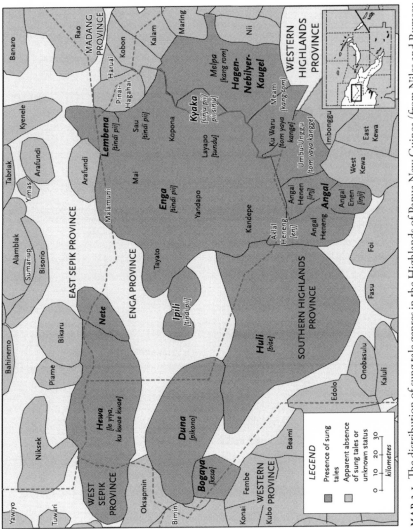

MAP 3.1 The distribution of sung tale genres in the Highlands of Papua New Guinea (from Niles and Rumsey 2011:3)

Duna *Pikono* Tales

As a first example, let us consider an excerpt from a performance in the *pikono* genre of sung tales that is practiced among the Duna, in this case a performance by Kiale Yokona. The words of it are shown in text 3.1 with free translation, as rendered by Kirsty Gillespie and Lila San Roque with the help of Richard Alo. The line-breaks in this representation, as for *pikono* in general, are determined according to a "combination of features including breath breaks, grammatical units and melodic contour" (Gillespie and San Roque 2011: 53). As can be seen, the lines vary considerably in length. Groups of lines are sung in what Gillespie and San Roque (2011) call melodic "phrases." In Kiale's performance the lines shown in text 3.1 comprised a single phrase, which is shown in a musical transcription in figure 3.1. An audio recording of this phrase may be found at http://press.anu.edu.au/wp-content/uploads/2011/10/Online-item-02-Gillsepie-San-Roque1.mp3.

As can be heard in the audio file and seen in the transcript, there is an overall downward movement across the first part of the phrase, followed by a long series of syllables centered on a single pitch (shown here as C below middle C). This is typical of *pikono* phrases, which in Gillespie and San Roque's (2011) terms comprise a "descent" followed by "ground" section. The end of the phrase is marked

---

Text 3.1. Except from a *Pikono* Sung Tale Performance by Kiale Yokona (from Gillespie and San Roque 2011:54)

hiwakuya kata yaritia	they are all coming out *it was heard*
ake yaritia sopa aipe ruwanania	*what then it was heard* who is below, he will speak
mm yaritia sayanda sayape yaritia etona	*mm it was heard* Sayanda Sayape *it was heard* across
pei popo ndu sutia kena	there you will see the *pei* Hewa *popo* feathers shake
palu pelei popo ndu sutia kenania	you will see the *palu pelei* Hewa *popo* feathers shake
vana ayano popo ndu sutia kenania	you will see the *yana ayano* Hewa *popo* feathers shake
{keno nganda!}	{we two will go!}
	(from recording by Kirsty Gillespie 2005: vol. 3.2, track 3, 0.27–0.44)

hi wa-ku-ya ka-ta ya-ri-tia a-ke___ ya-ri-tia so-pa___ ai-pe ru-wa-na-nia

mm ya-ri-tia sa-ya-nda sa-ya-pe___ ya-ri-tia e-to - na pei po-po ndu su-tia ke-na___

pa-lu pe-lei po-po ndu su-tia ke-na-nia ya-na a-ya-no po-po ndu su-tia ke-na-nia

FIGURE 3.1 Musical transcription of the excerpt shown in text 3.1 (from Gillespie and San Roque 2011:55)

by a lengthened final vowel on the last syllable, as can be heard in the recording. Here as in most *pikono* phrases there is a pause before the next phase begins.

As shown by Gillespie and San Roque, the division between the descent and ground sections of the *pikono* "phrase" is more than a purely sonic one; it is matched by corresponding differences in the thematic content of the text. They explain as follows:

> While the melodic direction of the descent section can be generally anticipated, each descent within a *pikono* phrase is different. The ground section, however, presents a repeated and predictable melodic formula. . . . Working in tandem with this, textual lines within the descent section are normally quite different from each other, with little repetition occurring from line to line. However the ground section is built around a repetitive textual frame . . . containing parallel iterations of specialized *kēiyaka* vocabulary terms.[4] (Gillespie and San Roque 2011: 53)

The authors add that

> It is generally true to say that each phrase in a *pikono* introduces a new item or activity, and advances a notch in the narrative. Since the ground section of the *pikono* is generally built around a repetitive sequence as pointed out above, it is unsurprising that this new information tends to be communicated in the

---

4. The authors explain that *kēiyaka* are "praise names," which in *pikono* texts "can be used in a variety of ways, for example replacing common vocabulary items in the descent section of a phrase or enriching the identity and history of characters in the narrative. . . . In the ground section of a *pikono* phrase *kēiyaka* occur as part of a sequence, in which several *kēiyaka* terms for a single item (typically a landscape feature) are used in a conventional order. . . . A *kēiyaka* normally occurs within a framing phrase, and at each iteration of the frame a new *kēiyaka* is substituted for the one preceding" (Gillespie and San Roque 2011: 53).

descent section of the phrase, and that the ground section does not normally introduce new narrative content. (Gillespie and San Roque 2011: 55)

What is most relevant about these aspects of musical and textual organization in relation to issues of dialogue and dialogicity is that in the actual performances of *pikono*, members of the audience often respond with spoken interventions after the end of the phrase or during the "ground" section of it. This occurs in the sample of *pikono* performance. As shown in text 3.1 in curly brackets, and as is faintly audible in the sound file,[5] at the end of Kiale's sung phrase the words *keno nganda* "we two will go" are spoken. The speaker of them is a member of the audience. In order to understand what he means by them one needs to know a little about the thematic context, which is as follows:

> At this point in the story one of the main female characters, Kundaleme, is trying to persuade one of the heroes, Kaloma Koli, to go on a journey with her to meet the spirit of his close companion Sayanda Sayape (who has recently been killed by man-eating giants). She explains that Sayanda Sayape is going to appear to him, accompanied by a group of female spirits, and deliver an important message. (Gillespie and San Roque 2011: 53)

When the audience member says *keno nganda* "we two will go" he is identifying with a character in the narrative, namely with Kaloma Koli, and speaking *for* him in response to Kundaleme's argument that the two of them should go together (Gillespie and San Roque 2011: 61). This is typical of many such interventions by *pikono* audience members in that they are often voiced from the point of view of characters in the story with whom the speaking audience member identifies. That his intervention should come at the end of the "ground" section of the phrase is consistent with Gillespie and San Roque's observation that "the text of the ground section . . . tends to be imaginatively evocative, building on the 'information' outlined in the descent section, and provoking the hearer to engage with the story as something to construct for themselves" (Gillespie and San Roque 2011: 60).

Ku Waru *Tom Yaya Kange* Tales

I now turn to the sung tales from the Hagen region, and in particular to the Ku Waru area within it, and the genre of sung tales there, known as *tom yaya kange*,

5. Unfortunately for present purposes, only a single, directional microphone was used for this recording and it was much closer to the performer Kiale than to the audience member who responded.

which can be loosely translated as "loud praise tales." As shown in map 3.1, this region is at the eastern end of the overall region within which genres of sung tales are found (i.e., at the opposite end of the overall region from the Duna *pikono* genre). The musical structure and textual organization of *tom yaya kange* are quite different from *pikono*, in ways that turn out to be related to differences of mono-logic versus dialogic voicing.

Unlike *pikono, tom yaya kange* have repeating melodies, each of which has a fixed number of lines of text. Each line ends with an added vowel—what musicol-ogists call a "vocable"—which has no semantic value, but is an essential element of the musical structure of the line. Also unlike *pikono, tom yaya kange* have fixed, repeating rhythms, with an equal number of rhythmic units ("feet") in each line, most of the feet in any given performance being associated with a single word. These features of *tom yaya kange* are exemplified in text 3.2, which shows the first sixteen lines of a sung performance by Paulus Konts, a leading practitioner of the genre.[6] These lines may be heard online at https://vimeo.com/204817758 (password: Konts).

As can be heard in the online audio, the lines in text 3.2 are sung within two successive iterations of the melody. Each iteration spans eight lines of text, each of which in turn can be thought of in musical terms as comprising one measure or bar. In those terms the melody can be represented as in figure 3.2.[7]

This same melody is used throughout Konts's performance, which took approximately 23 minutes and included 1,068 lines. What is most relevant to note here is that in marked contrast to Kiale's *pikono* performance, during that entire performance there was not a single interjected utterance by any member of the audience. Nor have there been any in any of the approximately thirty *tom yaya kange* performances I have recorded over the past thirty-three years. When asked whether it would acceptable for that to happen, performers have answered that it definitely would not be. Consistent with these facts, at least three aspects of the musical, prosodic, and textual organization of *tom yaya kange* seem to make it less conducive to such intervention than Duna *pikono*.

First, the pauses between repetitions of the melody, where they occur at all, are far shorter than in Duna *pikono*. In general they are only as long as needed

---

6. For details concerning Paulus Konts and his performance style, see Rumsey (2006: 324–330).

7. I have labelled this a "rough" transcription because it does not include the rhythmic divisions of some notes that would be necessary to show how words with more than one syllable are sung. Notwithstanding the rhythmic differences at that level, all the syllables within a given note-length musical unit (corresponding to the textual items within each column in text 3.2) are sounded at the same pitch. Accordingly, figure 3.2 represents the melody used in this *tom yaya kange* performance at an abstract level that captures what is invariant to the melody across all its soundings.

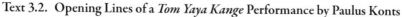

Text 3.2. Opening Lines of a *Tom Yaya Kange* Performance by Paulus Konts

1	*puku*	*tópa*	*lku–d*	*urum*	*e*	'He jumped and came into the house.'
2	*dali*	*pula*	*manya*	*lyirim*	*e*	'He removed his banana leaf apron'
3	*ola*	*pula*	*wal*	*lyirim*	*e*	'And put on his cordyline kilt.'
4	*ngi*	*kapola*	*mari*	*tekin*	*a,*	'Well done, my lad, well done!'
5	*kanab*	*a*	*kélipa*	*púpa*	*a*	'As I watched he went on his way'
6	*koroka*	*komunga*	*Kai*	*kanunga*	*a*	'Headed for Koroka Mountain.'
7	*ola*	*púpa*	*mólupa*	*mel*	*e*	'He climbed to the top and stayed'
8	*tubal*	*kop*	*ekeda*	*lyirim*	*e,*	'With a jew's-harp in one hand'
9	*kulaip*	*mingiyl*	*ekeda*	*lyirim*	*e*	'And a bamboo flute in the other.'
10	*kanab*	*ku*	*Kéla*	*purum*	*e*	'As I watched he went on his way.'
11	*toku*	*nóba*	*lkaib*	*turum*	*e*	'Where he smoked his tobacco and spat'
12	*toku*	*wale*	*pora*	*purum*	*e,*	'Fields of tobacco plants sprouted'
13	*toku*	*ikilya*	*purum*	*kanuma*	*a*	'And the smoke that went up in the sky'
14	*waru*	*kupa*	*pungla*	*nyirim*	*a*	'Billowed like clouds round the mountain.'
15	*i*	*kapola*	*mari*	*tekin*	*a*	'Well done, my lad, well done!'
16	*kanab*	*taka*	*taka*	*nyiba*	*a,*	'In my mind's eye the story unfolds.'

FIGURE 3.2 Rough musical transcription of the excerpt shown in text 3.2

for the performer to breathe. That can be clearly heard in Paulus Konts's performance, where the places in which he pauses are shown in text 3.2 by commas.

Second, in many *tom yaya kange* performances (unlike in the one by Konts discussed here), there is usually no pause at all between the end of one round of the melody and the beginning of the next. Rather, the performer sings for as long as he can on a single breath then quickly inhales, sometimes with an audible gasp.

Third, whereas in *pikono*, the full-melody-sized units that Gillespie and San Roque call "phrases" are of varying length and are associated with thematically discrete, well-bounded segments of text, the melody used in any given *tom yaya kange* performance repeats across a fixed number of lines that tend not to comprise discrete thematic units. This can be seen in text 3.2, where the boundary between successive soundings of the melody comes between lines 8 and 9. Far from being a break in the thematic content, this comes in the middle of a thematically cohesive pair of lines "with a jew's harp in one hand / and a bamboo flute in the other."

Huli *Bì Té* Tales

Having discussed some musical-cum-textual aspects of the Duna *pikono* and Ku Waru *tom yaya kange* genres, their performance conventions regarding audience participation, and some possible relations between the former and the latter, I will now more briefly discuss corresponding aspects of the genre of sung tales that is found among the Huli, who live in a region between the Duna and Ku Waru. The genre is called *bì té*, which translates literally as "talking story." Its tonal organization is very different from that of either *pikono* or *tom yaya kange*. It does not have a repeating melody of any kind. Rather, its pitch patterns are closely related to those of the Huli language, which is a tone language.[8] This has been demonstrated in fine detail by ethnomusicologist Jacqueline Pugh-Kitingan, who finds that across the entire range of Huli musical genres

> Melody is generally dominated by speech-tone. This domination is so great that Huli melodic movement appears to derive its essential motivation from the tonal patterns of the words and lines articulated. (Pugh-Kitingan 1984: 118)

Accordingly, within *bì té* the highest-level melodic unit is what Pugh-Kitingan (2011) calls the "sentence" or "section," with falling intonation at the end, usually ending in "linking expressions" such as *lāya* "said," or *lārugo ábiyani-ō* ("which I said that-o") (Pugh-Kitingan 2011: 112). An example may be found at http://press.anu.edu.au/wp-content/uploads/2011/10/Online-item-10-Pugh-Kitingan1.mp3, from a *bì té* performance recorded by Pugh-Kitingan in 1975. The words of the first 42 seconds of the performance are shown in text 3.3.

---

8. Huli has three tones—low-rising, high-falling, and mid-level—each of which extends over the entire word. In the orthography used here the tone for the entire word is shown with a mark over its first vowel.

Bĩ té mbira larogo.   Ndē   húlu   wãndari mbira-ò, wãndari mbira béreneya   lãya.

Story one   I'm saying, see. So then person girl   one-o,   girl   one   was sitting   said.

Listen, I'm going to tell you a story. Once there was a girl, a girl was living there (said).

Ndē   wãndari mbira béreneyàgo,   ĩbu ndē píyiya lãya. Pialu   hēaria,

And then girl   one   which was sitting, she then went   said.   When she had gone   she stayed,

Then one day the girl who was living there went for a walk (said). When she had gone, she stopped

ài   nē   lãyagola.   Ãgali balamãnda   mbīra wĩniyago,   hãnda wãlia hōwa,

then twilight because it was saying. Man man's house one   which was there when   she   found,

because night was approaching,   She found a man's house there with bundles of

ōbíagoha   dù   mbāria mbúla hēago   ãnda pūwá,   ōbíagoha bírayiya lãya.

that place sugar-cane one   tied up there house when went, that place she sat   said,

sugar cane tied up, and she sat down near that place (said).

Ãni   biaria   ãgali wãhe mbīra ira   bóyalu   ibuwa īra   ibira háyiya   lãya.

Then while doing man   old   one   wood carrying came   wood came put down said.

While she was there an old man came along carrying firewood, he came and put it down (said).

(*continued*)

TEXT 3.3. Translation of the First Part of a *Bì Té* Performance by Bebalu (from Pugh-Kitingan 2011:148)

Īra ìbira háyagola   īra   bíago gābiyaria   hàrane mbīra púwa, wāndari bíago
Wood came when put down wood that one while he chopped chip   one   went, girl   that one
While he was chopping the wood that he had brought, a chip flew off and struck that girl

bérearia   pú bilina háyiya   lāya. Āni bìyagola   mànda āgali bíagome īra   hàrane
while sitting go hit   put down said. Then because it did that wig   man that one wood chip
who was sitting there (said).   Because the chip flew off, the man (haroli) went to get it

bíago mò äi   ibiyaria   wāndari bíago hánda wāli háyagola
that one get then while he went girl   that found   said. When he   found
and in doing so he found that girl (said).   When he found her, he picked her

ìbu míni yálu púwa ību īgini dúria yágo.   Pāliaguha   ūlu wāhowa ūlu
her picked carried   his sons five were.   Place where to lide down hole found hole
up and carried her to where his five "sons" (students) were. He found a hole where she could lie down

The first 25 seconds of the same performance by Bebalu are shown in a musical transcription in figure 3.3.

Clearly audible at intervals throughout the recording, and visible in the first and seventh lines of figure 3.3, is a repeated interjection *é* by an audience member. Interventions by the audience at *bì té* performances are not only allowed but, in principle, required. But they take that particular, highly constrained form:

> The story-teller usually begins by instructing the listeners "You say *ẹ́* [yes]" or even "You say *ẹ́*, or my parents will die." This ensures a regular interjection of the word *ẹ* chanted on a level pitch by one of the listeners, which tells the performer that the story is not being wasted on a sleeping audience in the dark. It also serves as a prompting device to help the performer continue with the development of the story. (Pugh-Kitingan 2011: 112)

Dialogue versus Dialogism in the Three Regional Genres

Having compared three regional genres of sung tales within the Papua New Guinea Highlands in certain relevant respects, I now turn to the question of the extent to which they are dialogical versus monological in both the ordinary senses of those terms and the Bakhtinian ones. For purposes of this comparison, it is useful to return not only to Bakhtin but also to the dimensions of contrast in forms of "dialogicality" developed by Urban as discussed in the introduction. *Pikono* are clearly dialogical in the ordinary sense of the word, in that at certain key junctures they involve back and forth alternation between the performer and members of his audience. In that sense their dialogicality is "form-defined" in Urban's terms and also "content-defined" in that, as we have seen from the examples, the audience interventions are semantically responsive to what is going on in the narrative.

Huli *bì té* also involve "form-defined" dialogicality in that there is back and forth alternation between performer and audience members, but not "content-defined" dialogicality, since the audience interventions are not semantically responsive. Indeed, their interventions contain little semantic content at all, being limited to the one-word utterance *ẹ* "Yes." In that respect, they are highly formulaic (the third of Urban's analytical dimensions)—much more so than those of *pikono* audience members, which are quite varied and sometimes highly creative.[9]

Ku Waru *tom yaya kange* are not dialogical in the ordinary sense at all, as they involve no back and forth alternation between the performer and anyone else.

---

9. For examples drawing on observations by Lila San Roque, see Rumsey (2005: 67–69).

FIGURE 3.3 Musical transcription of the first part of the *bì té* performance by Bebalu (from Pugh-Kitingan 2011:141)

But they are dialogical in Bakhtin's sense. To see how, let us consider some aspects of their plots and performative framing. The plots are various, but cluster around a canonical one in which a young man sets out from his home to court a young woman he has heard about in a far-away place, undertakes a long and arduous journey to her home, wins her hand, but then encounters various obstacles in his attempt to bring her back to his home and marry her, sometimes succeeding and sometimes not. Although the stories are set in a fantasy world where, for example, fields of tobacco plants can instantly spring up from the ground where the hero spits—as in lines 11-12 of text 3.2—it is not the case that, as in Bakhtin's understanding of epic, "an absolute epic distance separates [the narrated world] from contemporary reality."

To see why not, let us consider some of the genre conventions of the overall category of *kange* ("tales") of which *tom yaya kange* are the sung version. One of the ways in which the world of narrated events in *kange* is placed in relation to the here and now is through the use of what Merlan (1995) has dubbed "techniques of verisimilitude," by which the characters and places in the story are likened to ones in the contemporary local setting. This is carried further by some performers, who import the tales into the local setting, casting local figures in leading roles. This is exactly what is done in this story by Paulus Konts, who in his story has the young suitor start out from his—Konts's—own home ground at a place called Ambukl, then make his way through a number of named places along the Highlands Highway and the provincial capital at Mt. Hagen, still without being identified. Finally when he reaches Tangapa's home at Ambra he is identified by her as none other than the narrator himself, "Konts, the lad from Ambukl."

While the plot of this particular story is the usual one of courtship and marriage, in some others the *tom yaya* performance style and its standard imagery are used for presenting narratives with non-canonical, distinctly contemporary plots and themes. For example this same performer Konts has also composed and performed a tale about a trip to the coast to buy betel nut to bring back to the highlands for sale. The story again casts himself in the leading role, but this time traveling not on foot to Ambra, but by bus to Lae, then on a boat to the port at Finschhafen. There he buys a thousand kina's worth of betel nuts and takes them back with him, beyond the Nebilyer Valley where he lives, to Wabag, the capital of Enga Province to the west. When he discovers that there is already an ample supply of betel nut in the Wabag markets, he continues on through the mountains to Porgera—a much more remote locale, where prices are higher, and more cash on hand because of the mining operations there. He sells his betel nuts there at a huge profit and returns triumphantly to Ambukl.

Notwithstanding its distinctly contemporary subject matter, this story was cast in classic *tom yaya* form, using the same rhythm and melody as for the performance excerpted in text 3.2, and many of the same standard *kange* thematic motifs as in other performances. For example, when preparing for his trip, Konts washes himself in a river, and dresses himself splendidly in a woven belt and bark belt hung with cordyline leaves, both standard motifs in the tales of courtship. When traveling on the bus to Wabag he carries with him a long *dagla* spear and a pronged *timbun* spear, described in parallel lines, just as the more standard narratives of quest and courtship.

In addition to *tom yaya kange* motifs such as these, which Konts uses in standard form in his tale of the betel nut trade, there are others which he artfully adapts to fit with its contemporary subject matter. An example is the following passage, which was spoken by the hero to the betel nut wholesalers in Finschhafen.

na buai lyibu ud a	"I've come to get betel," he said.
eni lyi naa lyibu e	"I haven't come to get you."
eni ya molai nyirim e	"You all can stay," he said.
nanga buai kenginsai nyirim a	"Just bring me my bags of betel."

To an audience familiar with *tom yaya kange*, those lines are thematically reminiscent of a saying which is commonly used in them used by hosts when welcoming first-time visitors from afar, namely:

kung koiyl kiulu lelym e	We've an oven for roasting pigs.
yabu koiyl kiulu naa lelym e	We've no oven for roasting people.

In other words, "Relax, we are not cannibals who intend to eat you, but friends who intend to feed you." Within the canonical *tom yaya* narrative of courtship, the point at which this remark typically occurs is when the hero has completed his long journey and arrived at the home of the young lady whom he has gone to court. Her place and its people are beyond the ken of his own, and therefore, like everyone at the edge of the known social universe, suspected of being cannibals (cf. Rumsey 1999).

The same remark is sometimes also made by the hero to his hosts, to put them at ease about the prospects for their daughter among his own people. For example, in a performance of one of the canonical tales of courtship, it was said by the young lady Tangapa to her suitor Tagla just after he arrives at her place, and then, as they are about to leave for his place, he says the same thing to her, followed immediately by the following lines:

na nu lyibu ui naa udiyl	I haven't come to get you.
nunga laikiyl nyikin akiyl-ya	You're doing what you've chosen to do.

In his betel nut story, by having the hero say "I haven't come to get you" at an analogous point at the outer end of his journey, Konts is both creating an implicit parallel to the more standard plot involving courtship and playing humorously upon coastal people's stereotype of highlanders as more savage than themselves, and perhaps even inclined to cannibalism.

All of these examples show that the *tom yaya* genre is dialogical in the Bakhtinian sense, rather than monologic, as in Bakhtin's characterization of epic as reviewed. That is, rather than an absolute separation between the story world and the contemporary one, a two-way relationship between the two is established, whereby the audience is invited not only to imagine the present in terms of the past but also to reimagine the past in terms of the present. This is done both by bringing the poetic and musical resources of *tom yaya kange* genre to bear on the subject matter from the contemporary world, but sometimes also by the narrator casting himself as a character within the stories.

Interestingly, by contrast, neither of those things has ever happened in any of the performances of *pikono* that have been recorded among the Duna, and when asked about the possibility, Duna people say that it would be wrong for a performer to do either because the stories have come down from the past and should not be tampered with (Lila San Roque and Kirsty Gillespie, personal communication, 2003; cf. Kendoli 2011: 46).[10] Rather, as we have seen, in the Duna region the linkage between the story world and the present is established not through any deliberate modification of the received traditional stories by the performer, but through spoken interventions by members of the audience addressed to the performer and/or the characters in the story.

In this respect, just as we have seen to be the case regarding dialogicality in Urban's sense, Huli *bì té* is intermediate between Duna *pikono* and Ku Waru *tom yaya kange*: at the level of content, Huli performers are not expected to recast *bì té* stories into contemporary settings as in Hagen, but unlike the Duna *pikono* form the *bì té* form with its specific musical and prosodic properties is used for other

---

10. Kendoli (2011: 46), a Duna man with long insider experience of *pikono* does note that

> One small change is that performers now include places like Port Moresby, Rabaul and Buka when they are counting places and so on. Before, our ancestors did not count these places. Then people started going to Port Moresby and returning, or going to Buka or Rabaul and other coastal places and coming home. At this time people started to include them in the counting, they heard the travellers' descriptions and included these places.

non-traditional purposes including settings of Roman Catholic liturgy (Fr. G. C. Lomas, personal communication, 2006).[11]

Conclusion

From the comparisons in this chapter, we can see that across the sung tales region there is an inverse relation between dialogue in the ordinary sense (or its Urbanian senses) and dialogicity in the Bakhtinian sense: Duna *pikono* performances are the most dialogic in the ordinary sense, but also the most monologic in the Bakhtinian sense, in that there is a strict separation between the story world and the contemporary one, and a notion of received narrative content that should not be altered. Performer and audience together strive to conjure up that story world in an authentic way. Hagen performers, on the other hand, perform in a manner which is strictly monologic in the ordinary sense, but thoroughly dialogical in the Bakhtinian sense, bringing the story world and the here-and-now one into a two-way interaction with each other. That there could be such a big difference in this respect across a distance of only about 200 kilometers seems remarkable. How is it to be understood?

One relevant consideration is that, though 200 kilometers may seem like a short distance "as the crow flies," the terrain in that part of Papua New Guinea

---

Citing this passage Kirsty Gillespie (personal communication, February 2015) points to a *pikono* performance discussed in Gillespie (2010: 138-140) that refers to Rabaul, Bougainville, and Port Moresby, and offers the view that "in mentioning those places, what happens at those places—what they are best known for (e.g. Bougainville for mining, Moresby for business etc.)—is evoked." She adds, and I agree, that "the important distinction here with the Ku Waru material is that any reference to contemporary times is indirect, evocative and subtle, rather than an integral part of the story."

11. In this connection, after reading a draft of this chapter Jacqueline Pugh-Kitingan (personal communication, March 2015) offered the following interesting recollections and observations:

Following on from the use of *bi te* for reciting the Catholic liturgy, I once asked my Huli research assistant (a member of the Evangelical Church of Papua) to tell one of the parables of Jesus from the Gospels in *bi te* form, to see the reactions of people. He decided to tell the parable of the rich man and Lazarus (he was surprisingly good at doing the *bi te* style). I recorded him on cassette and we played the recording back in a focus group session at the local Bebenete market. Since both parables and *bi te* are stories that can give some form of instruction, I was interested to see whether this would be acceptable to the Huli.

Everyone agreed at the time that the *bi te* format might be used for telling Biblical parables (but not other parts of Scripture) because Jesus was storying when he told them. But it never took off at all as a church practice in the Huli ECP and other non-Catholic churches. The reason later became apparent as I analysed all the *bi te* I had recorded—silly me!

is very rugged, and, until recently, direct social contact among people from the three regions has been rare, especially between Ku Waru and the other two. Another relevant consideration is that the difference between the Duna and Ku Waru forms of dialogism that I have discussed here can be related to other differences that I have discussed elsewhere (Rumsey 2001), between Ku Waru linguistic and aesthetic ideologies and those of the Kaluli people to the southwest of Duna as described by Steven Feld (1984, 1990), which valorize "collective texture and coordination of layered parts" over virtuosic solo performance (Feld 1984: 392). The Duna, who are geographically closer to Kaluli than Ku Waru, are also typologically closer insofar as their sung tale performances allow for and encourage interaction between performer and audience.

Finally, it should be borne in mind that what I have been discussing here, and characterizing as dialogical versus monologic in certain respects, are specific performance genres, not whole ways of life. This is especially important to note in contrast to a tendency which was evident in Bakhtin, and even more so in the work of other influential theorists of "orality" such as H. M. Chadwick (1926), and later Walter Ong (1982), to regard "epic" as the canonical narrative genre in "oral cultures," and to attribute to it a number of characteristics that were seen to be diagnostic of a whole of life as it was lived before the "dawn of literacy." Contrary to this tendency, in order to characterize the role of dialogism and the monologic per se in the areas Papua New Guinea that I have been discussing here one would have to look beyond the epic-like genres that I have focused on and take account of a much wider range of other genres and their social contexts. But I hope this chapter will at least have demonstrated that even within regional variants of what can for some purposes be treated as a single genre there can be considerable differences with respect to the canonical forms of dialogism and monologue that one finds in them.

Bi te are nearly always improvisatory, made-up stories with fantastic and fairy-tale elements—I only recorded one that was based on (morally shocking) events that had allegedly happened in the distant past. From the Huli point-of-view, bi te are essentially forms of entertainment based on make-believe, while parables are not. Jesus probably told his parables as entertainment too, but they were real-life stories intended to teach people and did not contain fantastic make-believe elements (even if the rich man in Hell could see Lazarus in Heaven after they had both died, this was considered a real-life event in the spiritual afterworld).

Anyway, I suppose the use of the *bi te* format for the Catholic liturgy indicates the adaptability of the genre, or at least its melodic and formal structure.

Acknowledgments

For detailed comments and corrections to drafts of this chapter based on their expert knowledge of genres discussed in it, and for years of exciting collaborative interdisciplinary research on those genres I am greatly indebted to Kirsty Gillespie, Don Niles, Jacqueline Pugh-Kitingan and Lila San Roque. Heartfelt thanks to all of them! Thanks also to all our other collaborators in that research, including both academics and practitioners of the genres; to participants at the "Monologic Imagination" conference and American Anthropological Association meeting where I presented versions of the paper; and to Matt Tomlinson for his advice and meticulous editorial work on it. For funding the research on which the chapter is based, including my own and that of the collaborators named above, I gratefully acknowledge the Australian Research Council.

References

Bakhtin, Mikhail M. 1981. *The Dialogic Imagination: Four Essays*. Ed. Michael Holquist, trans. Caryl Emerson and Michael Holquist. Austin: University of Texas Press.

Chadwick, Hecter Munro. 1926. *The Heroic Age*. Cambridge: Cambridge University Press.

Feld, Steven. 1984. "Sound Structure as Social Structure." *Ethnomusicology* 28:383–409.

Feld, Steven. 1990. *Sound and Sentiment: Birds, Weeping, Poetics and Song in Kaluli Expression*. 2d ed. Philadelphia: University of Pennsylvania Press.

Gillespie, Kirsty. 2010. *Steep Slopes: Music and Change in the Highlands of Papua New Guinea*. Canberra: ANU Press. http://press.anu.edu.au/titles/monographs-in-anthropology/steep_slopes_citation/.

Gillespie, Kirsty, and Lila San Roque. 2011. "Music and Language in Duna Pikono." In Rumsey and Niles (2011), 49–63.

Kendoli, Kenny. 2011. "Yuna *Pikono*." In Rumsey and Niles (2011), 39–47.

Merlan, Francesca. 1995. "Narrative Genres in the Highlands of Papua New Guinea." In *Proceedings of the Second Annual Symposium about Language and Society*, Texas Linguistic Forum 34, ed. Pamela Silberman and Jonathan Loftin, 87–90. Austin: University of Texas.

Niles, Don. 2014. "Traditional Knowledge and Sung Tales in the Highlands of Papua New Guinea." In *Traditional Knowledge and Wisdom: Themes from the Pacific Islands*, International Information and Networking Centre for Intangible Cultural Heritage in the Asia-Pacific Region under the auspices of UNESCO (ICHCAP), 70–85. Jeonju: ICHCAP. http://ichcap.org/eng/contents/book_list.php?mode=view&code=B0000586.

Niles, Don, and Alan Rumsey. 2011. "Introducing Highlands Sung Tales." In Rumsey and Niles (2011), 1–37.

Ong, Walter. 1982. *Orality and Literacy: The Technologizing of the Word*. London: Methuen.

Pugh-Kitingan, Jacqueline. 1984. "Speech-Tone Realization in Huli Music." In *Problems and Solutions: Occasional Essays in Musicology Presented to Alice M. Moyle*, ed. Jamie Kassler and Jill Stubington, 94–120. Sydney: Hale and Iremonger.

Pugh-Kitingan, Jacqueline. 2011. "An Ethnomusicological Discussion of Bi Té." In Rumsey and Niles (2011), 109–149.

Rumsey, Alan. 1999. "The White Man as Cannibal in the New Guinea Highland." In *The Anthropology of Cannibalism*, ed. L. Goldman, 105–121. Westport, CT: Praeger.

Rumsey, Alan. 2001. "Tom Yaya Kange: A Metrical Narrative Genre from the New Guinea Highlands." *Journal of Linguistic Anthropology* 11:193–239.

Rumsey, Alan. 2005. "Chanted Tales in the New Guinea Highlands of Today: A Comparative Study." In *Expressive Genres and Historical Change*, ed. P. J. Stewart and A. Strathern, 41–81. London: Ashcroft.

Rumsey, Alan. 2006. "Verbal Art, Politics and Personal Style in the New Guinea Highlands and Beyond." In *Language, Culture, and the Individual: A Tribute to Paul Friedrich*, ed. C. O'Neil, M. Scoggin, and K. Tuite, 319–346. Munich: Lincom.

Rumsey, Alan, and Don Niles, eds. 2011. *Sung Tales from the Papua New Guinea Highlands: Studies in Form, Meaning and Social Context*. Canberra: ANU E Press. http://epress.anu.edu.au/titles/sung_tales_citation.

Urban, Greg. 1986. "Ceremonial Dialogues in South America." *American Anthropologist* 88:371–386.

Urban, Greg. 1991. *A Discourse-Centered Approach to Culture*. Austin: University of Texas Press.

Voloshinov, Valentin Nikolaevich. 1973. *Marxism and the Philosophy of Language*. New York: Academic Press.

DISCUSSION

IS IT MONOLOGIC? IS IT DIALOGIC? WHAT DIFFERENCE DOES IT MAKE?

Don Kulick

Is it monologic? Is it dialogic? What difference does it make? What does it matter? The three chapters in this section ask those questions, and they all come to similar conclusions through different emphases, and by examining very different kinds of ethnographic material.

Alan Rumsey approaches the question of monologic versus dialogic in terms of performance genre. He compares genres of epic-like sung narratives in three groups in the Highlands of Papua New Guinea, and he concludes two things. The first is that Mikhail Bakhtin's characterization of epic as an archetypically monologic genre is not universal. The stories narrated by Ku Waru speakers in their versions of epic tales adhere to (locally conventional) epic structure and form. But whereas Bakhtin described epics as genres that narrate a vast distance between the epic world and contemporary reality, Ku Waru epics happily recount events that take place in the contemporary world, such as traveling by bus to purchase betel nut. The epics sometimes insert the narrator himself into the story as a protagonist.

Rumsey's second conclusion is that there is a complicated relation between monologic versus dialogic because a formally monologic set of utterances (e.g., a story enunciated by a single person, or by pairs of speakers who recite set texts) may be dialogic in Bakhtin's sense—that is, the story may intermingle distinct social "voices" (i.e., interested ways of speaking) in the telling. Contrariwise, a story that is told cooperatively with audience members and that needs audience participation for it to be recognizable and successful may be monologic in Bakhtin's sense, because the cooperation serves to collectively construct a unitary, transcendental voice that suppresses novelty and flattens out difference.

Similar complexities are discussed in Jon Bialecki's chapter on prophecy among people who participate in the Vineyard, a Pentecostal charismatic church that originated in southern California. Like Rumsey, Bialecki shows how the formal features of a particular speech genre may be monologic—his most telling example is of a male pastor receiving a message from God about the immorality of a teenage female church member—but the substance of the message, for the Vineyard congregants, is constructed through dialogue: the prophecy needs to be interpreted by the person it addresses, and by others, it can be rejected, and it can be mistaken or wrong.

Bialecki is interested in how the dynamic relationship between monologue and dialogue can achieve different kinds of political effects. He says that there is a tendency since and, indeed, *because* of Bakhtin, to regard monologue with suspicion, as a force that forecloses, distorts and abuses. In the material Bialecki discusses, however, the monologic utterance—prophecy—actively enables the dialogic: it sustains the community that strives to interpret it. His conclusion is that monologue and dialogue might best be thought of as variants of one another, as "some crisis of authority", he says, "that at some moments wears the mask of a permissive welter of different voices, and at other moments wears the mask of a universal coding, extending to the furthest horizons."

Greg Urban's contribution suggests a similar kind of linkage between power and the monologue-dialogue contrast. Urban argues that monologism (by which he means both (a) a metacultural valuation of sameness and (b) language that suppresses conflict and different voices) may co-occur with actual social diversity, and dialogism (a metacultural valuation of heterogeneity and novelty, and language that highlights diversity) may overlay social sameness or conformity. Urban's point is that particular socio-historical circumstances seem to encourage specific metacultural emphases that are the inverse of actually existing relations. So in conditions of great social diversity, metaculture will emphasize the importance of speaking in a single voice (Urban uses the example of "the length to which modern collectivities, especially nations, go to try to produce agreements, to speak with a single voice"). And under conditions where actual diversity is not great (Urban's example of this is modern consumer culture, which encourages everyone to be individuals by buying variants of the same things) metacultural emphasis will fall on discursive heterogeneity. Metaculture, he writes is "a way to encourage the ideals it promotes in a world out of sync with those ideals."

This is a testable hypothesis; one that could be pursued by historians, sociologists, and anthropologists. As all three authors indicate, however, it would be a difficult hypothesis to test, if for no other reason than the fact that there are many different genres of language in any society. Rumsey ends his contribution by explicitly saying that the observations about monologue and dialogue that he offers only apply to the genre of sung narratives he analyzes, and that any attempt to say anything more expansive and substantial about dialogism and monologism among Highlands groups would have to take into account a wide range of speech genres and their social contexts. Bialecki, similarly, makes it clear that he is discussing a specific genre (prophecy), even if his conclusion that monologue and dialogue have political effects is an observation with wider scope. And Urban himself discusses examples from the contemporary United States that exhibit *both* the tendencies he describes (i.e., the value of monologue against the backdrop of diversity *and* the value of dialogue against the backdrop of conformity). All this makes it hard to imagine how a broader look at the relationship between metacultural values and linguistic practice would come up with anything much more than some version of what all the authors already say here; namely, that monologue and dialogue are intertwined with and enable one another in various ways, and with various effects.

Urban's chapter goes beyond a discussion of Bakhtin's concepts, though, and his central theoretical argument concerns social and semiotic processes that he calls "replication." Replication, he explains, is a description of how culture moves through space and time. It "involves copying some aspect of culture (a behavioral routine, a word, a way of speaking, a belief, a story, a pattern, an idea, etc.)." This act of copying "is the basis for all culture." There are two ways of thinking about replication, Urban says. One is to emphasize the extent to which the model and the copy are similar. This way of thinking about replication sees it as copying. The second way of thinking about replication is to emphasize the extent to which model and replica are different. This way of thinking about replication sees it as response. Urban's point is that Bakhtinian monologism is essentially concerned with copying, and dialogism is concerned with response.

Urban's concept of replication invites a number of questions that perhaps can extend his and the other authors' contributions into areas not explored by any of them.

One question about Urban's idea of replication concerns his remarks on what he mentions as "an obvious example of replication," namely first-language acquisition. At several points in his chapter, Urban returns to the idea that first-language acquisition does not entail response. "Conceivably," he writes, "response only arises in conjunction with the differentiation of self from other." Because babies have not yet effected that differentiation, they do not respond, and the language they produce is an example of . . . well, that isn't entirely clear. Urban says that "in early developmental phases, before the acquisition of recognizable linguistic ability, the copy is not a 'copy' at all because the self is not differentiated from the other." That is an opaque sentence. What does it mean? When exactly is a copy not a "copy"? How can one be confident that one can tell the difference? And if a copy is not a "copy", what, then, is it?

Urban's argument about replication rests on the contrast he draws between copy and response. A copy, in his view, seems to be a carbon copy, an exact replication of an original. He says, to be sure, that "the replica and its model need not be—indeed, probably rarely are—identical," but the "probably" and "rarely" in that sentence allow for a situation—an occasion, an occurrence, a moment— where the replica and its model in fact are identical. One might wonder about the circumstances under which such an exceptional state might occur. And, again, how can one know with certainty when it happens?

Copies of that nature contrast with responses. A response, in Urban's model, is a replication with a supplement: an addition, an alteration. Response, as I noted above, "only arises in conjunction with the differentiation of self from other," which is why Urban says that infants don't respond. But here is the problem, or conundrum: if "in early developmental phases, before the acquisition of recognizable linguistic ability," an infant's vocalizations are not copies (because they aren't exact replications of a model), and they aren't responses either (because the infant has yet to differentiate her or his self from the other), *then what are they*? What is the unnamed, third category in the model? Non-copies (which would mean what?)? Meaningless irritating noises?

That infants neither copy nor respond is important for Urban's argument because it allows him to suggest that "much of culture passes to individuals who do not respond to it but rather assimilate it, as in the case of first language acquisition by children" (27). This rather anachronistic claim, however, is empirically not correct. The idea that first-language acquisition is an example of assimilation, not response, harks back to the old Culture and Personality School notion of "enculturation," which meant that children were molded like passive clay figures into the personalities desired by their culture, and also to Pierre Bourdieu's concept of a habitus that gets transmitted to children through osmosis or through magic because, Bourdieu ([1972] 1977: 167) believed, "what is essential goes without saying because it comes without saying." These are ideas about first-language acquisition that the anthropological literature on language socialization has spent the last four decades carefully debunking. That literature documents in detail how the socialization to use language through language is an active process that consists of a delicate, persistent chain or matrix of responses: responses of caregivers to the bodies and vocalizations produced by infants and children, and the responses of those infants and children to the bodies and language directed at them and others by caregivers (for summaries, see Garrett and Baquedano-López 2002; Duranti, Ochs, and Schieffelin 2012). If Urban had taken studies of language socialization into account, his claim that children somehow "assimilate" culture rather than respond to it would be a difficult one to sustain.

Similarly precarious, it seems to me, is the whole central distinction between copy and response. Urban's apparent confidence that he can distinguish between the two is reminiscent of a similar assurance expressed by psychoanalyst Jacques Lacan in an article titled "The Function and Field of Speech and Language in Psychoanalysis" (Lacan [1953] 1996). That text argues that a crucial distinction between humans and animals is that whereas humans respond, animals only react: animals obey a fixed program when they engage with one another and with the world; humans respond to the desire of the other.

The boundary that Lacan maintains separates animal reaction and human response is the basis of a critical assault on Lacan's entire conceptualization of the subject launched by another Jacques: Derrida. In a discussion of Lacan's thoughts about animals, Derrida queries what, exactly, the precise basis of the distinction between response and reaction might be. Derrida recognizes that the two are not exactly the same thing. But there is a fundamental problem, he says, with a theory that insists on "the purity, the rigor and the indivisibility of the frontier that separates—already with respect to 'us humans'—reaction from response; and as a consequence, especially, the purity, rigor and indivisibility of responsibility that ensues" (2003: 127).

Derrida's criticism is to point out that a response always contains some dimension of automaticity (that is, reaction), and that the difficulty or, indeed, the impossibility, of demarcating a solid frontier between a reaction and a response reveals that the point of proposing such a border is not so much to describe the world as it is a rhetorical ploy to uphold certain dogmas. In Lacan's case, what is at stake is the Cartesian separation of humans and animals. Lacan is at pains to fortify that separation, but the distinctions that he insists on to do so, Derrida points out, actually undermine it.

Lacan's defense of anthropocentrism applies to Urban as well, since his distinction between copy and response, and his literally Lacanian contention that "response only arises in conjunction with the differentiation of self and other" effectively disqualify non-human animals from the capacity to respond (one can wonder whether non-human animals can even copy, in Urban's model, or whether their exclusion from signification is absolute). But animals are not Urban's concern: in his chapter, what seems to be at stake in declaring a boundary between a copy and response is the distinction between assimilating culture and responding to culture. I have already mentioned that such a distinction seems empirically misguided; I am not convinced that it is theoretically tenable either, since a rigorous frontier between copy and response must be illusory: any acquisition necessarily involves a response. A copy is always, necessarily, a response—which is an observation, surely, that is Bakhtinian as much as it is Derridean.

Derrida is also pertinent to the very notion of replication because one of Derrida's most well-known concepts is iterability, which means repetition + change. Signs—all signs, without exception—are iterable, which means that they have to be repeated in order to mean. But the very repetition that secures their signification also necessarily changes them, since no repetition can ever be a carbon copy—indeed, even a carbon copy is a copy of something, and therefore necessarily different from it.

What is the relationship of Derrida's iterability to Urban's replication? Why does Urban propose the notion of replication, when the venerable and demonstrably serviceable concept of iterability, which appears to do much of the same work, is already readily available (iterability is a tool-in-trade of deconstructionist reading; it is also a crucial element of many poststructuralist analyses, including ones like Judith Butler's extensions of performativity theory)?

Although Urban does not mention Derrida in his chapter, in another context, he has stated that he does not share "poststructural self-doubt about representation", and he calls Derrida's work "a self-doubt turned into method" (2001: 226). One should respect that position, but personally, I am much more inclined than Urban seems to be to regard self-doubt as a good thing; a positive stance, both in terms of a general orientation toward the world, and also in relation to theory: what, after all, is "reflexivity" in anthropology if not "a self-doubt turned into method"?

My own sense is that Derrida's attention to porosity, leakage, and indeterminacy, and his insistence that all signs are unavoidably marked by response—are, indeed, response—fit more comfortably with Bakhtinian understandings of semiotic and social dynamics than do attempts to adjudicate whether something is a copy or a response. All the chapters in this section demonstrate nicely how monologism and dialogism are not separate processes; they are achievements that involve and implicate one another, at the level of interaction, of discourse, of subjectification, sociality, and, as Urban observes, at the level of culture and metaculture. Separation is futile. For that reason, while is it important and productive to examine how different kinds of 'voices' are produced in different ways in different contexts and at different scales, it is perhaps less compelling to worry much about whether those voices are genuine responses or etiolated entropic copies.

Acknowledgments

I am grateful to Christopher Stroud for helpful comments on the first draft of this text, and to Matt Tomlinson for his constructive and graceful editorial skills.

References

Bourdieu, Pierre. (1972) 1977. *Outline of a Theory of Practice*. Trans. Richard Nice. Cambridge: Cambridge University Press.

Derrida, Jacques. 2003. "And Say the Animal Responded?," In *Zoontologies: The Question of the Animal*, ed. Cary Wolfe, 121–146. Minneapolis: University of Minnesota Press.

Duranti, Alessandro, Elinor Ochs, and Bambi B. Schieffelin, eds. 2012. *The Handbook of Language Socialization*. Malden, MA: Wiley-Blackwell.

Garrett, Paul B., and Patricia Baquedano-López. 2002. "Language Socialization: Reproduction and Continuity, Transformation and Change." *Annual Review of Anthropology* 31:339–361.

Lacan, Jacques. (1953) 1996. "The Function and Field of Speech and Language in Psychoanalysis." In *Écrits*, by Jacques Lacan, trans. Brian Fink, 197–268. New York: W. W. Norton.

Urban, Greg. 2001. *Metaculture: How Culture Moves through the World*. Minneapolis: University of Minnesota Press.

4 "WITH UNITY WE WILL BE VICTORIOUS!"

A MONOLOGIC POETICS OF POLITICAL "CONSCIENTIZATION" WITHIN THE CUBAN REVOLUTION

Kristina Wirtz

Introduction

I wish to probe our dialogical analytic by reconsidering what we take monologue to mean, relative to dialogue, which has long been understood as its opposite. This excavation into our intellectual history returns to the arguments of M. M. Bakhtin—and his confederate, V. N. Volosinov—for a dialogical understanding of discourse, based on its fundamental condition of heteroglossia, the multiplicity of voices. Bakhtin attends to monologue mostly to critique prior theorists' assumptions that the utterance neatly maps onto the individual, on the one hand, and represents an abstract system called a language, on the other. He instead argues for relegating monologue to the realms of ideology and (literary) genre, where it struggles against the natural social fact of dialogicality.

In turn, Jan Mukarovsky of the Prague Linguistic Circle, influenced though he was by the Bakhtinians, proposes that dialogue and monologue are better understood as equivalent and complementary tendencies whose never-ending dynamic tension is constitutive of consciousness itself. And so I ask what purchase we might get from re-examining our conceptual apparatus regarding dialogicality and monologicality, their ontological status, and their locatability and explanatory power in the social life of discourse. I will consider these questions from a theoretical perspective, as well as in light of an ethnographic case that highlights their potential analytical utility.

My ethnographic case considers the poetics and performativity of the Cuban Revolution's hortatory practices in constituting Cuban revolutionary subjectivity. In these, a mono-logic emphasizing political unity and a totalizing commitment to the Revolution is evident, one conceptualized as a never-ending process of "conscientization," meaning the cultivation of inner congruence as well as outward conformity to the principles of the Revolution. I also consider everyday responses to this mono-logic of revolutionary virtue.

The Cuban Revolution, originally led by Fidel Castro, has run Cuba's government since 1959, when the revolutionaries violently overthrew the US-supported dictatorship of Fulgencio Batista and instead embraced a nationalist and Socialist vision for a truly independent Cuba.[1] Tensions with the United States, exacerbated by a US embargo begun in 1961, drove the Cuban Revolution into the Soviet bloc until the demise of the Soviet Union in 1991. Since then, the Cuban Revolution has sought to develop the revolutionary commitment of a new generation of Cubans amid the hardships of the ongoing US embargo and its post-Soviet "special period" of neoliberal adjustments, even as the contradictions between Socialist principles and economic realities have widened and hardened.[2] Drawing upon my fieldwork in the eastern Cuban city of Santiago de Cuba since 1998, I ask what insight Cuban perspectives on the politics of revolutionary subjectivity might provide for our theoretical apparatus regarding the dynamic between dialogicality and monologicality.

Re-theorizing Monologicality-in-Dialogicality

One central theoretical question is what kind of work we ask of these two concepts. In literary theory monologue and dialogue distinguish formal features of texts and therefore kinds of texts, based on the presence of a single voice—canonically, the "author"—or plural voices, such as characters in a drama. Bakhtin deepened the analysis of "voice" by demonstrating the ways in which voices, understood as distinct social perspectives rather than simply as speaking turns, can intermingle, interpenetrate, and "double" into ever more complex polyphonic arrangements, so that one cannot simply map "voice" onto "person"

---

1. For a few notable perspectives on this history, see Domínguez (1978); Lewis, Lewis, and Rigdon (1978); Pérez-Stable (1993); Ibarra (1998); Pérez (1999); Fernandez (2000); and Kapcia (2008b).

2. Some significant ethnographic analyses providing a range of perspectives on the structures and social changes impacting everyday life and Cubans' responses during the past few decades of the Cuban Revolution include: Rosendahl (1997); Perna (2005); de la Fuente (2007); Henken (2007); Brotherton (2008); Weinreb (2009); Pertierra (2011); and Gámez Torres (2012).

(Hill 1995) nor even onto fractionated "participant role" (Goffman 1981; Hanks 1996; Irvine 1996). Bakhtin is dismissive of literary analysis that assumes that an author fully controls—and thus can be identified with—his words, arguing, on the one hand, that all words come to us already "half someone else's" (Bakhtin 1981: 345) and, on the other, that their meaning comes as much from their uptake as from their utterance, giving discourse an open-ended, emergent quality (see Mannheim and Tedlock 1995). In his analysis, it is not simply the presence of one or multiple voices that characterizes a text, but the relationship between voices, where voices represent socio-historically situated perspectives, and where their dialogical interaction produces subjectivities. Bakhtin's is what we would now call a performative theory, where semiotic processes are constitutive of social realities.[3]

Monologue, in an absolute sense, stands for the vanishing point of the isolated utterance—the one that either does not engage an addressee or that goes unheard. Although Bakhtin's early essay "Discourse Typology in Prose" (1971) thus suggests that monologue can originate from opposite poles of either absolute authority to speak or abject powerless to make one's voice heard at all, he focuses on monologue as a tendency of politically powerful forces such as the nation-state. An example Bakhtin gives of the latter case would be a direct authorial voice "expressing the ultimate conceptual authority" and brooking no response, no questioning from an addressee's perspective (Bakhtin 1971: 180, 191; Titunik 1973: 196). We might describe such an utterance as nomically calibrated—framed as a direct representation of Truth (Silverstein 1993).[4] But notice, as Bakhtin does, that as soon as the orientations of centralizing political authority are objectified in order to be expressed in direct speech (or text), the author of such a text is creating a dialogical relationship with that already-typified authoritative discourse. Typification must therefore be understood as a dialogical process that requires recognition of a type across separate instances, via interdiscursivity (Bauman and Briggs 1990: 328; Mannheim and Van Vleet 1998). He goes on to point out that, despite the doubling of "speech centers" through such idealized, nomically calibrated replication, and therefore the formal kind of dialogicality he calls "stylization," if there is no differentiation or confrontation between the objectified voice of Truth and its most faithful

---

3. See Butler's (1993, 2004) work on performativity, as well as Kulick's (2003) cogent analysis bridging between social theory and semiotic approaches—well explained by Parmentier (1997) and Silverstein (2006), among many others. See my book (Wirtz 2014) for a more extended discussion of this argument.

4. An absence of deictic anchors and a correspondingly "universalized" chronotope might mark such an utterance, so that it seems to represent a "view from nowhere" rather than a link in any particular interdiscursive web.

repetition, "the monologic context does not weaken or disintegrate" (Bakhtin 1971: 180). Formal dialogicality can thus be a mechanism for replicating a mono-logic.[5]

By moving from "monologue" as a descriptor of non-heteroglossic discourse to "mono-logic" as an account of ideological—and, more broadly speaking, semiotically performative—forces toward discursive (and linguistic) unification and homogeneity, I therefore wish to focus on interdiscursive and dialogical processes generating concurrence and congruence across voices, to various degrees, but where perfect congruence—exact replication, speaking in unison—is an asymptote, an extreme never quite reachable in practicality. We can locate monologic efforts in moments of purification, unification, alignment, silencing, constraining, containing, standardizing, norming, and normalizing, for example. Notice these are all verbs of social force being applied—in tension with counterforces emblemized by heteroglossia.

Although Bakhtin looked to ordinary language-in-use as the foundation of literature, it is Volosinov whose analysis delves into social discourse. Consider his vivid description of linguistic meaning itself as "an electric spark that occurs only when two different terminals are hooked together," such that linguistic analysis apart from "the current of verbal intercourse" is akin to an attempt to "turn on a light bulb after having switched off the current" (Volosinov 1973: 103). This suggests that even the most authoritative, nomic utterance enters into dialogicality through being received and understood (85–87). Even in addressivity—even before considering response—we must consider what monologue and dialogue mean in the context of reception. Volosinov's major contribution to my discussion is in theorizing the intersubjective and polyphonic nature of consciousness (e.g., as "inner speech") and from there, the relationship between psyche and society. So, we must ask: How have notions of monologue and dialogue been applied to characterizing the "inner self" in itself and in relationship to the intersubjective self that receives and understands, as part of the performed self-in-interaction? When and how is monologic congruence modeled for consciousness itself? And for the alignment between inner and outer speech that produces a totalizing socio-political conformity?

---

5. Mannheim and Tedlock (1995: 4) cite Bakhtin's example of Socratic dialogue as formally dialogic but functionally anacretic, presenting only a single, authoritative perspective, albeit with multiple voices. Mannheim's more politically trenchant example is of the Peruvian military's "dialogues" with peasants, which, much like the Stalinism of Bakhtin's time were anything but dialogical in the functional sense.

A Poetics of "Conscientization" in the Cuban Revolution

Such questions have practical value in the efforts of the Cuban Revolution to continually recruit its citizens into an ever-deepening, shared revolutionary commitment that is totalizing in how it is to organize life and consciousness as a Cuban citizen. As Fidel Castro, the Cuban Revolution's most charismatic voice, famously said in his 1961 "Words to intellectuals" speech, "inside the Revolution everything, against the Revolution nothing" (Castro 1961). The workings of state-sponsored political discourse in any nation—what outsiders call "propaganda"—would fill several volumes, and my aim is not to be encyclopedic, but instead to point out the dynamic between heteroglossia and dialogic concurrence that is directed toward a monologic project of unifying all Cuban citizens for the cause of their Revolution, where to be patriotic is to support the Revolution, to enact the Revolution, and thus to be the Revolution. One important dynamic to explore, then, will be the ways in which official political discourse seeks to overtly and implicitly model many voices united as one.

A second, related dynamic is captured by a verb much used in Cuban political discourse over the decades: *concientizar*, "to make conscious/aware," where *conciencia* is a specifically politicized consciousness (Bunck 1994; Ayorinde 2004; Frederik 2005).[6] Akin to that bygone feminist mantra, "the personal is political," the process of *concientización* involves reinterpreting one's personal experiences according to a broader, critical social analysis (Allen 2011: 13–14, 93–94). That is, inner understanding becomes congruent with political ideology, demonstrating the truth of that ideology. One is persuaded. This dynamic monologic process of aligning psyche and society in turn should produce an idealized alignment between inner speech and outer performance, where citizens do not simply go through the motions because of coercion but act in accordance with revolutionary precepts because they know these to be correct, moral, and perhaps even naturally superior, in accord with their *concientización*.

Examining this important angle on mono-logic, understood as the effort to produce exactly the congruence between individual and voice that Bakhtin and Volosinov critiqued, allows us to analyze the emphasis on dialogue and debate in official Cuban political discourse not (or at least not exclusively) as a cynical and purposely false political performance of a coercive authoritarian state but as a project employing dialogue in the service of producing a like-minded moral

---

6. See Paolo Freire ([1970] 2000; originally published in Portuguese in 1968) for an influential articulation of *concientización* in a broader Latin American Leftist politics of liberation. Especially relevant is his account of dialogue as the key to developing critical consciousness, where the radical educator's engagement with his (adult, peasant) students' experiences will necessarily produce that critical (read: Marxist) consciousness.

citizenry committed to the Revolution. Rather than interpreting revolution-ary virtue as an ontology, as one of my Cubanist colleagues suggests (Holbraad 2014), I instead suggest we examine revolutionary political discourse in terms of its semiotics of nomic and monologic calibration, in seeking a collective, reflexive recognition of itself as the Truth. And in the ongoing effort to win hearts and minds, revolutionary discourse also reinforces a particular (if familiar) construc-tion of a unified, biographically continuous consciousness in terms of what Mauss called the "responsible self" (Mauss [1938] 1950; Hill 1995: 137; Johnson 2014).

As the reader will surely agree, an overtly political monologic project remains easy to challenge, not least in whispers and indirect, double-voiced critiques. Such troubling of collective consensus can, in turn, suggest that our "selves" are not as continuous and coherent as all that either.[7] Political monologue succeeds not (or not simply) by outshouting or silencing other voices, but to the extent that many voices sound as one. That is to say, what counts as political mono-logue is not some notion of pure single-voicedness speaking only to itself, having silenced or erased all critics, but instead efforts to produce an ideal congruence across multiple voices, where we might imagine the links of a speech chain in which each addressee agrees and aligns with the prior speaker's utterance, such that these "concurrences" (to use Bakhtin's term) are replicated in the next itera-tion of the unfolding interdiscursive web, out across time, space, and ever greater numbers of participants, all sharing the same orientation. Clearly, Bakhtin was dubious that such perfect congruence could ever fully vanquish the inherent dia-logicality of social life. And yet, his own biography tragically demonstrates the political force that this model of political mono-logic can gain, caught up as he was in the Stalinist purges of the 1930s.[8]

In a lighter but related vein, and moving from Soviet Russia to Soviet-era Cuba, consider an image from Cuban filmmaker Tomás Gutiérrez Alea's 1966 film, "Death of a Bureaucrat," in which a brief opening animation shows a fac-tory assembly line producing endless marble busts of independent Cuba's patri-otic hero, José Martí (1853–1895). The machine malfunctions, busts fly through the air, and one kills the exemplary worker (the "bureaucrat" of the title) and sets up the travails of his nephew to give his uncle a dignified burial and his widowed aunt her inherited pension in an overly bureaucratized system of red

---

7. Although beyond the scope of this chapter, I point out that Cuban practices of spirit pos-session and other folk religious sensitivities to spirits offer an autochthonous challenge to the Western legally responsible self, see Johnson (2014); Wirtz (2014: 69–79); and Espirito-Santo (2015).

8. Bakhtin survived his exile to Kazakhstan and demotion to the relative anonymity of a small, provincial teaching college; others of the Bakhtin Circle did not survive this era.

tape (the Cuban idiom would be endless stamps of approval) rather than human sympathy. Gutiérrez Alea undoubtedly chose marble busts of José Martí because these are ubiquitous features of public parks and building lobbies, and it stands to reason that such a proliferation of sacred emblems—the concrete objectifications of the Revolution—must be mass produced (where the uniformity of mass production—echoes of mechanical solidarity!—diagrams perfect conformity under the Revolution).

José Martí the hero is, in fact, a monument to monologic discourse: as promoted by an entire field of "Martí studies" in the Cuban academy, he is universally acclaimed, and his words often-quoted as aphorisms expressing Cuban national ideals such as independence, unity, and equality. There is nothing extraordinary about such hero-worship, nor about the replicability and wide citationality of such hero figures whether in marble busts or quotable aphorisms, since similar examples can be found in the service of official history and national unity anywhere. And the figure of Martí as national hero epitomizes the apotheosis of a host of lesser national angels, including, of course, the heroes and martyrs of the 1959 Cuban Revolution, starting with revolutionary leader and former president Fidel Castro.

But replication itself, even mass replication, does not ensure monologic unity, as the fallen marble bust of Martí in Gutiérrez's film warns us. Consider the image in figure 4.1, a lithograph by Cuban naïve artist Luis El Estudiante (Luis Joaquín

FIGURE 4.1 "Lithograph," 2003, by Luis Joaquín Rodríquez Ricardo, number 8 in a series of 10, owned by K. Wirtz; photo by K. Wirtz

Rodríquez Ricardo, b. 1966), which depicts the iconic figures of José Martí and Fidel Castro playing a game of chess. Fidel, head up, is moving his queen, while Martí rests his head in his hands as he intently studies the board that is their shared national politics. Is that a look of consternation on his face, signifying perhaps a double-voiced message? You decide what you think.

Theoretical Approaches to Monologicality amid Dialogicality

Theorists of the Bakhtin Circle argue for a view of social communication predicated on a fundamental tension between the shared understandings arising through the interactional history of a collectivity (producing Ferdinand de Saussure's *langue*) and the social differentiation so obvious to Marxists, which inflects every utterance with a distinctive social perspective. Every word carries its history of prior utterances as "intentions" that dialogically interact with the intentions of the next utterer, such that language cannot escape its heteroglossia (see also Shotter 1992). In "Discourse in the Novel," Bakhtin critiques existing approaches to language (specifically in literary studies of the novel) that

> have all postulated a simple and unmediated relation of speaker to his unitary and singular "own" language, and have postulated as well a simple realization of this language in the monologic utterance of the individual. Such disciplines actually know only two poles in the life of language, between which are located all the linguistic and stylistic phenomena they know: on the one hand, the system of a *unitary language*, and on the other the *individual* speaking in this language. (Bakhtin 1981: 269)

Bakhtin on the Force of Monologic Ideologies

What role, then, can monologue have, except as the ideological alter of dialogicality? Bakhtin's account of monologue versus dialogue describes monologue as an ideological push for or emphasis on linguistic unification—monoglossia—and therefore as a political project closely identified with the centralizing forces of the state, in seeking norms, standards, and other markers of shared language, and by extension, a shared perspective. He does not accord monologue the same ontological status as dialogue, then, since it is not constitutive of language itself. And yet he states that monologue exerts a real "force for overcoming this heteroglossia, imposing specific limits to it, guaranteeing a certain maximum of mutual understanding and crystalizing into a real, although still relative, unity—the unity of the reigning conversational (everyday) and literary language, 'correct language'" (Bakhtin 1981: 270).

As Michael Holquist (2002) argues, Bakhtin saw danger in monologic forces, which tended toward totalitarianism at one extreme and autism—which he understood as the inability for the inner speech of consciousness to connect with external others, and therefore social isolation—at the other. Of the two, the forceful efforts of official languages to produce unity were of greatest concern, even in the utopian case of a "language so compelling that no one would speak anything else" (52). As Holquist sums up Bakhtin's position:

> Official discourse in its most radical form resists communication: everyone is compelled to speak the same language (outer speech is all) . . . the more powerful the ideology, the more totalitarian (monologic) will be the claims of its language. (52–53)

Bakhtin's model of monologue thus focuses on ideological force that compels conformity, through some combination of coercion and merit. But notice that to understand how a utopian discourse could be so compelling on its own terms that people embrace it as their own perspective, a model of evaluation, as well as replication, is needed.

Mukarovsky on the Poetic Tension between Monologue and Dialogue

Holquist compares Bakhtin's views on monologue to those of Jan Mukarovsky, an influential member of the Prague Linguistics Circle. Where Bakhtin accords dialogue a more fundamental ontological status than monologue, which he and Volosinov relegate to ideology as an "abstraction," "logical construct," or even "illusion" (Holquist 2003: 58–59, see Volosinov 1973: 72), albeit a potentially powerful ideology, Mukarovsky posits monologue and dialogue as equivalent, complementary forces that are fundamental to the dynamic and processual "contexturing" of language (Mukarovsky 1977: 46–47). In his discussion of poetic language, he says: "Monologue and dialogue are two basic aspects of the semantic organization of an utterance and at the same time two mutually opposed forms of a linguistic structure in the functional sense." And yet, monologic and dialogical "orientations" can interpenetrate, producing ever more complex contextures, or pragmatic effects.

Much like Volosinov, to whom I return below, Mukarovsky speculates on the role of dialogic and monologic speech in psychological and, to a lesser extent, psychosocial processes. It is worth quoting him at length regarding his conception of how monologic and dialogic forces interact to produce individual consciousness:

> Therefore the dialogic and monologic qualities are in fact both present at the very origin of every utterance, whether its apparent form is monologic or dialogic. Indeed, they are even contained in the very mental process from which an utterance arises. The relation between the 'I' and the 'you' on which dialogue is based does not require two individuals for its activation but only the internal tension, contradictions, and unexpected reversals provided by the dynamics of every individual's psychic life. The apparent and potential dialogue nature of utterances thus has its root in the hidden 'dialogic nature' of the course of mental life. (Mukarovsky 1977: 58)

In his analysis of the inner speech of the psyche, then, monologue is not the lone or single voice, but the constitutive drive of the self toward coherence and unity, in the face of dialogue's constant production of difference. He describes psychic processes as operating more by associative relations than by the semantic or syntactic relations of language, thereby creating another point of contact in which the tensions between monologic and dialogic forces play out in constituting consciousness. These oppositions of thought and language, dialogue and monologue, in turn, shape literary and poetic reflection (Mukarovsky 1977: 60–61). For example, he suggests that poetic attention to what feels inexpressible in words highlights the differences, even the lack of congruence, between inner speech and social discourse, while the poetics of concealment and indirectness obscure impolitic or simply private inner speech, thereby hiding its lack of congruence with what external, social discourse requires. Rather than understanding the self as a static interconversion between "thought" (the psyche) and "language" (the social) Mukarovsky proposes a dynamic model in which forces for concurrence versus differentiation bring the self into a dappled, constantly moving awareness as "I" counterposed to "other."[9]

Thus far, I have examined conceptualizations of the productive tension between monologue and dialogue, as well as their relative ontological status—whether, with Bakhtin, we understand dialogicality to be the "natural" state of discourse, or whether, with Mukarovsky, we accord monologicality, understood

---

9. Compare this dialogical model of subjectivity with George Herbert Mead's (1934) influential discussion of the constitutive dynamic of "I" versus "me" and related phenomenological accounts (e.g., Merleau-Ponty [1962] 1989).

as congruence or coherence, an equivalent ontological status as a force shaping consciousness itself. I conclude from this discussion that it will be essential to trace out, then connect, the different domains where we theorize its struggle with dialogicality to play out. In short, I want to point out that it is not just in ideological processes that we might locate monologue and dialogue. The very notion of the person—and particularly that domain of personhood the Bakhtinians and Prague School theorists designated as "inner speech"—is also a rich zone for theorizing the role of voice and its potentially evaluative role in receptivity.

As Mukarovsky's work suggests, our examination of monologue versus dialogue must therefore also consider the entailments for our very concept of personhood, which Bakhtin argues cannot be reduced to "the individual" any more than discourse can be reduced to an abstract account of a "unitary language." These theorists worked with a potentially radical notion of fractionated, layered, and emergent personhood, one that anticipated postmodern and semiotic accounts (see Tedlock and Mannheim 1995). What Bakhtin nonetheless refers to as the "individual consciousness" and what Volosinov and Mukarovsky designate the "psyche" are already always products of dialogical relations. Volosinov provides the most in-depth discussion of how speech mediates the intersubjective self, and so it is to his *Marxism and the Philosophy of Language* that I now turn.

Volosinov and Hill on Consciousness Constituted through Heteroglossic Alignments and Differentiations

Volosinov is concerned to show the failings of both Psychologism and Formalism (e.g., "abstract objectivism," including various schools of structuralism and functionalism) to study language. He forcefully argues that the psyche cannot be accorded the status of an a priori entity because socialization into a stratified (read: class) society shapes our very experience of ourselves as selves. This dialogical process producing self and society is mediated by language—or more broadly, by semiosis (Volosinov 1973: 26–29), which he understands to be necessarily the stuff of social interaction and the stuff of consciousness. Having first argued that speech, or what he calls "the word" is "the semiotic material of inner life—of consciousness" (14), he then proceeds to describe the material basis of social organization (and in particular, class struggle) that grounds all social interactions—including, centrally, "speech performances" (20)—in their social context. All utterances thus reflect and refract social positionality, meaning they necessarily are "socio-ideological" in nature, entering into dialogical relations with each other.

The inner speech of consciousness, taking up these signs to constitute its own awareness, thus cannot but engage in an internal dialogue, not unlike what characterizes external communication with others. But Volosinov, like Mukarovsky, suggests that the psyche "does possess a special unity," constituted in and through the process of relating experience to other inner signs—that is, through seeking coherence as much as contrast in formulating understanding, where understanding consists of "total impressions" (Volosinov 1973: 35–38). Notice that the direction of causality is not from the psyche outward into the world, so to speak, but quite the opposite, where consciousness arises from the outside in, mediated by speech. Volosinov vividly characterizes inner speech as echoing the inflections, intentions, and voices of the social environment, which provides these heterogeneous resources through which the psyche continually emerges as a self-awareness of coherence-amid-dialogicality, through its ongoing semiotic engagement with the world.

One difficulty of such models is, of course, that introspection is an imperfect source of empirical information, since it is hardly free of the very ideological processes posited to produce consciousness in the first place (Keane 2002). In any event, my consideration of consciousness has the very modest goal of broadening the locations in which we might consider monologic and dialogic processes to interact to include "inner speech." I suggest that we reconsider monologue and dialogue as judgments about the congruence of voices, such that different degrees of alignment produce (dis)unity and (dis)continuity, and where monologicality is the ideal of a perfect alignment among those inner voices, or between "inner speech" and "outer speech," whereas any differences, tensions, or even oppositions signal some degree of dialogicality.

It is this theoretical framework that Jane Hill (1995) elaborates in her analysis of the "many voices of Don Gabriel," in which she traces the variety of semiotic resources, including voicings, mobilized by a Mexicano-Spanish speaker telling a deeply felt personal story about his son's murder. She shows how the speaker laminates multiple voices (figurations, codes, moral and evaluative stances, intonations, etc.) to populate a complex social landscape of oppositions between rural–urban, agriculture–business, communality–capitalism, tradition–modernity, and propriety–immorality while morally positioning himself and the other figures of his story on their devastating trajectories toward tragedy and grief. So who is Don Gabriel, who like all of us can give voice to the full heteroglossic diversity of his social environment? Hill argues that his selfhood emerges in his ongoing, always-partial attempts to present a consistent orientation to events, one that aligns his narrated and performed selves with the moral uprightness of his Mexicano peasant identification, in contrast to the narrated and voiced figures of others, who populate the subjective positions he keeps at a distance. Hill concludes by invoking what Mauss (1985) called the "responsible" self of Western legal, contractual, and civic tradition:

> The narrative reveals a veritable kaleidoscope of "emotional selves," which are all art, distributed fragments across the rhetorical system of the narrative. But the narrative does give us evidence of the integrity of another self, the "responsible self," which we may call consciousness, and allows us a privileged glimpse of the moment of "active choice" when this consciousness orients itself as a voice in a heteroglossic universe. (Hill 1995: 139)

Although heteroglossia remains the prime, the forces toward coherence and biographical continuity that play out through dialogical relations are what I characterize as monologic. Monologicality thus is as deeply historical a social fact as dialogicality. Many ideological interventions promoting (or coercing) monologics are, in fact, as concerned with addressing the alignment between "inner" and "outer" speech as they are with enforcing conformity strictly as an issue of public performance.[10] My case of Cuban *concientización*, to be examined in the following sections, will illustrate this point. That is, committed revolutionaries (and functionaries of the bureaucratic system of the Revolution) deploy an array of semiotic techniques and modalities to recruit the Cuban populace to believe in revolutionary ideals and not simply act the part. And at times, during my fieldwork, my Cuban interlocutors have given voice to tensions arising in enacting a revolutionary "consciousness." As Martin Holbraad (2014) argues, marshalling perspectivism rather than Butlerian performativity or semiotic theory, it may be more useful to ask how the Revolution constitutes its subjects through its enunciative order, rather than applying a rhetorical model to ask how it "convinces" its populace.

Revolutionary Mono-Logics

Charismatic Calibration

Monologic projects seek to recruit addressees into ever-more-perfect congruence with the authoritative "voice," and to minimize differences so that an apparently "single-voiced" unity will be what is replicated and broadcast, harmonizing the responses within a shared orientation. In these complex and multifarious semiotic

---

10. Webb Keane's (2002, 2007) work on Protestant missionization is an especially important intervention in tracing the coordinated spread of historically specific Western, Christian ideologies of personhood and of language, such as the cultivation of sincerity as an alignment between an inner, moral self and the world (see also Robbins, Schieffelin, and Vilaça 2014).

processes, one moment to examine is a heightening of the contrast between roles of "speaker" and "addressee" so that the "speaker" becomes absolute, addressing an audience that receives the speaker's utterance in perfect agreement. Consider the authority commanded by a highly charismatic leader, whose distinctive voice, with all of its indexical anchoring in the particularities of individual biography, becomes the definitive voice of a political orientation. A different moment instead flattens those distinctions and generalizes the indexical anchorings of what is instead a universal or commonsensical voice, with the goal of aligning and harmonizing speaker and addressee positions in order to make each link of the interdiscursive web a perfect echo of the former, toward that ideal of exact replication. Greg Urban's (2001) case of "we the people" illustrates the entextualization practices that allow this deictic formulation to be replicated across time and space, encompassing ever wider subjectivities and even being repurposed to express the Truth uniting new political collectivities. Each of these possibilities, involving either nomic calibration or what I will call, somewhat tongue-in-cheek, charismatic calibration, can exert monologic force, and they are not necessarily mutually exclusive.

The most visible example of charismatic calibration is the striking image of (a younger) Fidel Castro giving a speech, open air to a giant enthralled crowd or in a broadcast studio before a smaller audience, where such events, formally delivered as monologues that could last up to a record seven hours in his heyday, were then broadcast and printed by state media (which constituted all legally accessible media in Cuba) to reach the entire national audience. This oft-repeated kind of event models that absolute distinction between speaker and audience, where the audience performed intense and silent listening to Fidel's message, without interruption. During my extended fieldwork in Cuba in 1999-2000, I was always struck by how I could step outside of my residence and even walk down the street and still hear the same speech synchronized from every television—a case-in-point of mass-mediated formal monologicality charismatically calibrated so as to point-source revolutionary moral authority in the voice of Fidel.

Nor were televised speeches and their transcripts published in state newspapers the only charismatically calibrated monologic forms: along highways and atop city buildings, billboards promoting the Revolution were a common sight, as were smaller placards and even roadside markers along more rural highways. Much like Fidel's speeches, these iconic images of and aphorisms attributed to Cuba's heroes and martyrs of its nineteenth-century struggles for independence from Spain and its twentieth-century Revolution conveyed a sense of monumental historical continuity, in which each current moment is simply another iteration along the coherent and monologic historical arc of Cuba's ongoing struggle toward its unwavering ideals of independence and patriotism at any

FIGURE 4.2 Billboard of Guillermo Moncada with slogan, "Fatherland First," Santiago de Cuba, July 24, 2011. Photo by K. Wirtz

cost. "All of our action is a war cry against imperialism. –Che" declared one billboard, citing rehabilitated revolutionary martyr Che Guevara.[11] José Martí, a prolific writer and poet, was another frequently cited figure. And figures 4.2 and 4.3 show two billboards located right across from each other at a busy city intersection that quite deliberately collocate patriotic images of Cuba's past and present. In figure 4.2, an image of nineteenth-century independence hero Guillermo Moncada (1841–1895) with a Cuban flag as backdrop accompanies the slogan "fatherland first." In figure 4.3, photos of octogenarian brothers Fidel and Raúl against a similar flag backdrop accompany Santiago's official slogan and the official black-and-red icon commemorating the July 26, 1953, attack on the Moncada garrison in Santiago that was led by Fidel—an event the 1959 Revolution claims as its official moment of origin as a "movement," while 1959 is called its year of triumph. Hence, "el 26" is known to every Cuban, as is its premise that a struggle may require years to achieve victory. The slogan for the city of Santiago on the billboard expresses the telos linking past, present,

11. Original Spanish: "Toda nuestra acción es un grito de guerra contra el imperialismo" (from https://secure.worldexpeditions.com/au/index.php?section=presentations&id=2229185). Before his death in Bolivia, Che had increasingly split from Fidel, but as a martyr he could be safely reclaimed as a revolutionary hero.

FIGURE 4.3 Billboard of Fidel and Raúl Castro with slogan, "Santiago: rebellious yesterday, welcoming today, forever heroic," Santiago de Cuba, July 24, 2011. Photo by K. Wirtz

and future across the two billboards: "Santiago: rebellious yesterday, welcoming today, forever heroic."

Thus, charismatic calibration was evident not just in the continual broadcast and publication of Fidel's (and other revolutionary heroes') words, but in the multiple channels of their uptake as quotations indexing the unimpeachable revolutionary and patriotic credentials of their original authors. I suggest that these iconic images and quotes model how Cubans are to express their patriotic sentiments by identifying with and channeling the charismatic voices of the Revolution's heroes, who urge long-term, daily commitment to revolutionary values. Although the quotation marks and attribution to a charismatic source clearly demarcate such quotes from surrounding discourse, those who cite charismatic sources can bask in the glow that crosses those boundaries of attribution and thereby burnish their own revolutionary credentials.

We can also better understand the proliferation of rather less memorable citations, such as the following quote attributed to President Raúl Castro and neatly framed on the wall of a bleak, windowless administrative office I visited:

The secret to achieving greater successes lies in the capacity of blocks to together encompass the complexity of the situation, establish priorities, organize work, unite forces, demand discipline, educate by example, explain the need for each task, convince, motivate, lift the spirit, and mobilize the will of the people. Raul Castro[12]

If anything, the dissemination of such stultifying quotes seems likely to achieve quite the opposite effects of uplifting and motivating, to the extent anyone actually reads them. Having long since "gone native" enough to tune out such ubiquitous quotations in workplaces and schools, I admit to attending to this one initially out of boredom, after being left to wait alone in that office for a while. But even with a passing glance, upon entering the office, one notices who is being quoted. In short, to dutifully display such a poster, an effortless enough task, was to align oneself with its speaker and his sentiments, however banal. In fact, the more commonsensical the message, the less there is to challenge, lending itself to agreement. Likewise, to turn on one's television set for the nightly political program, even if no one was watching, performed a similarly effortless alignment to the Revolution as hanging a poster, with the added advantage that the television's volume could mask private conversation.

Challenges to Charismatic Monologue in Receptivity

Of course, living there, I quickly came to know that many of the televisions broadcasting Fidel's voice in synchrony were on at 9 p.m. in the despairing hope that he would wrap his speech up in time for the telenovela or the always highly anticipated "movie of the night" still to be broadcast. I also knew that at least some of those whose televisions broadcast the speech were silently pointing chins, pursing lips, and rolling eyes at the image, perhaps adding a quick gesture of finger and thumb stroking chin to indicate "la barba" ("the beard," a common metonym for Fidel). Heteroglossia remained, but it was constrained to small silent gestures or whispers in private among confidantes.

And when I too was impatiently seated in front of a television set awaiting the telenovela, I always found grim fascination in observing the television studio audiences, whose job was to model idealized audience behavior to the broadcast audience, and who therefore needed to perform sitting calmly but in a way that demonstrated that they were absorbed in, if not enthralled by, the speech being delivered live before them. At any moment, the camera could pan for an audience shot or a close-up "reaction shot" and one could see how hard those lucky

---

12. Original Spanish in all caps, no accents: "El secreto para lograr mayores exitos esta en la capacidad de los cuadros para abarcar de conjunto la complejidad de la situacion, establecer las prioridades, organizar el trabajo, cohesionar las fuerzas, exigir disciplina, educar con el ejemplo, explicar la necesidad de cada tarea, convencer, entusiasmar, levantar el espiritu y movilizar la voluntad de la gente. Raul Castro."

audience members were working to not fidget or get distracted or nod off. Even in the air conditioning of their studio, some of those exemplary workers were sweating. In marked contrast to this rapt, silent audience behavior expected of political speeches, where loud engagement was to be saved for vigorous applause and congratulatory shouts at the end (¡Viva Fidel! ¡Viva la Revolución!), most other audiences I observed, certainly in concert halls and cinema houses, during classical ballet, and even sometimes during academic conference talks, were notably boisterous, happily engaging in offering feedback or interrupting while carrying on other social business among themselves. Solemn, silent spectatorship, it seemed, was cultivated mostly as a response to political speeches.

Here, I would be remiss not to point out that silent conformity can be performed polyvalently and even parodically, so as to offer a critique of the conditions coercing it: consider Monique Skidmore's (2003: 10) description of the "blank exterior persona: listless eyes in wooden bodies" that Burmese citizens of totalitarian Myanmar cultivated in part because "they find feigning enthusiasm for the [military] junta exceedingly difficult."[13] I once observed the adult residents of an entire neighborhood block act just this way when called out for a pre-election rally to nominate representatives to the Elections Assembly. The block's CDR (Committees in Defense of the Revolution, a block-by-block political organ of the revolutionary state) "president" and a few young political operatives (probably from the Juventud Communista—Communist Youth, another national organization) had set up a platform and loudspeakers in the middle of the street and played the national anthem, at which adults both outdoors and inside stood silently. The organizers then exhorted the crowd to nominate who would stand for this election. I had been visiting a friend's religious ceremony at a house on the block, and we had to halt the ceremony when interrupted by the anthem, and so I moved with the others to get a good view through the doorway into the street. During about five minutes of speech, the crowd stood silently. No one even moved. In desperation, one of those on the platform even turned to the young woman seated on the platform next to her, and therefore an organizer of the event, to publicly ask her to run. The young woman kept her composure while demurring that she could not possibly serve, since she was due to leave for her compulsory military service soon. Frustrated at the interruption of our religious ceremony, I left after another five minutes of impasse, during which the organizers' pleas for their comrades to remember their patriotic and

13. Skidmore also argues that this silent, calm demeanor helps maintain the (inner) numbness necessary to survive the otherwise overwhelming fear and terror systematically generated by the regime, but Myanmar is radically different from Cuba in this respect. While Cubans are quite aware of and even cautious about their state's surveillance and security apparatus, they are not, in my experience, fearful of or terrorized by it.

revolutionary duty were met by an increasingly deafening silence and stillness in the crowd. Heteroglossia—here, evident in the addressees' refusal to cooperate with a speaker—does not always require voices.

Attempts to monologically channel the Revolution's message could be derailed in any number of ways, as in one unfortunate speaker at a televised conference whose nervousness conveyed to those I was watching the program with that he was (as I wrote in my field notes) "parroting, not saying *his own* words." In other words, he inadvertently demonstrated a lack of alignment to the message he was simply supposed to be replicating. Briggs (2013) describes the apparent double-voicing of Cuban journalistic coverage of a dengue fever outbreak as perhaps posing as great a challenge to the Revolution's triumphalist narrative of progress as the disease outbreak itself.

And yet there was (and remains) a shared vision and political project that the election rally organizers I observed were appealing to, thereby aligning themselves with and channeling—replicating and disseminating—the Revolution's message. And so it is too that state media broadcast many people's voices—government and Communist Party officials, journalists, other newsmakers, and ordinary citizens, all "on message" (more or less convincingly) in propounding the Truth that is the Cuban Revolution. Akin to all the television sets broadcasting and amplifying the same voice, this kind of mono-logic attention to form models its political dominance but cannot, in itself and apart from other structures of coercion, do much to control receptivity in its audience.

Clearly, the dominance and authoritativeness of Fidel's voice alone would not a fifty-year Revolution make. Consider one instance in which a wife mocked her husband, who was trying to dominate a conversation and shushing everyone, by turning to her daughter-in-law and saying: "Quiet, María! Fidel is speaking!" Fidel's voice and that of other leaders, such as his rather less charismatic brother, President Raúl Castro, must align with the "voice of the people"; the official message must lose or loosen its indexical anchor in his persona to be voiced as shared patriotism, as common sense, held by all.

I now want to consider two aspects of monologic efforts to generate mass congruence to a revolutionary orientation. The first concerns the semiotic workings of various media and modalities for promoting the intrinsic correctness of the Revolution as a worldview, so as to recruit the Cuban citizenry to that orientation. The second specifically addresses widespread metacultural concern about the congruence between outer conformity and inner orientation, not only in official discourses about conscientization, and in the barrage of revolutionary messages seeking to ensure a conscientious population, but in the responses of that population, as evident in everyday conversations about revolutionary virtue texturing my ethnographic experience there.

Con Unidad Venceremos (With Unity We Will Be Victorious)

Although the Revolution's charismatically calibrated voicing—the monumentalized speech of its heroes and martyrs—was highly visible and audible, there was a parallel phenomenon of aphorisms presented without attribution. Not only in slickly designed billboards, but on banners and as "graffiti" spray-painted on exterior walls[14] one saw aphorisms whose pithy sentiments apparently required no indexical anchoring as quotes but were simply proclamations of nomically calibrated Truths. Here are a few examples I recorded over my years of moving around Cuban cities:

> "Con unidad venceremos" ("With unity we will be victorious")
> "¡Socialismo o Muerte!" ("Socialism or Death")
> "Patria es humanidad" ("Fatherland is humanity")
> "Hasta la victoria siempre" ("Forever onward toward victory")
> "Lo nuestro es lo nuestro" ("What's ours is ours")
> "Libertad sin honestidad es deshonra" ("Liberty without honesty is dishonor")
> "Siempre el 26" ("Forever the 26th").

The nomic calibration of these aphorisms is evident in their condensation of unimpeachably patriotic sentiments, their portability, their ubiquity, and their lack of attribution to any particular individual, however charismatic.[15] Walking or riding across a city, a person could encounter a dozen of these without even trying. Even on rural highways, one passed small signs and even roadside stone monuments of this sort. While these are hardly the spontaneous creations of ordinary citizens (and I enjoy imagining the coordination of graffiti-brigades, as surely occurred through workplace and mass-organization "voluntary labor" required by the state), I suggest that they function by voicing a familiar, shared truth and recruiting their addressee (whoever passes and reads one) to align with properly revolutionary sentiment, as an inner orientation.

For example, everyone in Cuba knows the significance of "the 26th" (of July) and so is interpellated to a knowing and belonging subject position within the revolutionary "movement" every time they encounter another reminder of "the 26th." At the same time, the continual reinvocation of "the 26th" suggests the

---

14. Graffiti of this sort was more prevalent at the end of the 1990s and is now much rarer and more faded, suggesting that it is no longer being created to the extent it once was.

15. As Bauman (2004) argues for his corpus of market calls and spiels, the poetic form of these short texts also calibrates their genre—as sloganistic aphorisms of the sort a crowd might recite at a rally.

ongoing relevance of this one date—July 26, 1953—and thus invites the revolutionary subject to approach every day with the fervor of that anniversary.

By being the words of no one in particular and by sheer repetition, such slogans bid to become the words of everyone. And not only do such aphorisms voice a monological political unity. It is the attempt to compel a complete alignment with the Revolution, both in performance and in inner speech, that interests me here. Consider a small sign along a highway that I spotted in July 2014: "If only one revolutionary remains in Cuba, it will be me," where the first person wording interpellates the reader into the position of being that last supporter standing in some hypothetical future.[16] Such slogans thus constitute one effort to model political unity and recruit their addressees to the presupposition that to be a good person is to be patriotic, and to be a patriotic Cuban is to be aligned with, for, and in the Revolution. In doing so, they index the persistence of their alter: the unconvinced, unmotivated, or just plain exhausted subject the Revolution must continually recruit.

Once again, the evidence shows the incompleteness of such efforts: Cuban wits have long since turned "Socialism or Death!" into "Socialism and Death," although never as graffiti that I saw. And the official discourse of the 1990s post-Soviet "special period" crisis, urging Cubans to collectively sacrifice in order to preserve their Socialist revolution, was quickly and collectively reappropriated to express a perspective orthogonal to, sometimes even (indirectly) critical of, the official mono-logic. For example, the official discourse of the "lucha" or "struggle" against imperialism became the ubiquitous expression of the "lucha" of everyday survival, as in the ironic (and exhausted) double-voiced reply to "How's it going?": "Aquí en la lucha" ("here in the struggle . . ."), often accompanied by a heavy sigh.

As I read Martin Holbraad's (2014) argument, such double-voicing is not necessarily against the Revolution, since the necessity of hardship and sacrifice for the Revolution seems constitutive of the Cuban revolutionary subject. He argues that the seeming contradictions between commitment to and critique of the Revolution are a paradox only from the perspective of the Western liberal political subject, which exists prior to "ideology" and therefore defines itself relative to the Revolution as ideology.[17] The paradox resolves, he argues, if a revolutionary self-sacrificing subject is instead posited (370). But I am not convinced

---

16. Original Spanish: "Si solo se queda un revolucionario en Cuba seré yo." Notice that the slogan works against the very future it posits. Of course, such sentiments also offer a critique of Cubans' lack of commitment to the Revolution in the present.

17. One might also question whether ordinary Western liberal political subjects are always so absolute and consistent in our commitments.

that revolutionary subjectivity is as monolithic as Holbraad suggests, nor that we can dispense with that peculiarly Western commitment to an inner self performatively enacted through its confrontation with ideologies, per Volosinov. Holbraad's very examples, in fact, are quintessentially dialogical encounters. So rather than an ontological approach, I argue for a performative approach attending to the semiotic constitution of inner selves who must ideally come into congruence with the Revolution. That is, revolutionary virtue is predicated on the dialogical encounter of both inner and external "voices."

It is precisely the Revolution's long-standing attention to developing revolutionary consciousness—to *concientización*—that suggests a modeling of inner speech in response to outer speech much like what Volosinov and Mukarovsky posit. Consider again Fidel's "Palabras a los intelectuales" speech:

> It is possible that the men and women who have a truly revolutionary attitude toward reality do not constitute the majority sector of the population. Revolutionaries are the vanguard of the people, but the revolutionaries must aspire to having all the people march along with them. . . . The Revolution must aspire to having everyone who has doubts become a revolutionary. The Revolution must try to win the major part of the people over to its ideas. (Castro 1961)

That is, the Revolution must be committed to dialogue with the goal of convincing the unconvinced.[18] Formally dialogic formats in use include "debate" and "round table" political programs, lively discussions at academic conferences and through blog sites and publications (such as *Temas*), and mandatory workplace and mass organization political orientation meetings, that at least sometimes take the format of discussions.[19] In domains of cultural production, such as film and popular music, and official political campaigns such as the "Battle of Ideas" announced in 2000 as "a fight for truth and justice" (Kapcia 2008a), competing and even critical perspectives can flourish.[20]

---

18. Note that Fidel applies a rhetorical, rather than performative, framework, although I am arguing for an analysis of the performative effects of such hortatory logics.

19. I know of mandatory workplace meetings only indirectly, from finding a workplace closed during business hours and from friends' and acquaintances' occasional comments about them, and I admit to being circumspect about pursuing the topic with direct questioning. Some acquaintances roll their eyes at the notion that there is anything "dialogical" about such meetings, emphasizing their mono-logic and even coercive function in ensuring "rectification" and conformity to official views, but others have spontaneously praised moments of open discussion encouraged in their workplace meetings.

20. Original Spanish: "Es una pelea por la verdad y la justicia, como dijera Fidel Castro, en su discurso durante el acto por el IV Aniversario de la Batalla de Ideas" ("It is a fight for truth and

Critics of Cuba's regime will point out the limits of permitted critiques, and historians of Cuba's Revolution, such as Antoni Kapcia (2008a, 2014) delineate periods of higher or lower official tolerance of critique (which so easily gets recontextualized as dissent, or worse, as counterrevolutionary). Cuba's current moment seems relatively open to public discussion of such thorny issues as racism, sexism, re-entrenched "class" disparities, and corruption, and many Cubans I know engage passionately in these discussions. Other topics—such as regime change or vocal support for dissident groups—remain off limits. My goal here is not to assess the political climate, however, but to point out that by the Revolution's own logic, political dialogue is to be encouraged because the inherent superiority of Socialist principles and values will inevitably win people to a revolutionary orientation. As one banner hanging over a main commercial street promised in reference to the hegemonic Cuban Communist Party (back in 2002), "The party is immortal."

Revolutionary Virtue in the Struggles of "Double Morality"

Privately, Cubans at times assess political "dialogue" as mere window-dressing for the same old propaganda.[21] They complain about economic hardships that they only sometimes follow official discourse in blaming on the imperialists to the north. But they are also usually quick to express patriotic pride in revolutionary values. Rather than try to resolve these seeming contradictions in favor of an "outer" performance masking a more honest but inexpressible "inner" view, I suggest that Cubans may at least sometimes be engaging in exactly the sort of heteroglossic dialoguing toward mono-logic Truth modeled in official political discourse.

A representative example from several years back occurred as I sat watching a televised speech by Fidel with a friend. The speech, made to the National Assembly, concerned the key role of education in the "battle of ideas" campaign. My friend dramatically pointed at the TV screen, saying "liar!" After some shared astonished laughter, he reminded me that this was a private conversation, and that publicly expressing such a response would cause problems—and here he grabbed his forearm, indicating being taken into custody by the police. After this silent gesture, accompanied by a meaningful look, he seamlessly segued into

---

justice, as Fidel Castro said in his speech during the action for the fourth anniversary of the Battle of Ideas"), from Radio Rebelde, http://www.radiorebelde.cu.

21. Amy Weinreb's (2009) ethnography of Cuban dissatisfaction insightfully discusses Cuban understandings of public-private boundaries, especially as these play out in the "double morality" of everyday life.

praising the accomplishments of the Revolution, especially regarding education and literacy, thereby aligning himself with the speech that continued in the background. He then praised Fidel, giving him credit for Cuba's achievements on the world stage, saying, "he is very well-read and knows about everything," and "he is not afraid to speak the truth in any situation, whatever the risks."

This and many similar conversations I have had over the years, with Cubans from many walks of life, do not lend themselves to any single interpretation. They seem to express fundamentally heteroglossic perspectives that cannot always neatly be reconciled, nor delineated according to "inner" or "private" versus "public" speech. The revolutionary "struggle" it seems, extends to wrestling with one's own doubts and counterarguments, as well as with the gaps between one's ideals and actions.

In the late 1990s, the idiom I often heard Cubans use for the contradictions that increasingly defined their individual and collective lives was "double morality," meaning the inherent contradictions between Socialist principles such as self-sacrifice and putting the collectivity first, and pragmatic choices people made to procure the necessities through dubious transactions and putting their own needs first (see Wirtz 2004). By coincidence, Fidel himself listed "double morality" as a significant problem in Cuba's struggle against poor morale when my friend and I turned our attention back to the TV. These contradictions percolate through every level of the system, such that the government's concerns about the accumulated individual decisions to cheat the Socialist system in order to get by or get ahead were at least sometimes echoed in the anguish my most committed revolutionary friends expressed to me—through 2000 anyway—about their own "double morality." And outside observers, notably Ayorinde (2004), Brotherton (2008, 2013), and Hencken (2000, 2007), have argued that the regime itself has come to quietly rely upon the very economic strategies (and moral economies) it has decried as illegal, counterrevolutionary, and capitalist, in order to address the failings of its beleaguered command economy, thereby practicing its own heteroglossic counterpoint to revolutionary mono-logics. Is it any wonder, then, that what Tanuma (2007) dubs "post-utopian irony" is a well-mined vein of humor in Cuba?

I argue that these dialogical counterpoints to the Revolution's officially monologic exhortations to total revolutionary commitment are what best characterizes revolutionary consciousness: it is an ongoing struggle at all levels, from the ideological "battle of ideas" to the daily prospect of moral compromises necessary to everyday household and national economics alike, to the shaping of consciousness itself as a quest for ever-more-perfect congruence to revolutionary ideals and ever-more-complete commitment that, as it is achieved, would negate the "double morality" of everyday life and, presumably, allow Socialism to win once and for all the "battle of ideas."

As a concluding example, I present a typical moment articulating this "struggle" so constitutive of revolutionary consciousness from my fieldwork, in this case no doubt related to my presence as a foreigner. A close friend who is a folklorist and cultural promoter had arranged for me to interview the director and two long-time drummers of a traditional Afro-Cuban "Carabalí" folklore society. We were two hours into a long afternoon sitting together in their rehearsal space, during which the interview had moved between relatively formal questions and answers about the group's history and music, led by me, and stretches of crosstalk and conversation, fueled by rum my friend—call him Emilio—ran out to buy after the first hour. My recorder was on throughout most of the afternoon.

Emilio and I had decided I would show my gratitude to the elders of the Carabalí society for allowing me access to study their society by sponsoring transportation for them and elders from the other Carabalí society to see a nightclub show that Emilio directs—an opportunity financially beyond the reach of ordinary Cubans, unless they have connections. Following Emilio's judgment, I usually opt for some variation on sponsoring a party, so that my contributions are apparent to all members of a group. In this case, by sending everyone the same night, both societies could see I was dealing with them "equally." I had learned that directors of groups usually do the same with, for example, prize money from Carnival, to cut down on suspicions that they are financially benefiting instead of sharing. To spend everything on plentiful drink and sweets right away is to demonstrate to everyone that they have shared the resource. For me to give no gift would be seen as ungrateful and exploitative, but too much, or even the suspicion of too much to one or a few persons, could create jealousy or suspicion of corruption, heightening the risk of someone denouncing someone else to the authorities.[22]

Mentioning the nightclub had gotten Emilio talking about his work evaluating various commercial folklore groups, as required for their continued government permission to work as commercial acts. That topic, in turn, prompted some direct questions from me about what kinds of folkloric groups could "commercialize," or work in the tourist industry for money, and whether a traditional group like the Carabalí would ever receive payment for performing in a commercial tourist setting (the short answer to this was no). Emilio and the Carabalí director had also compared notes about the difficulties of leadership, including the importance of being fair, inspiring, and transparent about the use of limited resources. In their discussion, they used the word *interés*, "interest," which for Cubans connotes financial benefits. For example, foreigners like me often gained

---

22. I am not speaking hypothetically but from firsthand experience in situations where such suspicions or jealousy have had this unfortunate result.

Cuban "friends" motivated by *interés*, or potential access to the money and resources a foreigner might share—like getting to visit a nightclub. All such relationships were, shall we say, tainted by the suspicion of *interés*—including mine with Emilio and with the Carabalí elders. Such ethical questions were necessarily emergent in our interaction.

Emilio had just emphasized that I was "a humble person committed to my work," not a "millionaire." He then complained that the nightclub show he directed was plagued by problems of low motivation and ethics and told a story about one young musician who had begged for time off to deal with a crisis at home, then returned two weeks later and handed Emilio 40 Cuban convertible pesos (equivalent to US$40) and worth more than two months' average salary, as thanks for letting him "resolve the problem," where this expression refers to practices of "double morality." Emilio described his surprise and refusal to accept the money, realizing only then that the young musician had taken time off to engage in some sort of illicit "commercialization" (the nature of the scheme was not clear to me from his account, which left a lot implicit, but the other Cubans undoubtedly understood it perfectly).

Emilio continued (in my abbreviated translation): "If I accepted that, there would be grave problems with my reputation, which would never recover, AND I'd be implicated in what he did." The others agreed, and Emilio summarized, "You can't purchase your reputation," stimulating yet more discussion of revolutionary morality, in which everyone expressed vigorous agreement. Notice that Emilio's story depicted an immoral character (the young musician) by associating the character with morally dubious actions (commercialization, attempted bribery) that the narrator then rejected, both as an autobiographical character in his own story and as an interactional stance that his interlocutors could then heartily support, simultaneously distancing themselves from the immoral actions of the character and creating camaraderie—monologic consensus—through mutual alignment with revolutionary virtue. I have witnessed many similar moments of congruence with revolutionary virtues among interlocutors in response to this kind of self-reporting, often amid similar ironies, such as accepting potentially morally comprising "gifts" like the rum and the nightclub outing. Irony, that most quintessential case of double-voicing, may be as necessary to the project of revolutionary conscientization as double morality is to meeting economic needs within the Revolution.

As these ethical double-binds play out (and get ironed out) interactionally, in moments like the one I described, the "responsible self" emerges as a moral subjectivity to which narrator and audience, alike, can align. Rather than a monolithic ideology, the Cuban Revolution as political entity, collective action, and conscious orientation is constituted and lived in the ongoing, necessary struggle for an ever-more-perfect unity amid unavoidable heteroglossia.

Conclusion

In providing a reconsideration of monologicality, I wish to avoid the irony of giving a monologic ethnographic perspective on life under the Cuban Revolution, which is after all a complex reality producing heterogeneous lived experiences and a great deal more heteroglossia, even within official discourse, than I have been able to represent here. With that caveat in mind, I have argued that the exhortatory practices of the Cuban Revolution illustrate the productive—indeed, the performative—tension between dialogicality and monologicality that plays out not only in ideology, as Bakhtin described, but perhaps more significantly in the semiotic processes generating subjectivities, both collective and individual. My ethnographic data demonstrate some degree of convergence between Volosinov's and Mukarovsky's accounts of consciousness and the Latin American Leftist political notion of "conscientization" that has been so influential in revolutionary Cuba—a convergence that a deeper intellectual excavation would surely trace to a shared Marxist framework.

Reframing the Revolution as a struggle toward the ideal of unity, that asymptote where the official narrative would become the utopian "language so compelling that no one would speak anything else," we can reconcile the seeming contradictions between the Revolution's totalizing mono-logic claim on Truth and its ongoing, dialogical process of conscientization. Monological processes, then, do not necessarily drive toward erasing all heteroglossia to enforce conformity, but rather push toward congruence amid dialogicality, and they do so not uniformly but through a variety of poetic and metapragmatic strategies. The Revolution's ontological premises—that heady combination of struggle, sacrifice, and triumphalism—unfold through discourse histories linking heroes and the masses of ordinary citizens alike, past, present, and future, into the telos of "conscientization." We might even see the success of the project in those tortured moments when ordinary Cubans confront the "double morality" around them—and perhaps implicating them as well.

In examining the poetics of some of the Revolution's most notable hortatory practices, I have shown how seemingly dialogical forms can produce monologic effects, as in the preordained winner of the "battle of ideas." And sometimes monological forms can nonetheless model "dialogue," as when authoritative pronouncements heighten the contrast between charismatic speaker and audience and therefore highlight the rhetorical efforts of persuasion. I have pointed out how some hortatory practices model an idealized revolutionary subjectivity through charismatic calibration. For example, the monumentalization of heroic revolutionary voices and figures works much like the ubiquitous statues of Martí to provide perfect replicas that can be widely disseminated. But if we trace out the uptake and further dissemination of such charismatically calibrated models, it becomes apparent that while receptivity provides the opportunity to display one's congruence to the model, there is also the risk of double-voiced or dissenting receptivity, as in the marble Martí bust that, through human error, topples and creates an industrial accident in Gutiérrez's film (and where the film itself, in presenting its humorous critique, also models the limits of reducing Socialist solidarity to perfect mechanical replicability of forms).

Alongside charismatic calibration, I have pointed out the workings of nomic calibration in revolutionary slogans that are not framed as heroic quotes, but as universalized Truths voiced by no one and therefore, potentially, by everyone, including you, the reader of this anonymous graffito or that banner. To encounter such messages is to be interpellated into a revolutionary subjectivity of unity in which many voices rise as one: *hasta la victoria siempre*.

As a postscript and testament to mono-logic power, after el Comandante Fidel Castro passed away on November 25, 2016, the international news media reported that his 500-mile funeral procession from Havana was met in Santiago de Cuba's Plaza of the Revolution by a massive crowd chanting, "yo soy Fidel," "I am Fidel."

References

Allen, Jafari S. 2011. *¡Venceremos?: The Erotics of Black Self-Making in Cuba*. Durham, NC: Duke University Press.

Ayorinde, Christine. 2004. *Afro-Cuban Religiosity, Revolution, and National Identity*. Gainesville: University Press of Florida.

Bakhtin, Mikhail M. 1971. "Discourse Typology in Prose." In *Readings in Russian Poetics: Formalist and Structuralist Views*, ed. L. Matejka and K. Pomorska, 176–198. Boston: MIT Press. Original edition, "Tipy prozai ̌ceskogo slova," in *Problemy tvor ̌cestva Dostoevskogo* (Leningrad, 1929), 105–135.

Bakhtin, Mikhail M. 1981. *The Dialogic Imagination: Four Essays by M. M. Bakhtin*, ed. M. Holquist et al. Austin: University of Texas Press.

Bauman, Richard. 2004. "'What Shall We Give You?': Calibrations of Genre in a Mexican Market." In *A World of Others' Words: Cross-Cultural Perspectives on Intertextuality*, 58–81. Oxford: Blackwell.

Bauman, Richard, and Charles L. Briggs. 1990. "Poetics and Performance as Critical Perspectives on Language and Social Life." *Annual Review of Anthropology* 19: 59–88.

Briggs, Charles L. 2013. "The Biocommunicable State: Dengue, Media, and Indiscipline in La Habana." In *Health Travels: Cuban Health(care) on and off the Island*, ed. N. J. Burke, 23–53. Berkeley: University of California Medical Humanities Press.

Brotherton, P. Sean. 2008. "'We Have to Think Like Capitalists but Continue Being Socialists': Medicalized Subjectivities, Emergent Capital, and Socialist Entrepreneurs in Post-Soviet Cuba." *American Ethnologist* 35(2): 259–274.

Brotherton, P. Sean. 2013. "Fueling *La Revolución*: Itinerant Physicians, Transactional Humanitarianism, and Shifting Moral Economies." In *Health Travels: Cuban Health(care) on the Island and around the World*, ed. N. J. Burke, 127–151. Berkeley: University of California Medical Humanities Press.

Bunck, Julie Marie. 1994. *Fidel Castro and the Quest for a Revolutionary Culture in Cuba*. University Park: Pennsylvania State University Press.

Butler, Judith. 1993. *Bodies That Matter: On the Discursive Limits of "Sex."* New York: Routledge.

Butler, Judith. 2004. *Undoing Gender*. New York: Routledge.

Castro, Fidel. 1961. "Palabras a los Intelectuales." In *Castro Speech Data Base: Speeches, Interviews, Articles 1959-1966*. Latin American Network Information Center, University of Texas at Austin.

de la Fuente, Alejandro. 2007. "Racism, Culture, and Mobilization." In *CubaInfo: A Project of the Cuban Research Institute*. Florida International University.

Domínguez, Jorge I. 1978. *Cuba: Order and Revolution*. Cambridge, MA: Belknap Press of Harvard University Press.

Espirito Santo, Diana. 2015. *Developing the Dead: Cosmology and Personhood in Cuban Spiritism*. Gainesville: University Press of Florida.

Fernandez, Damian J. 2000. *Cuba and the Politics of Passion*. Austin: University of Texas Press.

Frederik, Laurie Aleen. 2005. "Cuba's National Characters: Setting the Stage for the *Hombre Novísimo*." *Journal of Latin American Anthropology* 10(2): 401–436.

Freire, Paolo. (1970) 2000. *Pedagogy of the Oppressed*. Trans. M. Bergman Ramos. New York: Continuum.

Gámez Torres, Nora. 2012. "Hearing the Change: Reggaeton and Emergent Values in Contemporary Cuba." *Latin American Music Review* 33(2): 227–260.

Goffman, Erving. 1981. *Forms of Talk*. Philadelphia: University of Pennsylvania Press.

Hanks, William F. 1996. "Exorcism and the Description of Participant Roles." In *Natural Histories of Discourse*, ed. M. Silverstein and G. Urban, 160–202. Chicago: University of Chicago Press.

Henken, Ted. 2000. "Last Resort or Bridge to the Future?: Tourism and Workers in Cuba's Second Economy." *Cuba in Transition* 10:321–336.

Henken, Ted. 2007. "Dirigentes, Diplogente, Indigentes, and Delincuentes: Official Corruption and Underground Honesty in Today's Cuba." Florida International University. https://cri.fiu.edu/research/commissioned-reports/dirigentes-henken.pdf.

Hill, Jane H. 1995. "The Voices of Don Gabriel: Responsibility and Self in a Modern Mexicano Narrative." In *The Dialogic Emergence of Culture*, ed. D. Tedlock and B. Mannheim, 97–147. Urbana: University of Illinois Press.

Holbraad, Martin. 2014. "Revolución o Muerte: Self-Sacrifice and the Ontology of Cuban Revolution." *Ethnos* 79(3): 365–387.

Holquist, Michael. 2002. *Dialogism*. 2d ed. New York: Routledge.

Holquist, Michael. 2003. "What Is the Ontological Status of Bilingualism?," In *Bilingual Games: Some Literary Investigations*, ed. D. Sommer, 21–34. New York: Palgrave MacMillan.

Ibarra, Jorge. 1998. *Prologue to Revolution: Cuba, 1898-1958*. Boulder, CO: L. Rienner.

Irvine, Judith. 1996. "Shadow Conversations: The Indeterminacy of Participant Roles." In *Natural Histories of Discourse*, ed. M. Silverstein and G. Urban, 131–159. Chicago: University of Chicago Press.

Johnson, Paul Christopher. 2014. "Toward an Atlantic Genealogy of 'Spirit Possession.'" In *Spirited Things: The Work of "Possession" in Afro-Atlantic Religions*, ed. P. C. Johnson, 23–45. Chicago: University of Chicago Press.

Kapcia, Antoni. 2008a. "Batalla de Ideas: Old Ideology in New Clothes?," In *Changing Cuba/Changing World*, ed. M. A. Font, 73–88. New York: Bildner Center for Western Hemisphere Studies.

Kapcia, Antoni. 2008b. *Cuba in Revolution: A History since the Fifties*. London: Reaktion Books.

Kapcia, Antoni. 2014. *Leadership in the Cuban Revolution: The Unseen Story*. London: Zed Books.

Keane, Webb. 2002. "Sincerity, 'Modernity,' and the Protestants." *Cultural Anthropology* 17(1): 65–92.

Keane, Webb. 2007. *Christian Moderns: Freedom and Fetish in the Mission Encounter*. Berkeley: University of California Press.

Kulick, Don. 2003. "No." *Language & Communication* 23(2): 139–151.

Lewis, Oscar, Ruth M. Lewis, and Susan M. Rigdon. 1978. *Neighbors: Living the Revolution: An Oral History of Contemporary Cuba*. Urbana: University of Illinois Press.

Mannheim, Bruce, and Dennis Tedlock. 1995. "Introduction." In *The Dialogic Emergence of Culture*, ed. D. Tedlock and B. Mannheim, 1–32. Urbana: University of Illinois Press.

Mannheim, Bruce, and Krista Van Vleet. 1998. "The Dialogics of Southern Quechua Narrative." *American Anthropologist* 100(2): 326–346.

Mauss, Marcel. (1938) 1950. "Une catégorie de l'éspirit humain: La Notion de personne celle de 'moi.'" In *Sociologie et anthropologie*, by Marcel Mauss, 331–362. Paris: Presses Universitaires de France.

Mauss, Marcel. 1985. "A Category of the Human Mind: The Notion of Person, the Notion of Self." In *The Category of the Person*, ed. M. Carrithers, S. Collins, and S. Lukes, 1–25. Cambridge: Cambridge University Press.

Mead, George Herbert. 1934. *Mind, Self, and Society from the Standpoint of a Social Behaviorist*. Chicago: University of Chicago Press.

Merleau-Ponty, M. (1962) 1989. *Phenomenology of Perception*. Trans. C. Smith. London: Routledge.

Mukarovsky, Jan. 1977. *The Word and Verbal Art: Selected Essays by Jan Mukarovsky*. Trans. J. Burbank and P. Steiner. New Haven, CT: Yale University Press.

Parmentier, Richard. 1997. "The Pragmatic Semiotics of Cultures." *Semiotica* 116: 1–42.

Pérez, Louis A., Jr. 1999. *On Becoming Cuban: Identity, Nationality, and Culture*. Chapel Hill: University of North Carolina Press.

Pérez-Stable, Marifeli. 1993. *The Cuban Revolution: Origins, Course, and Legacy*. New York: Oxford University Press.

Perna, Vincenzo. 2005. *Timba: The Sound of the Cuban Crisis*. Burlington, VT: Ashgate.

Pertierra, Anna Cristina. 2011. *Cuba: The Struggle for Consumption*. Coconut Creek, FL: Caribbean Studies Press.

Robbins, Joel, Bambi. B. Schieffelin, and Aparecida Vilaça. 2014. "Evangelical Conversion and the Transformation of the Self in Amazonia and Melanesia: Christianity and the Revival of Anthropological Comparison." *Comparative Studies in Society and History* 56(3): 559–590.

Rosendahl, Mona. 1997. *Inside the Revolution: Everyday Life in Socialist Cuba*. Ithaca, NY: Cornell University Press.

Shotter, John. 1992. "Bakhtin and Billig: Monological versus Dialogical Practices." *American Behavioral Scientist* 36(1): 8–21.

Silverstein, Michael. 1993. "Metapragmatic Discourse and Metapragmatic Function." In *Reflexive Language: Reported Speech and Metapragmatics*, ed. J. A. Lucy, 33–58. Cambridge: Cambridge University Press.

Silverstein, Michael. 2006. "How We Look from Where We Stand." *Journal of Linguistic Anthropology* 16(2): 269–278.

Skidmore, Monique. 2003. "Darker than Midnight: Fear, Vulnerability, and Terror in Making Urban Burma (Myanmar)." *American Ethnologist* 30(1): 5–21.

Tanuma, Sachiko. 2007. "Post-Utopian Irony: Cuban Narratives during the 'Special Period' Decade." *PoLAR* 30(1): 46–66.

Tedlock, Dennis, and Bruce Mannheim, eds. 1995. *The Dialogic Emergence of Culture*. Urbana: University of Illinois Press.

Titunik, I. R. 1973. "Appendix 2: The Formal Method and the Sociological Method (M. M. Baxtin, P. N. Medvedev, V. N. Volosinov) in Russian Theory and Study of Literature." In *Marxism and the Philosophy of Language*, 175–200. Cambridge, MA: Harvard University Press.

Urban, Greg. 2001. *Metaculture: How Culture Moves through the World*. Minneapolis: University of Minnesota Press.

Volosinov, V.N. 1973. *Marxism and the Philosophy of Language*. Trans. L. Matejka and I. R. Titunik. Cambridge, MA: Harvard University Press.

Weinreb, Amelia Rosenberg. 2009. *Cuba in the Shadow of Change: Daily Life in the Twilight of the Revolution*. Gainesville: University Press of Florida.

Wirtz, Kristina. 2004. "Santería in Cuban National Consciousness: A Religious Case of the Doble Moral." *Journal of Latin American Anthropology* 9(2): 409–438.

Wirtz, Kristina. 2014. *Performing Afro-Cuba: Image, Voice, Spectacle in the Making of Race and History*. Chicago: University of Chicago Press.

5 FROM NEIGHBORHOOD TALK TO TALKING FOR THE NEIGHBORHOOD

Zane Goebel

Introduction

Mikhail Bakhtin's (1981) work has invited us to think about the relationship between dialogue, monologue, and heteroglossia. Heteroglossia refers to both diversity within a population and the diversity of interpretation that this engenders in dialogue, yet as Bakhtin and the scholars in Dennis Tedlock and Bruce Mannheim (1995) note, as dialogue ensues over time it can become a type of monologue in the form of a local language and culture. In some cases, these local practices become an important part of nation-building endeavors, resulting in a much more widely recognized monologic entity, such as a national language. The current chapter looks at both types of monologism and the relationships between them in a setting characterized by complexity. My empirical focus is talk that occurred in a women's neighborhood in Indonesia and the broader context in which these conversations occurred.

Drawing on Bakhtin and those who have paid close attention to everyday interactional practices and their relationship to broader ideologies about language and culture, I start by sketching out how everyday dialogue relates to monologism at different scales. To provide a broader context to the neighborhood talk that I examine in subsequent sections, I then look at nation-building efforts in Indonesia prior to my recording of this neighborhood meeting in 1996. This period is important because these major nation-building efforts enshrined unitary ideologies about the semiotic features that index Indonesian-ness. After introducing this neighborhood, which was made up of Indonesians from all over Indonesia, I then focus on one audio recording that was made by my Indonesian spouse during my twenty-eight months of fieldwork in this neighborhood. I show

how neighbors jointly formulated a neighborhood voice through replication of semiotic forms, such as language choice, content of talk, and the sonic qualities of talk. This voice included prescriptions about how one should interact in this particular neighborhood.

From Heteroglossia to Monologism

Scholars of the humanities and social sciences have, for a long time, been interested in the relationship between uniformity and diversity and the processes that enable each to become part of national imaginaries and everyday social practices. Early twentieth-century engagement with the circulatory nature of processes of uniformity and diversity can be found in Bakhtin's (1981) work. In the essay "Discourse in the Novel," he emphasizes how forces of decentralization and centralization put a unitary language in a circular relationship with heteroglossia. As a concept, heteroglossia refers to both a diverse population with multiple voices (Bakhtin 1981: 262–263) and the diversity that this affords in the interpretation of any word or utterance (Bakhtin 1981: 275–279). Movement from heteroglossia to a unitary phenomenon can be observed when we look at dialogues between members of a heteroglossic population where negotiation over the meaning of words used in dialogue produces new situational meanings for these words (Bakhtin 1981: 279–282). In a sense, dialogue has led to the emergence of a unitary phenomenon: in this case, a shared understanding about the meaning(s) of a set of words amongst those involved in a small participation framework. Habitual interaction among a certain population provides a context where these words can be reused, helping to form an emerging unitary language for those involved (Bakhtin 1981: 290–293), although these words with "new meanings" also continue to contain traces or "tastes" of the contexts that they were previously part of (Bakhtin 1981: 293).

While Bakhtin repeatedly points to the embeddedness of words and unitary languages in social and political life, the relationships between them and cultural reproduction are unclear. Other scholarship has helped clarify these relationships while providing explanations of why we might reproduce others' words. One explanation is grounded in work on reciprocity (Malinowski [1922] 1996; Mauss [1925] 1966; Goffman 1971) and subsequent development of this work. Deborah Tannen (1989) and Mary Bucholtz and Kira Hall (2004), among others, have argued that we repeat others' words or pursue forms of social sameness to establish and maintain social connections with others. From a more structural perspective that links unitary languages with social and political life, Pierre Bourdieu (1984) points out that social value accrues to a language through its usage by socially valued speakers in socially valued fields. This process creates a *habitus* that can be distinguished from others (Bourdieu 1984). Distinction creates hierarchies with those inhabiting a socially valued habitus often able to perpetuate their position through ensuring their unitary language is replicated in one-to-many participation frameworks, such as schooling and the mass media, and in many cases helping to form the language of a nation-state (Bourdieu and Passeron 1977; Bourdieu 1984, 1991; Hobsbawm 1992).

With some partial explanations in place about the relationship between language and social relations and "why" speakers replicate others' words and social practices, we can turn to the "how." Linguistic anthropologists working in the broad area of cultural reproduction have provided some keen insights into this question. Some of the "how"—not totally isolated from the "why"—can be linked to cases where replication of words and/or social practices has been imperfect or differs from common social practice. In the case of situated face-to-face interaction, difference in language practices or other social practices can engender "responses to" and "partial copies of" others' words (Urban 2001; see also Urban, this volume).

Work on narrative provides numerous examples of this type of "metaculture"—that is, reflexive commentaries about cultural practice (Urban 2001)—especially the narratives and gossip found in the everyday talk of caregivers, elders, and neighbors (e.g., Haviland 1977; Brenneis 1984; Ochs 1996; Ochs and Capps 2001; Besnier 2009). These narratives contain judgments or "responses to" another person's prior social practices and they are often used to teach novices or the judged about correct social practice. These judgments or complaints about another are often key to making stories tellable. Typically, this type of reflexive talk partially copies the offenders' words—discussed in the broader literature as "reported talk," "constructed dialogue," or "represented talk" (Tannen 1989, 1995; Agha 2007; Holt and Clift 2007)—while providing new words in the form of examples of more appropriate social practices. As work on ethnopoetics and narrative has shown (Hymes 1981; Tedlock 1983; Tannen 1995), it is not just the replication that makes a piece of talk noticeable, but how it is repeated. Greg Urban (2001) points out that the poetic structuring of text helps make contributions more noticeable and, when this co-occurs with complaints about others—one example Urban discusses is a litany of complaints against the government—helps to increase the chance of uptake through responses.

Narratives and gossip involve multiple tellers and participants, each of whom may partially copy some of the judged or other participants' words. While the involvement of multiple participants makes it hard to assign responsibility for the talk to any particular participant (Besnier 2009), the outcome of such talk is often a group who seemingly speak with one voice about a particular social practice. In short, dialogic practice can engender a form of monologism that encompasses not just words but other semiotic forms and norms of usage, which if repeated enough form a "type" (Silverstein 2005) or "genre" (Dunn 2006) that is recognizable by more than a few people. More recently, this complex of signs has been referred to as an emergent "semiotic register" (Agha 2007). A semiotic register thus includes linguistic fragments and ideas linking their usage with setting and social type.

These locale-specific registers sit in tension with and are constituted from fragments of a host of other registers, some of which become a unitary language of a nation (whether a state or ethnic grouping). Fragments of a particular semiotic register become a unitary language through practices of judgment, although typically via larger participation frameworks (e.g., mass schooling, mass media, etc.). This process is referred to as "enregisterment"; that is, the process whereby regular multi-sited responses to copies helps a sign constellation (i.e., semiotic register) become recognizable for larger populations who no longer need to be anchored to a locale. Those making responses or judgments are increasingly credentialed experts—often important figures such as national leaders, celebrities, sporting heroes, and so on, rather than just elders, kin, and neighbors—and responses are often temporally and spatially distant from the copies that have engendered these responses (Urban 2001; Inoue 2006; Agha 2007). The work of Miyako Inoue, Asif Agha, and Greg Urban together with Michael Lempert's (2014) recent critique of work on replication also reminds us that the larger participation frameworks tied to nation-building projects tend to blur links between copies and responses while sedimenting multiple indexical relations. Thus, understanding what happens in settings where we might find replication-as-precise-reproduction also requires understanding the relationship between these social practices and the indexical potentials of sedimented semiotic constellations (such as a national or ethnic language) that can be used in such settings.

Creating National and Ethnic Monologism in Indonesia

The beginnings of ethnic monologism in Indonesia can be traced back to precolonial times (Ricklefs 1981; Hefner 2001). While the colonial period increased the importance of ethnic and national monologism (e.g., Maier 1993; Sears 1996; Errington 2001; Moriyama 2005), the period from roughly 1968 to 1998 is especially notable. This is so because there was major massification in the mechanisms that enregistered monologism, especially schooling and media (Goebel 2015), a move back to older unitary pure models of language, and a change in models of exemplary leadership from the heteroglossic model inhabited by Soekarno (Indonesia's first president) to the more monologic model inhabited by Indonesia's second president, Soeharto (Hooker 1993; Sears 1996).

Indonesia experienced significant massification of education from 1966 onward with the number of primary school students increasing from 8 million in 1960 to 24 million in 1990, and the number of lower secondary school students increasing from 1.9 million to over 5.5 million in this same period (Bjork 2005: 54). During this period, successive central and regional government departments attempted to deliver a number of languages in primary and secondary schools (e.g., Soedijarto et al. 1980; Nababan 1991; Lowenberg 1992; Arps 2010). These languages included Indonesian, English, and a regional language (*bahasa daerah*), which was the language of the region where the school was located. While regional languages were ideologized as unitary languages of co-ethnic communication, Indonesian was ideologized as the main "vehicle for" doing unity among a diverse nation of strangers (Alisjahbana 1976; Abas 1987; Departemen Pendidikan dan Kebudayaan 1993; Dardjowidjojo 1998).

Indonesian mass media was also an important mechanism for the dissemination of unitary languages. For example, the introduction of television and the formation of a government broadcaster, *TVRI*, in 1962 rapidly introduced a new social domain for the replication of monologic ideologies. According to Kitley (2000: 38), after the initial setup of a broadcasting unit in Jakarta in 1962, regional stations were set up throughout the archipelago by 1978. The launch of the Palapa satellite in 1975 fueled an increase in television ownership and by 1978 there were 900,000 registered television sets in Java and a further 200,000 in the outer islands (Kitley 2000: 47).

Until 1989, television broadcasts were in Indonesian. These broadcasts regularly aired representations of encounters with sameness in the form of encounters with other Indonesian speakers (Kitley 2000). This (re)produced indexical relationships between Indonesian, Indonesian citizen, and the doing of unity in diversity via Indonesian. Television also reproduced other ideologies found in the school curriculum, such as the link between regional languages and ethnic social types (Kitley 2000; Sen and Hill 2000; Goebel 2008; Loven 2008). Radio broadcasts too helped to replicate this ideology through broadcasting news in twelve regional languages and village agricultural programs in forty-eight regional languages (Sen and Hill 2000: 93–94). Monologic ideologies of ethnic groups speaking an ethnic language were also replicated in other ways, including through the commoditization of ethnicity for domestic and international tourists (e.g., Adams 1984; Parker 2002; Erb 2007), and the sale of ethnic music recordings (Sen and Hill 2000: 170). These settings, along with regular dissemination of ideas about correct and proper Indonesian (Hooker 1993; Sears 1996; Errington 1998, 2000), provided models for normative language use.

An Urban Neighborhood with a Transient Population

The urban neighborhood (Ward 8) I focus on here was located in the northern parts of the city of Semarang, the provincial capital of Central Java. Central Java is one of the heartlands of Javanese, although there is much variation in how

Javanese is used in the region (Conners 2007; Goebel 2010b). This neighborhood was much like many of the estates that were emerging in the outer areas across the city. As a housing estate designed for low- to middle-income Indonesians, Ward 8 attracted many middle-income public servants who came from all over Indonesia. Many of them were transient, staying only a few years before moving. As with most housing estates in this sub-district (*kelurahan*), there was little infrastructure provided by the developers when it was established in 1988. Members of Ward 8 were thus responsible for the building and maintenance of lighting, drainage, and the two roads that serviced this ward, as well as rubbish collection and security.

Wards were also administrative units linked to the central government in a hierarchical manner. State development policy was disseminated from above, while it encouraged reporting from below. Family units (*Rukun Keluarga, RK*) of around five members constituted larger units of twenty to thirty *RK* referred to as a ward (*Rukun Tetangga, RT*). Units of eight to twelve wards constituted neighborhoods (*Rukun Warga, RW*), while around thirty-eight *RW* constituted a sub-district (*Kelurahan*). A number of sub-districts constituted a district (*Kecematan*), while a number of districts constituted a regency or city (in the case of Semarang) that was located within the Province of Central Java. Typically, the organization and collection of money used to pay for infrastructure and health initiatives were carried out at two regular monthly meetings (one for the men and one for the women). The remit of these meetings was not just about the development of ward infrastructure and the carrying out of government initiatives but also about socializing with neighbors. This was explicitly written on invitations (*sambung rasa* "to share feelings") distributed the day before.

In Ward 8, there were many uninhabited houses as well as rented ones, which had an impact on meeting numbers and the ability of the ward to collect fees for infrastructure needs. In addition, while there were twenty-three households in Ward 8, rarely more than fifteen would attend meetings. Ultimately a group of regular attendees and their families shouldered the burden of neighborhood infrastructure development and other initiatives. These conditions regularly entered the talk of these meetings. Of interest here is how these conditions figured in the formation of a monologic ideology among a heteroglossic population, where inhabitants had different backgrounds in terms of ethnicity, language, religion, generation, education, economy, and so on.

From Dialogism to Monologism in a Monthly Meeting

The talk I look at here occurred in a meeting that was held in July 1996. In this meeting there were thirteen participants from various ethnolinguistic backgrounds, all of whom had competence in Indonesian (Goebel 2000). Figure 5.1

shows where participants were seated. Participants with a name plus an asterisk (*) are those who self-identified and were identified by others as non-Javanese. Those who were initially involved in this talk are indicated via a shaded pattern in Figure 5.1. I will be especially concerned with talk about a non-present ward member, Bu Tobing, who is also non-Javanese. There were two newcomers to this ward, Abdurrahman and Zainuddin, my Indonesian spouse. Both had moved to the ward three months earlier. The meeting was held just a few weeks before Independence Day celebrations were to be held nationwide, and importantly, within this ward. It is important because the ward had some intractable financial issues and indeed much of the talk in this meeting was devoted to who had and had not paid contributions and how members could manage to organize celebrations on a limited budget.

The talk represented in the following extract occurs about ten minutes into the meeting. The talk is preceded by a group conversation which identifies by name and residence three members who have not paid contributions toward the upcoming Independence Day celebrations. This is done through the partial copying of the talk in prior turns and an evaluation of the content of these copies. Turning to the talk in extract 5.1, we can see that in response to the list of payers and non-payers, of whom the non-present Bu Tobing is just one, Bu Abdurrahman asks for clarification about Bu Tobing at line 1.

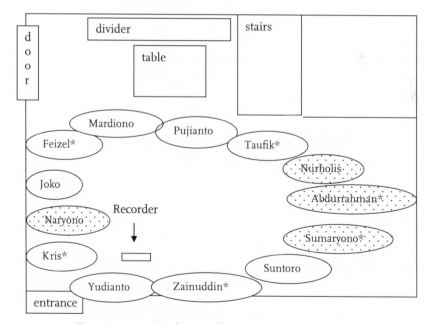

FIGURE 5.1 Participants at a Ward 8 monthly meeting

Extract 5.1 The Importance of Attending and Paying

Abdurrahman*

1	bu tobing tuh yang mana .	Which one is Mrs. Tobing?

Nurholis

2	[itu *loh* sebelah bu matius itu *loh*	*You know the one* beside Mrs. Matius.

Sumaryono*

3	[sebelah bu roni itu bu tobing *toh'*	The one beside Mrs. Roni is Mrs Tobing,
4	=	*you with me.*

Naryono

5	= + bu tobing + . tobing #tobing# (0.6)	Mrs. Tobing, Tobing, Tobing.

Nurholis

6	nggak pernah datang *kok'* =	[She] has never attended, *disappointingly*.

Naryono

7	= *lah iya* .	*That is right*, [she] has never attended a
8	arisan . [>nggak pernah datang>	meeting.

Nurholis

9	[>patungan sepuluh ribu>	[she] has never contributed her share of 10,000
10	#nggak pernah datang'# (0.7)	[rupiah toward celebrations] [at an arisan].

Sumaryono*

11	padahal rt penting butuh kenal ya (0.8)	But the ward is important [we] need
12	kalau (???) (???) [(???)	friends yes? If (???) (???) (???)

Orthographic conventions are as similar as possible to the standard Indonesian spelling system (Departemen Pendidikan dan Kebudayaan 1993). I use the following transcription conventions:

---

plain font	Indonesian (I).
bold	ngoko Javanese (NJ).
bold italics	forms that can be classified as NJ or I.
single underline	indicates the repetition of words or utterances between adjacency pairs.
double underline	indicates that the word or utterance was repeated in prior talk, although it may not always be in the immediately preceding turn.
. between words	indicates a perceivable silence.
brackets with a number (.4)	length of silence in tenths of a second.

=	no perceivable pause between speaker turns.
[	start of overlapping talk.
' after a word	final falling intonation.
? after a word	final rising intonation.
+ surrounding an utterance/word	raising of volume.
# surrounding an utterance/word	lowering of volume.
> at the start and end of an utterance	utterance spoken faster than previous one.
< at the start and end of an utterance	utterance spoken slower than previous one.
% signs around talk	stylized nasal type pronunciation.
@ signs around talk	major rise in the volume of an utterance.
: within a word	sound stretch.
Parentheses with three ?, i.e. (???)	word that could not be transcribed.
Double quotes in the English gloss	reported talk.

In the snippet of talk in extract 5.1, we get answers to Abdurrahman's query from three participants (Sumaryono, Nurholis, and Naryono). From line 7 onward, these answers increasingly resemble the talk of the previous speaker (copies are indicated by an underline in the transcript). At lines 7–8, Naryono copies Nurholis's *nggak pernah datang* "never attended" (line 6). The way these copies are performed also adds a poetic element to them that seems to engender further copies and responses. In particular, we see that copies are not just copies of words but also of the talk's tempo. For example, we see that at line 9 Nurholis copies the tempo of Naryono's talk at line 8. In this case, Nurholis speeds up her talk (indicated by > surrounding pieces of talk), as done by Naryono before copying the actual words "*nggak pernah datang.*" We also see that through what seems to be an innocent query about where Bu Tobing lives, now Abdurrahman is not just involved as a ratified participant but also partly responsible, in Besnier's (2009) terms, for the talk that follows. This responsibility also flows onto Sumaryono, whose response highlights why attending meetings is important. We also see participants' language choices resonating with the voice of the Indonesian state by doing unity in diversity in Indonesian, the ideological language of such practices.

Taken together, we see the beginnings of a monologic neighborhood voice that highlights participants' expectations about social conduct within this ward, namely attending meetings and paying dues, knowing your neighbors, and why this is important. In the talk that follows directly after the talk represented in extract 5.1, we will start to see how models of neighborship emerge as Bu Tobing is increasingly identified as someone who does not follow expectations about good neighborship. Here we see that these signs of good neighborship include paying neighborhood contributions without being chased, and appearing friendly when interacting with neighbors.

Extract 5.2 Becoming One Voice through Repetition

Joko

13	[ditarik waé:? . **ning**	**Just** ask for [contributions] **at her house!**
14	**umahé'** (0.9)	

Naryono

15	> **ning** <u>ditariki</u> **ning umahé** gé emben	[*I*] **went to her house** to ask for
16	ketoké piyé ya bu?> . %ya ***aku*** ra *enak*	contributions], **in the past, but she**
17	[*aku*%	**appeared unfriendly.** *Me, I didn't feel*
		comfortable.

Nurholis

18	[%>***aku*** ya **wegah** *ok* mono emoh> [	*Me* yeah *I* **couldn't be bothered,** [*I*] **don't**
19	#*aku*#%	**want to go there.**

Naryono

20	[%***aku***	[If] ***I* have** to ask for [contributions] *I*
21	meh narik **wegah**% [#*aku*#	**couldn't be bothered.**

?

22	[(??? ??? ???)	(??? ??? ???).

Nurholis

23	[%>***aku* meh** <u>narik</u>	[If]***I* have** to ask for [contributions] [*I*]
24	**wegah**%> #**ngono** *loh*# (0.4)	**couldn't be bothered, it's like that** *heh*.

Note that the talk in extract 5.2 involves another participant, Joko (lines 13–14), and that in copying her utterance *ditarik waé ning umahé* ("Just ask for [contributions] at her house!") Naryono adds a further response, this time about how Tobing appeared unfriendly and how she felt about this unfriendliness (lines 16–17).[1] Note too that again it is not just the talk, but also how it is delivered that helps ensure uptake. We can see two further poetic-type features being used here. The first is Nurholis's partial copying of Naryono's *aku ra enak aku* ("Me, I didn't feel comfortable"), which has a stylized pronunciation at lines 18–19 (this stylized pronunciation is indicated by the use of the percentage sign % surrounding pieces of talk). This poetic copying of the sonic qualities of participants' voices continues through to line 24. Table 5.1 highlights the extent to which others'

---

1. *Narik* has undergone a sound change here from its base form *tarik* which occurred at line 13.

Table 5.1 Copying other's talk (extract 5.2)

Joko	<u>ditarik</u> waé **ning umahé**
Naryono	**ning** <u>ditariki</u> **ning umahé**
Naryono	%ya *aku* ra *enak <u>aku</u>*%
Nurholis	%>*aku* ya <u>wegah</u> *ok* mono emoh> #*aku*#%
Naryono	%*aku* meh narik <u>wegah</u>% #*aku*#
Nurholis	%>*aku* meh narik <u>wegah</u>%> #**ngono** *loh*#

talk is copied in extract 5.2. In the table, I have underlined the copied words and sonic qualities.

The poetic copying, or pursuit of social sameness, can also be seen in their language choices. In contrast to their talk in extract 5.1, we now see increased use of Javanese fragments stereotypically associated with intimate co-ethnic talk (in bold). Of note also is the lowering of volume of the talk at the end of each turn (this is indicated by a hash # surrounding pieces of talk). Taken together, the copying of talk and the responses to these copies adds to an emergent monologic voice about good neighborhood by providing an example of what one should not do; that is, be chased for money and appear unfriendly.

As the talk continues (extract 5.3), Bu Naryono repeats much of what has been said before, but now with increased volume relative to her and others' earlier talk (I have indicated this increased volume by the @ sign). This raising of volume seems to be part of more public talk, which restates expectations about conduct in this ward, while positioning the non-present Bu Tobing as someone who does not follow such rules.

While copying others' talk is still a feature of the talk in extract 5.3, we also see copies of talk that are not temporally adjacent (i.e., Speaker A's talk copied in the immediately following turn by Speaker B). For example, we see partial copies of *nggak pernah datang* ("never attended") from extract 5.1 now reappearing in line 26's *ngga pernah ketemu*. I use a double underline to indicate this type of copying. We also see an instance at line 33, *ora tahu teko* "never attended," which in this case is in familiar Javanese or *ngoko*, as it is often referred to. We also see that in making a partial copy of talk involving the topic of debt-collecting (*ditarik* at line 25) at lines 27-29, Naryono adds her own response relating to ward responsibilities, and not being allowed to shirk ward responsibilities (lines 33–34).

Extract 5.3 Going Public

Naryono

25	@bu tobing@ **kui lho** . +<u>ditarik</u>+ **wong**	**That** Mrs. Tobing, [if] asked [for
26	kan? <u>ngga pernah ketemu</u> **yo** .	contributions] by **someone**, right? [she]
27	+ **ndeweké karepé kih**? . *lepas* >ngono	can never be found, **yeah her wish is** *to*
28	lho>+ . soko *tanggung jawab rt'* . iki	*let go you know, of ward*
29	ndeweké kih #<u>emoh</u>'#=	**responsibilities, [she] doesn't want to.**

Joko

30	= lho ojo	**Well don't live here** (???) (???)
31	**manggon neng kené** [(???)	

Naryono

32	[**anu opo**	**Ah what is it, she has never** *ever*
33	ndeweké <u>ora tahu teko</u> *loh*? . kan? ya	**attended**, right?, that's not allowed, *is it*.
34	nggak boleh *ok'* =	

Sumaryono*

35	= dia tuh dia statusnya di	She, what is her [residency] status here?
36	sini apa? =	

In addition to raising her voice—which, as we will see, helps increase the number of those who are involved in uptake—her talk is given extra authority by way of her status as ward head. We also see that Joko, who was marginally involved in extract 5.2, now becomes responsible for an evaluation of Tobing's behavior: "Well don't live here," at lines 30–31. By the end of this stretch of talk in extracts 5.1–5.3, Naryono, Nurholis, Sumaryono, and Joko are all involved in the creation of a monologic voice about bad neighborship (e.g., "non-paying," "non-attending," "unfriendly," and "irresponsible").

The language used in performing this voice is also important. This is so because except for Sumaryono, who reports being non-Javanese, it is done through the copying of language choice (in this case familiar Javanese), and sonic qualities. At this stage, it is worth highlighting that Bu Naryono appears to move between Javanese and Indonesian in two ways. The first is where both languages are found within a tonal unit. Tonal boundaries are indicated by a period surrounding talk, as in lines 25–26. Following synthesis of work on mixed language practices (Auer 1995; Alvarez-Cáccamo 1998; Gafaranga and Torras 2002; Goebel 2010b), I refer to this as "alternation as the medium." Alternation as the medium resembles the following pattern: AB1 AB2 AB1 AB2 (the upper case letters represent a particular medium and the numbers indicate Speaker 1 and 2). The second way is

where one language is used followed by a pause (indicated here by a period) and
then a different language, as in lines 32–34. In line with the above-mentioned
synthesis, I will refer to this as "codeswitching." Codeswitching can be illustrated
with the pattern: A1 A2 B1 A1 A2. Note also that this codeswitching seems to be
evaluative, that is to say, after commenting about Bu Tobing's non-attendance in
Javanese, Bu Naryono seems to make a clear judgment about such behavior where
she says *kan, ya nggak boleh ok* ("don't you agree you can't do that").

Codeswitching is also used in a number of other ways which help to add
further behavioral elements to emergent monologic ideas about good and bad
neighborship, as we will see in extract 5.4, which represents the talk immediately
following that represented in extract 5.3.

Extract 5.4 Giving Bad Neighborship an Indonesian Voice

Bu Naryono

| 37 | = *lah iya'* = | *That is right.* |

Bu Sumaryono*

38	= dia di sini	[if] she is here and asks for a ward letter
39	minta surat rt	right, don't give it [to her]
kan? jangan >+dikasih+'> =		

Bu Naryono

40	= **wong lagé**	**She,**
41	**emben ngené toh nang kené?** . saya tuh	**a while ago, came here and said** "<u>at</u>
42	sewaktu waktu #pind:ah'# =	<u>some time or another I will move."</u>

Bu Sumaryono*

| 43 | = <u>**kabeh**</u> | **All people** [move] |
| 44 | <u>+**w:ong+**</u>? = | |

Bu Naryono

| 45 | = *lah iya'* = | *That's right.* |

Bu Sumaryono*

46	= <u>semua +orang+</u>	All people, even office **workers**, none
47	**wong** kantor aja tidak ada menetap	stay forever (??? ???).
48	#(??? ???)# .	

The talk represented in extract 5.4 is important for a number of reasons. From the
perspective of language choice, we see that Naryono codeswitches from Javanese
to Indonesian to represent Tobing's talk in a previous encounter (lines 40–42).
Note too that following this Indonesian-speaking model of a deviant neighbor, we

see that the non-Javanese Sumaryono starts using Javanese in inter-ethnic encounter, which contrasts with reported inter-ethnic encounters between Naryono and
Tobing conducted in Indonesian (lines 43–44). Note too that this seems to be a
matter of choice rather than of not knowing the Indonesian equivalent. This is so
because Sumaryono says the same thing in Indonesian in her following turn (line
46). In interpreting "why this now," we can say that the non-Javanese Sumaryono
is pursing social sameness with co-present others who use Javanese. This contrasts
markedly with how the non-Javanese Tobing is represented—that is, as speaking
Indonesian in encounters with neighbors.

To be sure, we could interpret this codeswitching as achieving a change in activity type from "interacting with a co-present other" to "reporting another's talk,"
but this is too simplistic an interpretation for a number of reasons. First, Naryono
could easily have signaled this reported talk in many other ways, including using
fragments of the high variety of Javanese often referred to as *kromo* Javanese. She
had done this in other parts of the meeting and when being critical of another
neighbor. Second, otherness has strong indexical links with Indonesian vis-à-vis
Indonesian's role as the language of talk among strangers and Naryono's report
here seems to trope on this relationship. Sumaryono also seems to orient to this
specific interactional moment by offering a counter model through her actual
inter-ethnic talk that she now conducts in Javanese. When viewed over interactional time each conversational move is helping to build an emerging model of
good neighborship that includes speaking Javanese inter-ethnically.

The talk in extract 5.4 is important too because of how Sumaryono now
directly offers a response to Tobing's deviant behavior (non-attendance, etc.)
via her suggested sanction of not giving her a ward letter when asked. This is
important not only because these letters are essential for securing driver's licenses,
electricity, water and gas supplies, but also because through uptake of previous
talk Sumaryono's voice increasingly becomes one with the voices of Naryono,
Nurholis, and Joko. In short, the talk in extract 5.4 contributes to an emerging
model of good and bad neighborship in a setting where a mobile population
would not otherwise share the same ideas about good and bad neighborship. At
the same time, this talk also offers potential sanctions for deviant behavior. This
helps to further solidify an emerging monologic idea or semiotic register for this
constellation of participants about what constitutes good neighborship and how
to perform good neighborship.

Extract 5.5 represents further talk that contributes to the solidification of one
voice, while providing a behavioral description of how not to perform neighborship. This talk occurs immediately after that represented in extract 5.4.

Extract 5.5 Re-reporting Bad Neighborship

Sumaryono*
50 [laporan itu lah'   [she is only seen??] when she has to report
                                                        [to the ward]

Nurholis
51 [dijaluki sebelahnya itu *loh* bu matius =   [If] **asked for** [monetary contributions]
                                                        from the one beside Mrs. Matius, [you]
                                                        know who I mean.

Joko
52   = "I will be moving house."
53   saya tuh mau pindah tempat =

Naryono
54   = oh gitu *toh* =   Oh
55   [it's] like that *is it*?

Nurholis
56   =
57   heeh =   Yes.

Naryono
58   = >dijaluki #opo *anu* #> sepuluh   [If] **asked for what**
59   ribu:? . >ketoké *anu* + sinis kaé *loh* bu?   *what is it* **10,000 she looks really**
60   aku yo ora enak ngemis + ngono loh>.   *sour-faced* Bu [Nurholis and others
61   #wegah aku#(5.0)   present] **yeah** *I'm* **not** comfortable begging
                                             it's like that, *I* don't want to.

In this talk, we see repetitions of whole utterances that occurred in the previous talk, which point to a further movement toward a neighborhood voice. For example, we see that Bu Naryono's apparent conversation with the non-present Bu Tobing is repeated by Bu Joko at line 53, as if she had the same conversation with Bu Tobing. Through other partial copies on lines 58–61 we also see Bu Naryono continuing her representation of Bu Tobing, this time as an unfriendly and unapproachable neighbor, by giving a behavioral description about what the characteristic of being "unfriendly" noted earlier means—namely, being sour-faced. In doing so, she also provides one further prescription for neighborship in this ward. In the next extract, we will see again how another participant contributes a response. The talk represented in extract 5.6 occurs immediately after that represented in extract 5.5.

Extract 5.6 Widening Participation and Responsibility but Being One Voice

---

Sumaryono*

62 (??? ???) lagi . ya jadi dikucilkan aja'	(??? ???) again, yeah just don't include
63 nggak usah' . [apa tujuh belasan juga	[her] it's not necessary. What if for the
64 nggak usah .	17th [August celebrations] [we] also don't invite her

Naryono

66 [*dianu* dia itu **karepé iki**? .	*We will-* Her **wish is like this**
67 <u>nggak mau</u> urusan gini gini itu . #nggak	"I don't want to be involved in these sorts
68 <u>mau</u># =	of matters (organizing celebrations), [I] don't want [to]."

Kris*

69 = <u>oh</u> ya <u>ndak boleh</u>? =	Oh that's not allowed.

Naryono

70 = kumpul juga	[She] also doesn't want to socialize.
71 <u>nggak mau</u>' =	

Sumaryono*

72 = kenal **baé wong** . <u>nggak</u>	**Just saying hello to others** [she] **doesn't**
73 **gelem ok**' . lewat aja? [nggak	know, [she] doesn't **want to**, she just walks by, heh? doesn't . . .

In the talk in extract 5.6, Sumaryono now become more involved in listing potential sanctions for Tobing's deviant behaviors (lines 62–63), while on line 69 Kris too becomes involved in producing an emerging monologic neighborhood voice through her partial copying of Naryono's earlier response *ndak boleh* ("That's not allowed, is it," lines 33–34 of extract 5.3). We also see Tobing's Indonesian voice again copied at lines 67–68 through Naryono's representation of Tobing's thinking as being "in Indonesian," as in *nggak mau urusan gini gini itu, nggak mau* ("I don't want to be involved in these sorts of matters"). For the same reasons given in my analysis of Naryono's codeswitching into Indonesian (extract 5.4), Naryono's codeswitching here further contributes to the solidification of an emerging monologic model of bad neighborship that includes speaking Indonesian rather than Javanese. This sits in contrast to good neighborship that is done in Javanese and again here modeled as spoken in fragments of Javanese by both Javanese (Naryono at line 66) and non-Javanese (Sumaryono at lines 72–73). As the talk continues, we are provided with further insights into what Bu

Naryono and Bu Sumaryono see as normative neighborship in this ward through their accounts of Bu Tobing's deviant neighborship, in this case her unwillingness to socialize (line 70) or even engage in reciprocal phatic communication with neighbors (lines 72–73).

The type and form of neighborhood dialogue discussed so far continue for several more minutes with subsequent copies and responses being made by new participants, Zainuddin (my spouse) and Pujianto. The ensuing dialogue continues to represent Tobing as Indonesian-speaking and neighbors as Javanese-speaking, with the behaviors of not attending meetings and not paying contributions being reframed as behavior of which one should be ashamed. At the end of meeting, there is one further episode of copy and response where further undesirable behaviors of Tobing are listed, including: ignoring neighbors, pretending to be wealthy, pretending not to know one's neighbors in other contexts, and an evaluation of this as being treated like a rotten egg (e.g., being avoided by the antagonist). In short, Tobing continues to be represented as someone who cannot get on with her neighbors nor work together for the good of the neighborhood. This sequence involves Abdurrahman whose query started the sequence in extract 5.1 and Suntoro, both of whom offer evaluations and solutions. In so doing, the "we who speak with one voice" includes the majority of participants at the meeting (Abdurrahman, Nurholis, Naryono, Joko, Sumaryono, Kris, Pujianto, Zainudin, and Suntoro).

From Neighborhood Talk to Talking for the Neighborhood

It is now well established that dialogue creates local forms of culture (Mannheim and Tedlock 1995), but culture can be seen in some ways as monologism. I provided an example of this process in an understudied participation framework—that of a large meeting of those of different ethnolinguistic backgrounds. In doing so, I explored the tensions between dialogue and monologue at the local level by focusing on a series of dialogues in a neighborhood meeting and how they figured in the emergence of a form of monologism, in this case an ideology about the behavioral signs that signal good and bad neighborship. I was especially concerned with these neighbors' replication of others' words, the ways others spoke these words, and the languages they used to do this (namely, Indonesian or Javanese).

There were three features of this talk that seem to engender uptake and monologism. First, we see much replication-as-precise-reproduction (table 5.1). Second, we see a combination of poetic replication and complaint. Third, nearly all those present have made responses to the prior talk of just three participants: Naryono, Nurholis, and Sumaryono. As these multiple dialogues aligned over interactional time to form a monologic neighborhood voice, there were also tensions around the ideology of doing unity in diversity via Indonesian, because good neighborship was modeled as done inter-ethnically in fragments of Indonesian and Javanese rather than just Indonesian. In contrast, bad neighborship was modeled through reports of an Indonesian-speaking Tobing, who provided further evidence of an inability to get along with neighbors by not using the language of the neighborhood.

Acknowledgments

I am deeply indebted to Julian Millie and Matt Tomlinson for inviting me to participate in a workshop on monologism and then providing detailed feedback on this chapter, all of which has helped me rethink some of my earlier work (Goebel 2010a, 2010b). I am also indebted to all the participants in the workshop for engaging with the ideas presented here, though all errors and misrepresentations of their responses are my sole responsibility.

References

Abas, Husen. 1987. *Indonesian as a Unifying Language of Wider Communication: A Historical and Sociolinguistic Perspective*. Canberra: Pacific Linguistics.

Adams, Kathleen M. 1984. "Come to Tana Toraja, 'Land of the Heavenly Kings': Travel Agents as Brokers in Ethnicity." *Annals of Tourism Research* 11: 469–485.

Agha, Asif. 2007. *Language and Social Relations*. Cambridge: Cambridge University Press.

Alisjahbana, S. Takdir. 1976. *Language Planning for Modernization: The Case of Indonesian and Malaysian*. The Hague: Mouton.

Alvarez-Cáccamo, Celso. 1998. "From 'Switching Code' to Code-Switching." In *Code-Switching in Conversation: Language, Interaction and Identity*, ed. P. Auer, 29–48. New York: Routledge.

Arps, Benjamin. 2010. "Terwujudnya Bahasa Using di Banyuwangi dan peranan media elektronik di dalamnya (selayang padang, 1970-2009)." In *Geliat bahasa selaras zaman: Perubahan bahasa-bahasa di Indonesia pasca-orde baru*, ed. M. Moriyama and M. Budiman, 225–248. Tokyo: Tokyo University of Foreign Studies.

Auer, Peter. 1995. "The Pragmatics of Code-Switching: A Sequential Approach." In *One Speaker, Two Languages: Cross-Disciplinary Perspectives on Code-Switching*, ed. L. Milroy and P. Muysken, 115–135. Cambridge: Cambridge University Press.

Bakhtin, Mikhail. 1981. *The Dialogic Imagination: Four Essays*. Ed. M. Holquist. Trans. Caryl Emerson and Michael Holquist. Austin: University of Texas Press.

Besnier, Niko. 2009. *Gossip and the Everyday Production of Politics*. Honolulu: University of Hawai'i Press.

Bjork, Christopher. 2005. *Indonesian Education: Teachers, Schools, and Central Bureaucracy*. New York: Routledge.

Bourdieu, Pierre. 1984. *Distinction: A Social Critique of the Judgement of Taste*. Trans. R. Nice. Cambridge, MA: Harvard University Press.

Bourdieu, Pierre. 1991. *Language and Symbolic Power*. Trans. G. Raymond and M. Adamson. Cambridge, MA: Harvard University Press.

Bourdieu, Pierre, and Passeron, Jean-Claude. 1977. *Reproduction in Education, Society and Culture*. Trans. R. Nice. London: Sage.

Brenneis, Donald. 1984. "Grog and Gossip in Bhatgaon: Style and Substance in Fiji Indian Conversation." *American Ethnologist* 11(3): 487–506.

Bucholtz, Mary, and Kira Hall. 2004. "Theorizing Identity in Language and Sexuality Research." *Language in Society* 33(4): 469–515.

Conners, Thomas J. 2007. "Lexical Remnants in 'Peripheral' Javanese Dialects." Paper presented at the First International Symposium on the Languages of Java (ISLOJ), August 15–16, Graha Santika Hotel, Semarang, Indonesia, Semarang.

Dardjowidjojo, Soenjono. 1998. "Strategies for a Successful National Language Policy: The Indonesian Case." *International Journal of the Sociology of Language* 130:35–47.

Departemen Pendidikan dan Kebudayaan. 1993. *Tata bahasa baku bahasa Indonesia* [Standard Indonesian grammar]. Jakarta: Balai Pustaka.

Dunn, Cynthia D. 2006. "Formulaic Expressions, Chinese Proverbs, and Newspaper Editorials: Exploring Type and Token Interdiscursivity in Japanese Wedding Speeches." *Journal of Linguistic Anthropology* 16(2): 153–172.

Erb, Maribeth. 2007. "Adat Revivalism in Western Flores." In *The Revival of Tradition in Indonesian Politics: The Deployment of Adat from Colonialism to Indigenism*, ed. J. Davidson and D. Henley, 247–274. London: Routledge.

Errington, Joseph. 1998. "Indonesian('s) Development: On the State of a Language of State." In *Language Ideologies: Practice and Theory*, ed. B. B. Schieffelin, K. A. Woolard, and P. V. Kroskrity, 271–284. New York: Oxford University Press.

Errington, Joseph. 2000. "Indonesian('s) Authority." In *Regimes of Language: Ideologies, Polities, and Identities*, ed. P. V. Kroskrity, 205–227. Santa Fe, NM: School of American Research.

Errington, Joseph. 2001. "Colonial Linguistics." *Annual Review of Anthropology* 30:19–39.

Gafaranga, Joseph, and Maria-Carme Torras. 2002. "Interactional Otherness: Towards a Redefinition of Codeswitching." *International Journal of Bilingualism* 6(1): 1–22.

Goebel, Zane. 2000. "Communicative Competence in Indonesian: Language Choice in Inter-Ethnic Interactions in Semarang." PhD diss., Northern Territory University, Darwin, Australia.

Goebel, Zane. 2008. "Enregistering, Authorizing and Denaturalizing Identity in Indonesia." *Journal of Linguistic Anthropology* 18(1): 46–61.

Goebel, Zane. 2010a. "Identity and Social Conduct in a Transient Multilingual Setting." *Language in Society* 39(2): 203–240.

Goebel, Zane. 2010b. *Language, Migration and Identity: Neighborhood Talk in Indonesia*. Cambridge: Cambridge University Press.

Goebel, Zane. 2015. *Language and Superdiversity: Indonesians Knowledging at Home and Abroad.* New York: Oxford University Press.

Goffman, Erving. 1971. *Relations in Public: Microstudies of the Public Order.* New York: Basic Books.

Haviland, John B. 1977. "Gossip as Competition in Zincantan." *Journal of Communication* 27(1): 186–191.

Hefner, Robert W. 2001. "Introduction: Multiculturalism and Citizenship in Malaysia, Singapore, and Indonesia." In *The Politics of Multiculturalism: Pluralism and Citizenship in Malaysia, Singapore, and Indonesia*, ed. R. W. Hefner, 1–58. Honolulu: University of Hawai'i Press.

Hobsbawm, Eric. 1992. *Nations and Nationalism since 1780: Programme, Myth, Reality.* 2d ed. Cambridge: Cambridge University Press.

Holt, Elizabeth, and Rebecca Clift. 2007. *Reported Talk: Reporting Speech in Interaction.* Cambridge: Cambridge University Press.

Hooker, Virginia M. 1993. "New Order Language in Context." In *Culture and Society in New Order Indonesia*, ed. V. M. Hooker, 272–293. Kuala Lumpur: Oxford University Press.

Hymes, Dell. 1981. *"In Vain I Tried to Tell You": Essays in Native American Ethnopoetics.* Philadelphia: University of Pennsylvania Press.

Inoue, Miyako. 2006. *Vicarious Language: Gender and Linguistic Modernity in Japan.* Berkeley: University of California Press.

Kitley, Philip. 2000. *Television, Nation, and Culture in Indonesia.* Athens: Ohio University Press.

Lempert, Michael. 2014. "Imitation." *Annual Review of Anthropology* 43(1): 379–395.

Loven, Klarijn. 2008. *Watching Si Doel: Television, Language, and Cultural Identity in Contemporary Indonesia.* Leiden: KITLV Press.

Lowenberg, Peter H. 1992. "Language Policy and Language Identity in Indonesia." *Journal of Asian Pacific Communication* 3(1): 59–77.

Maier, Hendrik. (1993). "From Heteroglossia to Polyglossia: The Creation of Malay and Dutch in the Indies." *Indonesia* 56(October): 37–65.

Malinowski, Bronislaw. (1922) 1996. "The Essentials of the Kula." In *Anthropological Theory: An Introductory History*, ed. R. J. McGee and R. L. Warms, 157–172. Mountain View, CA: Mayfield.

Mannheim, Bruce, and Dennis Tedlock. 1995. "Introduction." In *The Dialogic Emergence of Culture*, ed. D. Tedlock and B. Mannheim, 1–32. Urbana: University of Illinois Press.

Mauss, Marcel. (1925) 1966. *The Gift: Forms and Functions of Exchange in Archaic Societies.* Trans. I. Cunnison. London: Cohen and West.

Moriyama, Mikihiro. 2005. *Sundanese Print Culture and Modernity in Nineteenth-Century West Java.* Singapore: NUS Press.

Nababan, P. W. J. 1991. "Language in Education: The Case of Indonesia." *International Review of Education* 37(1): 113–131.

Ochs, Elinor. 1996. "Linguistic Resources for Socializing Humanity." In *Rethinking Linguistic Relativity*, ed. J. J. Gumperz and S. C. Levinson, 407–437. Cambridge: Cambridge University Press.

Ochs, Elinor, and Lisa Capps. 2001. *Living Narrative*. Cambridge, MA: Harvard University Press.

Parker, Lyn. 2002. "The Subjectification of Citizenship: Student Interpretations of School Teachings in Bali." *Asian Studies Review* 26(1): 3–37.

Ricklefs, Merle. 1981. *A History of Modern Indonesia since c.1300*. Basingstoke, UK: Macmillan.

Sears, Laurie. 1996. *Shadows of Empire: Colonial Discourse and Javanese Tales*. Durham, NC: Duke University Press.

Sen, Krishna, and David T. Hill. 2000. *Media, Culture and Politics in Indonesia*. Oxford: Oxford University Press.

Silverstein, Michael. 2005. "Axes of Evals: Token versus Type Interdiscursivity." *Journal of Linguistic Anthropology* 15(1): 6–22.

Soedijarto, Lexy Moleong, A. Suryadi, Darlis Machmud, F. Pangemanan, A. F. Tangyong, N. Nasoetion, and R. Murray Thomas. 1980. "Indonesia." In *Schooling in the ASEAN Region: Primary and Secondary Education in Indonesia, Malaysia, the Philippines, Singapore and Thailand*, ed. T. Postlethwaite and R. M. Thomas, 48–96. Oxford: Pergamon.

Tannen, Deborah. 1989. *Talking Voices: Repetition, Dialogue, and Imagery in Conversational Discourse*. Cambridge: Cambridge University Press.

Tannen, Deborah. 1995. "Waiting for the Mouse: Constructed Dialogue in Conversation." In *The Dialogic Emergence of Culture*, ed. D. Tedlock and B. Mannheim, 198–217. Urbana: University of Illinois Press.

Tedlock, Dennis. 1983. *The Spoken Word and the Work of Interpretation*. Philadelphia: University of Pennsylvania Press.

Tedlock, Dennis, and Bruce Mannheim, eds. 1995. *The Dialogic Emergence of Culture*. Urbana: University of Illinois Press.

Urban, Greg. 2001. *Metaculture: How Culture Moves through the World*. Minneapolis: University of Minnesota Press.

6 MONOLOGUE AND AUTHORITY IN IRAN

ETHNIC AND RELIGIOUS HETEROGLOSSIA IN THE ISLAMIC REPUBLIC

James Barry

In this chapter, I examine monologue in the Islamic Republic of Iran, understanding monologue as a form of "unitary language" per Bakhtin (1981: 270–271). Unitary language exists in tension with heteroglossia, the former designed to set limits on the latter in the name of a purified social unity. In Iran, there are two distinct but interrelated monologues: the unitary language of state ideology and the unitary language of community solidarity. In the first half of this chapter, I analyze unitary language at the state level, focusing on religious and political discourse; in the second half, I examine discourse of ethnicity and national identity among Armenian Christians. I will argue that monologue, as it is expressed by Armenian Christians, often draws on the same symbols used to position religious minorities as loyal contributors to the Revolution and the Iran-Iraq War. However, Armenian Christian monologues are also designed to serve the needs of the local community and therefore exclude non-Armenian Iranians.

This chapter is based on fieldwork I have conducted since 2010. Most of the data comes from recent work in Tehran, where I conducted research for six months in 2010 and a shorter stint in 2014, and interviews that I conducted in 2012 and 2013 with Iranian Armenian migrants in the Los Angeles area, particularly in Glendale, California.

Monologue, Heteroglossia and Authority in the Islamic Republic of Iran

In Iran, particularly among the political leadership, authority is believed to come from God through his revelations in the Qur'an.

Authority is also drawn from Mohammad through the recognized Hadiths (the sayings and acts of the Prophet Mohammad that are meant to guide his followers), alongside similar accounts from the lives of the twelve infallible descendants of Mohammad, the imams of Shi'ism. Twelver Shi'a believe that the sixth imam, Ja'far, codified their legal systems in reference to Hadith, and the Ja'fari school is therefore the main source of jurisprudence. Clerics, known as the *ulama*, occupy a central position in the approval of legislation guaranteed by the Constitution of the Islamic Republic. The constitution is based on the philosophy of *velāyat-e faqīh* (the guardianship of the jurists). Traditionally in Shi'a legal practice *velāyat-e faqīh* specifically referred to the responsibilities clerics had toward the weakest members of society, such as widows, orphans, and the mentally ill (Abrahamian 1993: 19). However, Ayatollah Ruhollah Khomeini, known as the father of the Islamic Republic, reinterpreted its meaning, turning *velāyat-e faqīh* into a political doctrine in which the Shi'a clergy sit at the center of decision-making (Gheissari and Nasr 2006: 86). Because of Khomeini's reinterpretation, the *ulama*, especially the high ranked clerics known as *marjaʿ taqlīd* (meaning sources of emulation, for they seek to emulate God, the Prophet, and the Imams), have a direct political role in deciding whether laws passed by the Majles (parliament) adhere to Ja'fari Sharia. Clerics, therefore, are a very visible source of authority in Iran today. Even those Shi'a clerics who disagree with the system of *velāyat-e faqīh* do not disagree that they carry a responsibility to uphold God's rule among the citizens of their country. As Ghobadzadeh (2015) has noted, many *marjaʿ taqlīds* turn to a quietist approach rather than supporting or openly criticizing state policies.

Leaders of religious and political establishments in Iran therefore speak with the kind of guaranteed authority that potentially gives them license to speak unitary language. Much like Fiji's Frank Bainimarama, however, many of these figures are not so much the authors but rather the animators of statements (Tomlinson 2014: 93). Any deviation from officially sanctioned positions leads to open questions about an individual's commitment to the Islamic Republic and the Revolution. Matters are further complicated by Iran's difficult relations with many countries, particularly the United States. The anti-imperialist paradigm adopted by Ayatollah Khomeini during the 1960s, which specifically targeted the United States' interference in Iranian politics and economy, coupled with several confrontations such as the 1979 embassy takeover and the implementation of sanctions, means that politicians and other relevant state employees are required to adopt a unified approach on relations with the United States, even if they are working to mend these relations. Politicians and clerics who are comparatively moderate—like the current president, Hassan Rouhani—recognize these rules and act within them. Indeed, the Iranian constitution, alongside the statements of Khomeini and of the current Supreme Leader, Ayatollah Ali Khamenei, are often approached as authorities similar to what Tomlinson (2014: 117) notes for the People's Charter in Fiji or Mao's "Little Red Book," although with far less fanaticism. Very often statements regarding what Islam says about a certain issue or "what we as Muslims believe" is directly contradicted in action. For example, despite placing Muslim nations at a higher priority than non-Muslim nations in international disputes, Iran has refused to condemn Russian action against Muslim separatist groups in the North Caucasus (Akbarzadeh 2014: 66). Issues of contradiction and compromise can create problems for the Islamic Republic by potentially exposing monologue to criticism. Therefore, one solution to these problems is simply not to acknowledge that they exist (compare Fountain, this volume).

In terms of the employment of monological discourse, the Iranian revolutionary vocabulary is full of "self-evident truths" and "facts that speak for themselves" as well as the admonition to "do as I do by saying what I say" (see Tomlinson 2014: 103). Many in the leadership expect no answer, even though listeners will always turn monologue into dialogue. The Majles, the parliament elected through universal suffrage, speaks monologically by crafting unitary language. Even though members of parliament speak of different factions in Iran (namely, "principalist" [*eytelāf-e farāngīr-e osūlgarāyān*] and "reformist" [*eslāh-e talabān*]), both factions consider themselves to be upholding the same system in a drive for fundamental unity. However, their disagreements in recent years have become violent; at the time of writing, the reformist group is politically sidelined and many of its members have been accused of sedition since the 2009 election controversies. The values they claim to uphold are similar and are based on the same authorities: the constitution and the Qur'an. However, because of this similarity, their radical differences in interpretation on issues such as the role of religious jurists in governance (see Ghobadzadeh 2015) make their disputes much more heated than if one side openly opposed religion or the Islamic Republic entirely. In other words, the members of the Iranian Parliament, wherever they sit with reference to the principalist-reformist nexus, still acknowledge the same ideological force and are always determined to point this out to others and to each other in order to prove their credentials. Although they often differ over interpretation of the definition and responsibilities of the Islamic Republic, and do so at times quite violently, they usually deny that they are introducing innovations but rather argue that they are following the single correct path.

The boundaries of what is permissible in this political discussion are defined by the concept of "red lines" (*khatūt-e qermez*), topics that must not be mentioned and positions that must not be taken. The concept of red lines is very important in Iran, in both state censorship and also public behavior. Normally the boundaries are unremarked, blurry, and intuitive, but at times they are given a concrete form. Khamenei, for instance, outlined eleven such red lines in specific terms when directing Iran's nuclear negotiation team on how to deal with Western negotiators (Khamenei 2014). The importance of red lines is evident in their pervasiveness in Iranian society, where they act as a mechanism of unitary language that opposes "the realities of heteroglossia" while also acting as a "force for overcoming [it]" (Bakhtin 1981: 270). Red lines are noticeably Bakhtinian in that they explicitly call for a unified, centralized, ideologically sound, shared opinion among the political elites; however, red lines openly acknowledge the space of heteroglossia and are intent on countering it with ideological notions of "truth." The hazard is that heteroglossic speech can infiltrate the unitary language, leading to a complete subversion of the centralized authority. The menace of disruption to the monologue is among the principal reasons why the reformists have not only been sidelined by the government but are now considered to be a threat to it. The red lines create a black-and-white division which calls into question the loyalties of reformists who otherwise appear in allegiance with the Islamic Republic, by pointing to the areas on which reformists are willing to compromise. Social policies including personal freedoms and women's rights, as well as relations with Western nations, form key points of disagreement between reformists and conservatives (including the principalist faction). The red lines divide these policies in two, creating a clear distinction of what is correct and what is forbidden.

The reform movement has been plagued with serious accusations of sedition and wanting to overthrow the Islamic Republic. A key moment came in the 2009 presidential election, when Mir-Hossein Mousavi and Mehdi Karroubi disputed the election's results and, in doing so, gained a following that became known as the Green Movement. Even non-reformist hardliners can cause problems for themselves by crossing red lines. For example, the conservative politician Ali Motahari was physically attacked, in what he termed an assassination attempt, on his way to a public engagement in Shiraz mainly for his criticism that proper procedure in the detention of Mousavi and Karroubi for their sedition had not been enforced (Motahari 2015). This issue is a red line; both of these leaders were put under house arrest without a legal process being undertaken. In other words, even a conservative politician who is otherwise not sympathetic to the fate of the Green Movement can face consequences if he mentions this sensitive issue.

As the cases of Mousavi, Karroubi, and Motahari show, red lines help to mark the borders of unitary language, both silencing dissent and pointing to an ultimate consensus. The tensions between religious ideology and nationalism are extensive in Iran, as has been noted with regard to how successive presidents, with the notable exception of Mahmoud Ahmadinejad, have played to nationalist sentiments from a distance while being careful not to resort to the rhetoric of the previous Pahlavi regime or openly contradict the Islamic identity of the state (Ansari 2012: 280). Nationalism can be applied to religious contexts; the Supreme Leader of Iran, Ayatollah Seyyed Ali Khamenei—who is the highest religious and political figure in the country—relies heavily on the first person plural when discussing issues that affect Iranians or Muslims in general. In addition, he also uses the more distant third person plural as a means of building solidarity, or uses proper nouns such as the "Iranian nation" (*mellat-e īrānī*) or Muslim *ummah* to achieve precisely the same effect.

For example, the sensitive issue of relations with Western nations, especially with the United States, is hardly a matter of consensus among Iranians, yet Khamenei presents the official position as the only position. During a speech at the Imam Reza Shrine in Mashhad in 2013, the crowd rose to their feet chanting approval when the Supreme Leader said that "for thirty-four years, whenever the word 'enemy' is mentioned, 'America' immediately comes to the minds of the Iranian people" (Khamenei 2013). These chants are in unison and roughly the same in structure. For example, a standard chant involves phrases such as "*allahu akbar, khāmeneī rahbar*" (God is greatest, Khamenei is leader), "*marg bar zed-e velāyat-e faqīh*" (down with the opponents of the *velāyat-e faqīh*), "*marg bar monāfaqīn*" (down with the hypocrites, a play on the name of the terrorist group Mojahedin-e Khalq), and of course "*marg bar āmrīkā*" (down with America) and "*marg bar esrā'īl*" (down with Israel). These chants appear when Khamenei broaches topics such as Iran's greatness, Iran's resistance to American aggression, and the resistance of the Palestinians to Israel's occupation (see, e.g., Khamenei 2015c). Khamenei speaks of Muslim people as a collectivity sharing the same goals, particularly with regard to key issues, such as the Palestinian cause, which he stated is the most important issue for all Muslims (Khamenei 2015a).

Statements like these, however, are contradicted by Iranians in general discussions and by politicians themselves. For example, Esfandiar Rahim-Mashai, a close confidant of President Ahmadinejad, brought strong condemnation from members of the religious and political establishments (including the Supreme Leader) when he stated that the Iranian people were friends to all including the Israelis (Ezhārāt-e gheyr-e montazereh-e mashāyi darbāreh-e dūsti bā "mardom-e esrā'īl" 2008). Mashai's continual habit of innovating policies that either contradicted established norms in the Islamic Republic or were considered religiously insensitive or offensive were attempts by him and President Mahmoud Ahmadinejad to reshape Iranian monologue along the lines of their peculiar political and eschatological beliefs. The condemnation that Mashai's comments engendered demonstrate the difficulties that occur when one monologue is substituted for another.

An important aspect of Iranian culture which calls attention to the inescapable dynamics of heteroglossia is the notion of private and public personas. This has been a central subject in the works of William Beeman, perhaps one of the most widely read anthropologists to write about Iran in the English language. Despite at times exaggerating the prevalence of some of his examples in order to meet his argument, his work remains useful in outlining the boundaries of key cultural concepts in the Persian language. For example, one useful, if simplistic, distinction in language usage and power relations that Beeman makes is that of *bāten* and *zāher* (Beeman 1986: 11). *Bāten*, Beeman writes, is the field of the *andarūn*, the private section of a house, where the reactions of other interlocutors are predictable and in which individuals can feel free to express themselves openly. In contrast, *zāher* is the external, the field of the *bīrūnī* or outer part of a house, where interactions are not predictable and individuals are encouraged to hide their true feelings or opinions. On one level, this distinction mirrors the expectations of private-public personas that exist in many societies; however, the Iranian conceptions of internal-external circumstances are not confined by physical space, and it is possible to encounter an "internal" situation in a public space (Beeman 1986: 11). These findings can be compared to those of Gal (2002: 82), who noted that spaces deemed public according to one context can be recalibrated as private through "indexical gestures" that change the referential meaning of the space in the public-private dichotomy. Iranians often talk about how it is common for people to display two personalities (foreigners frequently observe this as well, but understand it in less detail) and Beeman's distinction is one way to describe the phenomenon. In the broadest possible terms, *zāher* is therefore the field where monologue as unitary language is most prevalent, as consensus and harmony are of particular concern, while *bāten* is a field of heteroglossia. Additionally, Beeman argues that *bāten* and *zāher* represent informal and formal positioning, respectively; this is expressed in the contrast between colloquial and standard speech. He qualifies this by noting that these are not polar opposites but rather exist on a continuum, giving examples where both forms of speech were combined, particularly when friends on socially equal standing were discussing an anecdote about someone of higher standing.[1]

Many Iranians are critical not only of authoritarian state monologues but also of the established rules of the society, those of family and of class, inclusive of the hierarchical aspects described by Beeman. The point is that there are multiple fields in which the centripetal forces of unitary language cause tension. As Bakhtin (1981: 279) argued, all discourse is oriented toward that which has

---

1. Interestingly as an aside, I have asked several Iranian interlocutors to describe *bāten* and *zāher* to me and none have confirmed Beeman's association of these words with informal-formal behavior, although they acknowledge that this sort of behavior is vital in Iran, and significant for me as a researcher to learn.

already been uttered and that which is expected in response, and therefore is inherently dialogic. Thus, unitary language—the monologic tendency—always exists in tension with language as people actually use it. There is a great amount of literature on this topic relating to Iran; Ahmadi and Ahmadi (1998: 218) write of how many Iranians describe themselves as experiencing a state of cultural schizophrenia or identity crisis, especially in regards to balancing a modern lifestyle with traditions. Many popular books in Iran focus on the balancing of traditions and modernity in Iranian culture. One example is *Cherā Darmānde'īm?* (Why are we helpless/stuck?) by Hassan Naraqi, a sociological critique of many aspects of Iranian culture, now in its twenty-second edition. Chapter titles include "We are alienated from (our) history"; "Our escape from the truth and secrecy"; "Our hypocrisy and opportunism"; and "Iranians and constant illusions of conspiracy," which give the impression of a culture in crisis. Publications like *Cherā Darmānde'īm?* in Iran show a deep concern for the future of the nation but also take aim at aspects of tradition, such as chapter three, *zāher-sāzī-ye mā* (Our pretence), which refers specifically to the practice of *zāher*.

Publications that directly contradict official discourse are effectively banned in Iran, but remain popular through modern means of samizdat. Those that criticize Islam's influence on Iranian society, such as Abdolhossein Zarrinkub's *Do Qarn-e Sokūt* (Two centuries of silence)—in which the author argued that Islam had worked to eradicate Iranian culture—are popular examples of this heteroglossic critique. Nevertheless, the state's attempt to restrict these publications represents their willingness to enforce red lines. For this reason, the general understanding of state discourses is that they cannot be directly challenged with any real hope of success and, for this reason, it is not worth listening to them. In the realm of heteroglossia, they exist as background noise, an exercise that all are able to recognize but to which only a few pay close attention. Of particular interest here is how this plays out regarding community identity.

Monologue and Heteroglossia in Armenian Tehran

The Armenian community of Iran is comparatively small but remains influential, mainly due to their contributions to Iranian society in terms of commerce, industry, and entertainment. From a peak of 250,000 before the Revolution (Sanasarian 2000: 176n16), the population was perhaps as low as 30,000 when I conducted fieldwork in 2014, although official estimates are far higher. They live mainly in the capital city Tehran, especially in the northeastern suburbs of Majidieh and Narmak, although historically important communities remain in Esfahan, Tabriz, and a few other regional centers. Armenians are predominantly non-Chalcedonic Orthodox Christians and speak their own distinct language, making them both a religious and an ethnic minority. Because of their unique status, they provide an informative case study of the ways that the monologic consensus around ethnicity and religion in Iran exists alongside heteroglossia. By monologue I mean the projects of unitary language developed not only by the government, itself strictly Islamic and Persian-centric, but also by Armenian leaders. Armenian leaders in Iran include the two elected officials who represent the Armenian community in the Majles, as well as the religious leadership of the Armenian Apostolic Church and lay leaders in the autonomous government apparatus of the community. These groups generally present Armenians as essentially Iranian, pleased that the Islamic Republic provides them with the freedom to practice their own religion, and as neither suffering discrimination nor having any problems with their Muslim neighbors or the government. Any suggestion of difficulties with the system are deflected by Armenian elites as propaganda from Iran's enemies, especially the United States and Israel.

Iran is a diverse country linguistically, with perhaps only 50% of the population speaking the national language as their first language. The actual number is difficult to determine for several reasons: first, the Iranian government does not gather exact data on language; second, the numbers we do have are often inflated depending on which organization has published them (Elling 2013: 28); and third, many among the linguistic minorities, such as Azeris, actually speak Persian as their principal language but still consider Azeri to be their mother tongue (Nercissians 2001: 68). Iranian identity is centered on Shi'ism and being an Iranian nation. Khomeini sought legitimacy for the state from both Shi'ism and Iranian nationalism, specifically playing to notions of the exceptional nature of the Iranian people past and present. The late Ayatollah saw the Iranian state as a fulfilment of the wishes of God, and therefore considered the protection of the nation to be a religious duty (Abrahamian 1993: 15).

From the 1979 Revolution onward, ethnic groups were considered indistinguishable by the official discourse of the Islamic Republic, and the concept of "ethnicity" was derided by religious and political leaders as part of a European attempt to undermine the *ummah*, the global Muslim community. Until the presidency of Mohammad Khatami, the subject of ethnicity in Iran was largely taboo. During Khatami's presidency, in which many marginalized groups were given important positions in government, the discussion changed (Elling 2013: 59). One of the issues with the discussion of ethnicity in Iran is the ambiguity around whether or not the issue was addressed in the 1979 Constitution.[2] Article 19,

---

2. The Islamic Constitution of 1979. Persian translation: http://www.moi.ir/Portal/File/ShowFile.aspx?ID=ab40c7a6-af7d-4634-af93-40f2f3a04acf. English translation: http://www.servat.unibe.ch/icl/ir00000_.html.

which prohibits discrimination, is often cited, with the term *qowm* usually being translated in English as "ethnic group." This term, Arabic in origin, is vague as it can refer more broadly to a people, a nation, or a tribe. Although *qowm* has been used to describe ethnicity, a new word—*qowmīyat*—was adapted from Arabic more recently mainly to deal with the impreciseness of the various words used to describe the concept (*nezhād, tabār*, and *aqvām*, the last of these being the plural form of *qowm*), all of which have multiple applications (Elling 2013: 17).

Due to the relative openness of discussion during Mohammad Khatami's presidency, the subject of ethnicity has remained present in political discourse, albeit within the limits of red lines. Khatami's successor, Mahmoud Ahmadinejad, did attempt to reverse some of the reforms but the cat was out of the bag, so to speak, and even Ahmadinejad made promises during the 2009 presidential campaign that linguistic rights—which are not necessarily the same as ethnic rights—would be upheld if he were re-elected. The failure of the state to directly address ethnolinguistic rights is evident in the fact that the current president, Hassan Rouhani, made the same promises during his 2013 election campaign. Initially, Rouhani has seemed intent on pushing through by appointing Ali Younesi as the special advisor to the president on minority affairs, and his announcement in January 2014 that languages other than Persian could be taught in schools and used in public broadcasts in areas where Persian is not the dominant language. The latter move was greeted with outrage by the conservative elite, who accused the Rouhani administration of working to divide the nation and of implementing policies that contradict Sharia. The debate is not about what the rules are, as both sides claim to be reading from the same document (the Iranian constitution), but rather it is about which rules take precedence. In this case, the loyalty of Iranians to Islam is the dominant discourse of the ruling authority. The fingerprints of Khomeini are all over this trend; Khomeini had argued that the division of the *ummah* into nation-states was the result of the divide-and-rule policies of Western colonial powers (Khomeini 1981: 48–49). Therefore, discussions of ethnic rights are often tied to the assertion that "ethnicity" is a divisive invention of the West.

In truth, the taboo around the use of languages other than Persian seems to be a hangover from the nation-building project of the unified state championed by Iran's great modernizer, Reza Shah Pahlavi (reigned 1925–1941), who was the first to ban the use of Azeri in schools, for example. However, through the authority of Khomeini's words, division of the nation is primarily understood as division of the *ummah*. For this reason, Rouhani has backed down somewhat, qualifying that he has no intention of changing the status of Persian, citing the language as crucial for national unity (Rouhani 2014).

This political debate, and the corresponding decisions about languages and metalanguages of unity, directly affects the Armenian community of Iran. The

Armenian community often mirrors the state-crafted national consensus in its own way. In the Armenian language, there is a tendency to use the passive voice to achieve the illusion of consensus. For example, in a standard interaction in the field, I would generally ask "why is this done" (*inčow kʿënwe*) as opposed to "why do you do this," as it is more effective in gaining a positive response, since I have noticed that the latter made interviewees uncomfortable. Correspondingly, a common response to this inquiry would be "it's done/ they do this because" (*anwowm e/ en orhedew*). On one hand, these are norms of politeness that can be found in many languages, but on the other, my frequent encounter with this use of passive voice has led me to conclude that it also works as a distancing mechanism for Armenians when encountering others. In other words, Armenians can use this technique to explain their culture without having to justify it.

At an official level, the Iranian government finds it difficult to be inclusive of non-Muslim minorities in the national narrative. The way they commonly get around this is by emphasizing the role of religious minorities in the Revolution and especially the sacrifices of minority soldiers in the Iran-Iraq War. Visiting the families of Armenian martyrs on Christmas has become an annual event for both the president and even the Supreme Leader (*Hanr. naxagahi aycʿë hay nahatakner Movsiseanneri ew partadreal paterazmi tarineri viraworwaç Albert Mahmowdeani bnakaranner* 2013). The Supreme Leader never fails to mention this sacrifice when meeting with minority members of parliament (Khamenei 2015b). But this categorically positions non-Muslims in Iran as supportive of the Islamic Republic and therefore not concerned with their lesser legal status. In the Armenian community, clerical leaders, such as the archbishop or the members of the Majles, speak more directly, using the first person plural "we" (*menkʿ*) to refer to the Armenian community to the exclusion of all other Iranian citizens. This can be seen in a speech given by the archbishop at an event in October 2014, where he stated that "we have one and a half million reasons to remember the Genocide," referring to the number of victims of the Armenian Genocide. Similarly, during a speech for the commemoration of the Armenian Genocide in April 2010, he railed against the issue of emigration in Iran, saying "only in the Islamic Republic can we be Armenian," meaning that those who migrate to Western countries complete the work of the Genocide by assimilating.

However, the "we" of this discourse is more often used as a form of defining sameness and difference among my interlocutors in Tehran. Consider this statement made in 2010 by Aram, a 23-year-old male from Tehran:

Īn keshvar keshvaremūn nīs; injā zendegī mīkonīm, valī īrānī nīssim. Vaqtī begam armanī'am, mīgan: "īrānī nīstīn?"

This country is not our country; we live here, but we are not Iranian. When I say I am Armenian, they say "you're not Iranian?"

The language is colloquial Tehrani Persian. As mentioned in the discussion of Beeman's work, this form of Persian is used to indicate familiarity between speaker and audience; but here it is also used to create distance between the speaker and the subject. On the one hand, Aram states he is not an Iranian, while, on the other, he complains that other Iranians do not consider him to be an Iranian and uses the colloquial form of the Persian language as a means of demonstrating his proficiency. Aram could have used Armenian to make this statement, but chose Persian in this instance to amplify his point: that he clearly spoke like other Iranians but these other Iranians still do not consider him to be Iranian. I have noted this in other instances, often when non-Armenian Iranians were present. The important point is that the way community leaders situate the Armenian community in Iran differs from the way their own community members situate themselves, which is not always consistent.

Several younger Armenians whom I met in Tehran distanced themselves from Iranian identity, stating that since they were not Muslims, they were not Iranians. For example, Sarkis, a 30-year-old engineer from Tehran, stated unequivocally that he was Armenian and not Iranian on the grounds that a Christian could not be an Iranian. Sarkis's views mirrored that of the statement by Aram: "this country is not our country." Alice, a 30-year-old office worker who had moved to Los Angeles from Tehran in 2012, stated that her feelings of exclusion in the United States were normal to her, since she was used to not belonging in Iran, and cited an instance where she was told when applying for a job at a library that she should not waste her time as the position would go to a Muslim. In all areas, religion was cited as a reason for exclusion although none of the participants described themselves as overly religious. Sarkis identified himself as an atheist and Alice was from a leftist family. However, Christianity is emblematically part of being Armenian, whether individuals consider themselves believers or not, and this is reinforced by the unitary language of the Islamic Republic's leaders. It is also part of the Armenian community's own discourse about who they are, and even those who are on the margins of the Armenian community agree on this.

Language is also important and this gives them clear ideas of ethnicity which, despite being played down by the official ideology, clearly exists in the minds of the people themselves. In other words, Armenian speakers sometimes conflate ethnicity and language for other groups besides their own. For instance, Alice complained about a colleague, a dishwasher at her workplace (therefore in a socially lower position), who would call her "the Armenian bitch" behind her back. Although she explained that his dislike of her stemmed from her habit of overturning her coffee cup to read her fortune, thus making his job more difficult, she stated that the heart of the matter was that she was an Armenian and he was an "Ardabili Turk." In colloquial language, she meant he was an Azeri-speaker from the city of Ardabil (the term "*azari-zabān*" or "Azeri-speaker" is not commonly used in Iran, where the words "*tork*" and "*torki*" are used as the ethnonym and language name, respectively). In this instance, language is used to identify what type of Iranian both people are, since Azeri-speakers are not religiously distinguishable from most other Iranians, as well as confirming the Armenian belief that all "Turks" are prejudiced against Armenians.

In the ideological alignment of language with community loyalty, accent is extremely important for the Armenian community in Tehran. The debate around accent, belonging, and loyalty shows a concern among some community members for the need to adhere to the "unitary language" of the Iranian state and to participate in the "socio-political and cultural centralisation" in an Iranian context (Bakhtin 1981: 271). The Tehrani Armenian accent is identifiable, notably for its retroflexed pronunciation of the letter "r" (Vaux 2004) and the long pronunciation of the letter "a." For this reason, it is often heard when Armenians from Tehran speak Persian, especially as Armenians sometimes pronounce the short Persian "a" as a lengthened "ā." Ani, a woman in her forties from one of Tehran's wealthier suburbs, complained that younger Armenians had this accent. She applauded a younger woman speaking at an event in Tehran where both Armenians and Muslims were present, saying that it provided a good image of the community as well integrated into the Iranian nation. Discourse about the responsibilities of being an Armenian—especially the indexes of being Christian, marrying within the group, speaking the language, and affiliating with particular institutions—coexists with discourse about being a loyal national citizen, knowing the Persian language, and being aware of Islamic norms. But to see these discourses as heteroglossic would be to miss the point: they are competing but co-present monologues, each its own unitary language.

The official position of community leaders conforms to the unitary language of state ideology. The Armenian community's leadership wants Armenians to recognize that they are in fact loyal Iranians who supported the Revolution and gave their lives for it in the Iran-Iraq War. The Rouhani administration has listened to the community's leadership in some instances in their endeavor to be more inclusive of religious minorities specifically. For instance, Rouhani has moved to replace the term *aqaliyat* (minorities) with *īrānīyān-e gheyr-e mosalmān* (non-Muslim Iranian), which has also been adopted by his administration (Fereydoun 2013). This appears to be a result of lobbying from the Armenian community specifically. Armen Nazarian, a candidate for the Tehran city council elections in

2013, stated in an interview that he disliked being called a minority, as his community has participated in all aspects of Iranian society, including fighting and dying for Iran in the war with Iraq, and therefore should be considered the same as other Iranians (Nazarian 2014). However, in a typical sign of heteroglossic engagement with official discourse, I have found that not all Iranian Armenians share Nazarian's point of view and during fieldwork in Tehran in 2014, I discovered that most found the term "minority" offensive only when used contemptuously, while others saw it as positive, citing it as guaranteeing their rights.

Obviously, the feeling of separateness from the majority is due to their being doubly separate in national discourse: both outside the dominant religion as well as being an ethnic minority. It is important to mention that while the Islamic Republic has emphasized the religious divisions between the state and its Armenian minority, it does not mean that this problem of identity is a result of the Revolution. Instead, Armenians in Iran have sought to blend their Armenian and Iranian identities carefully, especially on an official level, throughout the modern period beginning with the Constitutional Revolution in 1906. The scouting wing of the Ararat organization, one of the pillars of Iran's Armenian community, carries a motto that exemplifies this point. Yaghoubian (2014: 365) argued that the slogan of "*astsus, azgis yev hayrenikis*" (for my God, my nation, and my homeland) is "purposefully vague" as it can be "interpreted as being applicable to Iran or Armenia or both." Thus, there exists an official position that aims to incorporate the multiple voices of Iranian Armenians in heteroglossic identity discourse. On the one hand, the official position of the Armenian community takes into account that the unitary language of the government ("Iran is Muslim") and the unitary language of the community ("Armenians are Christian") are separate monologues, even though their community members will utter both. On the other hand, the leadership of the Armenian community acknowledges the incongruence and ambiguity in the heteroglossic space which all community members occupy, as belonging to Iran while being outsiders at the same time.

Concluding Remarks

There are no shortages of state and community discourses in Iran that seek to define the boundaries of society—what is acceptable and not acceptable, marked vividly in state discourses by the figure of red lines—setting apart the authentic from the imported. The reality is that members of the society at times resist monologic discourse, although Iranians will still unconsciously seek to uphold these points of view. The concluding point of the previous section, where Iranian Armenians either create their own parallel unitary language or engage heteroglossically with an identity that is Iranian and Armenian at the same time, is characteristic of the ambivalent discourse of most community members. Nevertheless, even those who are "part of the system," such as Esfandiar Rahim-Mashai (who was condemned for saying that Iranians could be friends with Israelis), can ad-lib rather than read from the script, causing controversy and testing boundaries. Interestingly, for many Iranian Armenians, especially those born after the 1979 Revolution, their points of view generally contradict those of their community leadership. This is in part the result of a generation gap that is increasingly considered a countrywide phenomenon, and the topic of several academic studies (see, e.g., Kamarbeigi 2002; Tajik 2003). This contradiction is also related to the nature of their identity as Christians in an Islamic Republic and as a people with two homelands.

In future research, I intend to address two topics that have emerged in my current project. The first is Iranian state ideology. By looking directly at the rhetorical techniques of Iranian leaders in this chapter, I have already reached areas of sensitivity and inevitably crossed the *khatūt-e qermez* (red lines). My intention has been to gain a better understanding of monologue in identity discourse, and in the future I intend to extend this to the way that Iranians, including minority groups like Iranian Armenians, talk about the Iran-Iraq War. The trauma of this war is eroding as a generation with scant (if any) memory of the dark days of the 1980s sees the war in terms of Iranian self-reliance, independence, and exceptionalism. Second, as the centenary of the Armenian Genocide is commemorated around the world, from Armenia to the Diaspora, the monologic narrative of this tragedy, developed over decades as a means of countering Turkish denials, has formed modern Armenian identity. An equally taboo subject, the narrative of the Armenian Genocide provides a useful example of unitary language where even those who disagree on the methods of Armenian political institutions still agree on the importance of Genocide recognition.

References

Abrahamian, Ervand. 1993. *Khomeinism: Essays on the Islamic Republic.* London: IB Tauris.

Ahmadi, Nader, and Fereshteh Ahmadi. 1998. *Iranian Islam: The Concept of the Individual.* Basingstoke, UK: Macmillan.

Akbarzadeh, Shahram. 2014. "Iran's Policy towards Afghanistan: In the Shadow of the United States." *Journal of Asian Security and International Affairs* 1(1): 63–78.

Ansari, Ali. 2012. *The Politics of Nationalism in Modern Iran.* Cambridge: Cambridge University Press.

Bakhtin, Mikhail. 1981. *The Dialogic Imagination: Four Essays by M. M. Bakhtin*. Ed. M. Holquist. Trans. Caryl Emerson and Michael Holquist. Austin: University of Texas Press.

Bakhtin, Mikhail. 1986. *Speech Genres and Other Late Essays*. Trans. V. McGee. Austin: University of Texas Press.

Beeman, William. 1986. *Language, Status and Power in Iran*. Bloomington: Indiana University Press.

Elling, Rasmus Christian. 2013. *Minorities in Iran: Nationalism and Ethnicity after Khomeini*. New York: Palgrave Macmillan.

"Ezhārāt-e gheyr-e montazereh-e mashāyi darbāreh-e dūsti bā 'mardom-e esrā'il'" [Unexpected comments about friendship with "the Israeli People"]. 2008. *Tabnak*, July 19. http://www.tabnak.ir/pages/?cid=14024.

Fereydoun, Hossein. 2013. "Dastiār vīzheh ra'īs jomhūrī dar bāzdīd az darmāngāh kheyrīeh arāmāneh: Vāzheh aqalīyat rā nemīpasandam" [Special advisor to the president in a meeting with the Armenian Benevolent Society: I do not use the term "minority"]. *ISNA*, December 29. http://isna.ir/fa/news/92100804508/.

Gal, Susan. 2002. "A Semiotics of the Public/Private Distinction." *Journal of Feminist Cultural Studies* 13(1): 77–95.

Gheissari, Ali, and Vali Nasr. 2006. *Democracy in Iran: History and the Quest for Liberty*. New York: Oxford University Press.

Ghobadzadeh, Naser. 2015. *Religious Secularity: A Theological Challenge to the Islamic State*. New York: Oxford University Press.

"Hanr. naxagahi ayc'ë hay nahatakner Movsiseanneri ew partadreal paterazmi tarineri viraworwaç Albert Mahmowdeani bnakaranner" [President of the Republic meets the families of the Movsisian martyrs and of Albert Mahmoudian, a victim of the imposed war years]. 2013. *Alik*, December 28. http://www.alikonline.ir/hy/news/community/item/7494-.

Kamarbeigi, Khalil. 2002. "Khānevādeh va shekāf-e naslī" [Family and the generation gap]. *Farhang-e Qowmes* 19:37–60.

Khamenei, Ali. 2013. "Bayānāt dar haram-e motahar-e razavī" [Statement at the Holy Shrine of Imam Reza]. *Khamenei.ir*, March 21. http://farsi.khamenei.ir/speech-content?id=22233.

Khamenei, Ali. 2014. "Bāztāb-e 11 khat-e qermez-e rahbarī barāye mozākereh konandegān-e haste'ī-ye īrān dar rasāneh-ha-ye jahānī" [Reflections on the leader's eleven red lines for Iran's nuclear negotiators in the global media]. *Bultan News*, October 10. http://www.bultannews.com/fa/news/223919/.

Khamenei, Ali. 2015a. "Javānān qat'an beh samar neshastan ārmān-e felestīn rā khāhad dīd" [The youth will definitely see the Palestinian cause bear fruit]. *Kayhan* January 26. http://kayhan.ir/fa/news/35954/.

Khamenei, Ali. 2015b. "Supreme Leader's Speech in Meeting with MPs of Religious Minorities." *Khamenei.ir*, January 26. http://english.khamenei.ir/index.php?Itemid=4&id=2009&option=com_content&task=view.

Khamenei, Ali. 2015c. "Dīdār-e mardom-e āzarbāyjān" [Meeting the people of Azerbaijan]. *Khamenei.ir*, February 19. http://farsi.khamenei.ir/video-content?id=28968.

Khomeini, Ruhallah. 1981. *Islam and Revolution*. Trans. H. Algar. Berkeley: Mizan Press.

Motahari, Ali. 2015. "ʿAlī Motaharī: Beh qaṣd-e koshtan āmadeh būd" [Ali Motahari: They had come intending to kill]. 2015. *Entekhab*, March 10. http://www.entekhab.ir/fa/news/193821/.

Naraqi, Hassan. 2001. *Cherā Darmānde'īm?* [Why are we stuck?]. Tehran: Akhtaran Books.

Nazarian, Armen. 2014. "Zendegī rūzmareh arāmāneh īrān dar goft-o-gū-ye shafaqnā bā ārmen nazarīyān" [The daily life of Iran's Armenian community in a *Shafaqna* interview with Armen Nazarian]. *Shafaqna*, July 11. http://www.shafaqna.com/persian/dialogue/item/79520-.

Nercissians, Emilia. 2001. "Bilingualism and Diglossia: Patterns of Language Use by Ethnic Minorities in Tehran." *International Journal of the Sociology of Language* 148:59–70.

Rouhani, Hassan. 2014. "Rowhānī: Zabān-e fārsī ʿamel-e mohem-e vahdat-e mellī-ye īrānīān ast" [Rouhani: The Persian language is an important element of the unity of the Iranian nation]. *Aftab News*, August 27. http://aftabnews.ir/fa/news/258837/.

Sanasarian, Eliz. 2000. *Religious Minorities in Iran*. Cambridge: Cambridge University Press.

Tajik, Mohammad-Reza. 2003. "Jāmeʿeh-e īrān shekāf mīān-e nasl" [Iranian society and the gap between generations]. *Rahbord* 25:264–280.

Tomlinson, Matt. 2014. *Ritual Textuality: Pattern and Motion in Performance*. New York: Oxford University Press.

Vaux, Bert. 2004. "Persian Armenian: The Third Literary Dialect of Armenian." Paper delivered at the UCLA Armenian Studies Conference on the Armenian Communities of Iran. May 15, 2004.

Yaghoubian, David. 2014. *Ethnicity, Identity and the Development of Nationalism in Iran*. New York: Syracuse University Press.

Zarrinkub, Abdolhossein. (1957) 2012. *Do Qarn-e Sokūt* [Two centuries of silence]. Los Angeles: Ketab Corporation.

DIVING INTO THE GAP

"WORDS," "VOICES," AND THE ETHNOGRAPHIC IMPLICATIONS OF LINGUISTIC DISJUNCTURE

Krista E. Van Vleet

Introduction

Taking up cases of political discourse in Cuba, Indonesia, and Iran, and drawing their ethnographic examples from television broadcasts and community meetings, government documents and graffiti, Kristina Wirtz, Zane Goebel, and James Barry investigate the monological. They, and other contributors to this volume, recalibrate just how we understand the mutual embeddedness of language and social life by highlighting the contexts, forms, and processes that create coherence, erase or elide alternate views, or enable the appearance of unity. The questions pursued in these chapters speak to how political consciousness develops through multiple channels, what effects the repetition of utterances has in concrete situated performances and more abstract circumstances of circulation, and how individuals and collectivities (states, community organizations, religious and ethnic groups, etc.) attempt to promulgate coherent discourses of identification or exclusion. The authors' insights suggest new angles from which to appraise just how certain understandings come to dominate at particular historical moments and in particular cultural, social, and political economic contexts. Blurring the background of "the dialogical," the authors bring the "monological" into focus.

In the comments that follow, I do not take up a comparative discussion of the ethnographic convergences and divergences of monologism in the diverse national contexts described in these chapters, nor do I trace the similarities and differences in what each author means by "monologism," "monologue," "mono-logic," or monological "forces," "traces," "tendencies," and "projects." Instead I reflect on two metaphors—"words" and "voices"—which emerge in definitions and conceptual descriptions across each of these articles. Of course, metaphors pervade scholarly writing—including this commentary—and everyday talk among speakers in the United States and elsewhere. Metaphorical language is not in itself problematic. However, I am intrigued by how an emphasis on "words" and "voices" shapes anthropological analyses of monologism (and, perhaps, dialogism as well).

Thus, after briefly noting some instances in which "words" and "voices" appear in the chapters of this section and the Introduction to the volume, I offer some thoughts about how "word" and "voice" constrain our understanding of language as a social activity and a social resource. I draw upon linguistic anthropological approaches, mostly developed since the 1980s, which have emphasized the historically and socially situated performances and material practices of language.[1] I point to the conundrums of using "words" and "voices" as starting points for analysis of talk when more precise analytical concepts might allow for an understanding of the ways "people can and do try to speak monologically" (Tomlinson, this volume) in everyday embodied interactions and communicate monologically through linguistic forms mediated in other ways. As shorthand for representing a complex and dynamic system, the figurative language of "words" and "voices" may be necessary. However, this metaphor also blurs the gaps between the various levels at which language circulates and obscures the differential theories and methodological issues anthropologists face in analyzing these levels. Bringing attention to the intersection of embodied talk and the multiple publics of mediated texts is crucial to understanding specific social, political, and economic contexts. Developing anthropological theories and methodologies that discern the variabilities of linguistic processes and ethnographic representations that highlight the disjunctures as well as the convergences of analysis at multiple scales also must be a part of this effort (cf. Hanks 1995).

On "Words" and "Voices" in Monologue

A few examples of the ways that authors use "words" and "voices" figuratively will suffice before turning to my more substantive reflections. The emphasis in each case is mine.

---

1. Among many others, see Bauman 1977; Basso 1985; Bauman and Briggs 1990; Gal 1991; Urban 1991; Duranti and Goodwin, eds. 1992; Ochs 1992, 2012; Tedlock and Mannheim, eds. 1995; Hanks 1996; and Irvine 1996.

In an excellent Introduction, Tomlinson defines monologism as including "the erasure of multiple *voices* within speakers' utterances" and "controlled verbal performances in which, whatever the number of participants, there is meant to be only a single *voice* representing a single opinion."

Based on research in Cuba since 1998, Wirtz examines the "ways in which official political discourse seeks to overtly and implicitly model many *voices* united as one," and at the same time asks how "inner understanding becomes congruent with political ideology." She suggests that monologue and dialogue be reconsidered "as judgments about the congruence of *voices*, such that different degrees of alignment produce (dis)unity and (dis)continuity, and where monologicality is the ideal of a perfect alignment among those inner *voices* . . . whereas any differences, tensions, or even oppositions signal some degree of dialogicality."

Goebel's analysis delves into the micropolitics of interaction in a neighborhood meeting in an urban ward in Java. He asks how a dialogical interaction might create a form of monologicality "that encompasses not just words but other semiotic forms and norms of usage," producing a unified understanding among interlocutors. "While the involvement of multiple participants makes it hard to assign responsibility for the talk to any particular participant," he writes, "the outcome of such talk is often a group who seemingly speak with one *voice* about a particular social practice."

Finally, Barry explores interrelated monologues, drawing on Mikhail Bakhtin's notion of "unitary languages." He focuses on state discourses that drive toward a fundamental national unity and Armenian Christian discourses of community solidarity, both at work in the Islamic Republic of Iran. As Barry notes, "the Iranian Revolutionary *vocabulary* is full of 'self-evident truths' and 'facts that speak for themselves' as well as the admonition to 'do as I do by saying what I say'" (see also Tomlinson 2014: 103).

The figurative use of these terms may, at least in part, derive from Bakhtin. In fact, Wirtz and Tomlinson draw upon one of Bakhtin's most quoted phrases, "The *word* in language is half someone else's. . . . In all areas of life and ideological activity, our speech is filled to overflowing with other people's *words*" (Bakhtin 1981: 293, 337). As Tomlinson continues, "within a single utterance, there are always multiple *voices*." A detailed discussion of what these metaphors do within each chapter, or the degree to which the symbolic extension of "word" and "voice" in the chapters of this volume may overlap with the scholarship of Bakhtin and his Circle is beyond the scope of this commentary. However, it is noteworthy that the metaphorical use of "word" and "voice" has troubled other scholars.

For instance, in an article on language and gender, published more than twenty years ago, Susan Gal (1991: 176–177) draws attention to "a currently widespread and influential metaphor in both feminist and nonfeminist social sciences." She continues in the following way:

> Terms such as "women's language," "voice," or "words" are routinely used not only to designate everyday talk but also, much more broadly, to denote the public expression of a particular perspective on self and social life, the effort to represent one's own experience, rather than accepting the representations of more powerful others. And similarly, "silence" and "mutedness" ... are used not only in their ordinary sense of an inability or reluctance to create utterances in conversational exchange, but as references as well to the failure to produce one's own separate, socially significant discourse. It is in this broader sense that feminist historians have rediscovered women's words. Here, "word" becomes a synecdoche for "consciousness."

Gal goes on to challenge social scientists to illuminate the relationships between gender, language, and power by attending to everyday talk, the actual interactional practices in which people are engaged, and the rootedness of linguistic practices in broader political and economic contexts. Unsatisfied by discussions of women's consciousness that are reliant on symbolic analyses, Gal (1991: 177) argues for an understanding of the ambiguous and contradictory ways individuals, including women, might mobilize various linguistic strategies within broader systems in which some linguistic forms are more valued or credible than others.

Recently Elinor Ochs (2012) has echoed some of Gal's challenges in an article reflecting on the opportunities offered by linguistic anthropology for understanding "experience." Directed primarily to psychological and cultural anthropologists, Ochs is not concerned so much with the metaphorical use of "words" and "voices" as with the overemphasis on the "symbolic capacity of language" and the heavy reliance on words as a privileged entryway to meaning. She points out that language has multiple capacities: indexical, performative, and phenomenological (143) as well as symbolic. Linguistic anthropologists, she writes, "look deeply into the manifold ways in which the temporal unfolding of language in and across situations—not just words but phonology, morphology, syntax, and discourse—is implicated in moment-to-moment thinking, feeling, and being in the world" (144). Like Gal, she encourages scholars to take seriously on-the-ground interactions that rely on concrete situations and broad historical and social contexts for their meaning.

On Pragmatic Meanings and Participation

Although I do not want to overdraw the reliance on "words" and "voices" in these excellent chapters, I am inclined to agree with Gal and Ochs that scholars—and perhaps especially cultural anthropologists—would gain much from mobilizing the analytical perspectives on language developed in linguistic anthropology. Below, I briefly consider some ethnographic examples, drawn from the chapters in this section, and discuss how concepts of meaning (that do not rely solely on words) and concepts of participation (that recognize multiple levels at which "voices" operate) might enrich representations of monologism. Linguistic anthropologists have demonstrated that analysis of everyday talk is necessary but insufficient for understanding social life. Following from this discussion, I suggest that the metaphors of "words" and "voices" bridge a gap between embodied talk and mediated texts; in doing so, these metaphors obscure significant theoretical and methodological issues that remain for us to address.

Scholars of language and communication have long understood that words are not the only, or necessarily the primary, unit of meaning. Over the past several decades, linguistic anthropologists interested in talk as social action also have explored pragmatic meanings, those tied to situational context. One aspect of pragmatic meaning is indexicality, in which meaning of a linguistic form depends on the interactional context (e.g., Silverstein 1976; Ochs 1992). Words such as "I" or "you" shift in meaning each time a speaker enunciates them, but even those utterances that seem to primarily be referential in content, have the capacity to shift meaning based on context.

For instance, Goebel's discussion of a neighborhood meeting in a ward of Semerang, a city in Central Java, Indonesia, offers a detailed analysis of a conversation in which talk about an absent neighbor works to reinforce agreement about just what good neighborliness entails, in this case attendance at meetings and payment of dues. When one participant switches from Javanese to Indonesian to creatively represent the talk of Tobing, the absent neighbor, that participant indexes Indonesian's hegemonic ideological position as the language of talk among strangers, and the meanings of Tobing's words shift. Through his close analysis of conversational exchanges, Goebel demonstrates that multiple interlocutors repeat or copy words and phrases, drawing a previous speaker's words into their responses and copying the sonic qualities of participants' voices including speed, volume, and pronunciation. In this analysis, the production of a dominant understanding of neighborliness relies on non-referential content, including the stylistic aspects of performance that emerge in the social interaction; words alone are not "cultural keys to fathoming the ethos of a community" (Ochs 2012: 148).

Gesture and facial expression, bodily positioning and spatial organization, patternings of speech and silence, and many other non-referential as well as referential aspects of language contribute to meaningful interaction. Wirtz's ethnographic illustrations also indicate that "words" and "voices" are insufficient analytical concepts. She remembers being called away from a ritual celebration by the playing of Cuba's national anthem. Wirtz and other members of the household and neighborhood stand silently during the anthem and during subsequent speeches in which young political operatives exhort the crowd to participate in political nominations. Not only does Wirtz show how silence is patterned in culturally significant ways (through her discussion of people listening to Fidel's speeches broadcast on television and radio), but she also signals that interlocutors—the crowd—may play on normative patterns to engage with or avoid other social activities (such as nominating representatives to the Elections Assembly). Wirtz does not elaborate on the talk of her interlocutors once they return to the ritual, or the status of neighbors in relation to the young speech-makers, or the histories of interaction among neighbors. Yet would a more detailed discussion of these embodied interactions, delineating participation as well as indexical meaning, shift understanding of just how a mono-logic "voice" is produced?

If everyday enactments of language are also modes of experiencing the world (Ochs 2012: 148), then not only the indexical and performative capacities of language but also the participation of speaking subjects are crucial to understanding the production of coherence. When Gal (1991) critiques the metaphorical and ideological use of the term "voice," she points to a reliance on the symbolic meanings of words and utterances, but implicit in her discussion is the recognition that speaking subjects are always members of larger communities. How interlocutors interpret spatial and temporal relations to the world around them, make use of material objects and other people, and access unequally shared material and symbolic resources are crucial aspects of participation that link interactional practices to broader political and economic contexts.

Participation is, of course, another aspect of linguistic analysis that has potentially profound implications for analyzing monologism. Around the same time that Bakhtin's work was translated into English and published, sociologist Erving Goffman (1974, 1981) argued that involvement in conversation required living breathing interlocutors to play several different participant roles, among them: author, animator, figure, and principal; addressee and overhearer. These roles shift over the course of a conversation; sometimes over the course of an utterance. Extending Goffman's insight into the inadequacies of the speaker-hearer dichotomy, Judith Irvine (1996) has argued that we imagine multiple utterance events—each with their array of speakers performing various participant roles—as laminated or layered upon each other. Offering the example of

Wolof wedding songs, which often include derogatory images of the bride (the figure) but are authored by a group of senior women of the husband-to-be's family (so no individual takes the blame) and sung (or animated) by a low-caste griot to the bride-to-be and her relatives, Irvine (1996: 140) points out that "an utterance has implicit links to many dialogues, not only the present one." She emphasizes the dialogic relationships between intersecting participant frames, elaborating Bakhtin's notion that "words are half someone else's." Interlocutors, including anthropologists, interpret utterances and make sense of communicative events, by engaging in "pragmatic reasoning" that implicitly or explicitly links the ongoing talk "to other acts, including the past, the future, the hypothetical, the conspicuously avoided, and so on" (Irvine 1996: 135).

Certainly by now, it is clear that I have a difficult time thinking in terms of monologism. If we take seriously the perspective that language is intertwined with multiple dimensions of human experience, then analyses of language—whether monologic or dialogic—may productively begin from what people are actually doing together and acknowledge that the present moment is just one in a broader historical context. In analyses of Quechua speakers' narratives of *llik'ichiri* (beings who suck the life force from the bodies of Andean peasants) (Mannheim and Van Vleet 1998, Van Vleet 2008) and stories of *Santuku* (the devil) (Van Vleet 2011), gossip about lovers eloping and incidents of domestic violence (Van Vleet 2003, 2008), and accounts of masculinity and personal prowess in Andean ritual battles and economic crises (Van Vleet 2010), I have found that attention to participation is crucial to tracing the ways that talk is jointly produced and embedded in social and political economic arenas. Recognizing individual speaking subjects as at once fragmented by participant roles and simultaneously participants in broader communities of practice may transform our understandings of monologic "voices." Accounting for the indeterminacies of language and incorporating both situational and institutional contexts into our analyses, may complicate our representations of monologic "words" in specific cultural and historical milieux, and more generally.

Between Embodied Interaction and Multiple Publics

Yet the question of just how monologic projects are enacted—in concrete and embodied interactions and in the circulation of utterances through other means (e.g., print and visual media)—remains. If "voice" and "word" (and speaker and hearer) are insufficient analytical concepts for understanding ongoing talk, we must also acknowledge that the embodied social interaction of talk is not the only manner of communication in which humans engage. Goffman (1976; cited in Irvine 1996: 135) argued that "one cannot predict from the form of an utterance the aspects of its context that may be critical to its interpretation." William Hanks extends this insight by noting that language "mediates" among multiple levels—from face-to-face interaction, to multi-party interactions, to the multiple publics of radio and television broadcasting, print media, or digital networks—and that discontinuities exist between these levels. Whereas anthropologists encounter these various mediations of language in their research, we do not always integrate analysis of multiple levels in our analyses; nor is it clear that the same the methodological and theoretical tools may be mobilized to analyze language at each level (Hanks 1995: 202).

Barry's chapter brings attention to the ways that some "texts" circulate widely, are closely tied to political and economic power, and are shaped by a broader historical context extending beyond any particular event. His discussion of the unitary language of state ideology and of community solidarity in Iran focuses on the concept of red lines or "topics that must not be mentioned and positions that must not be taken." The Ayatollah Khamenei "outlined eleven red lines in specific terms when directing Iran's nuclear negotiation team on how to deal with Western negotiators," and these were circulated in the *Bultan News*, available in print and online to (certain) people in Iran and elsewhere. Barry makes clear that red lines may be understood in sometimes divergent ways or contested (as in the sometimes violent disagreements between factions of the parliament or the disputes over the outcome of the 2009 presidential election that led to some politicians being put under house arrest).

Such utterances clearly shape everyday interactions but just how they are received by people who are positioned differentially by gender, class, ethnicity, or religion is unclear. As Hanks notes: "Access to a discourse is not merely a given in social life but a matter of occupying a position through which the discourse circulates. The position and its occupancy outlive the act of reception" (1995: 218). Thus, understanding Iranian "red lines" or Fidel's orations might require both a close analysis of on-the-ground interaction and a close analysis of the multiple publics through which certain texts circulate. Wirtz and Barry draw upon examples of utterances that are disembodied and mediated through television and radio broadcasts, printed text, posters and (state sponsored?) graffiti, and that require a concept of multiple publics. Animated (in Goffman's terms) by social actors removed from the on-the-ground interactions of the anthropologists and their interlocutors, the relevancy of these utterances requires different kinds of negotiation than those utterances analyzed in Goebel's article. However, the circulation of utterances—the repetition of some more than others—is shaped by institutional structures and enduring relationships of power in all of these contexts.

Thus, although Wirtz states that the "monumentalized speech" of Cuba's heroes and martyrs on banners and as graffiti "required no indexical anchoring," such utterances may be analyzed in the context of larger social and linguistic encounters, or longer historical relationships and processes, or arrays of institutional power relationships, to gain an understanding of the project of interpretive control in which the state is engaged. The issue of institutional structures and enduring forms of power are significant to analyses of communicative events that are grounded in talk between embodied individuals as well. Goebel briefly notes that nearly all the participants in the meeting make responses to three participants through "replication-as-precise-reproduction" or "stylized replication." This leads to further questions: "Who are those three participants?" "What kinds of social, political, and economic weight, power, and status do they have?" "Do they have ongoing social, emotional, economic, or political relations with each other?" Even as the circulation of a discourse is shaped by social and political structures, the very movment of discourse (through overhearing, witnessing, uttering, reading, repeating, sharing) also creates publics. Barry's analysis of the unitary language of Armenian Christians might further elaborate how the circulation of some utterances (as opposed to others) requires the recognition that social actors (men and women, in Iran and in the United States) have unevenly overlapping arrays of knowledge as well as differential access to power and status, and how through both embodied interactions and mediated texts new publics are created.

Conclusion

Rather than assuming to know just what we mean when we use "voice" or "words," we might ask what concepts or practices or relationships the metaphor incorporates. Is it possible to replace "words" with analyses of the "temporal, epistemic, affective, modal, actional, stative, attributive, and locative meanings" (Ochs 2012: 148) that are intermeshed with semantic meanings? Is it possible to replace "voices" with analyses of participation that recognize face-to-face interaction and the multiple publics constituted by radio and television broadcasting, print media, and digital networks? As Tomlinson points out, Bakhtinian theories of dialogism have been profoundly generative of anthropological analyses. Asking what kind of analytical traction concepts—such as "words" and "voices" or of "monologue" and "dialogue"—provide in our efforts to understand the diverse cultural and historical contexts in which anthropologists conduct research is not inconsequential.

Perhaps one reason that the contributors rely on the metaphors of "words" and "voices" is that these concepts seem to span the gap between on-the-ground, embodied interaction between people and utterances that are produced and disseminated in other ways and circulate through multiple publics. Such bridging may be necessary to maintain a polar opposition between the monological and the dialogical or to blur the conceptual distinctions among the definitions of monologue mobilized by various authors. Whereas Wirtz argues for understanding monologue as an asymptote, never quite reachable, but as "natural" as dialogue and always in dynamic opposition with dialogue, other contributors, like Goebel, make sense of "monologue" through jointly constructed dialogue. Barry acknowledges that "unitary language—the monologic tendency—always exists in tension with language as people actually use it." Tomlinson writes, "There is no truly singular voice, and no truly one-way communication: there is only interaction, suffused as it is with multiple voices and accents." How then might we perceive, analyze, and represent linguistic engagement in the world while extending understanding of interpretive control, coherence, and power?

In considering "word" and "voice" in these discussions of monologue, then, I have arrived at another issue. That is, rather than blurring the differences between face-to-face interaction and circulation of linguistic objects, how might anthropological analysis turn toward the task of integrating both in our ethnographic representations? How do we represent the points where these communicative events diverge and converge in ethnographic situations? How do we represent the different methodological and theoretical tools that we might use to analyze communicative events at different scales? (See also Hanks 1995: 223.) These questions are relevant because as human beings, and as ethnographers, we are engaged in social contexts and historical moments in which utterances circulate through multiple modes. We have variable access to utterances. Our ability to access or receive certain utterances creates publics often in ways we do not completely understand. Yet in our ethnographic representations, we may not integrate these multiple aspects of communication or mark the ways we interpret embodied talk differently than broadcast speech.

In other words, during fieldwork or as we gather ethnographic data, we are immersed in the contingent, messy, uncontrollable, frustrating, exciting, and above all, dynamic interactions in the daily life of multiple "communities." Part of the process of anthropological analysis is figuring out the interrelationships among an array of issues. This array may incorporate the histories of interaction among participants and participants' variable understandings of what they are actually engaged in doing, interpretations of "an utterance's conversational 'reach,' backward and forward" (Irvine 1996: 135), and the simultaneously circulating texts upon which participants may draw. Yet in contrast to our interlocutors, anthropologists depend on a "shallower history of relationships, a different understanding of and ability to negotiate the verbal and non-verbal cues of interaction, and a variable social knowledge" (Van Vleet 2003: 512; also see Mannheim and Tedlock 1995). Our ethnographic analyses might conceivably bring attention to the ways in which talk extends from the context of a particular historical moment to institutions and enduring forms of power, including those of scholarship.

From another perspective, ethnographic research allows an anthropologist to have access to the ways that people talk about events in joint interactions, in which they may "clarify, reinforce, or revise what they believe and value" establishing a sense of the meanings of things as well as a sense of themselves (Ochs and Capps 2001: 46). However, if we do not include extended segments of talk into our analyses and representations, how can anthropologists assess the modes, forms, and forces of interpretive control or monologue? If ethnographic representations incorporate only singular utterances extracted from the situational and historical context, how do we assess the validity of claims about communication—about either the production of utterances or the reception of utterances? The constraints of disciplinary representation (i.e., entextualization) may shape how we analyze and represent these differently mediated texts. Considering monologism has implications for ethnography—both as fieldwork and as representational practice. An overarching analytical (monological) voice might emerge (even when different voices are included in our texts). By bringing attention to polyvalent, jointly constructed, and dynamic social interactions and to the multiple publics emergent in fieldwork, while acknowledging the methodological and theoretical disparities in our analyses, anthropologists may yet integrate facets of the monological and dialogical into our representations of language and social life.

References

Bakhtin, Mikhail M. 1981. *The Dialogic Imagination: Four Essays by M. M. Bakhtin*. Ed. M. Holquist. Trans. C. Emerson and M. Holquist. Austin: University of Texas Press.

Basso, Ellen B. 1985. *A Musical View of the Universe: Kalapalo Myth and Ritual Performances*. Philadelphia: University of Pennsylvania Press.

Bauman, Richard. 1977. *Verbal Art as Performance*. Prospect Heights, IL: Waveland Press.

Bauman, Richard, and Charles Briggs. 1990. "Poetics and Performance as Critical Perspectives on Language and Social Life." *Annual Review of Anthropology* 19:59–88.

Duranti, Allesandro and Charles Goodwin. 1992. *Rethinking Context*. Cambridge: Cambridge University Press.

Gal, Susan. 1991. "Between Speech and Silence: The Problematics of Research on Language and Gender." In *Gender at the Crossroads of Knowledge: Feminist*

Anthropology in the Postmodern Era, ed. Micaela di Leonardo, 175–203. Berkeley: University of California Press.

Goffman, Erving. 1974. *Frame Analysis: An Essay on the Organization of Experience*. New York: Harper and Row.

Goffman, Erving. 1976. "Replies and Responses." *Language in Society* 5(3): 257–313.

Goffman, Erving. 1981. *Forms of Talk*. Philadelphia: University of Pennsylvania Press.

Hanks, William. 1995. *Language and Communicative Practices*. Boulder, CO: Westview Press.

Irvine, Judith. 1996. "Shadow Conversations: The Indeterminacy of Participant Roles." In *Natural Histories of Discourse*, ed. Michael Silverstein and Greg Urban, 131–159. Chicago: University of Chicago Press.

Mannheim, Bruce, and Dennis Tedlock. 1995. "Introduction." In *The Dialogic Emergence of Culture*, ed. Dennis Tedlock and Bruce Mannheim, 1–32. Urbana: University of Illinois Press.

Mannheim, Bruce, and Krista Van Vleet. 1998. "The Dialogics of Southern Quechua Narrative." *American Anthropologist* 100(2): 326–346.

Ochs, Elinor. 1992. "Indexing Gender." In *Rethinking Context: Language as an Interactive Phenomenon*, ed. Alessandro Duranti and Charles Goodwin, 335–358. Cambridge: Cambridge University Press.

Ochs, Elinor. 2012. "Experiencing Language." *Anthropological Theory* 12(2): 142–160.

Ochs, Elinor and Lisa Capps. 2001. *Living Narrative: Creating Lives in Everyday Storytelling*. Cambridge, MA: Harvard University Press.

Silverstein, Michael. 1976. "Shifters, Linguistic Categories, and Cultural Description." In *Meaning in Anthropology*, ed. Keith Basso and H. Selby, 11–55. Albuquerque: University of New Mexico Press.

Tedlock, Dennis, and Bruce Mannheim, eds. 1995. *The Dialogic Emergence of Culture*. Urbana: University of Illinois Press.

Tomlinson, Matt. 2014. *Ritual Textuality: Pattern and Motion in Performance*. Oxford: Oxford University Press.

Urban, Greg. 1991. *A Discourse-Centered Approach to Culture: Native South American Myths and Rituals*. Austin: University of Texas Press.

Van Vleet, Krista. 2003. "Partial Theories: On Gossip, Envy and Ethnography in the Andes." *Ethnography* 4(4): 491–519.

Van Vleet, Krista. 2008. *Performing Kinship: Narrative, Gender, and the Intimacies of Power in the Andes*. Austin: University of Texas Press.

Van Vleet, Krista. 2010. "Narrating Violence and Negotiating Belonging: The Politics of (Self-) Representation in an Andean Tinkuy Story." *Journal of Latin American and Caribbean Anthropology* 15(1): 195–221.

Van Vleet, Krista. 2011. "On Devils and the Dissolution of Sociality: Andean Catholics Voicing Ambivalence in Neoliberal Bolivia." *Anthropological Quarterly* 84(4): 835–864.

7 ACTING WITH ONE VOICE

PRODUCING UNANIMISM IN ALGERIAN REFORMIST THEATER

Jane E. Goodman

On January 18, 1952, Messaoud Salhi requested permission from French authorities to present a play called *The Deluded Youth* (*Al-Maġrūr*) in the Constantine municipal theater in Algeria.[1] Salhi was the president of an artistic association called Al-Malhat Al-Jazā'rīyya or La Comédie Algérienne (The Algerian Comedy) as well as a teacher at Jām'iyat al-tarbīya wa 'l-talīm al-islāmiyya, a reformist madrasa (school) that the troupe's seven members also attended. His request was not out of the ordinary: every play performed by the indigenous population, as the French called the Algerian Muslims, required a visa, affixed to the text itself, before it could be staged. Even though the play had been authorized and performed in the central Algerian city of Blida five years earlier, it needed a new visa for performance in the department of Constantine. Following an initial rejection on grounds that the script contained nationalist rhetoric, and then a round of censorship and revision, Salhi's play was authorized on February 6, albeit with the standard caveat that the event "must unfold in the utmost calm and maintain the character of a purely artistic event."[2]

We know little about Al-Malhat Al-Jazā'rīyya. The group's president Messaoud Salhi was born in 1922. In 1952, he seems to have

---

1. Salhi to the Prefect of Constantine, January 18, 1952, Centre des Archives d'Outre-Mer, Aix-en-Provence, France, Fonds Ministériels (FR CAOM) 93 4224. According to Salhi, the play *The Deluded Youth* (*Al-Maġrūr*) was edited by Ali Marhoum, although it is unclear to me exactly what "editing" would have entailed. The script of the play is located in FR CAOM 93 4224.

2. Prefect of Constantine to M. Salhi, February 6, 1952, no. 860, FR CAOM 93 4224.

been more or less in the good graces of the colonial administration.[3] He was described by one administrator as "'ulama of moderate tendency"[4] and as having demonstrated "good faith" in revising the script.[5] A note from colonial police files (Service des Liaisons Nord-Africaines, or SLNA, which oversaw indigenous affairs) attests that the information they possessed on M. Salhi "was not unfavorable."[6] He appears to have enjoyed good relations with the artistic luminary Ahmed-Reda Houhou,[7] director of the renowned orchestra and theatrical troupe El Mazhar El Fenni El Qassantini.[8] One of Houhou's plays, *The Three Misers*,[9] had been staged between 1949 and 1951 by Al-Malhat Al-Jazā'rīyya throughout the Constantine region, and El Mazhar El Fenni had provided the musical portion of the program for at least one of the troupe's performances. Their audiences of around three hundred would have filled the Constantine municipal theater, where both *The Three Misers* and *The Deluded Youth* were performed. Although one police report characterized the 1949 performance of *The Three Misers* as "apolitical,"[10] the script of *The Deluded Youth* clearly indicates that by 1952 the troupe had nationalist inclinations. Members of the nationalist (and soon to be revolutionary) MTLD (Mouvement pour le triomphe des libertés démocratiques, or Movement for the Triumph of Democratic Freedoms) could be found in its audiences.[11]

---

3. In a note from the Bureau Chief of the Service des Liaisons Nord-Africaines (SLNA) to the Prefect dated February 5, 1952, he reports that on the basis of conversations with Salhi in which the latter demonstrated "good will," he recommended approval (no. 195, FR CAOM 93 4224).

4. Handwritten note, no. 445, affixed to letter from Prefect to General Commissary, May 4, 1949, no. 8134, FR CAOM 93 4224.

5. Bureau Chief of SLNA to Prefect, February 5, 1952, no. 193, FR CAOM 93 4224.

6. Bureau Chief of SLNA to Prefect, February 2, 1952, no. 193, FR CAOM 93 4224.

7. Ahmed Rédha Houhou (1911–1956) was best known as the founder and the director of Mazhar el Fenni el Qassantini. He was also a playwright and a contributor to *Al Baçair*, the magazine of the Association des 'ulamā musulmans algériens (AUMA), of which he was an active member. In 1956, he was tortured and killed by the French military. For more on Houhou, see Cheurfi 2007: 603; Merdaci 2008: 162.

8. For names of troupes that are well known in the literature, I adopt the spelling used in Merdaci 2008. Similarly, I retain common spellings of names of prominent individuals.

9. The "three misers" were the imam, the *muqaddam*, and the administrator, per a handwritten note in FR CAOM 93 4224. The French translation of the title *Les Trois Avares* clearly references Molière's *L'Avare*, one of the most popular canonical French comedies adapted for Algerian theater.

10. Report, Commissary of Constantine to Governor General of Algeria, May 7, 1949, no. 2973, FR CAOM 93 4224.

11. Report, Constantine Prefecture, May 7, 1949, no. 2973, FR CAOM 93 4224.

The themes of *The Deluded Youth* revolve around oppositions that were common at the time. One main character, the *muḥtadā*, is a model of Islamic reform—studious, disciplined, and committed to his nation. The other, the "deluded youth," or *maġrūr*, represents the vain young man caught up in the leisures and pretensions of European life. The play contrasts social space, mores, and cultural practices in relation to these familiar tropes. The "deluded youth" frequents bars, nightclubs, casinos, cinemas, and cabaret singers—signs of how deeply into decadence and debauchery Algerians had fallen.[12] In contrast, the *muḥtadā* and his colleagues enact the essence of reformist modernity: they entertain themselves through intellectual debates in the Arab Club, engage in daily practices of prayer and spiritual discipline, and are committed to education. The trajectory of this four-act play is one of conversion: gradually the deluded youth comes to his senses, joining the side of the *muḥtadā* and his fellow reformists, who include *al-ḥākim* (the arbiter), and several others, referred to as "brothers." Together, they develop a plan to create an institution with a tripartite mission:

(1) The diffusion of Arab culture and national education including sports of all kinds.
(2) The revival of the national economy; the encouragement and promotion of industry.
(3) The struggle against social scourges such as alcohol, adultery, and so forth.

Before they can enact their plan, however, they are foiled: overheard by spies, they are arrested by the French police and thrown into jail, where they languish for months. Here, scenes unfold whose primary interest to me is that the censor did not remove them. For instance, while in prison they recite nationalist poetry and read aloud an article from the smuggled newspaper *Al-Waḥda* (Unity) that is sympathetic to their cause. The charges against them resonate in Algeria to this day: that they plotted against the government and were a threat to the internal security of state. In the end, the prisoners are acquitted and released. They immediately resume their plans: they hold a general assembly, elect officers, and vote on their project to create an institution that they hope will lead them toward an independent Algeria (the term "independence," *al-istiqlāl*, is crossed out but legible on the archival script).

---

12. Two kinds of practices were the primary targets of reformist critique. First, the reformists took on the kind of debauchery engaged in by the protagonist of Salhi's play, who had adopted the worst of European social mores. Second, they attacked practices they considered backward or "superstitious," based in ignorance (*jahiliyya*), most notably, the entire sufi edifice. Reformists understood both groups to have fallen away from the true Islam.

What strikes me about this play—aside from the fact that it passed French censorship—is not its by then familiar coupling of reformism and nationalism, or the conversion story that it portrays, or even the fascinating trial. What I find most intriguing is a small detail that audiences of the time, and perhaps even today, may not have noticed: every vote, every decision, and every plan the characters consider was unanimously approved. In all, four votes were taken. The first was held in the home of the *muḥtadā* about their initial plan. This was the only vote preceded by a brief discussion. The other three took place at the general assembly. The first was a unanimous voice vote to approve a slate of temporary officers; the second and third were via unanimous showing of hands—initially to elect permanent officers, then to endorse the project of building an institution. (The *maġrūr* was elected treasurer; the *muḥtadā* was, of course, president; and a new, self-nominated volunteer became secretary, thus modeling the combination of experience and new initiative that would be needed to attain their collective goals.) In each of these votes, they not only agreed, but they agreed with one voice, without debate. Moreover, they delegated full power to the elected officials. The three officers were endowed with the authority to designate their assistants, advisors, and all subcommittee members. When the president asked the assembly if they concurred with this, the public unanimously assented. As one attendee put it, "the fact that we chose them . . . shows that we have confidence in them and that we agree with all their decisions."

What are we to make of these displays of unanimity? Knowing Algerians' propensity for a good debate, when I first read the script I took the unanimous votes as an artifice of this kind of pedagogical play, where the focus was obviously to exhort audience members to align with the reformist-nationalist cause.[13] Clearly, there would have been no political or didactic interest in representing dissent or divergence of opinion. The purpose of the play was not to linger on discord, but rather to demonstrate concord.

Had I not been working with several contemporary theater troupes in Algeria while reviewing this archival material, I might not have given the votes further thought. The play would stand as little more than a text of reformist pedagogy. But the emphasis on unanimity at key decision points resembled what I was finding in my field research with five troupes nearly six decades later. In these troupes, displays of unanimity were *de rigueur* at moments such as selecting group officers and determining annual programs. These were not perfunctory

---

13. As James McDougall (2006) and others have noted, the alignment of reformism and nationalism was always problematic, and reformists did not initially support armed struggle. By the early 1950s, however, independence through armed struggle was emerging as the only viable option.

endorsements: failure to reach unanimity could lead to schism and rupture, with some members leaving to join other troupes or form new ones.

Such performances of unanimous agreement are not limited to cultural associations, and point to what several scholars have identified as a fault line running through Algerian political life since at least the revolutionary period: the tension between unanimism and diversity (see especially Colonna and Daoud 1993; Colonna 1996a).[14] From 1962 to 1989, Algeria was a single-party state governed by the National Liberation Front (FLN); under the FLN, elections were essentially displays of unity rather than occasions for pluralist debate. Unanimism has pervaded many other domains of public culture as well. For Fanny Colonna, breaking with "the cardinal value of unanimism" represented an "impossibility" not only in political or ideological terms but, more significantly, in "cognitive" terms (1996b: 4).[15] As she put it, differences among Algerians—be they linguistic, religious, ethnic, gendered, or sexual—have been disavowed in public life via a kind of "blackmail of unanimity" (*chantage à l'unanimité*) that was "readily internalized by the social subjects themselves" (5). Colonna and her colleagues have productively troubled the presumption of unanimity by bringing to light some of the less visible diversity that animated Algerian society throughout the twentieth century. In the present chapter, I make the opposite move. I seek to understand how Algerian publics learned to produce unanimism as a social practice. Drawing on archival data from artistic troupes of the 1930s to the 1950s, I suggest that Algerians began performing unanimity well before the revolution, and I explore some possible reasons why this might have been the case. I also attend to the flip side of unanimism: rupture.

In focusing on practices of unanimism in reformist theatrical associations I am not suggesting that what made sense to Algerians in those decades somehow automatically transferred to independent Algeria. The social meanings of unanimism have no doubt shifted. Yet the "affinities of the [single-party] state with the Reformation" (Colonna 1993: 8) are clearly visible in the articles of faith on which the Algerian republic was founded: the unicity of religion (Islam) and official language (Arabic), both constitutionally enshrined,[16] were consolidated

---

14. Unanimism and its flip side, division, have long been visible at many levels of the Algerian political system. At lower levels, unanimism might lead to explicit fissioning. Just after the Fédération des élus musulmans was founded in 1928, for instance, it split into two groups (Cole 2009: 21).

15. Colonna locates the "end of unanimism" in 1989, with constitutional changes following the social unrest of 1988 that led to a multiparty system and lifted restrictions on freedom of expression and association. See Colonna 1996b.

16. Tamazight (Berber) was acknowledged as a national language in the constitution of 1996, but as of 2016 it had not been recognized as an official language.

during the rise of reformism in the 1930s and 1940s even as the country's pluralism was officially silenced.

In taking up the unanimist practices of Algerian civic associations in the early to mid-twentieth century, I seek to complicate a prominent line of argument in democracy theory, which has long accorded to voluntary associations a storied niche. Alexis de Tocqueville (2003) was among the first to argue that democratic societies operate horizontally, lacking the strong vertical ties that aristocratic societies provide, where one man can marshal around him a loyal following if need be. As he saw it, civic associations provided the strength in numbers that could counter the relative weakness of each individual. In a similar vein, Jürgen Habermas linked the emergence of a democratic public sphere to the kind of "rational-critical debate" fostered in Europe's literary clubs, coffeehouses, and salons, which were free, he contended, of the doxic authority of church and state ([1962] 1991). Habermas's work fueled a proliferation of scholarship conjoining voluntary associations, civil society, and a democratizing public sphere. For some scholars, the presence of voluntary associations has been used as a kind of litmus test to assess the democratic potential of non-Western regimes and, in its most extreme form, as a way to "differentiate states according to their potential for democracy and civilization" in the manner of Samuel Huntington (White 1996: 147, critiquing Huntington 1993). Indeed, the connection between voluntary associations and democracy has become so naturalized in some circles that voluntary or civic associations (now more often called nongovernmental organizations or NGOs) are being used prescriptively—that is, they are deliberately "injected" into a society by international aid organizations in order to foster democratic practice, as Steven Sampson has described for Albania (1996; see also Hann and Dunn 1996; Hann 2004).

While civic associations are often viewed as spaces for the promotion and management of the kind of diversity associated with pluralist democracies, they can articulate with the state in other ways. Pierre Rosanvallon has shown how associations could function as sites for "learning about unity and translating it into action" (2007: 234) within what he calls "the political culture of generality" in Jacobin France[17]—a culture that so aspired to the vision of "a single, unified society" (4) that it sought to tightly control intermediary bodies into the

---

17. Jacobinism describes a political philosophy and movement developed following the French Revolution that was dedicated to the promotion of a centralized republican state in which political power was concentrated in the center, as opposed to a more federalist organization. Rosanvallon finds the term "Jacobin" problematic and replaces it with what he terms "the political culture of generality." He examines generality "as a social form (the 'great national whole'), as a political quality (faith in the virtues of immediacy), and as a regulatory procedure (the cult of the law)" (2007: 4).

twentieth century. In the contemporary Algerian case, Andrea Liverani (2008) has demonstrated the ways voluntary associations have taken on the work of the neoliberalizing state, performing functions that the state no longer assumes. An adjacent body of scholarship offers an important corrective to the Habermasian focus on voluntary associations by identifying manifestations of civic practice in alternative arenas (e.g., Karlström 1996; the essays in Comaroff and Comaroff 1999; Chakrabarty 2000: ch. 7; Snyder 2001).

In this chapter, I expand on these lines of scholarship. I argue that while voluntary associations may well be sites for experimentation in democratic practice, this need not be their only or even primary function. I suggest that the Algerian theatrical and musical associations of the reformist period may anticipate another kind of civic history, a history of displays of unanimism in public life. In focusing on the artistic performances and the social practices of these associations, I hope to elucidate how expectations of unanimism both reverberated through and were constituted within local practice. I am interested in how and why Algerians learned to produce public displays of agreement for particular audiences (including themselves) at particular historical moments.

One reason scholars have sought to move away from a focus on voluntary associations as sites for the production of civil society has to do with the nature of colonial rule, which drew a sharp legal distinction between citizens and subjects that foreclosed any number of civic possibilities to those considered "subjects," which included most of the indigenous population (see Mamdani 1996; cf. Chatterjee 1993). Throughout Africa, whereas urban areas were typically governed under civil law, rural regions were placed under the rule of "custom."[18] Civil law was intended for rights-bearing European settlers, but a third group also fell under its purview: urban-based natives (Mamdani 1996: 19). Mamdani devotes little attention to this group, considering it "of limited significance" (20) and tangential to the dual form of power wielded by the colonial state. Here I make this group my focus. While Mamdani and others have demonstrated how colonial administrators used indigenous institutions (particularly via so-called "indirect rule"), my emphasis is on how indigenous populations appropriated European institutions of civil society, turning these institutions to their own ends. Moreover, the urban population I consider is by and large not the group generally characterized as the "native elites" or "*les évolués*," who may have been more practiced in the use of French institutions. Rather, I am interested in the

---

18. Algeria, of course, was a somewhat different case than equatorial and southern Africa, which were Mamdani's primary focus. The early decades of French rule in Algeria were indeed marked by the kind of split Mamdani describes. Once Algeria became juridically part of the French state in 1848, however, distinctions between colonizer and colonized revolved primarily around the issue of "personal status" rather than "custom."

Arabophone youth educated in the madrasas associated with the Islamic Reform or *iṣlāḥ* movement. In highlighting the ways in which this group made use of the institutional possibilities afforded them by French law, I aim to extend recent scholarship on "Africanized modes of civil society" (Comaroff and Comaroff 1999: 20) from its largely contemporary, post-independence focus to an earlier formative period.

In approaching unanimity in terms of performance, I consider both collective displays of unanimous agreement and the extensive social labor entailed in their production. In the material I examine, displays of unanimity are generally made manifest in moments of ritual such as voting. Such events constitute fleeting but potent symbolic occasions that Durkheim initially characterized in terms of collective effervescence and that anthropologists have analyzed as specially marked domains of reflexive display that can help to generate a sense of belonging and common purpose (e.g., Singer 1958). I examine how social actors helped to generate these moments through the specific ways they made use of language and gesture (Austin 1962). To so do, I draw on a line of scholarship in linguistic anthropology that views society and culture as communicatively constituted and focuses on social meaning as emergent in every interaction, from the most highly marked to the most mundane. From this perspective, I will be interested in the participant structure (the organization of interaction) of the associations, in the speech genres employed at meetings, and in the ways persuasive speech may have operated in generating unanimity.

Yet, focusing solely on displays of unanimity risks erasing from view the equally compelling practices that undergird such displays. To address these behind-the-scenes practices, I am inspired by a related approach, outlined in the work of sociologist Erving Goffman (1959), that employs theatrical metaphors to characterize the relationship between front-stage forms of social interaction (such as collective ritual) and the backstage forms of communication that can support and enable, or sometimes undermine, collective display. Differences and disagreements, for instance, may be relegated to a backstage that is rarely made visible. Without ongoing and purposeful backstage labor, I contend, front-stage unanimity risks losing its social force.

I begin by considering the cultural, political, and legal environments in which theatrical and other associations emerged. Next, I examine practices of unanimism engaged in by numerous theatrical associations at the time, as described in the archival records. I consider how unanimity was both represented in play scripts and enacted, however tenuously, at key moments in the social life of an association. My focus is on representations and practices of voting, as unanimous voting was both portrayed in Salhi's script and regularly practiced by association members in their annual meetings. In the second half of the chapter, I devote sustained attention to three factors that may have fostered the production and performance of unanimism: first, the reformist doctrine of *tawḥīd*, or unicity; second, consensus-based vernacular decision-making practices (such as those found in the Berber assembly or *tajmaʿat*); and third, specific measures instituted by the French colonial administration that may have encouraged Algerians to produce public displays of unanimity.

Cultural, Political, and Legal Contexts of Associational Life

Reformist plays like the one staged by Salhi's troupe lie on the margins of mainstream histories of Algerian Arabophone theater, which began in the years following World War I.[19] Religious and comic genres were not entirely separate in the early years. In 1921, the Lebanese-Egyptian actor and director Georges Abiad' put on two historical dramas in Algiers, both in classical Arabic. While these were not particularly well received, they did impress a group of madrasa students and Arabophone elites, who began to produce their own morality plays dealing with subjects such as alcoholism (Roth 1967: 22). The students came together under the auspices of voluntary associations that were forming at the time, such as the Association of Muslim Students, the theatrical association Al-Muhadiba, and the musical association Al-Mutribiyya (20).[20] Amateur actors affiliated with one or more of these associations began performing morality plays, historical dramas, and pedagogical skits at Muslim holidays. In 1926, a new genre of comic theater appeared, led by actors including comedians Allalou, Dahman, and Rachid Ksentini, as well as the important singer, actor, and, later, director and producer Mahiéddine Bachetarzi. In contrast to the madrasa students, these actors performed in *derija* (spoken Algerian Arabic) and focused largely on farces that operated as social critique. The Mahiéddine troupe would often perform for Muslim holidays (Bachetarzi 1968: 180–182). Local associations, including some reformist ones, often sponsored the Mahiéddine troupe's productions (218, 221; Roth 1967: 36), and the troupe's visits would sometimes inspire local youth to create their own associations (Bachetarzi 1968: 225).

---

19. Histories of early-twentieth-century Algerian theater include Roth 1967; Bachetarzi 1968; Cheniki 2002, 2006; Allalou 2004; Ben Achour 2005.

20. Al-Mutribiyya (El Moutribia) was an important association founded in 1909 by the renowned musician Edmond Yafil (1877–1928), which was known for its expertise in *andalous* (Algerian classical) music. Mahiéddine Bachetarzi initially studied with Yafil; see Bachetarzi 1968. On Edmond Yafil, see also Glasser 2012. On Al-Mutribiyya, see also Bouzar-Kasbadji 1988.

By the time Al-Malhat Al-Jazā'rīyya was founded in Constantine in the mid-1940s,[21] the city had a burgeoning associative sector. The 1930s alone had seen the birth of over one hundred associations (Merdaci 2007: 102, citing Benhassine 2005). These formed in an environment governed by two laws that would make available to Algerians new possibilities of sociability and solidarity: the French 1901 law on associations and the 1919 Jonnart law. The 1901 "Law relative to the contract of association" (Loi relative au contrat d'association)[22] was passed in the metropole in what appeared in retrospect as a pivotal moment in the struggle in France between what Pierre Rosanvallon has described as a unanimist Jacobin culture of "generality," which concentrated power at the center of the state, and the emergence of more particularistic and dispersed "intermediary bodies" that would allow citizens to congregate around discrete interests and agendas.[23] This law was not specifically targeted at Algeria, and it is unclear whether its potential repercussions in Algeria entered into the debate in France.[24] However, it is apparent from French archives that surveillance became one of the key applications of the law in Algeria, in keeping with the regime of exception (termed the Code de l'indigénat) that Algerians had been living under since 1881; the Code, building on groundwork previously laid in the 1865 Senatus-Consulte, had made Algerians subjects rather than citizens of France and subjected them to a different regulatory environment.[25] The 1901 law gave officials a means of keeping track of what associations were doing by requiring each to register with the police, supply the names, addresses, and professions of its officers, provide an annual report of its activities, and secure an official authorization before any meeting (Kaddache 1993: 36). Yet surveillance had its limits, and whatever its shortcomings, the 1901 law did provide a sanctioned means for Algerians to gather around a common set of concerns. Moreover, social practice did not always follow the letter of the law;

---

21. Archival records show that the troupe was active from at least 1947 to 1953, but do not provide the date the troupe was created.

22. *Journal Officiel de la République Française*, no. 177 (July 2, 1901): 4025–4027. The law was further elaborated in *Journal Officiel de la République Française*, no. 221 (August 16–17, 1901): 5249–5252.

23. As Rosanvallon (2007) makes apparent, well before passage of the 1901 law, citizens in France had developed many unofficial ways to congregate around mutual interests and agendas. The 1901 law did, however, provide a sanctioned avenue for the official development of new forms of civism.

24. Algeria appears nowhere in Rosanvallon's otherwise masterful account of the development of associative practice in France (2007).

25. The basis for the Code de l'indigénat had been established by the Senatus-Consulte of July 14, 1865, which codified differences in personal status between French settlers and Muslims, becoming "the cornerstone of a legal edifice that consigned Algerians to a status of permanent civil and political inferiority" (Ruedy 1992: 76). For more on this legislation, see Brett 1988.

I saw little evidence in the archives that theatrical or musical associations did in fact request authorization every time they met,[26] though they clearly did so for performances.[27]

The Jonnart law of 1919 did not directly target associations, but it attempted to address—albeit in a limited way—Algerians' desire for a fuller engagement in political life by attenuating some aspects of the unpopular Code de l'indigénat.[28] Most significantly, under the Jonnart law, some 425,000 Algerian subjects, or 43% of the adult male population (Ruedy 1992: 112), were allowed to vote for their own candidates in local elections, more than seven times as many as had been able to vote under previous legislation (Kaddache 1993: 44). In 1930, some of the local elected officials in Constantine came together to form the Fédération des élus musulmans de Constantine (Federation of Muslim Elected Officials of Constantine), affiliated with the national Fédération des élus. A year later, the Association of Algerian Muslim ʿulamā or AUMA (Association des ʿulamā musulmans algériens) formed, led by the prominent reformist Ibn Ben Badis. A year earlier, Ben Badis had founded the madrasa Jāmʿīyat al-tarbīya wa ʾl-talīm, which all of the members of Messaoud Salhi's troupe Al-Malhat Al-Jazāʾrīyya had attended and where Salhi himself was a teacher.

As the Fédération des élus and the Islaḥ movement gained strength during the 1930s, other formations were also taking shape. The Etoile Nord-Africaine (ENA), created in 1926, was forming among the Algerian immigrant community in France under the leadership of Messali Hadj. The ENA was the first party to voice nationalist demands, for which it was banned in France, only to reemerge as the Parti du Peuple Algérien (PPA), which had a presence in both France and Algeria although it, too, was eventually banned. In 1946, Messali Hadj formed a new movement, the Mouvement pour le triomphe des libertés démocratiques (MTLD), to serve as a front for the PPA (Ruedy 1992: 151). The Algerian Communist Party, formed in 1936 after a break from the French Communist

---

26. In 1924, a list of demands published in the newspaper *Ikhdam* by the Emir Khaled, active for a time in the Young Algerians movement, included "freedom of the press and of *association*" (Kaddache 1993: 109, emphasis added), suggesting that Algerians did experience restrictions on their ability to congregate.

27. The 1901 law was also the vehicle through which other associations came into being. Prominent among these was the Fédération des scouts musulmans algériens (SMA) (Federation of Algerian Muslim Scouts), which Mohamed Bouras founded in Algiers in 1935; in 1939 the SMA became an official 1901 association (Chikh and Mohamed 2000). During the early decades, the SMA maintained close ties to reformists, and indeed Ben Badis was among those who initially encouraged Bouras.

28. For more on the reforms instigated through the Jonnart law, see Ruedy 1992: 112; and Kaddache 1993: 42–45. On the Fédération des élus in the city of Constantine, see Cole 2009. On the history of the Fédération des élus in Algeria, see Ruedy 1992: 131–133.

Party, lacked a widespread following. However, the PPA later imitated some of its administrative and recruitment tactics, including the cellular, networked organization it adopted (148). The cellular model may have had some influence on the development of an expectation of unanimity among members, although this remains speculative. What is clear is that within the burgeoning associative climate in Constantine in the late 1930s and 1940s one thing police looked for when they received association membership lists was any potential party affiliation; most suspect was affiliation with the PPA (or PPA-MTLD).

Unanimity in Associative Practice

In the early years of associative practice, unanimity does not appear to have been a guiding principle. Consider Mouhibbi El Fen, the first musical and theatrical association created in Constantine in May 1933. At first its members were remarkably diverse. Some were loyal to Ben Badis while others, including its first president, Abdelmadjid Rahmouni, were affiliated with one of the many *zawāyā* (sufi brotherhoods) popular in Constantine at the time (Merdaci 2008: 166). Professionally, the members were a mixed group: six employees in local administrations, six in economic enterprises, five artisans, three landlords, and two teachers. While many were graduates of the French high school Jules Ferry, others came out of the Arabophone madrasas (210). Mouhibbi El Fen's statutes allowed for political diversity. Gradually, however, the group adopted a reformist orientation, described as "a subtle form of allegiance, essentially to the person of the shaykh Abdelhamid Benbadis" (Merdaci 2007: 103). This was clear in Mouhibbi El Fen's performance for the Ben Badis Institute following a speech by Ben Badis; this performance would likely have included the hymn "Ša'b al-Jazā'ir" ("The Algerian people"), a setting of Ben Badis's poem of the same title, which had been composed by Mouhibbi El Fen's music director, one Si Brahim Ammouchi, at the request of Ben Badis (104).

Mouhibbi El Fen's diversity was also its demise. It was one of the few associations for which I found a reference to a lack of unanimity at the general assembly. Indeed, according to Merdaci, the 1937 assembly featured "a head-on fight between those close to the *'ulamā*, led by Ahmed Bouchemal, and the president Abdelmadjid Rahmouni, who had declared his sympathies for the sufis" (2008: 166–167). At that point, the troupe ceased to exist as such; those members aligned with Ben Badis formed a new troupe, Chabab El Fenni (96), which had a more homogeneous membership. Chabab El Fenni lasted only a few years, until the outbreak of World War II in 1940. After the war, in 1945, some of its former members created l'Etoile Polaire, which in turned spawned El

Amal El Masrahi in 1949. The genealogy of Messaoud Salhi's troupe Al–Malhat Al-Jazā'rīyya is less clear. Given its close ties to Jām'īyat al-tarbīya wa 'l-talīm, it likely emerged directly out of this reformist madrasa. It would have overlapped in time with first Etoile Polaire and then El Amal El Masrahi.

Similar stories of splitting and reconstitution characterized other theatrical groups of the day. El Hilal Ettemthili El Qassantini, formed in 1938, had a fleeting existence (162). Like Mouhibbi El Fen, El Hilal Ettemthili initially included members of competing ideological tendencies. Of twenty-two members in February 1939, three were identified with sufis, ten with reformists (called *ulamā* in the police reports, though not all *ulamā* were reformists), and six with the Féderation des élus, and two were considered neutral; one *ulamā*-identified member was further affiliated with the communists.[29] Their audiences may have been similarly diverse, since on February 1, 1939, some eight hundred came to see their play "Crime of the Fathers." This audience included Dr. Bendjelloul of the Féderation des élus and Ahmed Bouchemal of the *ulamā*, who had served as president of Al-tarbīya wa 'l-talīm and as publisher of the *ulamā* newspaper al-Shihāb, and was a founder of the Algerian Muslim Press.[30]

Yet it appeared almost impossible to maintain such diversity; El Hilal Ettemthili reportedly was close to scission over a difference between the adjunct secretary (described as of "*ulamā* tendency") and the treasurer, who had reportedly turned the site of the association into a bar during the 'Aid festivities.[31] In 1941, after two years of inactivity due to disagreement among its directors, the troupe tried to come back together. They reportedly reached an agreement after what the French police report termed "an exchange of views" (*une échange de vues*),[32] but it did not last long. Other troupes went so far as to prohibit all political discussion, such as Jider El Masrahi,[33] or to expel members who were affiliated with particular parties. El Hilal Ettemthili, for instance, unanimously voted

---

29. Special Departmental Police of Constantine to Prefect, February 17, 1939, no. 507 (FR CAOM 93 4224).

30. Report, Special Departmental Police of Constantine, February 2, 1939, no. 403, FR CAOM 93 4224. On Ahmed Bouchemal, see Merdaci 2008: 85.

31. Report, Special Departmental Police of Constantine, November 29, 1939, no. 2940, FR CAOM 93 4224.

32. Special Departmental Police of Constantine to Prefect, December 9, 1941, no. 8787, FR CAOM 93 4224.

33. Article 3 of Jidar El Masrahi's statutes of April 13, 1952, reads, "All political discussion, as well as any intervention in a political question, is rigorously prohibited within the troupe" (FR CAOM 93 4224).

to expel its comptroller because of his affiliation with the PPA in July 1938.[34] Eventually El Hilal Ettemthili appears to have become entirely *'ulamist* and by 1944 was performing such well-known reformist plays as *Bilal Ibn Rabah*,[35] to be discussed presently.

Why did associations struggle so hard to reach unanimity? What made unanimity a more attractive option than, say, majority rule? What transpired in the 1930s that led to a "head-on battle" in an association like Mouhibbi El Fen, which had initially included both reformists and sufis? To address these questions, I consider three factors: first, the importance of *tawḥīd*, or unity, in the reformist imagination; second, local practices of decision-making, including the size and nature of elected committees as well as what Andrea Liverani calls "associative familism" (2008: 62); and third, the over-determining presence of the colonial apparatus, which, paradoxically, both sharpened the line between reformists and sufis and laid the groundwork for the emergence of a singular Islamic identity by making practice of the Muslim faith the key grounds for excluding Algerians from French citizenship.

Tawḥīd, or Unicity

A key rationale for discourses and practices of unanimity is no doubt linked to the reformist doctrine of *tawḥīd*, which derives from the Arabic root meaning "one" and can translate as unicity, unification, or union as well as belief in the unity of God.[36] Doctrinally, *tawḥīd* refers to the conviction, central to reformist thought, that Muslims must return to the source of their religion, to practices grounded in the belief in a single God and in the foundational authority of God's words as conveyed in the Quran, the Hadith, and the Sunna. The premise of *tawḥīd* led reformists to categorically reject the various intermediaries (sometimes referred to as marabouts or saints) who had long dominated popular practice throughout the Maghrib.[37] For the reformists, practices related to such intermediaries were considered "innovations" (*bidā'at*) that were at odds with Islam's basic tenets. Within the broader reform movement, which by the 1940s was emerging as

---

34. Report, Special Departmental Police of Constantine, July 20, 1938, no. 2438, FR CAOM 93 4224. Associations were required by law to prohibit political affiliation, as one reviewer pointed out to me.

35. El Hilal Ettemthili requested permission to perform the popular play *Bilal Ibn Rabah* in June 1944. Handwritten note, June 19, 1944, FR CAOM 93 4224.

36. Wehr [1979] 1994: 1236–1237.

37. On the sufi orders or *zawāyā*, see Dermenghem 1954; Clancy-Smith 1994; Colonna 1995; Cornell 1998; and Scheele 2007.

a dominant religious force across the Arab world, *tawḥīd* was also invoked to attenuate antagonisms between the four schools of Islamic jurisprudence, each of which elevated the teachings of its particular foundational *imām* over the underlying unity of the Islamic community, or *umma* (Commins 1990).[38] Divisions among Sunni and Shi'a Muslims were similarly subordinated, at least in theory, to the overarching unity contained in the notion of *tawḥīd*. In Algeria, which was primarily Sunni and almost exclusively aligned with the Maliki school of legal thought, the reformists concentrated their energies on the sufis and their many followers. The sufi organizations, called *zawāyā*, were built around a saint and his followers or adepts (sometimes called *ikhwān*, brothers), but they could bring together hundreds or, for the most popular saints, thousands of people for saint-day festivities and other ritual occasions. While some saints were associated with a single locality, others had regional and even national renown, and belonged to brotherhoods that stretched across the Maghrib and the Middle East. Although many sufi organizations had challenged colonial power during the early decades of conquest and occupation, by the 1940s, most had reached accommodation with the French ranging from mutual tolerance to working relationships to outright support. To the reformists, however, the sufi leaders were little better than charlatans who took advantage of an uneducated population to enrich themselves and their organizations. The doctrine of *tawḥīd* challenged the entire sufi edifice—both the presumed existence of intermediaries between Muslims and their god and the many kinds of miraculous or, from a reformist viewpoint, "superstitious" practices associated with these intermediaries.

Tawḥīd was not merely a theological doctrine. It was also a factor "at every level, and in all aspects of Islamic life." Indeed, *tawḥīd* was to serve as a unifying force for the Islamic community "in the moral, psychological, political, and even cultural sense" (Merad 1999: 238). As James McDougall put it, *tawḥīd* constituted "a theological principle to be rigorously applied to social life" (2006: 114). In its vision of a singularity of belief and purpose across the domains of philosophy, politics, and personal life, *tawḥīd* appears to constitute what Bakhtin identified as an idealist philosophy (see Bakhtin 1984: 79–85), in which "the affirmation of the unity of *existence* is . . . transformed into the unity of consciousness" (Bakhtin 1984: 80). With regards to the script in question, the narrative arc of the conversion story clearly aligns with the "ideological monologism" that characterizes idealist philosophy. The encounters between the characters of the *muḥ tadā* (a term with the same root as *tawḥīd*) and the *maġrūr* are portrayed in terms of the "single mode of cognitive interaction among consciousnesses" that characterizes idealist philosophy, wherein "someone who knows and possesses the truth instructs

---

38. I am grateful to Ethan Katz for this reference.

someone who is ignorant of it and in error" (Bakhtin 1984: 81). For instance, after initial scenes in which the *muḥtadā* chastises the *maḡrūr* for indulging in alcohol consumption and movie-going, the latter unexpectedly drops by the former's house and entirely subordinates himself to the religious leader. The *maḡrūr's* conversion entailed no scenes of self-questioning, no internal dialogue. Instead, he simply says: "I couldn't bear your absence and being away from you. Because I have become dependent on your ideas and opinions to solve my problems. That's why I came by . . . I have greatly reflected on your advice . . . and I have turned the page on my old life, in which I find nothing of merit . . . Give me guidance, I am under your orders and completely obedient."

Yet such an ideological and idealized representation of unicity is clearly not a direct reflection of social practice. How did the unifying or (in Bakhtin's terms) monological principle of *tawḥīd* articulate with the rich plurality of social experiences and political perspectives? How was agreement produced on the ground? If, in Omar Carlier's words, "community is placed under the sign of unicity while society itself unceasingly produces diversity," how was the resulting tension handled in practice? (Carlier 1998, cited in McDougall 2006: 234). Although Carlier was speaking of the resurgence of Islamism in Algeria in the 1990s, the question is equally relevant to the reformist period.

One way unicity was produced was via the pragmatics of speech, through speech acts that bring into being what they call for (Austin 1962). As Ben Badis toured the countryside in the 1930s, he called for "unitarism (*tawḥīd*), union, and generosity toward all human beings (*'ibād*), concord and mutual assistance (*ta'alūf, ta'āwun*) among all the inhabitants of Algeria, without distinction of race or creed" (Merad 1999: 127, quoting Ben Badis). This message was recast on a more intimate level in the play under consideration here, where it was performatively invoked at key decision points. During the general assembly, for instance, the *muḥtadā* (who had just been approved by voice vote as temporary president) evoked a divinely bestowed unity prior to the final two unanimous votes (held to elect the permanent committee and agree on the project): "I am grateful," says the *muḥtadā*, "that you granted me the honor of presiding over this general assembly. And I congratulate you for your honorable determination and your zeal in striving for the common good. You are driven by sincerity and goodness toward the flourishing of Arabness (*al-'arūba*). I thank God for bringing together our dispersed affairs and unifying the word of the disunifed *umma* in this blessed general assembly. 'What is brought together by the hand of God cannot be separated by the hand of Satan.'"[39] As a speech act, this may have worked to produce

---

39. FR CAOM 93 4224.

the very sense of oneness that it references: If God were on the side of unity, how could a member of the assembly dissent?

The *tawḥīd* model seems to have been adopted even by the AUMA at its creation. According to Merad, the association formed after five and a half years of discussion and debate (1999: 115). By the time of the AUMA's first general assembly, in May 1931, they had largely reached agreement. On the very first day, the statutes were adopted and the administrative council designated. The rapidity of these moves suggests that the details had been hammered out beforehand. In such a situation, the general assembly comes to resemble a ritual festival of unity more than a moment of electoral decision, which is how Malika Rahal characterized the general assemblies of the Union démocratique du manifeste algérien (UDMA) from 1945 to 1954. As she put it: "The systematic and repetitive character of the election of the committee gave it a surprising ritual value. . . . The number of these elections shows that they go beyond basic organizational necessities to constitute an activity in and of themselves, participating in the normal activity of members of the section and symbolizing the beginning of any collective action" (Rahal 2007: 66). The Muslim Scout organization appears to have worked in much the same way. Brahim Mamouchi reported in his memoirs that when he helped to bring the scout organization to Constantine he called a general assembly in April 1932 at which "comrade Belattar M'Hamed was *designated* president" (Mamouchi n.d.: 4, emphasis added).[40] It seems that once an association was at the point of selecting a slate of officers, its members had had so much advance back-and-forth discussion that they knew already who their representatives would be; in effect, they had reached unanimity before the general assembly took place, so that it became a rubber stamp of sorts.[41] The vote thus had a different significance than it would in an election governed by majority rule—it was not usually a moment of choice. Rather, it was a ratification of a decision that people had already labored long and hard to reach. Associations that could not reach prior agreement would often end up either splitting or ceasing activities altogether. Meetings and elections thus became celebratory occasions, "festive reunions" (Rahal 2007: 66) at which members celebrated their common vision in a Durkheimian moment of collective effervescence.

The public nature of the votes themselves also merits attention. Whether by voice vote or show of hands, association members were called on to publicly perform their allegiance to a common agenda. This is an entirely different use of the vote as social activity than voting by secret ballot, which became naturalized

---

40. I am grateful to Madjid Merdaci for bringing Mamouchi's manuscript to my attention.

41. For related perspectives on consensus decision-making, see Bailey 1965; Falk Moore 1977.

within Western democracies over the course of the nineteenth and twentieth centuries.[42]

Vernacular Decision-Making Practices

Members of artistic associations may also have been drawing on vernacular modes of decision-making found in adjacent forums for argumentation and debate, such as those found in the Berber *tajma'at* system. The *tajma'at*, commonly translated by the French as the *"assemblée du village"* (village assembly),[43] was an all-male body that met regularly (typically weekly, on Fridays or on the day following the regional market) to discuss matters of importance to the collective life of a village, ranging from the upkeep and development of public space to the issuing of fines for transgressions of social mores or violations of established rules (*al-qanūn*). Decision-making in the *tajma'at* typically operated via consensus: all able-bodied men of the village had to assent to the group's decisions before they could take effect.

In situating consensual decision-making practices in relation to the social organization of Berber villages, I follow William Murphy (1990) in adopting a Goffmanian rather than a Durkheimian lens. Consensual practices need not be interpreted, Murphy argues, as a communitas-like occasion to display solidarity or as "a mirror of social cohesion" (32). Instead, consensus-based decision-making may be more productively viewed in dramaturgical terms, as a strategy for building a "front stage" that appears consensual through "backstage" practices that might be anything but (25). From a dramaturgical perspective, the apparent equality of all voices present at the *tajma'at* can be seen as a strategic means of obscuring very real differences in power and status. For if in theory all voices were equal, in practice this was not the case. Historically, most *tajma'ats* had an *amīn* (president), a *wakīl* (adjunct), and various *tamen* who were appointed by and represented the patrilineages that made up the village (Mahé 2001: 80). This small group could act as a village council; they would set the agenda for the larger *tajma'at*, represent the village to outside authorities, and could come together outside of the weekly *tajma'at* meetings if there were urgent matters to discuss. As Mahé notes, some analysts have concluded that the true power in the village was

---

42. For an analysis of the secret ballot and its history, see Bertrand, Briquet, and Pels 2006.

43. For a fascinating reconstruction of the unfolding of dialogue at a Kabyle village assembly, see Lanfry [1946] 1959. On the *tajma'at* as an Algerian political institution, see Roberts 2003: 43–47. On consensus decision-making, see also Fernandez 1965; El-Hakim 1978. The *tajma'at*, of course, has undergone considerable change. See Mahé 2001: 546–553; Goodman 2005: 83–89.

located in this smaller group, with the full *tajma'at* acting merely as "a registration chamber or a solemn proclamation through which the citizen body unanimously ratified a decision that was already made" (81). Yet on the ground, things were not so straightforward: the *tamen* patrilineage representatives would have had to be able to garner the support of their respective kin groups. Moreover, "the restricted assembly [village council], like the plenary, was obliged to . . . achieve strict unanimity" (82). The achievement of unanimity in what Mahé calls the "plenary" *tajma'at* could thus be hard-won, the product of long negotiations among multiple parties and competing interests. Moreover, many *tajma'ats* anticipated the possibility of secession—that is, the constitution of a parallel village assembly—and would levy high fines on anyone suspected of or engaged in such a dissident action (84). The *tajma'at* also established fines for breaching codes of public conduct at the meeting, thereby preventing the kinds of fights that might otherwise break out during heated discussions (86).

Because consensus was the expected outcome, the *tajma'at* had no need to follow the kinds of voting procedures that have been associated with democratic practice since the advent of the secret ballot (see Bertrand, Briquet, and Pels 2006). It was governed not by a principle of majority rule, but by something closer to the Islamic *tawḥīd*, in practice if not in name. In the cultural associations of the 1930s to 1950s, however, the apparatus of voting had become increasingly familiar to members from the political elections that surrounded them, even as their participation in those elections was limited. Electoral practices seem to have taken hold in the artistic associations, where—as in the scenes of voting represented in Messaoud Salhi's play—a voting procedure appears to have been laminated into a consensus-based participation structure.

Consider, for instance, the election held by El Chabab El Fenni at its general assembly of October 21, 1940. The society had apparently been in some disarray, the former president was resigning, and there was a budget shortfall. The purpose of the meeting was to regroup and start afresh. After the "moral" and "financial" reports had been given, those present "participated in an exchange of views."[44] Only after this were new elections held. At the same meeting there was also an "exchange of views" concerning artistic activities, which culminated in a consensus decision to organize a concert for the upcoming holiday Aid al-Saghir. Another "exchange of views" took place at a meeting later that fall, where "each one gave his opinion about the play they were preparing."[45] The "exchange of

---

44. Special Departmental Police of Constantine to Prefect, October 22, 1940, no. 6337, FR CAOM 93 4224.

45. Special Departmental Police of Constantine to Prefect, December 24, 1940, no. 8046, FR CAOM 93 4224.

views," as the French termed it, seems to have been a key speech genre that would have documented the labor entailed in achieving unanimity; unfortunately, it is not elaborated in the archival records.

In noting resemblances between the decision-making structures at work in the *tajma'at* and the Constantine artistic associations, I am not suggesting that the *tajma'at* functioned as a self-conscious political model that the associations sought to imitate, as, decades later, the Berber *'arūsh* movement of the early 2000s tried to do.[46] Nor am I arguing that Algerians were somehow mired in vernacular forms of social interaction and unable to adopt other forms of civic practice. It is plausible, however, that association members were familiar with *tajma'at*-style modes of collective decision-making and that they turned them to new uses. Omar Carlier (1995: 151–162), for instance, has shown how older social bodies (such as the kinship faction known as *sof*) and their associated styles of interaction can inhabit newer kinds of civic association: "born of what already exists," associations can go on "to initiate another cultural practice" (159).

While the *tajma'at* is generally associated with rural, primarily Berber areas rather than urban, predominantly Arab environments, "rural" and "urban" were fluid categories in Constantine during the 1930s. The city of Constantine is located between the large Kabyle Berber region to its northwest and the Aurès Berber region to its south. The global depression that began in the late 1920s was by the early 1930s severely impacting Algerian agriculture, forcing rural residents to the cities.[47] Between 1931 and 1936, the indigenous Algerian urban population grew by over six hundred thousand people, or almost 11%, and during the same period, the indigenous population in Constantine increased by almost eight thousand, or 15%. The figures are even more dramatic if we take into account the previous five years: from 1926 to 1936 the indigenous Algerian urban population expanded by nearly 20%.[48] Yet in the *tajma'at* institution, strong familism and vertical ties extending from a patriarch down to his sons and nephews help to ensure continuity over time. When this kind of model was laminated onto artistic associations that lacked the *tajma'at*'s perduring familial relationships and vertical ties, it faced new challenges.

---

46. The *'arūsh* movement, formally the Coordination of 'Arush, Daïrat, and Communes, began in Kabylia in 2001 after police killed the Kabyle youth Massinissa Guermah; forty-two others died in subsequent riots. Organizing itself loosely around the village *tajma'ats*, the movement positioned itself outside traditional political parties and initially gained a good deal of popular support. See Roberts 2003: ch. 18.

47. Figures are drawn from Kaddache 1993: 273–275.

48. The urban population increased from 5,190,756 in 1926 to 6,201,144 in 1936, according to the Annuaire Statistique de l'Algérie, cited in Kaddache 1993: 271.

Unanimous votes in artistic associations may also have had to do with the large size of the elected committees, which resembled a community of participants more than a small number of electoral representatives. Mouhibbi El Fen's first administrative council (*conseil d'administration*), selected in 1933, had twenty-two members (Merdaci 2008: 212). Similarly, in October 1940, the newspaper *Dépêche de Constantine* reported that El Chabab El Fenni unanimously elected a slate of twenty-two officers.[49] Only thirty people attended El Chabab El Fenni's meeting,[50] meaning that more than two-thirds of those present became part of the governing body and thus were assured of having at least some voice in future decision-making. El Hilal Ettemthili elected a twenty-one-member Administrative Council, out of some forty total members, in 1939.[51] Records indicate a proliferation of titles and positions: president, vice president, and four designates; treasurer and one adjunct; secretary, one designate and one adjunct; a theater director; and nine assessors.[52] It seems that whoever wanted a say in the association's operations could probably secure himself a position.

A related avenue to consider is what Liverani calls "associative familism" (2008: 62), the tendency of civic associations in the Middle East and North Africa to be built around a core of individuals from the same family. Liverani is concerned primarily with contemporary, post-independence associations, and my work with theatrical associations from 2008 to 2011 is consonant with his argument. By far the most stable troupe I worked with, the thirty-year-old El Moudja Theater of Mostaganem, is built around a core of five people from the same family—the director and four of his children (his wife and two other sons had previously acted as well). Three of the other four troupes I followed each had two active family members. Was this also the case in earlier decades? For Salhi's troupe Al-Malhat Al-Jazā'riyya, three of the seven members (including the director) lived at the same address and two of those three shared the same last name.[53] Yet not all associations displayed this tendency. El Chabab El Fenni had two members of the same last name, but other associations showed few or no family connections.

---

49. *Dépêche de Constantine*, October 23, 1940, in FR CAOM 93 4224.

50. Special Departmental Police of Constantine to Prefect, October 22, 1940, no. 6337, FR CAOM 93 4224.

51. Special Departmental Police of Constantine Report, May 15, 1939, no. 1890, FR CAOM 93 4224.

52. Ibid.

53. Salhi to Prefect, April 7, 1949, no. 3378, FR CAOM 93 4224.

Colonial Discourses and Practices

Finally, the aspiration toward unanimity may have been in part a response to particular aspects of the French colonial apparatus. Police decided what plays these associations could and could not stage. They were present at every play, every concert, and even many meetings, looking for lurking nationalists who, the French feared, were using theatrical scripts and performances to advance an anticolonial agenda. The enveloping presence of the colonial state worked paradoxically. On one hand, by accentuating differences between reformists and sufis, it drove a sharp wedge between Algerians who might otherwise have found ways to work together. On the other, it grouped all Algerians into a monolithic category of "Muslims," thus making Islam emerge as the single factor around which the indigenous population could unite (McDougall 2006; compare Barry, this volume). This "rule of colonial difference" (Chatterjee 1993) was mapped onto and conjoined with the Islamic principle of *tawḥīd*, which came, in the Algerian case, to signify an expectation of sociocultural singularity that continues to exert force to this day.

As we have seen, when the first theatrical troupes formed in the early 1930s, it was common for them to include members of both reform and sufi persuasion, and even some who affiliated unproblematically with both. For instance, Brahim Mamouchi, one of Mouhibbi El Fen's founding members, reported that in 1932 he was both active in the Hansaliya sufi order and a member of the reformist madrasa Jām'īyat al-tarbīya wa 'l-talīm.[54] What happened during the 1930s that might have made it more difficult for reformists and sufis to occupy the same social space? The decade was problematic for many Algerian Muslims from its inception: in 1930, gala centenary festivities were held around the country to mark one hundred years of French colonial rule. While Algerian Muslims hoped that the French government would use the occasion of the centenary to announce new rights for the indigenous population, this did not transpire. A list of eleven desired changes drawn up by the Muslim Elected Officials of Algeria (Élus des musulmans d'Algérie) in 1931 went nowhere.[55] Meanwhile, as already described, Ben Badis began to tour the Algerian countryside in 1932 disseminating reformist ideas (Merad 1999: 127). The colonial administration took note, and in 1933 issued two decrees to isolate so-called "agents of reformist propaganda": they were forbidden to preach in the official state mosques, and they were put under

---

54. Mamouchi n.d.: 3.

55. Kaddache provides the list of demands, which included "integral representation of the indigenous population in parliament," and "increasing indigenous representation in the elected assemblies in Algeria" (1993: 251).

surveillance (132).[56] On the ground, these measures entailed "numerous closings of Arab schools, refusal to open new schools, limits on freedom of movement, and even jail time" (132).

As the decade wore on, the French did everything they could to accentuate divisions between the reformists, who were generally seen as threatening to the colonial state, and the sufi organizations, perceived largely as supporters if not collaborators. French police records insistently drew a sharp dividing line between reformists and sufis. Indeed, all members of theatrical or musical associations were repeatedly noted as being either one or the other: along with their names and addresses, the police would typically record each member's sufi ("marabout") or *salafi* ("'ulama") affiliation. Moreover, local disputes between reformists and sufis may have taken on larger significance by the very fact that they were mediated through the French police system. McDougall describes how what began as a relatively minor scuffle between *salafis* and *ikhwān* (brothers of a sufi order) in the town of Mila in 1936 was amplified by French administrators and through local rumors into a wider conflict between two opposing ideologies (2006: 116–120). This and other "small symbolic spectacles" (120) helped to produce what became, as the 1930s wore on, an intractable dividing line between salafism and sufism.

In this climate, one can imagine that it might have been difficult for someone like Ahmed Bouchemal—a frequent figure in police reports who was simultaneously a founding member of Mouhibbi El Fen, a director of El Chabab El Fenni, the president of the administrative council of the madrasa Al-tarbīya wa 'l-talīm (McDougall 2006: 132), and a founder of the important Algerian Muslim press (Merdaci 2007: 102)—to stay on good terms with Mouhibbi El Fen's first president, Si Abdelmadjid Rahmouni, himself a sufi and thus not subject to the same level of surveillance. How could a theatrical association sustain internal diversity when everything surrounding it, from the reformists' own emphasis on uniformity to colonial police practices, reinforced and polarized members' differences? Could Ahmed Bouchemal and Si Abdelmadjid Rahmouni have managed to relate to each other outside the intersecting *salafi* and colonial logics in which their lives were inscribed? If in the early years it was still possible for sufi adepts and reformists to work together in the same social space, it had now become far more challenging.

The colonial context also opened a symbolic and political space in which the principle of *tawḥīd* was able to take hold in the imaginations of Algerians (see McDougall 2006). Like all late colonial democracies, France faced the predicament of how to minimize the tension between its own republican proclamation

---

56. See also McDougall 2006: 124–125n92, on the "Michel circular."

of equality among all citizens and the imperial requirement to maintain the colonized population in a state of subordination (see, e.g., Chatterjee 1993; Cooper and Stoler 1997). This was not, of course, solely a colonial problematic: the liberal state itself was developed on a foundation of difference (Mehta 1999). As Immanuel Wallerstein has shown for the case of post-revolutionary France, although "the concept of citizen was intended to be inclusive . . . the other face . . . was exclusion. . . . The way to define citizenship narrowly in practice, while retaining the principle in theory, is to create two categories of citizens" (2003: 651). While in France the division between "active" and "passive" citizens had been constructed around property ownership, in Algeria the line was drawn differently. In 1848, with the advent of the Second Republic, Algeria's status had changed from a colony to an overseas extension of France itself.[57] As I have already noted, following the 1865 Senatus-Consulte decree, Algerians were accorded French nationality but were not granted citizenship; instead, they were considered "French subjects."[58] Although the Senatus-Consulte put in place a procedure through which Algerian Muslims could attain full citizenship, few sought to do so, largely because it meant relinquishing their civil status under Muslim law (Brett 1988: 453; Ruedy 1992: 76). In 1870, Algerian Jews were "naturalized" as French citizens (via the Crémieux Decree), but Algerian Muslims who refused to give up their "personal status" continued to be excluded from citizenship.[59] The French tinkered with this status over the decades and eventually accorded limited political rights to a handful of Muslim Algerians through mechanisms such as the Jonnart law, but these mechanisms ensured that the indigenous population would remain a political minority until very late in the game.

As McDougall has persuasively argued, the reformists entered into the space opened up under the personal status laws via the "recuperation and reformulation of the *statut personnel* as the key signifier of 'Algerian-ness'" (2006: 94). This, McDougall contends, "constituted a kind of discursive *tawḥīd*: the multiplicity of Algerian religious and cultural realities were . . . reduced to a single sign of 'authentic' selfhood" (94). The *'ulamā* essentially appropriated the Jacobin language of singularity that the French had been imposing on them for decades and seized for their self-definition the very category—Islam—into which they had already been uniformly slotted. By appropriating the French colonial category

---

57. Algeria's change in status from a military-ruled colony to an administrative extension of France began in 1848 with the Second Republic but was fully achieved only after the advent of the Third Republic in 1870.

58. On the 1865 Senatus-Consulte, see Julien 1964: 433–434; Brett 1988.

59. On exactly what "statut personnel" entailed, see Ioualalen, "Qu'est-ce au juste le statut musulman?" *La Voix des Humbles* 101 (July 1931): 11, reproduced in Kaddache 1993: 253.

of the statut personnel, the *'ulamā* were able to "construct new claims to unitary, sacred authority" built on "an exclusive conception of national community reduced to a unitary and unanimist 'essence'" (96). The colonial power itself, in other words, helped to generate the very category that Algerians would later embrace as their common rallying cry. The statut personnel became the symbolic space that was at once "the key site of exclusion from French citizenship" and "the key space in which an alternative, Algerian citizenship would be created" (92).

The reformist plays were among the cultural products that populated this alternative space. They constitute one of the media in which *tawḥīd* was discursively and performatively enacted. In this regard, Messaoud Salhi's play is of particular interest. Many aspects of the play represent the reformist message and invite spectators into the fold: from the conversion story to the portrayal of the *muhtadā*'s practices of spiritual discipline to the project to create an institution with education and social mores as its twin concerns. Yet at the same time, *tawḥīd* was viscerally embodied in this play as a social practice of unanimous decision-making: on four occasions, the actors are enjoined to perform their collective assent via a voice vote or a showing of hands.

Other plays of the period likewise represent the singularity of behavior, mores, and thought that Algerians were expected to embrace. Scripts regularly singled out two groups of Algerians for critique or comic ridicule: those who had pretentiously embraced European habits (such as the *maġrūr* or "deluded youth" in Salhi's play), and those who were seen as mindlessly following traditional or "backward" practices and were thus consigned to the realm of ignorance (*jāhiliyya*) that the reformists sought to combat (such as the sufis and their followers). Indeed, the plays may have provided a vocabulary in which these practices could be evaluated and critiqued in relation to the goals of *tawḥīd*. Some plays— among them, *The Story of Ignorants Who Call on Science: Bring the Flame*,[60] staged by the troupe "La Chabiba" (The Youth) in the central Algerian city of Blida in 1938—revolved around an exaggerated portrayal of a battle between modern, scientific knowledge and the kind of practical knowledge associated with rural folk practice. Those on the side of tradition are depicted as ignoramuses or buffoons, out of touch with the modern world.[61] La Chabiba's play invites rural sages who claim to have scientific knowledge to submit to a series of tests imposed by a Western-educated professor. If they fail, they agree to be burned on the forehead.

---

60. The script is located in Archives du Département d'Alger (ALG Alger) 21/41. Ben Ameur Cheikh translated it at my request into French.

61. The reformist plays were not alone in critiquing what they perceived as backward practices. The popular Mahiéddine Bachetarzi comedy troupe staged many plays making fun of rural or "uncivilized" ways. For a discussion of one such play, see Cole 2009, 2014.

Needless to say, the sages fail each test and must subsequently bear the sign of their ignorance. Clearly, only one kind of knowledge was to be valorized. Other plays were based on well-known stories from the Islamic tradition, such as the frequently performed *Bilal Ibn Rabah*, in which the protagonist, a slave named Bilal, initially hides his Muslim faith from his idolatrous Abyssinian masters. He is found out and tortured, but refuses to renounce his beliefs, instead uttering: "I believe in God alone . . . Allah is my destination, my refuge, my path, my source . . . the one I lean on." When Bilal, chained to a rock, is close to death, he continues to praise God, punctuating each line with "the only," "the unique." This phrase is then detached from its surrounds, echoing alone, repeatedly, as the scene ends.

Conclusion

To conclude, I return to the tripartite project that the characters in Salhi's script unanimously endorsed: the diffusion of Arab culture, national education, and sports; the revival of the national economy; and the struggle against social scourges. What does this outline if not a far-reaching program encompassing all aspects of society: from culture and education to the economy to social morality? This was a blueprint for a *projet de société*, as it would be termed following Algeria's opening to multiparty democracy in 1989. It was a vision of an alternative way of organizing civic life that conjoined the national interest with a kind of moral discipline that everyone was expected to embrace. Salhi's play offers a creative attempt to outline in performance the terms of an alternative civic sphere in which citizens can collectively reach agreement on a shared vision of public morality and the public good. In so doing, the play offers a model of unanimism in public culture that seems to anticipate contemporary practices.

The Algerian reformist theatrical associations brought into being a lively, multidimensional performance sphere in which participants were engaged in modeling and producing unanimism through various creative means. In the play I have focused on, the script highlighted speech acts designed to produce a feeling of collective unity preceding what would then turn out to be a unanimous vote, thus mirroring the forms of persuasive speech reformist leaders were using in appearances around the country. I alternately adopted Durkheimian and Goffmanian lenses in looking at the general assemblies that association members regularly engaged in, which were also modeled in the script. The assemblies worked on one level as ritual occasions for the festive celebration of unity. At the same time, these were clearly onstage moments when the social labor entailed in producing unanimity was momentarily masked. A potentially rich backstage discourse was hinted at in tantalizing archival references to a speech genre that

French surveillance officers termed an "exchange of views." I have also considered the large elected committees as a participant structure that could mitigate the unanimity apparent in their election. Throughout, my emphasis has been on unanimity as a social achievement that required considerable discursive and performative labor to produce and maintain. At the same time, by focusing on unanimism as a social practice, I hope to have troubled the easy linkages between voluntary associations and a democratizing public sphere that have long haunted the civil society literature. The Algerian theatrical troupes made use of voluntary associations to constitute alternatives to the practices of individual choice and majority rule that are often associated with democracy.

This material suggests that theories of democracy and civil society may not offer the sole or even the most helpful lenses through which scholars should approach civic associations. Indeed, such theories may work to obscure the social and performative labor that goes into the achievement of consensus. At the same time, however, a consensus model of public life need not be celebrated as a utopian alternative to a practice of majority rule. Indeed, achieving consensus is fraught with problems of its own. Such a model rests particularly uneasily in a nation-state framework, where the backstage labor entailed in its achievement not only is undercut by other powerful interests, be they military, political, or economic, but also leads necessarily to the exclusion or marginalization of those with divergent agendas. Yet despite unanimism's potential pitfalls, it is crucial to recognize it as a social accomplishment in and of itself. As scholars examine the practices of contemporary civic associations in states with unanimist models of public life, the theatrical associations of the 1930s to 1950s can remind us to look not only to ritual displays of consensus, or its flip side, fissure, but also to the far messier practices of social and linguistic labor entailed in the achievement of unanimity.

Acknowledgments

This research was generously funded by Fulbright-Hays, the American Council of Learned Societies, the Social Science Research Council, the National Endowment for the Humanities, the American Institute for Maghrib Studies, and the Indiana University New Frontiers Program. I am grateful to Latifa Krachai for her initial translation of the Arabic script into French; to Ben Ameur Cheikh, who translated into French one of the additional scripts I refer to; and to Hassan Lachheb, who assisted me with remaining translation questions. All translations from French to English are my own unless otherwise indicated. This article has benefited from critical readings at various stages by

Fanny Colonna, Ilana Gershon, Susan Lepselter, and Javier Leon. Anonymous reviewers provided incisive critiques that led me to reformulate key aspects of this essay for its original publication (see Jane E. Goodman, "Acting with One Voice: Producing Unanimism in Algerian Reformist Theater," *Comparative Studies in Society and History* 55(1)(2013): 167–197). Earlier versions of this paper were presented at the Centre des Etudes Maghrébines en Algérie in May 2009, the Middle East Studies Association Annual Meeting in November 2009, and the University of Michigan Anthropology and History Workshop in April 2010. I am grateful to conference and workshop participants for invaluable comments and questions. Any remaining errors of fact or interpretation are, of course, my own.

References

Archival Sources

Centre des Archives d'Outre-Mer, Aix-en-Provence, France Fonds Ministériels (FR CAOM) 93 4224.
Archives du Département d'Alger (ALG Alger) 2I/41.

Published Sources

Allalou, Selali Ali. 2004. *L'Aurore du théâtre algérien (1926–1930)*. Oran, Algeria: Editions Dar el Gharb.
Austin, J. L. 1962. *How to Do Things with Words*. Cambridge, MA: Harvard University Press.
Bachetarzi, Mahiéddine. 1968. *Mémoires 1919–1939, suivi de etude sur le théâtre dans les pays islamiques*. Algiers: Société Nationale d'Edition et de Distribution.
Bailey, F. G. 1965. "Decisions by Consensus in Councils and Committees, with Special Reference to Village and Local Government in India." In *Political Systems and the Distribution of Power*, ed. Michael Banton, 1–20. London: Tavistock Publications.
Bakhtin, Mikhail. 1984. *Problems of Dostoevsky's Poetics*. Ed. and trans. Caryl Emerson. Minneapolis: University of Minnesota Press.
Ben Achour, Bouziane. 2005. *Le Théâtre algérien: Une historie d'étapes*. Oran, Algeria: Editions dar el Gharb.
Benhassine, Karima. 2005. "La Vie associative à Constantine." PhD diss., Department of History, Université Mentouri, Constantine, Algeria.
Bertrand, Romain, Jean-Louis Briquet, and Peter Pels, eds. 2006. *The Hidden History of the Secret Ballot*. Bloomington: Indiana University Press.

Bouzar-Kasbadji, Nadya. 1988. *L'Emergence artistique algérienne au XXe siècle: Contribution de la musique et du théâtre algérois à la renaissance culturelle et à la prise de conscience nationaliste*. Algiers, Algeria: Office des Publications Universitaires.

Brett, Michael. 1988. "Legislating for Inequality in Algeria: The Senatus-Consulte of 14 July 1865." *Bulletin of the School of Oriental and African Studies* 51(3): 440–461.

Carlier, Omar. 1995. *Entre nation et jihad: Histoire sociale des radicalismes algériens*. Paris: Presses de Sciences Po.

Carlier, Omar. 1998. "D'une guerre à l'autre: Le Redéploiement de la violence entre soi." *Confluences Méditerranée* 25 (Spring): 123–137.

Chakrabarty, Dipesh. 2000. *Provincializing Europe: Postcolonial Thought and Historical Difference*. Princeton, NJ: Princeton University Press.

Chatterjee, Partha. 1993. *The Nation and Its Fragments: Colonial and Postcolonial Histories*. Princeton, NJ: Princeton University Press.

Cheniki, Ahmed. 2002. *Le Théâtre en Algérie: Histoire et enjeux*. Aix-en-Provence, France: Edisud.

Cheniki, Ahmed. 2006. *Vérités du théâtre en Algérie*. Oran, Algeria: Editions Dar el Gharb.

Cheurfi, Ahmed. 2007. *Dictionnaire encyclopédique de l'Algérie*. Rouiba, Algeria: Editions ANEP.

Chikh, Bouamrane, and Djidjelli Mohamed. 2000. *Scouts musulmans algériens (1935–1955)*. Algiers, Algeria: Dar El-Oumma.

Clancy-Smith, Julia A. 1994. *Rebel and Saint: Muslim Notables, Populist Protest, Colonial Encounters (Algeria and Tunisia, 1800–1904)*. Berkeley: University of California Press.

Cole, Joshua. 2009. " 'To Each His Own Audience': Performing Politics and Culture in Interwar French Algeria." Paper delivered at the Middle East Studies Association annual meeting, November 23, Boston.

Cole, Joshua. 2014. "A chacun son public: Politique et culture en Algérie des années 1930." *Sociétés & Représentations* 38: 21–51.

Colonna, Fanny. 1993. "Comment ruser avec l'uniformité." In *Etre marginal au Maghreb*, by Fanny Colonna and Zakya Daoud, 3–10. Paris: Editions Centre national de Recherche Scientifique.

Colonna, Fanny. 1995. *Les Versets de l'invincibilité: Permanence et changements religieux dans l'Algérie contemporaine*. Paris: Presses de la Fondation Nationale des Sciences Politiques.

Colonna, Fanny, ed. 1996a. "Algérie, la fin de l'unanimisme: Débats et combats des années 80 et 90." Special issue, *Monde Arabe Maghreb-Machrek* 154.

Colonna, Fanny. 1996b. "Radiographie d'une société en mouvement." In "Algérie, la fin de l'unanimisme: Débats et combats des années 80 et 90," ed. F. Colonna, special issue, *Monde Arabe Maghreb-Machrek* 154: 4–10.

Colonna, Fanny, and Zakya Daoud, eds. 1993. *Etre marginal au Maghreb*. Paris: Editions Centre national de Recherche Scientifique.

Comaroff, Jean, and John Comaroff, eds. 1999. *Civil Society and the Critical Imagination in Africa: Critical Perspectives.* Chicago: University of Chicago Press.

Commins, David Dean. 1990. *Islamic Reform: Politics and Social Change in Late Ottoman Syria.* New York: Oxford University Press.

Cooper, Frederick, and Ann Laura Stoler. 1997. *Tensions of Empire: Colonial Cultures in a Bourgeois World.* Berkeley: University of California Press.

Cornell, Vincent J. 1998. *Realm of the Saint: Power and Authority in Moroccan Sufism.* Austin: University of Texas Press.

Dermenghem, Emile. 1954. *Le Culte des saints dans l'Islam maghrébin.* Paris: Gallimard.

De Tocqueville, Alexis. 2003. *Democracy in America and Two Essays on America.* London: Penguin.

Falk Moore, Sally. 1977. "Political Meetings and the Simulation of Unanimity: Kilimanjaro 1973." In *Secular Ritual,* ed. Sally Falk Moore and Barbara G. Myerhoff, 151–172. Assen, The Netherlands: Van Gorcum.

Fernandez, James W. 1965. "Symbolic Consensus in a Fang Reformative Cult." *American Anthropologist* 67(4): 902–929.

Glasser, Jonathan. 2012. "Edmond Yafil and Andalusi Musical Revival in Early 20th-Century Algeria." *International Journal of Middle East Studies* 44:671–692.

Goffman, Erving. 1959. *The Presentation of Self in Everyday Life.* Garden City, NY: Doubleday.

Goodman, Jane E. 2005. *Berber Culture on the World Stage: From Village to Video.* Bloomington: Indiana University Press.

Habermas, Jürgen. (1962) 1991. *The Structural Transformation of the Public Sphere: An Inquiry into the Category of Bourgeois Society.* Cambridge, MA: MIT Press.

El-Hakim, Sherif. 1978. "The Structure and Dynamics of Consensus Decision-Making." *Man,* n.s., 13(1): 55–71.

Hann, Chris. 2004. "In the Church of Civil Society." In *Exploring Civil Society: Political and Cultural Contexts,* ed. Marlies Glasius, David Lewis, and Hakan Seckinelgin, 44–50. London: Routledge.

Hann, Chris, and Elizabeth Dunn, eds. 1996. *Civil Society: Challenging Western Models.* London: Routledge.

Huntington, Samuel. 1993. "The Clash of Civilizations?." *Foreign Affairs* (Summer): 22–49.

Julien, Charles-André. 1964. *Histoire de l'Algérie contemporaine: La Conquête et les débuts de la colonisation (1827–1871).* Paris: Presses Universitaires de France.

Kaddache, Mahfoud. 1993. *Histoire du nationalisme algérien.* Vol. 1. Algiers, Algeria: Entreprise nationale du livre.

Karlström, Mikael. 1996. "Imagining Democracy: Political Culture and Democratisation in Buganda." *Africa* 66(4): 485–505.

Lanfry, Jacques, ed. (1946) 1959. *L'Assemblée du Village.* Vol. 280. Trans. J. Degezelle. Fort National, Algeria: Fichier de Documentation Berbère.

Liverani, Andrea. 2008. *Civil Society in Algeria: The Political Functions of Associational Life*. London: Routledge.

Mahé, Alain. 2001. *Histoire de la Grande Kabylie XIXe–XXe siècles: Anthropologie historique du lien social dans les communautés villageoises*. Paris: Bouchène.

Mamdani, Mahmood. 1996. *Citizen and Subject: Contemporary Africa and the Legacy of Late Colonialism*. Princeton, NJ: Princeton University Press.

Mamouchi, Brahim. n.d. "Mémoires, Brahim Mamouchi, Professeur de Musique." Unpublished ms.

McDougall, James. 2006. *History and the Culture of Nationalism in Algeria*. Cambridge: Cambridge University Press.

Mehta, Uday S. 1999. *Liberalism and Empire: A Study in Nineteenth-Century British Liberal Thought*. Chicago: University of Chicago Press.

Merad, Ali. 1999. *Le Réformisme musulman en Algérie de 1925 à 1940: Essai d'histoire religieuse et sociale*. Algiers, Algeria: Les Éditions El-Hikma.

Merdaci, Abdelmadjid. 2007. "Djam'iyat Ettarbiya Oua Etta'lim (1930–1957): Au carrefour des enjeux identitaires." *Insaniyat* 35–36 (January–June): 97–107.

Merdaci, Abdelmadjid. 2008. *Dictionnaire des musiques citadines de Constantine*. Constantine, Algeria: Les Éditions du Champ Libre.

Murphy, William. 1990. "Creating the Appearance of Consensus in Mende Political Discourse." *American Anthropologist* 92(1): 24–41.

Rahal, Malika. 2007. "Prendre parti à Constantine: L'UDMA de 1946–1956." *Insaniyat* 35–36 (January–June): 63–77.

Roberts, Hugh. 2003. *The Battlefield, Algeria 1988–2002: Studies in a Broken Polity*. London: Verso.

Rosanvallon, Pierre. 2007. *The Demands of Liberty: Civil Society in France since the Revolution*. Trans. Arthur Goldhammer. Cambridge, MA: Harvard University Press.

Roth, Arlette. 1967. *Le Théâtre algérien de langue dialectale, 1926–1954*. Paris: Maspéro.

Ruedy, John. 1992. *Modern Algeria: The Origins and Development of a Nation*. Bloomington: Indiana University Press.

Sampson, Steven. 1996. "The Social Life of Projects: Importing Civil Society to Albania." In *Civil Society: Challenging Western Models*, ed. Chris Hann and Elizabeth Dunn, 121–142. London: Routledge.

Scheele, Judith. 2007. "Recycling Baraka: Knowledge, Politics, and Religion in Contemporary Algeria." *Comparative Studies in Society and History* 49(2): 304–328.

Singer, Milton. 1958. "From the Guest Editor." *Journal of American Folklore* 71(281): 191–204.

Snyder, Katherine A. 2001. "Power and Politics among the Iraqw of Tanzania." *Africa* 71(1): 128–148.

Wallerstein, Immanuel. 2003. "Citizens All? Citizens Some! The Making of the Citizen." *Comparative Studies in Society and History* 3:650–679.

Wehr, Hans. (1979) 1994. *The Hans Wehr Dictionary of Modern Written Arabic*. Ed. J. M. Cowan. Urbana, IL: Spoken Language Services.

White, Jenny B. 1996. "Civic Culture and Islam in Urban Turkey." In *Civil Society: Challenging Western Models*, ed. Chris Hann and Elizabeth Dunn, 143–154. London: Routledge.

8 CREEDAL MONOLOGISM AND THEOLOGICAL ARTICULATION IN THE MENNONITE CENTRAL COMMITTEE

Philip Fountain

Monological Theology?

In July 2013, anthropologist Jon Bialecki uploaded a blog post entitled "Anthropology and Theology, Difference and the Monological." Included was the following:

> There seems to be a big push as of late to take up Joel Robbins' challenge regarding the relationships between theology and anthropology.[1] There are several pieces in the pipeline suggesting that anthropology would do well to take up theology as offering useful insights. The problem with this is that theology tends to be monological, and while it would be going too far to say that anthropology is solely about human difference, that certainly is one of the poles that gives shape to the field. If we take up theology as having insights for different aspects of human behavior, then that pole collapses [and] we end up trying to explain a variable with a universal, which is analytically misguided.

What interests me here is Bialecki's warning that anthropologists should be wary about theology, and more specifically his reason for

---

1. Bialecki refers to Robbins's (2006) article on the "awkward" relationship between anthropology and theology. Robbins's paper has indeed inspired a remarkable series of anthropological engagements with theology. See Howell 2007; Fountain 2013; Fountain and Lau 2013; Meneses et al. 2014; and Tomlinson 2014. This literature has been matched with theological engagements with anthropology. See Jørgensen 2011; Scharen and Vigen 2011; Scharen 2012; Ward 2012; and Banner 2014.

advising caution: theology's propensity for (misguided) monologism. I suggest that the argument that theology inclines toward monologism is, impulsively or instinctively, broadly shared among contemporary anthropologists.[2] Given the formative nature of the separation from Christian theology undertaken by early leading anthropologists (Larsen 2014), this ongoing dismissal of theology should be seen as an active reinscribing of a founding myth of the discipline. The identification of theology-as-monologic, and its negation on the basis of that analysis, reverberates with the echoes of Enlightenment critiques of religion.

Against this line of argument it is worth recalling that Mikhail Bakhtin, the preeminent philosopher of dialogue, imagined theology in a rather different light. Ruth Coates (1999: 21) argues that while the Christian elements have been "suppressed" in scholarly treatments of Bakhtin's work, Bakhtin nevertheless was deeply indebted to—and, it could be argued, thoroughly fixated on—Christian theology. His famous analysis of the dialogic concept emerged out of his understanding of the relationship between people and God. The equally celebrated notion of carnival derived from The Feast of Fools of Catholic tradition and remained indelibly associated with these roots. For Bakhtin, "the gospel, too, is carnival" (Coates 1999: 8).

Yet Bakhtin clearly also adhered to a forthright anticlericalism and regarded certain forms of theological discourse as inimical to carnivalesque laughter, irony, parody, and indeterminacy. Some forms of theological articulation are, indeed, presented as bona fide monologues. Particular genres of theological articulation appear monological because they are performed to look that way. But in analyzing such monological performances two analytical temptations should be resisted. First, we should not assume that such monologic performances are representative of theological discourse as such, and therefore attention must be given to differences within theology. Second, we also should not simply take monological performances at face value. This carries the implication that analysis should focus on practices of monological construction. Accordingly, Bialecki's (2011: 680) earlier analysis of Christian language ideologies—that "Christian language is not as monolithic an object as it may first appear to be"—is, I think, right on the mark because it calls for methodological attentiveness beyond mere appearances.

---

2. This is not to say that this excerpt is a definitive summary of Bialecki's thought on the subject. As a blogpost, it should be read as "occasional," which may in part account for its particularly sharp juxtaposition of the two disciplines. Importantly, a number of Bialecki's published papers characterize theology in quite a different light, as involving the co-presence of monologism and dialogism (see esp. Bialecki 2011, 2014a, 2014b, and his chapter in this volume). The original blogpost also includes the disclaimer that monologism "isn't a problem with all theology," and Pentecostal theologian Amos Yong is presented as an example.

This chapter is an ethnography of the articulation of Christian theology. Rather than presuming that theological discourse has an inherent propensity for monologue, I seek to analyze the ways in which theological forms are expressed, negotiated, and conversed with. I examine both the practices of theological articulation and its avoidance—each of which should be seen, I argue, as a discursive strategy. My central concern is to explore how theological articulation works in practice. To do so I focus on a specific genre of theological discourse: the creed.

The Creedal Form

In his seminal analysis of *Christian Moderns*, Webb Keane (2007: 67–72) presents a nuanced analysis of what he calls the "creed paradigm." His approach is to look at "the creed and its implications" as part of a wider investigation into the semiotic ideologies of Protestant, and more specifically Calvinist, Christianity.[3] My analysis of the creedal form draws on Keane's approach and, as with Keane, my appreciation for the creed has been greatly enhanced by the writings of doctrinal historian Jaroslav Pelikan. In *Credo*, his monumental historical assessment of the creeds, Pelikan (2003: 7) observes the "sheer repetitiveness" of creeds over time.[4] Later creedal statements frequently reference, quote, and incorporate earlier creeds, especially the Apostle's Creed and the Niceno-Constantinopolitan Creed.[5] Creeds constitute a particular genre of theological articulation and they share a similar aesthetic. Although there is some variation among creeds and

---

3. Keane argues that the creedal form is "a characteristic practice of Christianity" (2007: 67) and "unique to the evangelizing, scripture-based religions" (69). However, he also notes that parallel semiotic forms can be identified in the American Pledge of Allegiance, the UN Universal Declaration of Human Rights, and the Boy Scout's oath. These connections are illustrative of genealogical continuities: "Such small, repeated, habitual semiotic practices are some of the ways in which the capillary effects of historical forces can be felt well beyond the category of religion as conventionally understood" (76).

4. Creeds make "the same points over and over again, often in the same esoteric and archaic terminology, citing the same biblical passages as proof texts, and pronouncing the same condemnations upon the same old heresies (or upon each other's new heresies)—and all with the same sense of total self-confidence and utter rectitude" (Pelikan 2003: 7).

5. The Apostle's Creed was an eighth-century reworking of The Roman Symbol, a baptismal creed used in Rome since the second century. It has attained "near-universality" as a statement of Christian faith (Pelikan and Hotchkiss 2003a: 667–668). Between 325 and 787 C.E. a series of influential ecumenical councils were held which, taken together, produced an authoritative precedent for creedal discourse. The Second Ecumenical Council was convened in Constantinople in 381 and produced the Niceno-Constantinopolitan Creed. This council expanded on the earlier Nicene Council of 325, and was also preoccupied with the language for understanding Trinitarianism (Pelikan and Hotchkiss 2003a: 155–156, 160–161).

related "confessions," "symbols," and statements of faith, it is through these common features that the creedal form is identifiable.[6]

Creeds are structured by a blow-by-blow progression, which is sometimes enumerated and which details a formulaic codified listing (Keane 2007: 70). They are concise and systematic renditions of the core propositions of the faith. That "religion" today is frequently thought to be propositional in nature and to be primarily concerned with matters of belief, as Talal Asad (1993: 40–41) has argued, is in no small measure due to the normative role that creeds have played in establishing imaginations of the nature of Christianity (which has frequently been taken as the archetypal form of religion). While, as Pelikan (2003: 130–136) points out, creeds have scriptural antecedents, including the Jewish *Shema*[7] and various declarations in the Gospels and epistles that may have been used within (or as) early liturgies, it is nevertheless also the case that most Christian Scripture is recorded in narrative or poetic genres, rather than as propositional doctrine (Anderson 2004: 51).[8]

Concomitant with their propositional form, creeds also deploy radically brief, minimalist language. Creeds are summaries, condensed versions of what are invariably expansive and complex ideas.[9] They seek to index these concerns without unwieldy explication, and frequently also via scriptural citation. Their concise "modular form" renders them highly portable, and indeed creeds have proved adept at traveling across time and space (Keane 2007: 69; see also Ingram 2014). Their minimalist brevity leads to a related density. Creeds are intense distillations

---

6. Dyck (1985: 15–16) argues that creeds and confessions ought to be differentiated, with the latter decidedly less monological than the former: "creeds tend to denote timeless, classic, and universal statements . . . [whereas] Confessions tend to be more particularistic, personal, and occasional, that is, written for a specific purpose at a particular time and place." However, it is not always clear that this distinction holds in practice. Moreover, as Pelikan (2003: 458) argues, the demarcation between the two is "somewhat arbitrary and historically inconsistent." In any case, the similarities are such that they may be regarded as constituting a single creedal genre.

7. "Hear, O Israel: The LORD is our God, the LORD alone" (Deut. 6:4).

8. Pelikan seeks to diminish the distance separating dogma and Scripture in order to argue for their essential continuity. He therefore regards creeds as being propelled by the inner logics of Christianity that "require that there be some sort of formula for the confessing of that faith" (2003: 124). See especially his commentary on *Acts* (2005), which brings the narrative text into direct dialogue with the Nicene-Chalcedonian creedal tradition. But while creeds and Scripture should not be seen as occupying opposing positions, and while there are clear continuities of substantive content and terminology, it is nevertheless also the case that in terms of genre much of Scripture—even the creedal fragments Pelikan identifies—are very different kinds of discourse than the creeds.

9. If not unspeakable. See, e.g., Sarah Coakley (2013) on the long history of apophatic theology and contemplative practice for understandings of the Trinity, which she argues deserves attention alongside institutional concern with creedal articulation.

of concepts and words that are deemed indispensable. Creedal language bears substantial moral weight and much is invested in the precise choice of terminology. The classic case in point is the Filioque controversy of the sixth century, which concerned changes to the formulation of Trinitarianism in the Niceno-Constantinopolitan Creed. The disputation resulted in enduring schism between the Eastern and Western Church. As this example amply illustrates, there is an "utter seriousness" that inheres in the creedal form, such that they are treated "as, quite literally, a matter of life and death" (Pelikan 2003: 70). Their solemnity is further enhanced by the fact that creeds are, implicitly though sometimes also entirely explicitly, organized attempts at boundary-making.[10] The effect of these dynamics is to evoke a peculiarly authoritative tone, and indeed creedal statements are generally only taken as definitive after they are formally adopted by an ecclesial hierarchy. Creeds are "authorizing discourses" that seek to subject doctrine to "a unified authority" (Asad 1993: 37).

It is not hard to see, therefore, how the creed could be imagined as an archetypal monologic form. Perhaps even more than the epic, the creed appears as an anti-novel in Bakhtin's (1981: 3–40) sense: it is wrapped in an undeniable "official air"; it maintains a "rigidity and canonic quality"; it appears "completed, conclusive and immutable" and resembles "an utterly finished thing"; it is fixing and static rather than "unfolding"; and it lacks a sense of comedic laughter and ludic excess.

The authoritative and monovocal register of the creed is performed in their use within liturgies of worship. In the context of church ritual, where the creed is spoken in unison with the entire congregation following not only the same words but also the same tone, tempo, and rhythm, creedal recitation enacts a communal singularity. The refrains "I believe" or "We believe" perform and embody a monological script which leaves little space for diversity and differentiation. And yet, it is also within this liturgical context that the limits to the monologic ambitions of creedal forms also become apparent. These limitations emerge historically in the way in which liturgy and doctrine have been indexed with each other through a "creative interplay" (Johnson 2013: 128).[11] The communal nature of creedal

---

10. Though see also Chris Anderson's (2004: 166–167) suggestion that "dogma exists to prevent dogmatism," precisely because the heresy which dogma seeks to prevent is inherently reductionist: "Doctrine exists to establish boundaries so broad that what is most excluded is the effort to exclude, the effort to reduce. This is what all the heresies have sought to do, to reduce the mystery of Jesus Christ, from one end or the other, to flatten the vertical beam or raise the horizontal, to reduce the man to a God or the God to a man rather than keeping that paradox and mystery intact."

11. Johnson (2013: 131) argues that the Early Church used creeds primarily for prebaptismal catchesis and baptism and it was only in the sixth century at Constantinople and the eleventh century at Rome that the Niceno-Constantinopolitan Creed was included in Eucharistic

recitation also introduces a marked linguistic ambiguity. Drawing on Bakhtin and Wittgenstein, Keane's (2007: 71) insights are germane:

> There is an apparent paradox here, since the creed takes the *form* of a proposition, and thus seems to put the speaker in an exterior third-person relationship to her own beliefs, as that of a subject to an object world. As Wittgenstein remarks, belief statements are peculiar since they seem to invite the notion of having more than one voice: "'Judging from what I say, *this* is what I believe.' . . . One would have to fill out the picture with behaviour indicating that two people were speaking through my mouth." . . . The sense of paradox, however, depends on a prior normative linguistic ideology that one speaker should have only one voice.

A polyvocality inheres within creedal articulation. The trajectory of the creedal form might be monological, but in its performance this begins to unravel. The observation that creeds are only ever articulated in the midst of multiple competing alternatives further enhances the pertinence of this insight. The earliest creeds sought to delineate between orthodox and heterodox positions, thereby inscribing this recognition of plurality within their very text.[12]

Creedal multiplicity has only increased over time. The Reformation in particular sparked a remarkable profusion of creeds such that creedal assent today is enacted only "after Babel" (cf. Steiner 1975). Certainly, Mennonites have displayed a remarkable propensity for creed-making during and after the Reformation. Because of this recent proliferation, the creed and close correlates are often regarded as illuminating a particularly modern dynamic. Although the *longue durée* of Christian creedal construction clearly complicates this association, it is nevertheless not without its merits. Attention to changing patterns of creedal use over time at the very least facilitates attentiveness to the different sorts of ways that creeds have been deployed and interpreted.

---

liturgy. Nevertheless, even prior to formal incorporation the influence of creeds was apparent in liturgy. Likewise, the formal creeds drew upon liturgical practices for their terminology and structure. See also Banner (2014: 174–175), for whom the inclusion of creeds within the rituals of worship was a "liturgical happenstance with its origins in the rough and tumble of early Byzantine ecclesial politics."

12. For example, the First Ecumenical Council of 325 c.e. was convened to combat the Arian heresy which held that Christ was created and that there was a time in which Christ did not exist. The opposition to Arianism was inscribed into The Creed of Nicaea through the emphasis on "the Lord Jesus Christ . . . [as] true God from true God, begotten not made" as well as within the final sentence: "And those who say 'there once was when he was not,' and 'before he was begotten he was not,' and that he came to be from things that were not, or from another hypostasis or substance, affirming that the Son of God is subject to change or alteration—these the catholic and apostolic church anathematizes" (Pelikan and Hotchkiss 2003a: 155–156, 159).

Theological Articulation in the Mennonite Central Committee

My key concern in this chapter is to examine how theological articulation works in practice. To do so I examine three case studies. Two are episodes in the history of the Mennonite Central Committee (MCC). MCC is a North American peace, justice, and development organization in the Anabaptist tradition. The third case concerns Christian Aid Ministries (CAM), another Anabaptist service organization. In 2007-2008, I carried out 22 months of ethnographic fieldwork focused on MCC, primarily in the context of Indonesia. A central line of inquiry over the course of this research was to examine how Christian theologies of service were enacted in the practices of the organization.

A distinctive feature of MCC is that it is saturated in Christian symbolism. MCC's logo—in MCC slang fondly known as "the pregnant pigeon" (see figure 8.1)—combines images of cross and dove which are thick with scriptural allusions. MCC publicity material frequently refers to biblical texts and deploys certain keywords—"service," "love," "peace," "non-resistance"—which are pivotal in the ethical theology of the historically pacifist Mennonites.[13] Moreover, donors are appealed to in explicitly theological terms with donations being located as acts of Christian compassion for distant others.

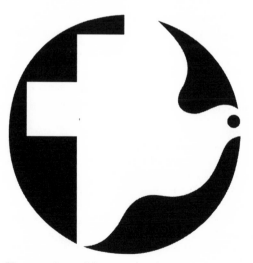

FIGURE 8.1 The "Pregnant Pigeon" logo

---

13. As with much Mennonite theology, biblical references focused particularly on the New Testament and especially the four Gospels. Mennonite readings of the Bible privilege the

---

BOX 8.1   The 'Rusty Nail' Mission Statement

MCC seeks to demonstrate God's love by working among people suffering from poverty, conflict, oppression and natural disaster;

MCC serves as a channel of interchange by building relationships that are mutually transformative;

MCC strives for peace, justice and dignity of all people by sharing our experiences, resources, and faith in Jesus Christ.

Source: MCC 1999; emphasis in original.

The organization's carefully crafted mission statement is explicit about MCC's Christian affiliation. The 1999 version of the mission statement (see Box 8.1), in what is colloquially known as the "rusty nail" document on account of a vertical band of reddish-brown adorning the front cover of the brochure,[14] locates MCC squarely within the Christian tradition, carrying out a specifically Christian agenda (Mennonite Central Committee 1999). The statement opens by framing MCC's work as a demonstration of "God's love" and closes by affirming that MCC is committed to "sharing . . . faith in Jesus Christ."

Christian ritual too permeates the organization. At a two-week orientation for new MCCers, which I attended in mid-2008 in Akron, Pennsylvania, we began each morning with devotions and participated in communal sung worship.[15] During our visit to Akron, my wife and I were asked to lead a devotion for the international staff team as part of their regular (optional) weekly practice.[16] A month earlier I attended MCC's (binational) Annual General Meeting (AGM) in Waterloo, Ontario, during which prayers were offered for MCC's work around the world. An opening speech at the AGM described the organization

---

person and teaching of Jesus Christ as the hermeneutical key through which to understand the rest of Scripture. John Howard Yoder (1984: 37) characterizes this emphasis on Jesus as "a canon within the canon." Myles Werntz (2014) describes Yoder's hermeneutics, especially as outlined in *The Politics of Jesus* (1972), as "axiological Christology," an approach which resonates broadly among Mennonites.

14. The "rusty nail" document replaced the previous mission statement known as the "purple egg."

15. See Fountain (2011) for further discussion of practices of orientation in MCC.

16. My wife, Iris, volunteered with MCC for the duration of my fieldwork and we attended this orientation together.

as an "outpost of the church." The summary of international programs provided by senior administrators explicitly referred to biblical texts; for example, Matthew 10:42, which refers to provision of a "cup of cold water," was used to support sending material aid, including canned meat, as a form of relief work.[17] We also heartily sang Christian hymns in four-part a cappella. Congregational singing is a prominent ritual practice among ethnic Mennonites. According to Mennonite academic and poet Julia Kasdorf (2009: 91), in such singing practices a Mennonite community "simultaneously produces and consumes an aesthetic whole." She continues, "Maybe in this, the quintessential communal activity, Mennonites most keenly feel what it is to *be* the Body of Christ."[18] The practice of singing together in harmony—orchestrating the intertwining of difference to produce aesthetic coherence—evokes and enacts an ideal ecclesial corporeality of a diverse-yet-common peoplehood.

Christian ritual and discourse likewise permeated the gatherings of the 20–30 person MCC team in Indonesia. The team meetings and team retreat, both annual events, included time for communal prayer, worship singing (including a cappella hymns in four-part harmony), theological reflection, communion, and ritual foot-washing alongside discussions about strategic plans and development projects. In the MCC Indonesia country office, the small group of expatriate and Indonesian staff concluded their meetings with communal prayer, with the prayer giver selected according to a rotating roster of the office staff.

That MCC Indonesia's communal space should be so pervaded by Christian language and practices is in large part explained by the vetting process through which prospective MCCers join the organization. Around the world, expatriate service workers with MCC are required to meet three "screens" to work with the organization: (1) exhibit a commitment to personal Christian faith, (2) be active members of a Christian church and (3) be committed to the teaching of nonviolent biblical peacemaking. In MCC Indonesia, the same screens were also used in hiring local staff. With this boundary policing mechanism adjudicating membership in the organization it is hardly surprising that communal practices in MCC Indonesia were pervasively Christian.

---

17. MCC operates a mobile canner which makes an annual circuit of Mennonite rural heartlands. Volunteers gather at each designated stop to prepare canned meat for relief. The process is frequently accompanied by Christian prayer and ritual. The can's label entextualizes Christian identification through the refrain "In the name of Christ" (Fountain 2014).

18. Music made by Mennonites is very diverse (Epp and Weaver 2005). Nevertheless, four-part a cappella music has a long history and particular resonance within many Mennonite communities. Without understatement, Kasdorf (2009: 90–91) notes the "remarkable quality of passion and joy that makes heavy Anabaptist bodies almost levitate during congregational singing."

And so, when I asked MCCers "What is MCC's theology of service?" I expected a fairly straightforward answer. My expectation was entirely misplaced. In their responses various MCCers confessed to not knowing what the answer was. Others said that although once they thought they knew what MCC's theology of service was, now they were actually engaged in MCC work in the field they were much less sure. Still others informed me that MCC had never articulated a definitive theology of service. While MCC was indeed infused with Christian discourse and ritual it had no formal, official, publicized, and systematically framed creedal statement that could serve as a benchmark of its Christian identity. Instead, MCC relied on vague allusion to a sacralized mission and a plethora of opaque spiritual associations.

Creeds have, in fact, historically held an awkward location in Mennonite church practices, with long-standing ambivalence among Mennonite communities about the creedal form (Roth 2005: 28–30).[19] For early Anabaptists this ambivalence reflected a theological critique of authoritarian and hierarchical church structures which backed up their orthodoxies through the use of coercive force (Urry 2006: 31–32). This unholy alliance is frequently dismissed by Mennonite theologians as "Constantinianism," and it is seen as a serious ecclesial error (Yoder 1984: 135–147). The Mennonite critique of creeds was also informed by a broader Protestant embrace of *sola scriptura*, such that Mennonite biblicism frequently downplayed the authority of (extra-biblical) creedal statements. This is apparent, for example, within the anti-creedalism of the Church of the Brethren, an Anabaptist denomination, which historically identified itself as having "no creed but the Bible" (Longnecker 2007). Another criticism of the creed is that the focus on propositional belief downplays ethics and practices: the Mennonite movement "was much more an ethical response than a creedal one" (Redekop 1989: 55). Indeed, Mennonite confessions often include attention to faithful practice as well as correct belief with Amish and Old Order Mennonite *Ordnung* (discipline, rules) providing prime examples.

As these critiques suggest, a recurring concern among Mennonites is creedal monologism. Discussing the adoption of the *Confession of Faith in a Mennonite Perspective* in 1995 by the (now amalgamated) General Conference Mennonite Church and the Mennonite Church, Susan Biesecker-Mast (2007) examines an "inherent tension" between imperatives to clarify and "fix" convictions in a timeless authoritative text and attempts to leave space for messianic rupture and for confessing "God's truth-on-the-move" which confounds all attempts to nail it down.[20] Leading Mennonite theologian John Howard Yoder exemplified this

---

19. For historical discussion of Mennonite creeds and confessions, see especially Loewen 1985; Neff et al. 1989; Pelikan 2003: 466–472; and Urry 2006: 17–38. Loewen (1985) and Pelikan and Hotchkiss (2003b) both also include full texts of various Anabaptist confessions.

20. On the *Confession of Faith in a Mennonite Perspective*, see also Finger 2007; Mathies 2007; and Wright 2007.

creedal quandary by affirming Nicene and Chalcedonian orthodoxy but also adopting a "narrative and relativizing approach" to the creeds. Yoder argued against the anti-creedalism of some of his co-religionists, but he proposed not less but rather the production of more creeds so as to affirm that no creed "should be a last word or filter between us and the Scriptures" (Parler 2012: 75–99). And indeed, despite their hesitations and even in their ambivalence, Mennonites have been remarkably prodigious producers of creedal statements with Mennonites constructing and affirming many different confessions over the years, so much so that this proliferation is rightly seen as ludic in its excess.[21] So, why did MCC lack any such statement? Archival research in North America furnished some possible answers.

A Missiology for MCC

In the early 1990s, Ray Brubacher, at the time Director of MCC's Overseas Services, published a short article in the internal MCC newsletter *Intercom* calling on the organization to develop a formal missiology.[22] Brubacher's (1991) article, titled "A Missiology for MCC," was not atypical for the newsletter. Rather than a formal expression of official policy or a polished declaration of normative intent, Brubacher's tone, content, and style were conversational. The article sought to evoke discussion, and the substantial quantity of files in the archives in response attests to a vibrant and vigorous correspondence.[23]

In his article, Brubacher states that as a "personal interest" he had intended for a while to examine MCC's missiology and, after receiving encouragement from other MCCers, he began considering the possibility of an "institutional exercise" in the matter. Brubacher took for granted that MCC had a Christian identity. He was, however, concerned with whether this identity was properly grounded in a systematic, thorough, and coherent theology. "I sense sometimes," wrote Brubacher, "that we draw up plans using social science theories and then paste

---

21. "It is generally true that the Anabaptists and later Mennonites have been and are non-creedal" writes Cornelius Dyck (1985) in the Foreword to Loewen's compendium of Mennonite Creeds, "It is surprising, therefore, to find that the Anabaptists and especially the Dutch Mennonites wrote many confessions . . . probably more than any of the other three Reformation traditions."

22. One way to understand missiology is a sustained reflection on the nature and practice of mission. It is generally conceived as a theological exercise.

23. The archival material I draw on in this section is drawn from Nancy Heisey's personal collection of documents, which she kindly gave me permission to peruse, and the official MCC files archived in Akron, Pennsylvania. Given the nature of the material, I have not used pseudonyms for authors of the archived documents.

a Bible verse at the end to make it feel religious. . . . I fear we sometimes run the risk of proof-texting." Brubacher's concern was primarily with MCC's work in the field. A key advantage of clearly articulating an organizational theology is the provision of "adequate guidance" to field workers in carrying out their work for a "church agency that does not plant churches."[24] However, Brubacher assumed that in addition to emerging from the contexts "in which we live and work" the planned missiology would also draw from an "understanding of who we are" and the distinctives of the Mennonite tradition of biblical reflection. Although the exact genre of this desired missiology is not clearly articulated, a creedal statement was one possibility.

With the publication of Brubacher's article the process of constructing a missiology for MCC began. A missiology file was initiated to house the accumulating documents and correspondence that arose in the wake of Brubacher's reflections. Field workers, church leaders, and MCC administrators were invited to contribute their views, and many did so with enthusiasm. Discussions were held and meetings were called. Well-known Mennonite missiologist Wilbert Shenk was invited to Akron to present a one-day seminar to MCC staff on Mennonite missiology and mission praxis. The results of a survey of MCC workers' values and perspectives, conducted by graduate students in development studies at Eastern University, were added to the mix.[25]

The actual task of drafting the missiological statement was delegated to Nancy Heisey. Heisey was well placed to guide the process given her many years of work with MCC, her familiarity with Anabaptist theology including ongoing graduate studies at Eastern Mennonite Seminary, and her previous involvement in a major two-year listening project seeking to learn from the voices of those on the receiving-end of MCC and Mennonite mission board activity. Heisey wrote four drafts and each was reviewed and critiqued. The drafts were analytical, rather

---

24. In a letter to Heisey, who was assigned the task of writing the draft missiological statements, Brubacher (1992) wrote: "I would like the statement to be above all practical and useful as opposed to theoretical. I would like the final product to be a useful document for all workers within MCC. I see it primarily as an internal document, but if, at the end, there seems to be reason to share it more broadly, we can then make that decision. . . . [T]he document should help all of us understand our role in the world as a mission agency with the rather unique mandate not to plant churches (although to say that reflects a fairly narrow view of mission and of church)."

25. See the "Research Survey Report on MCC Missiology Dialogue" by Foster and colleagues (1992), in the MCC archives. A similarly protracted and intensively dialogical process was a feature of the lead-up to the *Confession of Faith in a Mennonite Perspective* in 1995: "The new confession of faith was written amidst extensive conversation, ongoing debate, critical exchange, and responsive revision not only within the joint committee [assigned to oversee the process], which met often during those *ten years*, but also across the church" (Biesecker-Mast 2007; emphasis added).

than merely prescriptive. While parts use abstracted, depersonalized language, other sections make use of the first person pronoun and assume a personal tone. Accordingly, in a letter to John A. Lapp, then MCC Executive Secretary, sent toward the end of the drafting process, Heisey (1993b) wrote that much of the text could simply be filed as "my end-of-term report."

Although the title of the final draft—"MCC Missiological Statement: Draft 4" (Heisey 1993a)—appears to indicate a formal organization-wide document, Heisey quickly dispels such preconceptions (left open by Brubacher's initial *Intercom* article); the draft is merely "an in-house missiological working document." Written for an internal audience, devoid of formal status and lacking a sense of definitive standing, the missiological statement had become more modest in intent. The purpose of the text was to "codify . . . who MCC is and why we do what we do." Although the statement has a number of distinctly creedal features, ambiguity over the genre of the statement is never entirely resolved. It is part theological essay, part historical survey, and—with its brevity, modular and systematic form, and enumerated paragraphs—it is also part creed.

In her text, Heisey addresses two long-standing MCC mottos: "In the Name of Christ" and "A Christian resource for meeting human needs." Both were indicative of how MCC is embedded in a Christian identity and its work premised on the basis of a tacit Trinitarian theology. As an "inter-Mennonite" organization, MCC had played an important role in bringing together diverse Anabaptist groups. Still, despite this Christian identity, Heisey suggests that MCC's work has historically been based in "action rather than theological reflection." Heisey proceeds to address a diverse set of concerns intended to help orient field practice. In these she charts a delicate route between the liberal-evangelical binary that has dominated twentieth-century missiological debate in North America.[26]

Despite being reworked multiple times, and despite a careful and sophisticated examination of theological concerns within MCC, Heisey's statement went no further than this fourth draft; it was never published and did not garner a wide readership. None of the MCCers I talked with during my field research

---

26. That is, Heisey avoids reducing Christian mission to just evangelistic "soul saving" or "societal transformation." The liberal-evangelical binary (and related, if not synonymous, distinctions between "ecumenical" and "mainline" vis-à-vis "conservative" and "fundamentalist") is an inadequate frame for analyzing twentieth-century North American Protestantism (Wellman 2008). While this distinction was influential in shaping debates and practices, both "evangelical" and "liberal" camps were diverse and shifted over time (Bosch 1991). For recent anthropological analyses of liberals and evangelicals in North America, including their relationships with each other, see especially Bielo 2011; Elisha 2011; Harding 2001; Klassen 2011; and Luhrmann 2012. Mennonites have been influenced by both tendencies but, as per Heisey's approach, have often sought to weave between each (see Shenk 2000; and also Rempel 2000; Sawatsky 2006).

in Indonesia and only a very few in North America had ever heard of the failed project. After all the effort to produce the text of Heisey's carefully crafted statement, the process fizzled out. The conversations dried up. The missiology file was closed and the correspondence archived. The project of constructing a missiological statement was abandoned amid fading enthusiasm among all involved. Rather than clarifying its theology this was a disarticulation of MCC's theology of service. It was a proactive avoidance of a systematic, concise theological statement; an evasion of creedal clarity.

The documents in the file on the missiology of service hint at the reasons why the project was abandoned. As the process went on frequent doubts were posed about its worth and viability. In a letter to Brubacher and other MCC administrators just prior to submitting her final draft, Heisey (1993b) notes her own wavering support:

> I do want to underline what I said to Ray [Brubacher]. . . . That is, I am less and less convinced that a missiology statement is what MCC needs. More in-house conversation, absolutely yes. In some formal process, good! But an effort at definition that goes beyond the documents we have already hashed through seems to contradict what has been the genius of MCC's service vocation.

A similar tone is expressed in a letter from Brubacher (1993) to two senior MCC administrators. This was also one of the last pieces of correspondence to be archived into the missiology file. The letter provides Brubacher's guidance on how the statement should be read:

> Attached is a missiological statement written by Nancy Heisey. Although it is titled "MCC Missiological Statement" neither Nancy nor I claim this to be MCC's definitive statement. In fact, there are some who say MCC should not have one at all. Two reasons are given: 1) MCC is a flexible and adaptive entity and should not be tied to something fixed. 2) MCC should not do a definitive statement without extensive consultation with "the field" and its network of partnerships. I agree with number two, but have questions about number one. I feel that it is appropriate to work at a missiological statement even at an "in house" level. We do too little of that. Nancy's paper, for the time being, is an in house document for purposes of discussion and discernment by MCC persons, whatever their context (leadership or primary assignment).

Brubacher and Heisey's eventual hesitancy to pursue a formal theological articulation is revealing. MCC's "genius," in Heisey's account, is to fail to produce a comprehensive definition of its own theological identity and instead focus on enacting service. Brubacher's two reasons for not having a formal missiology are the need for flexibility in the field and the difficulty of adequately consulting all the appropriate stakeholders.

The attempt to articulate a missiology for MCC should be seen as an articulation of organizational policy. In order to understand this endeavor I turn, therefore, to David Mosse's (2005) study of development policy. According to Mosse, the purpose of development policy—defined broadly to include "all kinds of development models, project designs and strategies"—is not primarily to direct or guide an organization's practice (14). Instead, policy is oriented in the opposite direction. Development policy has the social task of "legitimation, persuasion, and enrolment" of a supporting constituency (21). Organizational policy is "a bid for political support" (35). However, for those constituencies that are amalgams of diverse and contradictory interests, effective policy cannot afford to be too explicit, too direct. Instead, it must be ambiguous and equivocal, deploying largely vacuous terms, such as "participation," to mediate between divergent interests (46). In so doing, otherwise incommensurable groups may all willingly participate by reading such buzzwords as conforming to their predilections.

As organizational policy, the crafting of a missiology for MCC failed on a number of fronts. It failed first as a consequence of providing too much clarity. The 11-page document was too specific, too detailed. It lacked those features that Mosse regards as essential to making policy work: ambiguity, opacity, vagueness. The problem was not that Heisey sought to chart a course in-between liberal and conservative theologies as such. It was, rather, that a course was charted at all. A clear theological statement potentially excludes existing MCC supporters who might not be willing to continue to support the particular theological stance provided. A substanceless missiology might have been practicable, but Brubacher didn't want a vacuous statement. He sought a document that could help guide MCC workers through ethical and theological challenges. The distance between guidance and ambiguity constituted an insurmountable obstacle.

MCC's problem was that it already had a defined constituency—the Mennonite "peoplehood" of the United States and Canada—and this constituency is marked with profound theological heterogeneity (Kraybill 2011). Within MCC too there are a variety of implicit missiologies (Green and Krabill 2011). Despite powerful coalescing forces, no attempt at theological clarity could succeed in enrolling these disparate groups. Theological candor was therefore antithetical to achieving "a high degree of convergence" among the "disparate interests" of this constituency.

The "Statement of Faith" of Christian Aid Ministries

The case of Christian Aid Ministries (CAM) provides a comparative example that further illuminates MCC's approach. CAM is a large Mennonite-Anabaptist aid agency founded in 1981 as a channel of relief aid for Beachy Amish, Old Order Amish, and conservative Mennonites. It is a direct competitor with MCC for those portions of the Mennonite constituency. CAM has expanded rapidly and now has a global reach across multiple continents.[27]

CAM's "statement of faith" is a remarkable list of twenty-three separate affirmations in explicit creedal form (see Box 8.2). The first four affirmations concern the Trinitarian nature of divinity and the centrality of the sacred scriptures—the "divinely inspired Word of God." These are followed by declarations on humanity (created by God but depraved by sin), salvation ("by grace through faith in Christ"), and the church ("those who are born again"). Ten ritual practices and prescriptions for behavior follow, including: the holy kiss, "the woman's head is to be veiled, and her hair uncut," modest personal appearance, a nonresistant lifestyle, and grounds for excommunication. The final section outlines belief in the Second Coming of Christ and the promise of "eternal bliss in heaven" for believers and "eternal damnation in hell" for the unrighteous. The statement resonates with adherents of a particular mix of traditional Anabaptist concerns, American fundamentalism, and cultural practices distinctive of conservative Mennonite and Amish sects. Here therefore is an example of an articulation of a forthright and systematic creedal monologue by an Anabaptist NGO.

Yet the statement is striking for how little of the content directly relates to the practices of delivering CAM's relief aid. Its lack of specificity in this area is such that it could easily be transferred without modification to an entirely different sector or organization. Indeed, the Statement is substantively the same as one previously published in the Beachy Amish publication *Calvary Messenger* and much of the content is a reworking of "the rather uniform progression" characteristic of earlier Anabaptist creeds (Loewen 1985: 35).[28] Clearly, this statement too is an example of theology-as-policy with the goal of articulation being to enroll a constituency rather than to dictate field practice. Whereas MCC's ambiguous

27. Nolt (2011: 144–152) notes that in 2008 CAM delivered material aid and other services to eighty-nine countries. Cash donations to CAM totaled $24.8 million, compared to $36.6 million to MCC that same year. But gift-in-kind contributions far outweighed this, amounting to 86% of contributions to CAM. Among these gifts are food stuffs (including canned meat), medical supplies, clothes, food parcels, Bibles, and doctrinal books.

28. Compare especially with the Brief Statement of Mennonite Doctrine, which is a summary of the Mennonite Confession of Faith adopted by Mennonite General Conference in 1963 (Loewen 1985: 78). While the order of the articles is somewhat different, and while the language on some points diverges, the two statements are substantively the same.

BOX 8.2 Christian Aid Ministries' Statement of Faith

1. **We believe** in one God, eternally existing as Father, Son, and Holy Spirit. Matthew 28:19; Galatians 4:4–6; Ephesians 2:6, 13–18; 1st John 5:1–13

2. **We believe** that Jesus Christ is the Son of God, and that He was conceived of the Holy Spirit and born of the virgin Mary. Luke 1:35; Matthew 1:20–25

3. **We believe** that the Holy Spirit convicts of sin, effects the New Birth, gives guidance in life, empowers for service, and enables perseverance in faith and holiness. John 16:7–11,13

4. **We believe** that the Bible is the divinely inspired Word of God, revealing God and His will, both in the Old and New Testaments. Luke 1:70; 2nd Timothy 3:16; 2nd Peter 1:20, 21

5. **We believe** that in the beginning God created all things. He made man in His own image, with a free will, a moral character, and a spiritual nature. Colossians 1:16,17; 1st John 1:1–13

6. **We believe** that man, through unbelief and disobedience fell into sin, bringing depravity and death upon the human race; that man as a sinner is self-centered and self-willed, unable to redeem himself. Romans 3:10–18,23, 5:12

7. **We believe** that there is one Mediator between God and man, the Man Christ Jesus, Who shed His blood and died on Calvary to redeem us from sin, was resurrected from the dead, ascended to heaven, and is sitting at the right hand of the Father interceding for us. John 3:16; Hebrews 9:12–14, 10:12; Colossians 1:20–22

8. **We believe** that salvation is by grace through faith in Christ—a free gift bestowed by God on all who believe in Christ, repent of their sins, are born again, and walk in newness of life. Ephesians 2:8,9; John 3:3,5; Romans 6:1–7, 10:9, 10

9. **We believe** that the church is the body of Christ, and that all those who are born again and walk in obedience to the Word of God constitute the true church of which Christ is the head. Ephesians 1:22,23; Colossians 1:18; 1st John 1:7; 1st Timothy 3:15

10. **We believe** that God provides the church with the necessary leadership, such as bishops, ministers, evangelists, and deacons, to shepherd the flock, teach the Word, administer the ordinances, and lead the church in the exercise of discipline. Ephesians 4:11–16

11. **We believe** that Christ commissioned the church to: evangelize the world, make disciples of all men and teach them to follow Him in a Biblical walk of life, and to minister to the needs of all people. Mark 16:15; Matthew 28:19,20; 1st John 3:17

12. **We believe** that those who repent and believe should be baptized with water as a symbol of: new birth, baptism of the Spirit, cleansing from sin, commitment to Christ, and separation from evil. Matthew 28:19; Acts 2:38, 10:44–48; 1st Peter 3:21

13. **We believe** that the church should observe the communion of the Lord's Supper as a symbol of His broken body and shed blood, in a common union of believers with Christ and one another. 1st Corinthians 10:16–21, 11:23–26

14. **We believe** that Christ taught both by example and by commandment that feet-washing is a symbol of brotherhood, service, and humility, and should be observed literally. John 13:3–17

15. **We believe** that the holy kiss should be practiced as a symbol of Christian love among the believers, brother with brother and sister with sister. Romans 16:16; 1st Peter 5:14

16. **We believe** that God has established unique roles of authority for man and woman. Therefore, a man's head is to be uncovered in praying and prophesying, and the woman's head is to be veiled, and her hair uncut, signifying their acceptance of God's order. 1st Corinthians 11:1–16

17. **We believe** that the anointing with oil, accompanied by the prayer of faith, is honored by God in the restoration of physical health, in accordance to His will. James 5:14,15

18. **We believe** that marriage is intended by God to be the union of one man and one woman for life, and that the believer shall marry only in the Lord. Hebrews 13:4; Mark 10:6–9

19. **We believe** that the personal appearance and lifestyle of Christian men and women should be modest, free from worldly fashion and adornment, maintaining simplicity in all areas of life, living as strangers and pilgrims in this world, seeking a city not made with hands, eternal in the heavens. Romans 12:1,2; James 4:4; 1st John 2:15–17

20. **We believe** that Christians should not take part in any destruction of human life, nor in any acts of retaliation. Instead, they should live a nonresistant lifestyle, demonstrating the love of Christ in their daily walk. Matthew 5:39–46; John 18:36; Romans 12:19–21

21. **We believe** that the church and state are ordained of God as separate entities in His divine plan, and that believers should honor rulers and be subject to their authority and pray for them. Romans 13:1–7; 1st Peter 2:13–17

22. **We believe** that the unrepentant, fallen brother or sister shall be excommunicated from the body of Christ in the spirit of love, and shall be received back into fellowship upon repentance and amendment of life. 1st Corinthians 5:1–13; 2nd Corinthians 6:14

23. **We believe** in the second coming of our Lord Jesus Christ, the blessed hope of believers, and that upon His return He will resurrect the righteous to eternal bliss in heaven, and the unrighteous to eternal damnation in hell. He will sit on the throne of His glory, judging all nations in the last day. 1st Thessalonians 4:16,17; Matthew 25:31–46

Source: CAM, https://christianaidministries.org; emphasis in original.

and unstated theology of service helped to recruit a diverse constituency, this operates in the opposite way. It is avowedly conservative and sectarian. Because CAM's constituency occupies a narrower niche, the work of enrolment through policy can afford to be much more specific. Those on the conservative end of the spectrum of MCC's supporters—perhaps frustrated with MCC's theological ambiguity and seeking a clearer statement of theological affinity—could be drawn to CAM's approach of unambiguous theological articulation.[29]

The contrasting approach of CAM vis-à-vis MCC illustrates different ways in which the creed can be treated. It also provides an example of some of the reasons for deploying monological forms. The sheer diversity of MCC's constituency required certain kinds of theological articulation to sustain support. CAM, as the more recent arrival, did not seek to engage the whole breadth of the Mennonite peoplehood but rather a specific and limited segment. It did so through creedal articulation.[30] But even while CAM's Statement of Faith enrolls conservative and traditionalist Amish and Mennonites, it does not constrict or guide the actual practices of relief work in any meaningful sense. The monologic in this case is deployed as a marker of difference, but this is directed primarily at a domestic constituency rather than in order to guide its field operations.

Shared Convictions

My final case returns to MCC. This episode took place after I had completed my fieldwork. During the final year of my fieldwork, MCC undertook an extensive organization-wide consultation process called "New Wine/New Wineskins" using a method of organizational analysis called Appreciative Inquiry. The stated

---

29. An even clearer, in fact decidedly blunt, statement of theological clarity is apparent in CAM's Billboard Evangelism program which, since 2006, has erected billboards across the United States. Signs have included such messages as "If you die tonight? Heaven or Hell. 855-FOR-TRUTH. John 3:35" (accompanied by images of fluffy white clouds and infernal flames) and "The Holy Bible. Inspired. Absolute. Final. 855-FOR-TRUTH. Psalm 119:89" (accompanied by an image of a black-covered Holy Bible). See https://christianaidministries.org/programs/6 and https://gospelbillboards.org/category/billboards/. Such billboards are ethically and theologically unimaginable within MCC.

30. Although CAM occupies a narrower niche in the Anabaptist spectrum, it too is an assemblage of different groups. In his brief history of CAM, Nolt (2011: 148) suggests that its "genius" is found in how it manages its own diverse constituency. In much the same way that MCC provides myriad avenues of service for its constituents, so too CAM has proliferated different mechanisms for participation: "Its promotional literature repeatedly emphasizes that donors can choose the type of projects they wish to support—in effect, implying that CAM does not determine a particular agenda so much as makes available an array of possibilities from which donors can choose."

goal was to reconfigure MCC for the twenty-first century.[31] In mid-2009, as one of the outcomes of this process, and for the first time in its history, MCC proposed to introduce a creedal statement of "convictions" as an officially sanctioned, publicly accessible theological articulation (see Box 8.3). These convictions, along with other reformulated statements of identity, were formally approved by the end of the year (Terichow 2009). This creedal statement affirmed a Trinitarian theology including an orthodox Christology and ecclesiology, and various ritual (baptism, worship, Lord's Supper) and ethical practices (service, peacemaking, seeking justice, caring for creation, sharing possessions). The adoption of this statement begged the question as to whether my analysis of MCC was being overtaken by events.

Of course, organizations are never static. They are always becoming. At times they follow expected paths and at others they assume unanticipated trajectories. Just because MCC had disarticulated its theology of service for almost ninety years, this was not a prescription for continuing to do so. This said, I came to see the adoption of the Shared Convictions statement as something rather more modest than the radical disjuncture it first appeared. Rather than negating the argument I had formed while working through the archives of the missiological project in the 1990s, this was in fact a perpetuation of the status quo. Three key issues are at stake.

First, the convictions statement was an example of masterful use of ambiguous language. It was not the kind of statement that would ensure conformity of theology or practice. The details were not clear and specific enough to be seen as especially normative. While the statement certainly identified those who owned the convictions as "Christian"—with explicit references to Christ, the Holy Spirit, the Church, Christian Scriptures, and various religious rituals—it did not provide any substantial advance on MCC's existing mission statement. With seven quite general statements, this document remained much less specific and extensive than CAM's weighty list of twenty-three edicts. By adopting this statement MCC continued to be sacralized in the same vague sorts of ways as previously.

Second, the statement was clearly not meant to provide any meaningful direction for MCC's field programs. Indeed, the statement itself was adopted verbatim from the Mennonite World Conference, the global umbrella group of Anabaptist-Mennonite churches, which in March 2006 approved the "Shared Convictions" document. This was the first statement of beliefs to be adopted by

---

31. Three questions were used to guide the consultations: "What is the task that God is calling MCC to in the 21st century (our purpose)? To whom is MCC accountable (who is the 'keeper of the MCC soul')? What is the appropriate structure for ensuring that the values and principles held by MCC are effectively expressed at every level and drive exemplary programming?"

BOX 8.3   Convictions

MCC is part of the larger mission of the church and embraces the "Shared Convictions" of global Anabaptists,* inspired by Anabaptists of the 16th century who modeled radical discipleship to Jesus Christ.

By the grace of God, we seek to live and proclaim the good news of reconciliation in Jesus Christ. As part of the one body of Christ at all times and places, we hold the following to be central to our belief and practice:

- God is known to us as Father, Son and Holy Spirit, the Creator who seeks to restore fallen humanity by calling a people to be faithful in fellowship, worship, service and witness.
- Jesus is the Son of God. Through his life and teachings, his cross and resurrection, he showed us how to be faithful disciples, redeemed the world, and offers eternal life.
- As a church, we are a community of those whom God's Spirit calls to turn from sin, acknowledge Jesus Christ as Lord, receive baptism upon confession of faith, and follow Christ in life.
- As a faith community, we accept the Bible as our authority for faith and life, interpreting it together under Holy Spirit guidance, in the light of Jesus Christ to discern God's will for our obedience.
- The Spirit of Jesus empowers us to trust God in all areas of life so we become peacemakers who renounce violence, love our enemies, seek justice, and share our possessions with those in need.
- We gather regularly to worship, to celebrate the Lord's Supper, and to hear the Word of God in a spirit of mutual accountability.
- As a world-wide community of faith and life we transcend boundaries of nationality, race, class, gender and language. We seek to live in the world without conforming to the powers of evil, witnessing to God's grace by serving others, caring for creation, and inviting all people to know Jesus Christ as Saviour and Lord.

In these convictions we draw inspiration from Anabaptist forebears of the 16th century, who modeled radical discipleship to Jesus Christ. We seek to walk in his name by the power of the Holy Spirit, as we confidently await Christ's return and the final fulfillment of God's kingdom.

* As adopted by Mennonite World Conference General Council, March 2006.

Source: MCC 2011.

leaders of the global Anabaptist church. Adopting the statement did not require any particular changes of missional practice among MCCers. It was not designed to operate as "a missiology for MCC" or a "theology of service" in the same sense as Brubacher had called for in *Intercom*.

Third, the adoption of shared convictions was clearly a political strategy of enrolment. At the time, one of the pressing issues facing MCC was the question of the extent to which it should engage in internationalization. This was closely related to attempts to broaden the understanding of the Mennonite "peoplehood" beyond North America and beyond ethnic Mennonites. Questions about whether MCC should be made accountable to a global Anabaptist body, and the Mennonite World Conference was the only viable candidate for this, rather than only to Canadian and American Mennonite churches, were being actively debated. During interviews in North America and Indonesia, this issue frequently emerged as a prominent concern. Many within MCC felt a strong moral imperative to rethink how a North American organization could interact Christianly with partners in developing countries. The wholesale adoption of Shared Convictions was symbolic of a wider process of attempting to realign MCC's relationship with global Anabaptism. These dynamics are made clear in an article by an MCC staff writer who notes that soon after Shared Convictions was adopted by MCC it was also proposed that MCC would "facilitate relationships between and among Anabaptist service agencies worldwide" (Walker 2011). This statement implicitly raises the question of global Anabaptist ownership. However, this goal was soon downgraded so that MCC merely sought to participate in a "Global Anabaptist Service Network." Regardless of the outcome of the Wineskins process, the adoption of this creedal statement was primarily a mechanism of political recruitment and a means of realigning MCC with other political-ecclesial shifts. The theological content of the statement was less important than the relationships it signaled and enabled.[32]

Because the statement's rhetoric was designed to be innocuous and thereby exclude as few as possible, and because many Canadian and American Mennonite churches had already accepted Shared Convictions as an official creed (among others), most of MCC's constituency was able accept the statement without difficulty. But while the introduction of Shared Convictions was largely a non-event, it was not entirely so. Some portions of MCC's constituency did respond

---

32. Compare with Biesecker-Mast's (2007) discussion of the political function of *The Confession of Faith in Mennonite Perspective*. The creation of this Confession was "crucial for constructing unity among the two denominations [General Conference Mennonite Church and the Mennonite Church] in preparation for merger and for sustaining unity within the new denomination, because it gave the church the experience of having one voice, one word, one authority to which it may turn as questions and issues inevitably arise."

critically. In 2013 the *Canadian Mennonite* magazine reported that the conservative Sommerfeld Mennonite Church, consisting of thirteen congregations in Manitoba, had decided to pull out of active participation in MCC Manitoba and MCC Canada (Braun 2013). Among the reasons given was that the Shared Convictions statement was not definitive enough in its language regarding the Trinity. Specifically, the statement "God is *known to us* as Father, Son and Holy Spirit" (emphasis added) was regarded as too vague, too innocuous. Desiring a more forthright proclamation of Trinitarian ontology (perhaps more in line with CAM's statement of faith), the Sommerfelders left the MCC family. The effect of articulating theology through creedal monologue was therefore divisive and disassembling of support for at least some portions of MCC's constituency, much as Heisey and Brubacher had anticipated two decades earlier.

Conclusion: Creeds, Theological Articulation, and the Monological Imagination

As a particular genre of theological articulation the creed presented both a problem and an opportunity for the Anabaptist service organizations discussed in this chapter. For most of MCC's history senior administrators have actively avoided adopting a formally sanctioned and normative statement of theological orthodoxy. Instead, they relied on vague allusion, polyvocality, proof texting, storytelling, and spiritual insinuation. Such strategies trumped monologue as effective practices for enrolling its constituency to participate in the organization. This avoidance of the creedal form was also an eliding of the monologic. In doing so, MCC drew on Anabaptist ambivalence toward authoritarian Christianity.

But the creed can also have its uses. CAM's statement of faith with its sectarian appeal has worked well for the organization, enabling the active enrollment of a particular Anabaptist constituency. MCC leadership implicitly accepted the potential usefulness of monologism in their adoption of Shared Convictions in 2009. In contrast to CAM, this statement's origins in the Mennonite World Conference worked against sharp demarcation. The statement was intended to be readily acceptable for as broad a range of Mennonites as possible. Yet even this broad statement could prove divisive, as is shown with the withdrawal of the Sommerfeld Mennonite Church from MCC. It is revealing, however, that both CAM and MCC's creedal articulations were not directed at field practices. The ownership of their respective creeds helped sacralize their organizations, but neither was aimed at shaping field practices. Creedal monologism was useful for some purposes but elsewhere other forms of theology—including non-propositional faith, ethical praxis, and active disarticulation—were put to work. Creedal articulation could be both fraught and compelling, divisive and assembling. It is in the tensions between these dynamics that monologism is put to work and where it meets its limits.

Acknowledgments

Grateful thanks for comments and suggestions on improving this paper from Bernardo Brown, Ray Brubacher, Michael Feener, Josh Gedacht, Patrick Guinness, Nancy Heisey, Julian Millie, and Matt Tomlinson. Earlier versions of this paper were presented at the 2010 Australian Anthropological Society Conference at Deakin University and in 2014 at the conference on The Monologic Imagination, Monash University. Attendance at the Deakin conference was possible through the Robyn Wood Travel Grant. Fieldwork was possible with generous grants from the Australian National University and the Religious Research Association's Constant H. Jacquet Award. Thanks especially to Mennonite Central Committee personnel for their participation in this research.

References

Anderson, Chris. 2004. *Teaching as Believing: Faith in the University*. Waco, TX: Baylor University Press.

Asad, Talal. 1993. *Genealogies of Religion: Discipline and Reasons of Power in Christianity and Islam*. Baltimore: Johns Hopkins University Press.

Bakhtin, Mikhail M. 1981. *The Dialogic Imagination: Four Essays*. Ed. Michael Holquist. Trans. Caryl Emerson and Michael Holquist. Austin: University of Texas Press.

Banner, Michael. 2014. *The Ethics of Everyday Life: Moral Theology, Social Anthropology, and the Imagination of the Human*. Oxford: Oxford University Press.

Bialecki, Jon. 2013. "Anthropology and Theology, Difference and the Monological." https://jonbialecki.com/2013/05/17/anthropology-and-theology-difference-and-the-monological/.

Bialecki, Jon. 2014a. "Does God Exist in Methodological Atheism? On Tanya Lurhmann's *When God Talks Back* and Bruno Latour." *Anthropology of Consciousness* 25(1): 32–52.

Bialecki, Jon. 2014b. "After the Denominozoic: Evolution, Differentiation, Denominationalism." *Current Anthropology* 55(S10): S193–S204.

Bielo, James S. 2011. *Emerging Evangelicals: Faith, Modernity, and the Desire for Authenticity*. New York: New York University Press.

Biesecker-Mast, Susan. 2007. "A Genealogy of the Confession of Faith in a Mennonite Perspective." *Mennonite Quarterly Review* 81(3): 371–397.

Bosch, David J. 1991. *Transforming Mission: Paradigm Shifts in Theology of Mission*. Maryknoll, NY: Orbis.

Braun, Will. 2013. "Sommerfeld Church Pulls out of MCC." *Canadian Mennonite* 17(1), January 2. http://www.canadianmennonite.org/articles/sommerfeld-church -pulls-out-mcc.

Brubacher, Ray. 1991. "A Missiology for MCC." *Intercom* 35(9): 8.

Brubacher, Ray. 1992. "A Missiology for MCC, Letter to Nancy Heisey." February 28.

Brubacher, Ray. 1993. "Missiology Statement, Letter to Ed Martin and Ed Metzler." April 14.

Coakley, Sarah. 2013. *God, Sexuality, and the Self: An Essay "On the Trinity."* Cambridge: Cambridge University Press.

Coates, Ruth. 1999. *Christianity in Bakhtin: God and the Exiled Author.* Cambridge: Cambridge University Press.

Dyck, Cornelius J. 1985. "Foreword." In *One Lord, One Church, One Hope, and One God: Mennonite Confessions of Faith in North America, an Introduction,* by H. J. Loewen. Elkhart, IN: Institute of Mennonite Studies.

Elisha, Omri. 2011. *Moral Ambition: Mobilization and Social Outreach in Evangelical Megachurches.* Berkeley and Los Angeles: University of California Press.

Epp, Maureen, and Carol Ann Weaver, eds. 2005. *Sound in the Land: Essays on Mennonites and Music.* Kitchener, ON: Pandora Press.

Finger, Thomas. 2007. "The Confession of Faith in a Mennonite Perspective as a Living Letter." *Mennonite Quarterly Review* 81(3): 309–326.

Foster, G., et al. 1992. *Research Survey Report on MCC Missiology Dialogue.* Philadelphia, PA: Eastern College.

Fountain, Philip. 2011. "Orienting Guesthood in the Mennonite Central Committee, Indonesia." In *Inside the Everyday Lives of Development Workers: The Challenges and Futures of Aidland,* ed. A. M. Fechter and H. Hindman, 83–106. Bloomfield, CT: Kumarian.

Fountain, Philip. 2013. "Toward a Post-Secular Anthropology." *The Australian Journal of Anthropology* 24(3): 310–328.

Fountain, Philip. 2014. "Development Things: A Case of Canned Meat." *Sites,* n.s., 11(1): 39–73.

Fountain, Philip, and Sin Wen Lau, eds. 2013. "Anthropological Theologies: Engagements and Encounters." Special issue, *The Australian Journal of Anthropology* 24(3).

Green, Stanley W., and James R. Krabill. 2011. "The Missiology of MCC: A Framework for Assessing Multiple Voices within the MCC Family." In *A Table of Sharing: Mennonite Central Committee and the Expanding Networks of Mennonite Identity,* ed. Alain Epp Weaver, 192–212. Telford, PA: Cascadia Publishing House.

Harding, Susan Friend. 2001. *The Book of Jerry Falwell: Fundamentalist Language and Politics.* Princeton, NJ: Princeton University Press.

Heisey, Nancy. 1993a. "MCC Missiology Statement: Draft 4." Akron, PA: Mennonite Central Committee.

Heisey, Nancy. 1993b. Missiology, letter to John Lapp, February 1.

Howell, Brian. 2007. "The Repugnant Cultural Other Speaks Back: Christian Identity as Ethnographic 'Standpoint.'" *Anthropological Theory* 7(4): 371–391.

Ingram, Brannon D. 2014. "The Portable Madrasa: Print, Publics, and the Authority of the Deobandi ʿUlama." *Modern Asian Studies* 48(4): 845–871.

Johnson, Maxwell E. 2013. *Praying and Believing in Early Christianity: The Interplay between Christian Worship and Doctrine*. Collegeville, MN: Liturgical Press.

Jørgensen, Jonas A. 2011. "Anthropology of Christianity and Missiology: Disciplinary Contexts, Converging Themes, and Future Tasks of Mission Studies." *Mission Studies* 28(2): 186–208.

Kasdorf, Julia S. 2009. *The Body and the Book: Writing from a Mennonite Life*. University Park: Pennsylvania State University Press.

Keane, Webb. 2007. *Christian Moderns: Freedom and Fetish in the Mission Encounter*. Berkeley and Los Angeles: University of California Press.

Klassen, Pamela. 2011. *Spirits of Protestantism: Medicine, Healing, and Liberal Christianity*. Berkeley and Los Angeles: University of California Press.

Kraybill, Donald B. 2011. "The Mystery of Broad-Based Commitment: MCC in the Eyes of Mennonites and Brethren in Christ in the United States." In *A Table of Sharing: Mennonite Central Committee and the Expanding Networks of Mennonite Identity*, ed. Alain Epp Weaver, 105–134. Telford, PA: Cascadia Publishing House.

Larsen, Timothy. 2014. *The Slain God: Anthropologists and the Christian Faith*. Oxford: Oxford University Press.

Loewen, Howard J. 1985. *One Lord, One Church, One Hope, and One God: Mennonite Confessions of Faith in North America, an Introduction*. Elkhart, IN: Institute of Mennonite Studies.

Longnecker, Carol. 2007. "Progressivism and the Mission Field: Church of the Brethren Women Missionaries in Shanxi, China, 1908-1951." M.A. diss., Clemson University.

Luhrmann, Tanya M. 2012. *When God Talks Back: Understanding the American Evangelical Relationship with God*. New York: Random House.

Mathies, David Kratz. 2007. "'Holding Fast' to Principles or Drawing Boundaries of Exclusion? The Use and Misuse of the Confession of Faith in a Mennonite Perspective." *Conrad Grebel Review* 25(3): 68–85.

Meneses, Eloise, Lindy Backues, David Bronkema, Eric Flett, and Benjamin L. Hartley. 2014. "Engaging the Religiously Committed Other: Anthropologists and Theologians in Dialogue." *Current Anthropology* 55(1): 82–104.

Mennonite Central Committee. 1999. *Principles that Guide Our Mission*. Akron, PA: Mennonite Central Committee.

Mennonite Central Committee. 2011. *Principles and Practices Guiding the Mission of Mennonite Central Committee in the Name of Christ*. Akron, PA: Mennonite Central Committee.

Mosse, David. 2005. *Cultivating Development: An Ethnography of Aid Policy and Practice*. London: Pluto Press.

Neff, Christian, John C. Wenger, Harold S. Bender, and Howard John Loewen. 1989. "Confessions, Doctrinal." *Global Anabaptist Mennonite Encyclopedia Online*. http://gameo.org/index.php?title=Confessions,_Doctrinal&oldid=117980.

Nolt, Steven M. 2011. "MCC's Relationship with 'Plain' Anabaptists in Historical Perspective." In *A Table of Sharing: Mennonite Central Committee and the Expanding Networks of Mennonite Identity*, ed. Alain Epp Weaver, 135–166. Telford, PA: Cascadia Publishing House.

Parler, Branson L. 2012. *Things Hold Together: John Howard Yoder's Trinitarian Theology of Culture*. Harrisonburg, VA: Herald Press.

Pelikan, Jaroslav. 2003. *Credo*. New Haven, CT: Yale University Press.

Pelikan, Jaroslav, and Valerie Hotchkiss. 2003a. *Creeds and Confessions of Faith in the Christian Tradition*. Vol. 1. New Haven, CT: Yale University Press.

Pelikan, Jaroslav, and Valerie Hotchkiss. 2003b. *Creeds and Confessions of Faith in the Christian Tradition*. Vol. 2. New Haven, CT: Yale University Press.

Redekop, Calvin. 1989. *Mennonite Society*. Baltimore: Johns Hopkins University Press.

Rempel, Peter. 2000. "The Shape of Global Anabaptist Missions for the 21st Century: The Whole Gospel to the Whole Broken World by the Broken Whole Church." *Mission Focus: Annual Review* 8:23–37.

Robbins, Joel. 2006. "Anthropology and Theology: An Awkward Relationship?." *Anthropological Quarterly* 79(2): 285–294.

Roth, John D. 2005. *Beliefs: Mennonite Faith and Practice*. Harrisonburg, VA: Herald Press.

Sawatsky, Walter. 2006. "The Many Faces of Anabaptism and Mission since 1860." *Mission Focus: Annual Review* 14:134–148.

Scharen, Christian, ed. 2012. *Explorations in Ecclesiology & Ethnography*. Grand Rapids, MI: Eerdmans.

Scharen, Christian, and Aana Marie Vigen, eds. 2011. *Ethnography as Christian Theology and Ethics*. London: Continuum Books.

Shenk, Wilbert R. 2000. *By Faith They Went Out: Mennonite Missions 1850-1999*. Elkhart, IN: Institute of Mennonite Studies.

Steiner, George. 1975. *After Babel: Aspects of Language and Translation*. Oxford: Oxford University Press.

Terichow, Gladys. 2009. "New Wine: Shared Statements a Major Step as MCC Reshapes its Future." *Mennonite Central Committee*. http://mcc.org/stories/news/shared-statements-major-step-mcc-reshapes-its-future.

Tomlinson, Matt. 2014. "Bringing Kierkegaard into Anthropology: Repetition, Absurdity, and Curses in Fiji." *American Ethnologist* 41(1): 163–175.

Urry, James. 2006. *Mennonites, Politics, Peoplehood: Europe-Russia-Canada 1525 to 1980*. Winnipeg: University of Manitoba Press.

Walker, C. Z. 2011. "Church Summit Points Way Ahead for MCC." *Mennonite Central Committee*. http://mcc.org/stories/news/church-summit-points-way-ahead-mcc.

Ward, Pete, ed. 2012. *Perspectives on Ecclesiology and Ethnography*. Grand Rapids, MI: Eerdmans.

Wellman, James K. 2008. *Evangelical vs. Liberal: The Clash of Christian Cultures in the Pacific Northwest*. Oxford: Oxford University Press.

Werntz, M. 2014. "On the Knowledge of God: John Howard Yoder, Peter Ochs, and the Limits of Communal Dialogue." *Journal of Scriptural Reasoning* 13(2). https://jsr.shanti.virginia.edu/volume-13-number-2-november-2014-navigating-john-howard-yoders-the-jewish-christian-schism-revisited/on-the-knowledge-of-god-john-howard-yoder-peter-ochs-and-the-limits-of-communal-dialogue/.

Wright, Jeff. 2007. "Teaching Position or Conversation Starter? The *Confession of Faith in a Mennonite Perspective* and the New Mennonites of Southern California." *Mennonite Quarterly Review* 81(3): 437–441.

Yoder, John H. 1972. *The Politics of Jesus: Vicit Agnus Noster*. Grand Rapids, MI: Eerdmans.

Yoder, John H. 1984. *The Priestly Kingdom: Social Ethics as Gospel*. Notre Dame, IN: University of Notre Dame Press.

9 THE PUBLIC METACULTURE OF ISLAMIC PREACHING

Julian Millie

Since commencing field research about Islamic oratory in Indonesia's West Java Province in 2007, I have frequently sought explanations from Muslims in the province about the nature and function of this important religious medium. According to the answer I have most commonly received, preaching consists of the circulation of Islamic knowledge—Qur'an and Sunna (acts and utterances of the prophet)—to listeners who are challenged to implement it. I found a similar conception in the Indonesian preaching manuals I consulted. The manuals' definitions of preaching emphasize two concepts derived from Qur'an and Hadith: preachers convey (Arabic, *balagha*) Islamic teachings, and they challenge (Arabic, *da'a*) Muslims to obey them. These ideas of conveying and challenging are prominent in Indonesian Islamic awareness, for the two Arabic words Indonesians use to mean "preacher"—*da'i* and *mubaligh*—are cognate forms of those terms. The abstract nouns they use to mean "preaching" are also cognates, namely *da'wa* and *tabligh*. And the conveyance of Islamic knowledge is a prominent part of public life. About 98% of the Province's 43,000,000 residents are Muslims,[1] and for many of these, preaching is a preferred Islamic observance, for preachers are skilled at bringing acceptable and accessible Islamic content to all kinds of gatherings, including celebrations of life-cycle events and calendrical feasts, civil commemorations, study groups, and events held in corporate settings. Against this background, one is entitled to expect that preaching

---

1. According to the 2010 census, the population of West Java Province was 43,053,732 (http://www.bps.go.id). The census of 2000 (but no subsequent census) asked respondents to name their religious self-identification. According to that census, 97.65 of West Javanese residents self-identify as Muslim (Suryadinata et al. 2003).

would consist in the main of the circulation of Islamic knowledge through pious speech.

In practice, this is not the case. There is no doubt that pious speech is a basic element of preaching, yet I was constantly struck by the fact that orators succeeded by treating their listeners as subjects with a broader range of competencies than religious ones. By this I mean subjects familiar with and affected by a range of genres, ways of speaking, media forms, and cultural patterns and models. Preachers approach their listeners not only as Muslims respectful of Islamic learning but also as television viewers, as lovers of profane as well as religious songs, and as people prepared to laugh at themselves. Successful preachers were those with the skills to communicate in these terms. This meant that the reality of West Javanese preaching did not fully harmonize with the explanations I had been given: preaching is a pious speech genre full of impious speech.

In other words, I encountered a contrast between the actual practice of preaching and its metaculture. Following Greg Urban (this volume, and Urban 2001), I understand metaculture as "reflective culture and evaluative discourse" and the "kind of culture [that] influences how individuals cognize instances of replication." The metaculture of Islamic preaching in West Java is largely monological, limiting its character and texture to pious communication. And when the metaculture does refer to impious speech, it generally does so in a guarded way. According to some dispositions, it has no place in oratory. According to others, it has a potential that needs to be monitored and restrained. This chapter describes and analyzes the conflict between preaching's monological metaculture and its multivocal reality, drawing on a number of examples from West Javanese preaching performances. I identify a public utility in this conflict: the inconsistency between preaching's metaculture and its practice works in two ways: it bolsters public respect and admiration for Islam while at the same time enabling the frequent circulation of Islamic messages through preaching.

Two Interactions

I start with a general outline of two contrasting interactions that Islamic preachers of West Java master and mobilize to varying degrees in every one of their orations. The examples to follow illustrate how they successfully combine them. In my introductory paragraphs, I mentioned these two interactions as pious and impious, but a more accurate pair of terms, recognizing that this analysis proceeds from empirical observation of spoken language, is constrained and multivocal.[2] Constrained and multivocal interactions differ in their constitutive

2. This pairing of terms is highly similar to those adopted in the previous major work on preaching on the island of Java (Keeler 1998). Keeler uses a number of terms. For the interaction

linguistic resources and also in the relations they imply between listeners and Islamic norms. The constrained interaction is invariably comprised of the verbalization and translation of Islamic norms, most often in the form of Arabic language entextualizations of Qur'an and Hadith. The preacher recites chunks of Arabic text verbatim and provides accompanying translations into one of the two vernacular languages used within this bilingual community. (Almost all West Javanese are competent in the national language of Indonesia, Indonesian, as well as their ethnic language, Sundanese. Both languages are used in preaching, although as my analysis reveals, they differ in their non-referential significances.) Even if they do not understand the referential meanings of the chunks of Arabic, listeners recognize these as revelation. Most West Javanese Muslims have at least some Qur'anic literacy, and the rare ones who do not are familiar with the distinctive sounds and appearance of Qur'an and Hadith from their constant circulation in oral and written genres. The preacher's ability to work with these Arabic texts signals his or her authority to mediate a field of knowledge valued by preachers and listeners.

I regard this as constrained for a number of reasons. First, the subject matter requires a certain decorum that imposes a weight on the interaction. Although the verses and Hadith are short and compact, and thus are able to be recalled in small fragments, their status as revelation limits the range of strategies for their verbalization. It is not acceptable to treat these textual fragments with puns or word games, for example. Similarly, the roles of speaker and listener are fixed in this interaction: the preacher discharges a weighty responsibility of admonition, while the listener must accept the norms as obligatory, or at least appear to do so. The resultant solemnity constrains the relationship between speaker and listener. Apart from that, constraint arises from unavoidable repetition. The corpus of texts able to be recalled, Qur'an and Hadith, is large but limited. These cannot be replaced by other texts. Certain verses and Hadith are commonly recalled at occasions or feast days to which they are relevant. After years of attending life-cycle and calendrical celebrations, many

---

I label as multivocal, Keeler uses "entertaining mode" and "contrasting voices." For what I label "constrained," Keeler uses "heavier, more monologic," "highly serious mode," "monotone, impressive and authoritative." I have preferred the word multivocality over dialogism. The latter term has become inseparable from Bakhtin's theorizing of voice in the polyphonic novel (Bakhtin 1984). In his scheme, the emergence of dialogism in the novel was significant because it heralded a new era in the representation of the "thinking human consciousness" (Bakhtin 1984: 270). When considered against this scheme, preaching must appear as a "naïve and simplistic" genre (Bakhtin 1984: 271), for the utterances of preaching events give unanimous support for the collective's subordination to the ultimate authority of Islam. Any plurality of voices, decentering of authority and double-voiced discourse within a sermon do not at all dialogize the fact of listeners' submission. When that monologism is not present in a specific instance of preaching, that instance can surely no longer be called preaching.

listeners develop familiarity with the texts appropriate to specific calendrical moments.

While the pious, constrained interaction consists of chunks of language sourced from texts that are found in almost precisely the same form anywhere in the Islamic world, and would be more or less equally recognized in their Arabic forms by Muslims anywhere, the multivocal interaction is highly oriented to context, and to the here and now of the dialogical interaction. Recognizable and accessible linguistic and cultural materials from a wide range of genres feature heavily: narrative, song, reported dialogue, mimicry, idioms, specialist registers, and so on. In creating this multivocality, preachers display a range of verbal skills that contrasts with those displayed in the constrained interaction. As a result of the expanded range of thematic possibilities enabled by this interaction, multivocal preaching is peopled not solely by the figures of the Islamic pantheon (the Prophet Muhammad, his house, and successors), but by characters and caricatures recognizable from everyday life, including stereotypes of village life as well as characters known from artistic genres and media culture.

The relative status of preacher and listener changes during the multivocal interaction, as the preacher moves to a more sympathetic equality with listeners. This movement is achieved in various ways, for example, through the appropriation of linguistic materials just mentioned, which are less heavily laden with didacticism. It is also achieved through the preacher's frequent switch to the inclusive third person pronoun, a positioning that contrasts with the imperative or admonishing footing of the first interaction. The preacher joins with his listeners in reflecting together on the norms that form the subject matter of the event or discourse, drawing attention to intra-community relationships and shared cultural references.

When creating multivocal interactions, preachers reveal a more ambiguous collective commitment to Islamic norms. During the constrained interaction, the preacher idealizes ways for leading a morally compliant Islamic life. By contrast, the shared reflections in vernacular genres frequently reveal Muslims failing to comply with those norms in recognizable ways. In striving to create affective recognition and humorous reactions in listeners, preachers invert Islamic norms. This brings a major decentering to the moralizing orientation of the sermon. While the first interaction sees norms idealized as goals of human endeavor, the second reveals violations of norms as a routine part of the life of the community.

I have outlined the distinction between constrained and multivocal styles by comparing the different linguistic and cultural resources that constitute them, and the contrasting footings they imply. But Indonesian Muslims usually bring the issue of propriety to the distinction. This is a point I make more strongly later in this chapter. In public discourse about preaching, the constrained interaction is evaluated positively, while the multivocal one is not.

A Multivocal Shariah Lesson

The vast majority of preaching performances incorporate both these interactive styles. For example, a preacher might verbalize and translate a Qur'anic verse and then follow that with a lengthy narrative, featuring a Sundanese location and cast, in which the relevant norm is illustrated.[3] The two examples I present here are contrasting shariah lessons made distinctive and acceptable by the play of voices through which the preacher presents them.

Kyai Al-Jauhari (b. 1971) is a popular preacher for village celebrations of life-cycle events and Islamic feast days. Most of his orations are delivered in Sundanese. His popularity is such that it is common for him to fulfil three invitations on a single day. He is known as a preacher with expertise in traditional Islamic learning, but his distinctiveness comes from his ability to surprise and amuse audiences with many kinds of vocal styles. He frequently sings songs from contemporary pop charts in his orations. These capabilities give him appeal for all age brackets. Recordings of his sermons in cassette and digital video formats circulate in West Java in authorized and unauthorized versions.

Example A is taken from a sermon Al-Jauhari delivered at a wedding celebration.[4] It is a shariah lesson in the form of a narrative retelling based on Qur'anic materials. In keeping with the theme of the situation, the event narrated is the first ever marriage, namely that between Adam and Hawa (Eve).[5] The relevant Qur'anic fragments, all from verses 35 to 37 of the *Al-Baqara* chapter, are entextualized within the narrative retelling. To assist in interpretation of the excerpt, it is necessary that I first give a basic synopsis of the Adam and Hawa story as it is known by Al-Jauhari's listeners: Allah grants the prophet Adam and Hawa a place in heaven. Allah informs Adam that he may remain in heaven as long as he refrains from going near the Tree of Eternity. Iblis (the devil) introduces himself to Adam and tries to entice him to eat the fruit of the tree. He refuses, so Iblis

---

3. My translation of a selection of sermons from the Sundanese preacher A. F. Ghazali (d. 2001) gives many examples of how a skillful preacher enhanced audience acceptance of his shariah-oriented sermons with multivocal strategies (Ghazali 2008).

4. I transcribed the example from an unauthorized video recording in DVD format purchased from a stall in a bus terminal in Bandung, the capital city of West Java (Pasar Inpres 2008). People commonly make illegal recordings of Al-Jauhari's sermons and retail them for profit.

5. The narrative of Adam and Hawa, as it is found in the Qur'an (2:35–38 and 20:115–123), is brief, and lacks many of the narrative features appearing in Al-Jauhari's retelling.

corrupts Hawa, who then uses her feminine wiles to convince Adam to climb the tree and pick the fruit. He does so, and they eat it. Allah expels them from heaven and separates the couple. Adam repents over a period of two hundred years and is then reunited with Hawa.

Al-Jauhari used three languages in the excerpt. The dominant language is Sundanese. I have italicized his Arabic, but left it untranslated, as his Sundanese text gives the meanings of those words. The third language is Indonesian, the national standard, which appears as italicized English text in the translation. The excerpt commences with Al-Jauhari answering a contrived question from an imagined interlocutor. This device is commonly used by preachers to maintain listeners' attention and to give forward motion to their performances. Quotation marks are used to indicate the switches between contrived voices that are a hallmark of Al-Jauhari's style, which is also characterized by high-speed delivery and rapidly executed bodily gestures.

Example A

"Are you sure, Mr. Al-Jauhari, that the prophet Adam was married to Eve?" That's right. "How do you know it?" The Quranic verse I read to you just know. *Wa qulna ya Adam uskun anta wa zaujuka.* That's the one.

"Hi Adam, live with your wife *al-jannata*, in paradise, *wa kula minha*
5 *raghadan haithu shi'tuma.* You can eat together, do whatever you wish. You are free to choose what you want. Only one thing is not allowed. *Wa la taqraba hadhihi al-shajarah.* Do not approach this tree. If you keep trying to approach it, to climb it to pick its leaves and take its fruit, *fa takuna min al-dzalimin,* you will be considered among the wrongdoers."

10 The Prophet Adam went right on enjoying his life together with Eve. That's the meaning of *uskun anta. Uskun* means living a peaceful life, we can also call it *sakinah.* While the prophet Adam was enjoying paradise, along comes Satan. If we tell this as a story it could go like this:

"Hi, what's your name?"
15 *"Adam."*
"And you?"
"Eve."
"I'm Satan." [audience laughter] *"You are new residents here, aren't you?"*
"Yes."
20 *"I'm your senior,"* Satan said. "What are you doing here, 'dam?" *"I am free* to do whatever I want. One thing is not allowed; approaching that tree."

After Eva was seduced, then Satan started to persuade Adam. If I tell it as a
story, it could go like this:

"Adam, come here!"

25 *"What's up, honey?"*

"Do you still love me?"

"Of course, I do, Eve. I love no woman but you."

Of course there weren't any other women then, just one [audience laughter].

"If you really love me, how do I appear to you?"

30 If the Prophet Adam acted like a youngster of today, he might have sung it
[like this]: [Indonesian pop song]

You are like a song in my heart

That summons my longing for you, ooh . . .

Like the air I inhale, you are always there, Ha . . . ha. . . .

35 That grandma looks confused again [points to audience member]. She doesn't
know the song! [audience laughter]. That song is Dealova, Grandma, the
singer is Once.

*"Do you know everything, Al-Jauhari?" Hang out, man! So what, that's just
how it is . . . !* [Marked Jakarta style of Indonesian; audience laughter]

40 *"If you really love me, prove your love for me!"*

*"How can I show my love to you? Do you want my life? Or can I give you the
life of a duck?"* [nonsense joke, audience laughter]

"No. I only want that fruit," said Eve. *"I want you to pick that fruit for me."*

"Don't ask me to pick that fruit. You know Allah has forbidden it. Ask for

45 *something else."*

*"No . . . I only want that. If you don't pick it for me, I will commit suicide
. . ."*

The example commences as a constrained lesson in shariah. Al-Jauhari flags
the multivocality to follow in line 13, as if saying "I am about to take this verse
somewhere unexpected." I draw attention to three examples of multivocality
following this: two replays of imagined conversational dialogue and one performance of a pop genre.

The first conversational replay is Iblis's introduction to Adam and Eve (lines
10–21). Al-Jauhari performs this in the language conventional for the introduc-
tions that occur when newcomers come into a neighborhood, or when students
meet in a dormitory. Such communications would frequently unfold in the
national language, Indonesian, because of the necessity for interethnic communication implicit in such encounters. In this exchange, Al-Jauhari mimics the
polite casualness that would dictate the tone of such an encounter. It is a skillful
translation of the Qur'an into an identifiable conversational register, conveying its emotive-affective aspects through his full attention to the timbre and

intonation of those recognizable voices. Listeners sense the incongruity: Satan and Adam conduct their meeting in the conversation styles of contemporary Indonesians.

In the second conversational replay (23–46), which relates Hawa's seduction of Adam, Al-Jauhari's mimicry crosses over boundaries of gender and genre. This is performed in a mimesis of the voices of prime-time Indonesian romantic tele-drama, and specifically its breathy romantic exchanges. Al-Jauhari's mimicry of these is a highly stylized one, being more breathy, more coy, more feminine, more alluring than the actual television dramas, and this brings irony to the perfor-mance. The parodies tap into shared emotional dispositions, for they express the shallowness and general fallibility that people recognize in the roles and charac-ters of romantic drama. Hawa is caricatured as vain, and Adam as weakened by infatuation. The reports succeed by confronting listeners with colorful images of something at once recognizable and humorous: the failings of humans affected by romantic love.

The final multivocal element to be mentioned here is the performance of the pop song in lines 32–34. Being a talented singer, Al-Jauhari's singing of popular tunes surprises audiences with its quality and resemblance to the originals broad-cast through national media. The use of contemporary songs invites a high level of audience identification but also creates a risk of alienating older people who form a substantial segment of his audience. Al-Jauhari employs tricks to mitigate this risk, such as the intervention in lines 35–37 in which he steps outside his narrative to point out an old lady who does not recognize the song. This interven-tion succeeds on a number of levels. The teasing metacommentary affectionately points out the older generation's disconnection from contemporary Indonesian culture, generating humor among the audience as it does so, but at the same time, is a very inclusive move in their direction. They feel acknowledged. This strategy enables him to maintain a close and satisfying interaction between himself and his audience.

This passage forms part of a shariah lesson about a text very well-known to members of the audience. Their familiarity with these materials is so high that an unreflective delivery might risk disengagement and boredom, so Al-Jauhari replays the Qur'anic events through dialogic encounters that ironically carica-ture voices recognizably belonging to everyday Sundanese life. The didacticism of this passage has no banality for his audience, for the succession of dialogues has audiences in suspense about the identity of the next voice or everyday situation they will encounter in the retelling. This is Al-Jauhari's skill: the narrative and lesson might be repetitions, but he transforms them into a gripping exercise in multivocality.

The Islamic Association

My second example is from another Sundanese preacher, Shiddiq Amien (d. 2009). He worked within a contrasting Islamic environment to Al-Jauhari, who is most frequently engaged to preach at festive events. By contrast, Shiddiq Amien was an office bearer and preacher for an Islamic activist organization dedicated to Islamic development of self and society. The Islamic Association (Ind., *Persatuan Islam* or *Persis*) was founded in Bandung by Muslim traders in 1923, partially as a response to the burgeoning Western modernity of that colonial center (see Federspiel 2001). It has an Islamic political and social vision that relies quite heavily on scriptural literalism. It is central to the Association's program that Muslims must accept and implement the prescriptions for conduct in daily life (*fiqh*) that are set out in the sources of Islamic law (especially Qur'an and Hadith). The group also foregrounds an insistence that Islamic norms are accessible and not difficult for ordinary Muslims to study, and that these norms are wholly compatible with rational modes of thinking (Ind./Arabic, '*aql*). It has between three to four million followers on Java.

Between 2008 and 2011, I attended a number of the Association's weekly public gatherings (*pengajian*) held at a mosque in central Bandung. The Association calls these "The Sunday Jihad Meeting." They attract listeners from within Bandung but also from the rural areas around Bandung. The speaker is always a cleric of high rank within the organization. The speaker delivers his sermon from within the mosque, but because the audience is so large, usually numbering between 3,000 and 6,000, most listeners sit on the road outside the mosque and listen to the sermon as it is broadcast through loudspeakers. The Bandung police close the roads around the mosque every Sunday morning to enable this to happen.

Shiddiq Amien was the Chairman of the Association in West Java and nationally. He had dedicated his life to the group and received wide approval as an orator. He was not a virtuoso performer in the manner of Al-Jauhari. The Association favors orations in what appear to be "simple" forms and does not approve of preaching—like that of Al-Jauhari—in which speakers demonstrate virtuosity in non-religious genres. This preference makes the Islamic Association a valuable case study for examining the metaculture of Islamic preaching: its followers told me that Amien was an exemplary preacher in the constrained style. Nevertheless, I noticed that they did not realize the extent of his oratorical skill. Although they understand him to be speaking in an everyday register, in fact he makes skillful use of low-key humor, and skills in narrative and other verbal structures. The Association's listeners generally do not have the metalinguistic sensibility necessary to recognize this.

The sermon included a lesson on "things forbidden to women during their menstruation."[6] In this lesson, Amien referred to a number of well-known Hadith on this topic, which is not a strange one for West Javanese Muslims. From their earliest years Sundanese Muslims, male and female, listen to admonitions on this topic. Women in Islamic West Java do not generally consider it improper for a male preacher to raise these issues and make admonitions about them.

The dominant code used in Amien's sermon was Indonesian. His multivocality, however, relied heavily on Sundanese. The switches to Sundanese have a pronounced meta quality because he uses these to share with his listeners informal reflections about the themes of the unfolding discourse. As I have argued elsewhere, the Sundanese language enables the preacher to address listeners from a less authoritative and more equal footing. The switches to Sundanese "enable Amien to reach into the shared cultural context in a playful preaching voice and to establish a more intimate and less formal rapport than the one speaking through the national standard, which remains faithful to the strict letter of the Islamic Association's programme" (Millie 2012a: 391).

In the transcript in Example B, I have left Amien's Arabic entextualizations in Arabic, for he translates almost all of these into Indonesian. The non-italicized English text is translated from Indonesian, the dominant code in this sermon. The italicized English text was delivered in Sundanese, the first language of Amien and his listeners. The ◄ symbol indicates rising intonation intended to draw an affirmation from listeners:

Example B

---

1   The third and fourth things forbidden to menstruating women are ritual prayer and fasting.
     'An Abi Sa'id Al-Khudri qala [According to Abu Said bin Hudri, the Prophet said],[7] *kharaja rasul 'ullah* the Messenger of Allah left his house, *fi adha au*
5   *fitrin*, probably forgetting whether it was the festival of adha or fitri, but it was certainly a feast day, *ila al-musalla* and went to the *musalla*. We often translate this among ourselves as "went to the mosque," but in fact *musalla*, in this context, is the name of a field in the eastern part of Medinah.

---

6. I have used a video disc (Amien 2009) of the Sunday sermon as source material for this analysis.

7. This phrase marks the Arabic text as a Hadith. In their written forms, Hadith commence with a statement of the person who originally heard or observed the content of the Hadith. In his entextualizations, Amien faithfully preserves this earliest point in the Hadith's chain of authority. At the Islamic Association's events, listeners are provided with a photocopied sheet of relevant Hadith. Occasionally, Amien would refer directly to the sheet by referring to Hadith by the numbers with which they were marked on the handout.

10   *Fa marra 'ala al-nisa'*, the Prophet then went towards the place where the
women were. Ladies, at that time it was probable that, because there were no
sound systems, or because he had special advice for women, after giving his
sermon to the men, the Prophet descended from the rostrum then went to
the back rows to give a special sermon for the women.
The content of that sermon [was], "*Ya ma'shar al-nisa'.* Oh women!

15   *Tasaddaqna* increase your alms, *fa inni* for verily, *uritukunna* it was revealed
to me that you all, *akthara ahli al-nar* most of you will go to hell." *The
Messenger of Allah said, "Women! Increase your alms*, for I have seen into hell,
and most of its inhabitants are women."
In reality, don't be shocked, ladies! For we need to pay attention to the first

20   sentence, *tasaddaqna* [give alms], only that one. If you don't wish to dwell in
hell you must increase your alms.
At this point, the women were surprised, *fa qulna* so they asked,
"*wa bima ya rasul 'ullah,* why is that, Oh Messenger of Allah?"
Qala the Prophet explained, "Firstly *tuqthirna al-la'na* you often speak ill of

25   others." Women often speak ill of others. They curse people. Perhaps because
their thoughts, not feelings, come first. *They feel a bit of resentment, so they
wish misfortune upon someone else.*
"*I pray that your life be full of misfortune! That a cockroach will crush you! That
your wajit* [a Sundanese sweet] *will stick to its wrapper!*" [audience: smiles and

30   mild laughter]
Secondly, *wa takfurna al-'ashir*, they frequently *disobey* their husbands.
Disobedience to husbands, not to Allah. This has been explained in another
hadith, ladies, where the Prophet explains what he means by *disobedience, lau
ahsanta ila ihdahunna al-dahra kulla*, if a husband behaves well towards his

35   wife for a whole year, *thumma ra'at shay'an qatt* and then she sees the smallest
mistake from him, all the goodness of the husband is then erased.
A year of drought . . . how do we say it? Is soaked by a day of rain. After all, there
are wives who say to their husbands,
"*All you* [Sundanese, *sia* = coarse pronoun] *do is cause me pain!*"

40   [audience: laughter]
"*What do you mean, I cause you pain?*"
"*You never make me happy.*"
Her husband says, "*If you want to be happy* [*senang*], *fart in the steamer.*
[audience: laughter] *The sound will be 'senang.*"[8]

45   *That's what he says.*

---

8. The audience members' laughter after the word "pain" is partly brought on by "the wife's"
use of the coarse second pronoun *sia* (you) to address her husband. The steamer joke refers to

In lines 16–18 and 31–36, Amien verbalizes and translates two potentially oppressive statements of the Prophet (these respectively form the content of two Hadith). In the first, the Prophet observes that most of the occupants of hell are women. In the latter, the Prophet states the ease with which a woman can erase the rewards earned by a man's virtuous behavior. The preacher follows both of these with direct addresses to listeners that evaluate and qualify those norms, and which defuse the severity of the Hadith. To do this, the preacher draws very heavily on the repertoire of everyday Sundanese sociability in order to relocate the interaction into the world of everyday, informal, intimate communication. In lines 26 to 29, Amien produces a string of Sundanese idiomatic expressions, verbalizing in the "voice" of a woman, drawing high recognition from the audience and conveying humorous affect.[9] In lines 37 to 43, he summons up a very recognizable cultural form: a dialogue between spouses in which speakers project a graphically honest rather than idealized view of married life. A coarse joke concludes his representation of the earthy realities of domestic life.

These examples of multivocality rekey the normative implications of the Hadith. The entextualizations of Hadith and Qur'an bear witness to the Association's fundamental principle: humans are obliged to comply with the norms expressed in the Qur'an and Hadith. But with his variations into Sundanese, Amien addresses an ethnic collective prepared to look upon normative obligations through an ironic and playful lens. The vernacular idioms signal a heightened inclusiveness between preacher and listeners in these passages. Indeed, all uses of Sundanese in this excerpt point to a more equal and informal footing. The collective signaled in these switches is not inhabited by the exemplary figures encountered in the Hadith literature. It is peopled by Sundanese subjects who speak to each other in intimate and playful ways that acknowledge the human tendency to err.

Bauman's treatment of the concept of rekeying is useful here, for it helps us deal with the inversion issue: how can preachers simultaneously advocate for idealized norms and treat them ironically in the one speech event? How can the genre sustain piety and impiety in the same message? How does the preacher's authority as religious specialist survive the inversion? In his 1986 work on storytelling, Bauman analyzed conversational anecdotes in which people pass on to

---

the resonance the steamer gains from its shape and depth. People commonly joke that breaking wind in the steamer will produce the sound *se-nang*, resembling the Indonesian and Sundanese word *senang*, meaning "to be happy."

9. An indication of the distance between the styles of Al-Jauhari and Amien is that Amien does not reproduce the timbre and intonation of the styles he copies. Even when speaking as a woman, he does not mimic a female voice, but retains the same intonation as he used in the rest of the sermon.

their neighbors stories about moral issues involving known figures in the neighborhood. In narrating wayward behavior by neighbors and family, storytellers relativize behavioral norms in jokes:

> The anecdotes achieve their effect by rekeying the situation, overturning the apparent direction of the interaction and the moral alignments and attitudes that have seemed to control it and establishing an ironic alternative, not as a substitute but as a coexistent perspective. The effect of the punch line is to that extent subversive, a breakthrough both on the part of the one who is reported to have spoken it and on the part of the narrator into a kind of scepticism and relativism that takes pleasure in refusing to take ideal, normative moral expectation too seriously—a "comic corrective," in Burke's apt phrase, "containing two-way attributes lacking in polemical, one-way approaches to social necessity." (Bauman 1986: 75)

West Java is a society where Islamic norms are constantly circulating in preaching and other media. The population assents to this ongoing admonition, but for this circulation to take place at such high volume and frequency, preachers must enable listeners to engage positively with their religion. If women left these events bearing a negative impression of their own capabilities and qualities as moral subjects, preaching would not be the attractive Islamic media form that it is. At the most potentially oppressive moments of his oratory, Amien's multivocality reorients his interaction with listeners. He turns to the repertoire of Sundanese idiom, so rich in expressions highlighting human specificity (kinship roles, physical features, moral failings, emotional states, personality traits, etc.), and takes a "backward" step away from the potential burden on individuals. Instead, a shared position is affirmed: where the collective is concerned, norms are relative things. This example indicates that it takes more than doctrine to sustain high participation in Islamic preaching. The constrained interaction alone is not sufficient.

The Metaculture of Islamic Oratory

Preaching succeeds through the co-occurrence of constrained and multivocal interactions. Without entextualizations of Qur'an and Hadith, spoken discourse is unrecognizable as preaching. Without multivocality, preaching events fail. But West Javanese and Indonesian discourse about oratory presents a different impression of preaching. At the metacultural level, multivocality is distanced and even excluded from the scope of the activity. In public representations, West Java's Muslims support a generic model for preaching that is monological, constituted almost solely by the constrained interaction. As Ward Keeler puts it, listeners "devalue sermons that include familiar voices, voices like their own" (1998: 171).

Preaching manuals effect concealments and distancings of multivocal interaction. I have yet to read a preaching manual that gives instructions about anything resembling the multivocal styles discussed here.[10] As noted in my opening paragraphs, normative descriptions of preaching practice generally proceed from the Qur'anic terms that Indonesians have borrowed for talking about preachers and preaching. According to these, the preacher conveys and exhorts. The manuals do give some attention to variations in voice, mentioning one or more of a number of Quranic verses and Hadith that encourage the use of language appropriate to situation (see Millie 2102b), but the skillful multivocality revealed in the examples does not appear as an element of the preacher's task.

Some preaching manuals go further to explicitly criticize multivocal preaching on religious grounds. One of Indonesia's most famous modernists, Mohammad Natsir (1908–1983), an ideologue of the Islamic Association, wrote a preaching guidebook that has constantly been in print since its first publication in the mid-1960s (Natsir 2000). He explicitly critiqued preachers who satisfy large audiences through verbal artifice. These preachers were victims of their own "desiring self" (Arabic, *hawa ananiyah*). The same applied for preachers who hoped for financial rewards from preaching. The proper reward in Natsir's vision is a meaningful emotional connection between preacher and audience, expressed in the Qur'anic term *al-mawaddah fi al-qurba* (loving kindness among kinsfolk).[11] Charles Hirschkind observed followers of Cairo's mosque movement upholding a similar decorum. Listeners connect the conduct of speaking with virtues, and Hirschkind's pious informants expected that its public performances would be "conducted in a calm, respectful manner, protected from the kind of passions that would vitiate the act and the social benefit that it seeks to realize" (2006: 132).

But it is not solely religious reasoning that underpins the exclusion of multivocality from preaching's metaculture. A second cause is Islam's status as a progressive category in Indonesian public awareness. As a result of developments that started before Indonesian independence in 1945, Islam has been integral to imaginations of Indonesian modernity.[12] In current times, the most prestigious

---

10. A number of Indonesian works are discussed in Millie (2012b).

11. The Qur'anic source cited by Natsir is Al-Shura 23, which Pickthall interprets as, "This is it which Allah announceth to His bondmen who believe and do his good works. Say (O Muhammad, unto mankind): I ask of you no fee therefore, save loving kindness among kinsfolk [*al-mawaddah fi al-qurba*]."

12. The historical emergence of Islamic modernity is well covered in Geertz (1973), Atkinson (1983), and Bowen (1993). For the implications of this for oral preaching and its meanings, see Keeler (1998) and Millie (2013).

conceptions of Islam are those that tie the religion to progress toward better Indonesian national futures. Images of "passive" listeners emotionally engrossed in clever verbal artifice are not compatible with those meanings (Keeler 1998; Millie 2013). These images disrupt the conception of Islam as a means for achieving better futures for Indonesian communities.

The social power of these norms emerges from time to time in critiques aimed at preachers on the basis that their success is based too heavily on their performance skills. These critiques were prominent in public discourse of the early 1990s, when media deregulation was enabling the emergence of preachers who were capable of reaching audiences through electronic media including cassette recordings and television. In 1992 a major national current-affairs magazine ran a lengthy feature asking whether the broadening of the acceptable range of preaching competencies was acceptable (*Tempo* 1990). Much of the discussion focused on the financial success of the emerging stars, including criticisms of high-profile preachers who obtain financial benefit from their speaking abilities. In contemporary times, when the electronic mediation of preaching stars is more voluminous and speedier than ever, a steady critique of the propriety of virtuoso preaching continues to appear.[13]

The monologic metaculture emerges plainly when an oration moves from oral to written form. This involves a transformation that replicates the hierarchy in which the constrained style is held to be superior to multivocality. Because preachers are well known public figures, publishers of West Javanese print media like to publish written versions of their orations as copy. Shiddiq Amien was a constant contributor to print media such as newspapers and mosque bulletins. I noticed that the multivocality through which preachers achieved success with their face-to-face audiences was never or rarely reproduced in the written versions of the oratories. Little of the artifice by which the preachers create good outcomes in performance survived the transition from oral to written text.

When an orator consents to the transformation of an oration into written publication, he or she is aware that the circulation of written texts holds differing implications to those arising from oral ones. An oration is a negotiation between a speaker and a willing, co-present audience. Speaker and audience attend with more or less matching conceptions of what is proper for the situation. A newspaper article is a public Islamic expression which circulates into contexts that cannot be foreseen. Within the oratorical situation, the preacher has some measure of control over the communicative interaction, but this control is lost when the preacher's text enters the circulatory flows of the print media. If the wrong

---

13. A recent example, one of many, is the 2006 book by Solichul Hadi entitled "The Celebrity Preacher" (Ind., *Dai Selebritis*).

kind of material were to circulate in written form, the preacher risks appearing as a buffoon or disrespectful of Islam. Amien's image would suffer if his fart jokes circulated through the print media, and so would the image of the specific media concerned. In other words, preachers do not want to be represented before unknown reading audiences for what they really are, namely religious authority figures who are not only learned in religion but are also skilled verbal performers. When a sermon is reproduced in print, it is reshaped in accordance with the monologic metaculture of Indonesian Islamic oratory.

Discourse about preaching is not totally dominated by the metaculture just outlined. I have occasionally encountered expressions of approval for multivocality. These were usually expressed in private conversations by Muslims who made it clear that they did not claim to be authoritative speakers on the topic. In discussing my project with taxi drivers, for example, they would sometimes express a preference for preachers with highly multivocal styles, but at the same time emphasize their lack of knowledge on the topic. A further exception to the public metaculture about preaching is the peripheral genre of publication known as "religious humor." Books of this genre, which are cheaply made ephemeralia, are compilations of jokes spoken by Islamic leaders (e.g., Anwar 2015). Readers appreciate the easily recognizable and original humor collected in such books. They can be considered as positive recognition of preaching's multivocality, but cannot be considered as metaculture about preaching in a direct sense, for they generally contain no reflections on preaching, simply reproducing examples of Islamic humor without reflection on the contexts of their utterance.

Implicit approval for multivocal skill in preaching emerges clearly in the decisions made by organizers of preaching events. Despite the strength of the monological metaculture in public discourse, the committees that organize preaching events continue to engage preachers whose sermons range over many genres and ways of speaking. Such preachers ensure that calendrical and other celebrations are well-attended and conducted in the atmosphere of activity and festivity (Ind., *ramai*) that organizers desire. The engagement of a celebrity preacher can have economic benefits for a community, enabling it to collect small contributions from a large number of visitors. I once attended an all-night preaching event (*tabligh akbar*) held in a religious school in which the organizers had constructed a balanced program of alternating speakers. The sequence of preachers taking the stage from sunset to the morning prayer of the following day was deliberately arranged so that preachers whose styles consisted largely of comedic play and non-religious genres were alternated with more "serious" preachers like Siddiq Amien, whose impious strategies were low-key and less elaborate. This blended program illustrated how the practical conduct of preaching events encourages co-occurrence of the two interactions.

Final Words

I conclude by pointing out a clear logic in this discrepancy between the mono-logic metaculture about preaching that dominates public discourse, and the real preferences exercised in preaching events. This requires consideration of the West Javanese public's deep commitment to Islam. Almost everybody in West Java unites behind the conviction that Islam is a valuable public good. Ethnographers have noted that Islam is a crucial element of Sundanese self-identification, evidenced by a widely circulating idiom, "Sunda is Islam, and Islam is Sunda" (*Sunda itu Islam, dan Islam itu Sunda*; see Newland 2000). Throughout recent centuries, Islam has been a resource that has served as a positive counterpoint to processes of colonization, revolution, civil war, and economic hardship. In the present, West Javanese voters show a preference for Islamic political parties that is higher than the national preference. Against this background, the monologic construction of the genre supports Islam's status as a privileged sphere. The entextualizations of Hadith and Qur'an are metonyms for Islam, and hence for the well-being of the community more generally. They point directly to revelation and Allah's Prophet, and by extension to Indonesian modernity, and it is therefore fitting that the medium for their public circulation should be distinguished from other media forms by public recognition of its value and dignity. Islam's value and distinctiveness would be threatened if oratory's openness to multiple genres and voices were to be publicly acknowledged as one of its virtues. Its value as a revealed moral order would be harmed if its success were reduced to the verbal artifice of clever performers like Al-Jauhari and the affective responses they create. And the sanctity of its meanings would be diminished by recognition of the shared irony Amien works with in his translations of Hadith.

By uniting behind the monologic metaculture, West Java's Muslims maintain public respect for preaching and prevent that respect from suffering the kind of effect—described by Bakhtin—that novelistic discourse exerted on monologic literary genres. Bakhtin saw that the novel absorbed monologic genres, and that this threw the integrity of those genres into disarray. These previously authoritative genres "become more free and flexible, their language renews itself by incorporating extraliterary heteroglossia and the 'novelistic' layers of literary language, they become dialogized, permeated with laughter, irony, humor, elements of self-parody and finally—this is the most important thing—the novel inserts into these other genres an indeterminacy, a certain semantic open-mindedness, a living contact with unfinished, still-evolving contemporary reality (the openended present)" (Bakhtin 1981: 7).

This quote is quite an accurate characterization of a process that West Javanese Muslims would like to prevent from having any affect on Islamic genres. Bakhtin's words convey the decentering tendencies that hang threateningly over public Islam in West Java. The province's preachers convey Islam's normative textuality with certainty, but they also convey inversions, playfulness, travesty, and coarseness. Discursive recognition of this would reorient the status of Islam in the direction of more mundane realities. As a result, Islamic mediators cannot be publicly recognized and praised as comedians or brilliant verbal performers, even when they actually are. By ensuring that impious multivocality is kept away from public recognition, the domain of religion is discursively separated from the cultural realities that sustain participation within it. The resultant metaculture simultaneously protects and sustains the ongoing practice.

Acknowledgments

The author acknowledges the support of Australian Research Council Discovery Grant *Glocalisation and Sub-national Islams in Indonesia* (DP1094913), which funded the research on which this article is based. Gratitude is also extended to Dr. Ahmad Bukhori Muslim and Dr. Agus Ahmad Safei, who assisted with transcription of examples, and Mr. Jujun Junaedi, who assisted with field research in Bandung, West Java.

References

Amien, S. 2009. *Al-Quran dan Kejadian Manusia (Bag. 2): Pengajian Ahad, 3 Mei 2009*. Bandung: JIHAD/Pengajian Ahad Viaduct. [DVD Video Recording]

Anwar, Gus Chalis. 2015. *Humor para kyai: Menabur tawa menuai berkah*. Yogyakarta: Araska.

Atkinson, Jane Monnig. 1983. "Religions in Dialogue: The Construction of an Indonesian Minority Religion." *American Ethnologist* 10(4): 684–696.

Bakhtin, Mikhail M. 1981. *The Dialogic Imagination: Four Essays*. Ed. M. Holquist. Trans. C. Emerson and M. Holquist. Austin: University of Texas Press.

Bakhtin, Mikhail M. 1984. *Problems of Dostoevsky's Poetics*. Ed. and trans. C. Emerson. Minneapolis: University of Minnesota Press.

Bauman, Richard. 1986. *Story, Performance, and Event*. Cambridge: Cambridge University Press.

Bowen, John R. 1993. *Muslims through Discourse: Religion and Ritual in Gayo Society*. Princeton, NJ: Princeton University Press.

DDII. 2001. *Khittah Da'wah: Dewan Dakwah Islamiyah Indonesia*. Jakarta: Dewan Dakwah Islamiyah Indonesia.

Federspiel, Howard M. 2001. *Islam and Ideology in the Emerging Indonesian State: The Persatuan Islam (PERSIS), 1923 to 1957*. Leiden: Brill.

Geertz, Clifford. 1973. "'Internal Conversion' in Contemporary Bali." In *The Interpretation of Cultures*, by Clifford Geertz, 170–189. New York: Basic Books.

Ghazali, A. F. 2008. *The People's Religion: The Sermons of A. F. Ghazali.* Ed. and trans. J. Millie. Cupumanik: Bandung.

Hadi, Solichul. 2006. *Dai Selebritis.* Jakarta: Harmonie Publishing.

Hirschkind, Charles. 2006. *The Ethical Soundscape: Cassette Sermons and Islamic Counterpublics.* New York: Columbia University Press.

Keeler, Ward. 1998. "Style and Authority in Javanese Muslim Sermons." *Australian Journal of Anthropology* 9(2): 163–178.

Millie, Julian. 2012a. "The Languages of Preaching: Code Selection in Sundanese Islamic Oratory, West Java." *Australian Journal of Anthropology* 23:378–396.

Millie, Julian. 2012b. "Preaching over Borders: Constructing Publics for Islamic Oratory in Indonesia." In *Flows of Faith: Religious Reach and Community in Asia and the Pacific*, ed. L. Manderson, W. Smith, and M. Tomlinson, 87–103. Dordrecht: Springer.

Millie, Julian. 2013. "The Situated Listener as Problem: 'Modern' and 'Traditional' Subjects in Muslim Indonesia." *International Journal of Cultural Studies* 16(3): 271–288.

Natsir, Mohammad. 2000. *Fiqhud Da'wah: Jejak Risalah dan Dasar-Dasar Da'wah.* Jakarta: Media Da'wah.

Newland, Lynda. 2000. "Under the Banner of Islam: Mobilising Religious Identities in West Java." *Australian Journal of Anthropology* 11(2): 199–222.

Pasar Inpres. 2008. *Tausiyah K.H. Jujun Junaedi dina raraga Maulid Nabi Muhammad SAW sareng resepsi walimatul Titi Martini, S.Tp ka Yuda Anwari, S.Sos, pelaksanaan: Minggu, 8 April 2007, di lingk. Pasar Inpres-Sumedang.* (Unauthorized DVD).

Suryadinata, Leo, Evi Nurvidya Arifin, and Aris Ananta. 2003. *Indonesia's Population; Ethnicity and Religion in a Changing Political Landscape.* Singapore: ISIS.

Tempo. 1990. "Laporan Utama: Saya Ustad, Bukan Artis," *Tempo* 9, Th. XX, April 28, 74–83.

Urban, Greg. 2001. *Metaculture: How Culture Moves through the World.* Minneapolis: University of Minnesota Press.

THE MONOLOGIC IMAGINATION
OF SOCIAL GROUPS

Courtney Handman

Matt Tomlinson nicely situates what seems so paradoxical about the "monologic imagination" in his Introduction to this volume. In contrast to the multiple heteroglossic possibilities implicated by the "dialogic imagination" that Bakhtin (1981) so influentially articulated, the monologic seems less like an imaginative process of creative combination and more like a monolithic force bearing down on speakers as the voice of the sovereign. The monologic imagination is in that sense reminiscent of Durkheim's (1995: 16) depiction of the necessity of socially shared mental categories:

> having broader scope than all our ideas, they govern all the particulars of our intellectual life. If, at every moment, men did not agree on these fundamental ideas, if they did not have a homogeneous conception of time, space, cause, number, and so on, all consensus among minds, and thus all common life, would become impossible.... Does a mind seek to free itself from these norms of all thought? Society no longer considers this a human mind in the full sense, and treats it accordingly.

The monologic imagination (at least a certain aspect of it) similarly seems to emerge from transcendent and sovereign categories. Nestled along with Durkheim's vision of a supreme society, God and totalitarian states also speak with singular voices. Vološinov (1986: 71) adds to this list the monologic utterance of language theorized as a (Saussurean) system, "the study of defunct, alien languages preserved in written monuments." He makes this monologic form the origin of "civilization" as such: "This role of the alien word led to its coalescence in the depths of the historical consciousness of nations with the idea of authority, the idea of power, the idea of holiness, the idea of truth, and dictated that notions about the word be preeminently oriented toward the alien word" (75).

Following this line of thought, linguistic anthropologists have made aspects of heteroglossia the standard starting points for any analyses of situated linguistic interactions. In this model, interaction is always going to be plural, partial, and contested, with various actors taking up one voice or another to a certain extent. Theories of heteroglossia exclude the sovereign speaking subject as a possibility. Because speakers must use others' words, the autonomous, individual speaker can only ever be an unrealizable dream of the modernist subject (see Keane 2007). Yet the evocations of power and coercion in Bakhtin's or Vološinov's monologic imagination lend themselves to the reduction of heteroglossia to a sense of individualizable speaker voices, possibly even voices "owned" by sovereign subjects (see Slotta 2015). If monologue creates a singular sovereign voice, then this must be suppressing unique, individual voices.

Yet Tomlinson, both in his Introduction here and in other recent work (2014), resists this simplification of monologue, arguing for sustained attention to the different possibilities of monologue in the creative construction of singularity. Sometimes this is the work of erasure (Irvine and Gal 2000) in the blunt, coercive, or suppressive sense that Vološinov seems to be talking about—the project of making others shut up. But sometimes it is a matter of creating ambiguity, vagueness, or even a profusion of talk against which heteroglossic voices emerge. The three chapters that I discuss here can be read as arguing that monologues are better thought of as allowing certain kinds of social relations to exist rather than just stopping certain kinds of voices from being heard. What becomes clear after reading these three chapters is that monologism and heteroglossia are deeply intertwined with local concepts of what social groups are and what social groups ought to do. The preoccupation with an antagonistic opposition of free individuals and oppressive social groups that undergirds at least part of the common conception of heteroglossia and monologism is insufficient.

The ways in which monologism is not always a top-down process of silencing is particularly clear in Jane E. Goodman's paper on colonial Algerian theater groups. Goodman argues that democratic institutions like voluntary associations and voting are not necessarily heteroglossia-inducing mechanisms in which different voices are automatically heard and different perspectives are debated. Yet as she notes, "the connection between voluntary associations and democracy has become so naturalized in some circles that voluntary or civic associations . . . are being used prescriptively—that is, they are deliberately 'injected' into a society by international aid organizations in order to foster democratic practice." These assumptions are so naturalized that Goodman notes her own sense of disorientation when, in the midst of examining these Algerian theater groups, she could hardly find any examples of contestation that she was expecting in either meeting minutes or theatrical representations of group meetings. In her examples, meetings and votes are public enactments of unanimity rather than locations for Habermasian contestation.

In denaturalizing voluntary societies as breeding grounds of democratic impulses, Goodman also refuses to naturalize these performances of unanimity as Durkheimian facts of mechanical solidarity or coercive force. She situates them as products of religious reformist movements focusing on pious obedience to God, Berber political traditions of kin-based deference, and colonial hierarchies that reified the colonizer-colonized opposition as the supreme contrast. Using Goffman's dramatological metaphor, she examines meetings as public performances that often presupposed, but publically erased, the "backstage" work of disagreement and (ideally) consensus building. These backstage conversations were the prior texts within the natural history of a group's discourse but prior texts that were not supposed to leave overt traces (up to and including the fact that there are almost no minutes of these interactions for the historian to analyze). Like Judith Irvine's (1996) analysis of Wolof insult poetry, the final utterance at the official meeting had to come from the group as such. If a prior text was referenced overtly, the group often dissolved rather than work through the difference. Yet it is insufficient to call this simply a "silencing," since to do so would be to assume that what everyone intended to do in these events is voice their unique perspective.

But if Goodman's case seems to find monologue in unambiguous declarations made possible by the bracketing of prior texts, we can read Philip Fountain's chapter in terms of the many ambiguities of talk through which a monologue emerges. When the Mennonite Central Committee (MCC) is finally able to produce a creedal statement (after earlier failed attempts), the document is so vacuous and undemanding that any analysis that equated it with Durkheimian normativity would be ridiculous. Fountain suggests that this is in fact why this document was able to succeed where others before it had languished as unfinished drafts. By not making demands on the Christians who have to engage with it, no beliefs were questioned, no practices had to be amended. It was a "political strategy of enrolment." It may also be seen as a Mennonite comment on Mennonite institutionality. Like other Christian service organizations, they seem to imagine their work in terms of person-to-person impacts (or God-to-person-to-person impacts) in which the organization as such is relatively unimportant. The Bible translation organization known now as SIL International has a similar history of ambiguous belief statements that has allowed the same kinds of controversies to crop up repeatedly in the organization's history (Handman 2015: ch. 2). Yet there is little interest in resolving these ambiguities. Not only are they helpful in enrolling diverse members, but to focus too much on the nature of the organization itself would contradict their more overarching missiological claim that conversion is not mediated by external institutions so much as dematerialized spirits. Monologic creedal statements like the MCC statement Fountain analyzes are less expressions of sovereign power and more banalities acting as apologies for humans' incapacity to communicate like angels do.

At the same time, Fountain points out that creedal statements, when they do try to make non-ambiguous claims, do so not as singular statements shouted into an empty social space, but as critical comparisons that define denominational (or sub-denominational) differences. That is, when Christian groups are not being embarrassed about their sociality they are celebrating it. Fountain refers to this as a form of heteroglossia, where theological claims are made on contested ground. Fountain argues that this heteroglossia often goes unrecognized in secular social science accounts of Christian theology.[1] In two different senses, then, Fountain takes what would at first seem to be the most unassailably sovereign, monologic religious form—the creed—and describes the ambiguities and heteroglossia that go into it.

While Goodman and Fountain talk about the ways in which the monological is neither as sovereign nor as singular as it has been described in the past, Julian Millie demonstrates that local people may sometimes demand a sovereign, monological voice. West Javanese Muslims value a religious register that is divorced from mundane concerns, at least when they discuss sermonic oratory or when that oratory circulates in semi-official channels in print form. However, some of the most sought-after preachers are famous precisely for their skill in interweaving Hadith with local pop songs and the occasional fart joke.

This heteroglossic mélange of voices from across contemporary Indonesia would seem to flout the valuation of a separable sphere of religious piety. Yet it is in this example where the most Durkheimian model of the monologic seems to live, found in preachers' quests for relevance and the desire to make their messages palatable. These preachers seem to be working on the assumption that

---

1. In setting up his argument as a critique of secular social science assumptions of theological monologism, Fountain uses a comment that Jon Bialecki made in a blog post as his only example. Yet Bialecki's comment is not, to my mind, a statement about theology's monologism as the term is defined in this volume but theology's assumption of universality, especially in contrast with anthropological claims about human diversity. To be too glib in characterizing two disciplines, one could argue that theology makes universalizing claims while trying to obfuscate the ways that differences are sustained among people in practice, but anthropology makes particularizing claims while trying to obfuscate the ways that universalisms are smuggled into theories.

religious discourse as such is not part of lay people's everyday lives, and there has to be a form of "translation" into lower registers. Millie argues that some of this shift to heteroglossia is a matter of obfuscating a moment of coercive power, as when comments about women's qualities as moral subjects has to be broken by laugh lines. Thus, the West Java metacultural value placed on a separable religious sphere is evident not only in the editing that preachers do when they prepare written versions of their sermons for publication. It is also there in the very idea that religion has to go through a translation process in order to fit into the heteroglossic everyday world. It is there in the sense of having to couch moral demands on women in pleasant, undemanding terms. The assumption that seems to guide these rhetorical moves is that religion is not immediately relevant or natural to the everyday world, and that the preacher therefore has to do incredible verbal work in order to make it so. In that sense, the most direct use of heteroglossic forms from a domain of power is actually the most direct expression of the monologic imagined as coercive force.

Millie's chapter makes the important point that heteroglossia does not necessarily lead to a process of breaking down normative monologism. The obverse part of this point is that figuring something as monologic does not mean that it is the voice of power. That is, figuring a voice as monologic can be a kind of boundary-making that limits the power or possibility of various forms of talk to circulate and be the basis of interaction. A few brief examples can help make this point. Miyako Inoue (2006) analyzes early twentieth-century "school girl speech" in Japan as something that was rarely spoken by young women but endlessly quoted by men worried about emerging forms of gendered modernity. In their writing, these men derisively characterize the young women's speech as so much vacuous babble, but babble that they could not stop quoting. "As a speech act, the reporting of school girl speech produces the pragmatic effect of irrationality, incoherence, and garrulousness that contributes all the more to the imposed indexical meanings of *teyo* and *dawa* [utterance-final forms that were becoming linked with school girl speech]. Alterity is, thus, tamed and contained not by being silenced but on the contrary by being allowed to be loquacious" (Inoue 2006: 54). In the hands of male critics, school girl speech was a never-ending monologue of insipid, pointless talk against which their own writing could be judged as reasonable, modern, coherent, and thus masculine. In this case heteroglossia makes it impossible for the cited speakers to have a voice, since their endless, monologic speech says nothing at all.[2]

---

2. Films and TV in the United States make use of overdubbing technology to construct a similarly loquacious void when first person characters are presented as attending to their inner monologue while ostensibly listening to their conversation partner drone on. As with Inoue's

In colonial New Guinea a similar sense of meaningless voices comes across in missionary and administrator citations of Pidgin English (what is now known as Tok Pisin). In this case, the sense of meaninglessness came from colonial ideas about the structural inadequacies of pidgin and creole languages. It was "a kind of gibberish talk, where style and grammar do not matter" (Lehner 1930: 1). With relatively reduced morphological machinery, New Guinea Pidgin English became infamous in colonial circles for its lengthy and, to Euro-Australian ears, ridiculous circumlocutions used to create novel vocabulary items. Colonized "natives" prattled on in a linguistic anarchy that colonizers typified through absurd vocabulary lists: "hat belong finger—thimble; trousers belong letter—envelope" (1). The most famous lexical items circulated without any evidence that they were ever used by indigenous speakers: "mixmaster belong Jesus Christ" for "helicopter" or "bikpela bokis sapos yu paitim, em i krai" (big box, if you hit it, it cries/makes noise) for "piano." As with Inoue's school girl speech example, the colonized Pidgin speaker's voice is more cited than spoken and is characterized in this case by its extremely low length-to-content ratios: if Pidgin could be used to communicate at all, it required an incredible amount of talk to refer to and predicate about what the colonizers (but not the colonized) thought of as mundane objects. Monologues from speakers in what colonizers thought of as structurally deficient semi-languages take shape within heteroglossic acts of citation that keep "natives" monologically talking without stop but also without sense.

Taken together, the chapters here help develop an overall critique of the normalized sense of monologism's coercive force and heteroglossia's expressive power: monologues do not always oppress and dialogues do not always create the conditions for voices to be heard, as Peters (1999) argues. There are as many ways of constituting social groups as there are ways of imagining monologic communication.[3]

References

Bakhtin, Mikhail M. 1981. *The Dialogic Imagination: Four Essays*. Ed. Michael Holquist. Trans. Michael Holquist and Caryl Emerson. Austin: University of Texas Press.

Durkheim, Émile. 1995. *The Elementary Forms of Religious Life*. Trans. Karen Fields. New York: Free Press.

---

school girl speech example, the narrator is often male and the ignored (endlessly talking) person female.

3. I want to thank James Slotta for a number of insightful discussions that greatly helped me to develop these comments.

Handman, Courtney. 2015. *Critical Christianity: Translation and Denominational Conflict in Papua New Guinea*. Berkeley: University of California Press.

Inoue, Miyako. 2006. *Vicarious Language: Gender and Linguistic Modernity in Japan*. Berkeley: University of California Press.

Irvine, Judith. 1996. "Shadow Conversations: The Indeterminacy of Participant Roles." In *Natural Histories of Discourse*, ed. Michael Silverstein and Greg Urban, 131–159. Chicago: University of Chicago Press.

Irvine, Judith, and Susan Gal. 2000. "Language Ideology and Linguistic Differentiation." In *Regimes of Language: Ideologies, Polities, and Identities*, ed. Paul V. Kroskrity, 35–85. Santa Fe, NM: School of American Research Press.

Keane, Webb. 2007. *Christian Moderns: Freedom and Fetish in the Missionary Encounter*. Berkeley: University of California Press.

Lehner, St. 1930. "What Should Be the Attitude toward the Pidgin Language in Mission Work." Paper delivered to Lutheran Mission Annual Conference, Wau, Papua New Guinea. Archives of the Evangelical Lutheran Church of America (LMF 55/10).

Peters, John Durham. 1999. *Speaking into the Air: A History of the Idea of Communication*. Chicago: University of Chicago Press.

Slotta, James. 2015. "The Perlocutionary Is Political: Listening as Self-Determination in a Papua New Guinean Polity." *Language in Society* 44(4): 525–552.

Tomlinson, Matt. 2014. *Ritual Textuality: Pattern and Motion in Performance*. New York: Oxford University Press.

Vološinov, V. N. 1986. *Marxism and the Philosophy of Language*. Trans. Ladislav Matejka and I. R. Titunik. Cambridge, MA: Harvard University Press.

CONCLUSION

RELIGIOUS AND POLITICAL TERRAIN OF THE MONOLOGIC IMAGINATION

Matt Tomlinson and Julian Millie

In this volume, contributors have built a sustained case for taking the monologic imagination seriously. In doing so, we are also urging a reconsideration of the dialogic imagination. Bakhtin's influential work emerged from that historical moment in which social commentators began to identify positive value in the perceived ambivalence and decentered nature of modern life. His analyses were cogent initial statements of this ambivalence. Yet, as the authors in this volume have demonstrated and the broader ethnographic record shows convincingly, speakers in all sorts of sociopolitical contexts often deny language's dialogism in order to try to speak in a purified, singular voice. In this brief concluding chapter, we suggest that this tendency is seen especially often in markedly religious and political projects. Or, to turn this formulation around: we can approach religious and political contexts as ones especially conducive to the mobilization of monologue. These are contexts in which the ambivalent and decentered nature of modern life is often treated as something to be contained and opposed.

Consider two figures who might at first seem to have little in common: the founder of Methodism, John Wesley, and the North Korean dictator Kim Jong-il. Wesley offered advice on preaching which, we suggest, vividly illustrates the Protestant ideal of a subject for whom speaking itself can be an expression of purification. Part of Wesley's advice is explicitly dialogic in Bakhtin's sense, as he advocates speaking plainly to pious people, "to those who neither relish nor understand the art of speaking, but who, notwithstanding, are competent judges of those truths which are necessary to present and future happiness" (quoted in Outler 1964: 88). In other words, the speaker speaks in anticipation of the nature of his or her audience's engagement. Yet Wesley also endorses a full-blown Protestant model of the sincere speaker whose words reveal his or her soul. For Wesley, such sincere expression requires a kind of monologic construction:

> My design is, in some sense, to forget all that ever I have read in my life. I mean to speak, in the general, as if I had never read one author, ancient or modern (always excepting the inspired). I am persuaded that, on the one hand, this may be a means of enabling me more clearly to express the sentiments of my heart while I simply follow the chain of my own thoughts, without entangling myself with those of other men; and that, on the other [hand], I shall come with fewer weights upon my mind, with less of prejudice and prepossession, either to search for myself or to deliver to others the naked truths of the gospel. (Quoted in Outler 1964: 89; bracketed insertion in original)

In Wesley's model, the ultimate monological truth is God's word encountered in the Bible. Although speakers should express what is in their hearts, their hearts should be filled in the first place with divine monologic discourse. This kind of radical interiority need not motivate the construction of monological discourse, especially as any supposedly autonomous speaking subject is necessarily constituted dialogically (Keane 2002, 2007). Yet Wesley's attempted erasure of human interaction from the composition of his words does, we argue, show a monologic imagination fervently at work. "Naked truths" must be delivered in a purified channeling that connects divinity and humanity as directly as possible.

Kim Jong-il's North Korea is perhaps the limiting case of monologism in action, a remarkably thoroughgoing example of an attempt to create a single, unified national voice. The dictator led a cult of personality so complete and pervasive that there was reportedly almost no corner of society, self, or language that it did not reach. Although many political leaders, like Kim and his father Kim Il-sung, are known for hanging their portraits everywhere in public, the Kims' faces traveled even beyond those spaces, moving into private domestic ones: "precisely because it *was* the intimate privacy of your home, it was a sanctified place in which you would of course hang portraits of Kim Il-sung and Kim Jong-il" (Jin-Sung 2014: 108). Moving from the creepily intimate to the patently ridiculous, playlists in karaoke bars only contained songs exalting the Kims (149). The poet Jang Jin-Sung, employed by the government as a writer, discovered severe limits on artistic expression as all words were vetted by higher authorities, and authors were told what to write in the first place. When written materials from South Korea needed to be consulted, those sources arrived pre-censored in black ink (Jin-sung 2014: 64–65; cf. Demick 2009: 55). In fact, "every single writer in North Korea produces works according to a chain of command. . . . It is not the job of a writer to articulate new ideas or to experiment with aesthetics on his or her own whim" (Jin-sung 2014: 3–4).

One of the most disturbing manifestations of this thoroughgoing monologism was its expression in physical violence. "Death by firing squad to those who gossip!" declared a slogan on a market wall in Jin-sung's hometown, and he makes it clear in his memoir that this was not an empty threat (Jin-sung 2014: 56). The perfect emblem of Kim's monologism was a fiendish device meant to silence people so they could not speak at their executions. A spring was inserted into the mouths of the condemned so they could not say anything blasphemous about the Kims before being shot (Jin-sung 2014: 58; cf. Kang and Rigoulot 2001: 139). But in such a totalitarian state, even death was not meant to be a release, and "All cadres had to sign an oath of loyalty to Kim Jong-il when they were close to death, swearing that their single-hearted devotion would continue after they died" (Jin-sung 2014: 39–40).

Most attempts at monologue are not as extreme as Kim's red flags waving frantically at the outer limits of possibility, nor perhaps as thoroughgoing as Wesley's devout discursive erasure in planning his sermons.[1] But these two examples are useful for the bracing clarity with which they reveal monologism's value as a resource for religious and political projects. If dialogism defines language's natural life, per Bakhtin, speakers like Wesley and Kim show how it can be denatured in practice, sometimes ferociously. So much religious and political discourse depends for its force on a fiction of the sovereignty of authorship and the purity of voice. *Pace* Bakhtin, then, although all discourse is dialogic in its textual construction—the voices it marries—authors and speakers like Wesley and Kim seek a divorce from that dialogicality. Pure monologue is impossible, but this does not stop people from trying to create monologues through acts of creative erasure in which monologue serves as an asymptote, an ideal threshold never reached but sometimes—almost—touched with outstretched tongues in outsized effort.

In developing an argument about how political and religious speech might be understood primarily, rather than secondarily, in terms of the monologic imagination, we need to raise two implicated questions. The first concerns Bruce Mannheim and Dennis Tedlock's invaluable point, quoted in the Introduction to

---

1. Kim Jong-il died in 2011, but his son, Kim Jong-un, carries on the family line of work. In August 2015, enraged at South Korean loudspeakers broadcasting news and pop music, he threatened to have his soldiers attack the loudspeakers. The author of a *New York Times* article on the dispute referred to the loudspeakers as an "unlikely cause" for tension (Sang-Hun 2015)—but what could offend an autocrat more than insisting that he listen to you?

this volume, that the speaker of monologue "expects no answer" (Mannheim and Tedlock 1995: 1–2). To what extent does monological speech preclude answering, and to what extent does this preclusion depend on extralinguistic factors? Although the design of monologic speech is often explicit in its self-portrayal as singularly truthful, monologic speakers nevertheless often turn to tools of intimidation and suppression to enforce the public acceptance of this self-portrayal. Kim Jong-il's mouth-trap, shutting up the condemned so they could not speak against the regime as they died, is an illustrative example, if a frighteningly extreme one.

The second question is how and to what extent speakers move between relative emphases on monologic and dialogic tendencies at different historical moments. For example, a unit of "we, the people" might be shaped monologically so that it can afterward interact dialogically, as shown in Urban's analysis in this volume on the closed-door policy of the Constitutional Congress ensuring that "Congress [spoke] to the public with a single voice," defining "we, the people" partly by excluding the people and harmonizing dissonance among their elite representatives. It might seem obvious that the goals to which collectives aspire sometimes cannot be achieved without a strategic reliance on monologism, and this would apply as strongly to explicitly religious speakers as explicitly political ones. Brian Tamaki, quoted in this volume's Introduction for his insistence that he speaks God's truth rather than his own opinion, is a not-so-distant cousin of John Wesley seeking "to forget all that ever I have read in my life."

We are not arguing that religious or political speech can or should be defined exclusively in terms of monologism. The chapters in this collection, which demonstrate how monologism and dialogism implicate each other, underscore the fact that a focus on monologism alone would be inadequate. Rather, we argue that it is useful to ask when and how any project might be defined by its proponents primarily in monological terms, and why this seems to happen with notable frequency and intensity in religious and political ones. One way to begin such analysis is to ask how dialogism becomes an object of suspicion and a target of critique in the first place. In a chapter of a volume devoted to rethinking anthropology's "writing culture" movement (grounded in Clifford and Marcus 1986), Thomas G. Kirsch poses a relevant question about "how anthropologists deal with their interlocutors' self-identification as speakers," especially when anthropologists and their subjects do not share an understanding of who, precisely, is to be credited with speaking at a particular moment. This difficulty is seen clearly in cases of what Kirsch calls "theoglossia," "speech which says of itself that it is a 'monologue of the divine,'" and he observes that the topic "is of particular interest in cases in which the anthropologist's interlocutors accentuate not human speakership, polyphony, multivocality, dialogism and the partialness of truths, but instead divine speakership, monophony, monovocality, monologism and total truth" (Kirsch 2010: 90–92). When Kirsch conducted research with members of the Spirit Apostolic Church in Zambia, he was informed many times by interlocutors that they would speak to him "as the Holy Spirit" rather than as their human selves (104). He concludes wryly that many anthropologists, in seeking and embracing dialogism and partial truths, might completely miss the fact that their interlocutors "are happily seeking monovocality, monologism, and the total truth of theoglossia" (107).

The not-so-hidden danger in our approach is that although we are reluctant (for good reasons, we think) to pin down the "religious" and the "political" as easily identifiable categories, we must strenuously avoid the circular claim that if discourse is designed or expressed with monological tendencies, it must therefore be religious or political. And if we do want to keep using these categories (we do), we must pay attention to the ways they cross-fertilize each other: John Wesley had a political agenda, and the Kims' public veneration is a kind of divinization. Rather than set up the categories as firm units which require monological projects to stabilize themselves, then, we would rather begin with the monological imaginations at work and ask how and why they configure dialogism as something to be bypassed, downplayed, or overcome by and for particular kinds of agents, whether states, gods, or other ultimate authorities.

Narratives of golden ages are especially fruitful sites for investigating the interplay between monologic and dialogic ideals and practices. In stories of utopic pasts, people are said to have once spoken and acted properly, and these descriptions now serve to energize present-day religious and political projects. Courtney Handman (2015: 160) tells the story of a Guhu-Samane (Papua New Guinea) man, Henry, who laments that too many people talk too often nowadays: "Before there were no meetings," he says thrice, and then adds, "Before there wasn't a lot of talk. Just action. Only one man spoke, and he only said a little." Most linguistic anthropologists would take issue with Henry's decoupling of speech and action, but his point is clear. As Handman puts it, local history, "told from the point of view of the men's house, is silent, and . . . the present is so surprising for its constant talk." Similarly, Joel Robbins has written evocatively of Pentecostals in the Papua New Guinea highlands who, although they have embraced Christianity with great enthusiasm, complain that "God is nothing but talk." When Robbins asks what they mean, they consistently point to the Bible verse John 1:1, "In the beginning was the Word, and the Word was with God, and the Word was God." In the local language this is translated as "Long ago Talk existed. Talk existed alongside God. And Talk itself was God" (Robbins 2001: 905). Neither the King James Version nor the Urapmin version makes semantic sense, but for Robbins's interlocutors the verse points to their struggle with what they see as "the Christian promotion of speech to the center of religious life" (905).

As Handman and Robbins (and many other authors over the past two decades) make clear, understanding language's use depends partly on understanding language ideologies. Nowhere is this more the case than when examining understandings of monologism and dialogism, or more specifically, how monologic and dialogic tendencies are evaluated and what people count as monological and dialogical in the first place. On the first understanding, there is no doubt that monologism can be either friend or foe to differently placed subjects. An apparently monologic form can be taken to signal oppression (you're not letting me speak!) or perfect harmony (we all agree completely, with no discordant voices). An apparently dialogic form can be taken to signal harmony, but it can also be seen as harmful, fracturing, chaotic—too many voices sullying a clear and single meaning, as seen in the local visions of history described by Handman and Robbins.

On the second understanding—what counts as monologue or dialogue— consider the example of legislatively supported spaces of monologism called "exemptions" for which religious groups in Europe, North America, and Australia have argued despite some public opposition. Although these religious groups prosper within national communities in which dialogism is self-consciously cultivated as a beneficial principle of public participation and national identity, such groups insist that their educational and social infrastructure should be exempt from laws intended to foster the acceptance of a diversity of citizenship, such as those designed to prevent discrimination on grounds of sexual preference. The wrestle of monologism and dialogism is an intense one here. Supporters of legislative exemptions cite freedom of religion as the warrant for carving out monological spaces that curtail the dialogism supporting the groups' distinctive practices in the first place. This logic leads to a distinct view of dialogue as a species of monologue, as seen in recent statements of the Australian Catholic archbishop Christopher Prowse. After Pope Francis spoke to *Corriere della Serra* about homosexual civil unions, Prowse moved to dampen any speculation that the Pope endorsed them. The Pope had emphasized that marriage was meant to be "between a man and a woman," and, according to the *Canberra Times*, the archbishop declared that this was " 'hardly a green light for civil ceremonies.' . . . Archbishop Prowse said the Pope's interview showed his pastoral approach and a willingness to talk to followers about relationships. 'A willingness to dialogue isn't a willingness to compromise,' he said" (Nicholson, Cooper, and Carroll 2014).[2] Here is an ideal—perhaps curious to many readers, but seemingly self-evident to

---

2. We have reformatted this text, eliminating paragraph breaks.

the archbishop—of dialogue that does not require the possibility of compromise. As the Catholic theologian Catherine Cornille observes, "there is still a widespread perception within most religious traditions that dialogue is an extraneous activity that does not derive from or touch upon their own self-understanding" (Cornille 2008: 213).

With several caveats in mind, then, we can formulate our concluding question as follows: What if we bend Bakhtin and say that religious and political discourse is often characterized by the naturalization of monologue? In such discourse, might monologism be the naturalized "thing" and dialogism the project that requires the most effort—the emergent, fragile attempt that can never fully succeed? We can reformulate the question by asking to what extent markedly political and religious speech tends to be designed, in contrast to other kinds of speech, in ways meant to minimize the possibility that it will be transformed when it is taken up by audiences.

* * *

One of our motivations in preparing this volume has been to urge a rethinking of monologism as something other than the unwanted sibling of dialogism. If monologue inevitably fails (eventually, at least), explicit attempts at markedly dialogical speech can often fail, too. Yet many speakers push monologic projects to the point where they do achieve some of the effects they seek: shutting down other voices, erasing prior discourse, enforcing the expression of a unified voice. We hope this volume helps motivate new scholarship on these kinds of projects. And in that spirit, we are glad to conclude on a note of troubling ambiguity, with an invitation to responsive uptake. As noted above, dialogism is a positively evaluated metacultural principal—even "a vehicle for utopian social longing" (Urban and Smith 1998: 264). It has become a normative principle of authority in the democratic imagination, circulating as a sign in its own right of the popular canon of democratic principles, to the point where projects of monologism sometimes deliberately create scaffoldings of consultation to conceal their workings.

One of the most well-known and poignant expressions of dialogism's value is the German Lutheran pastor Martin Niemöller's reflection on Protestant complicity in Nazi Germany: "First they came for the Socialists, and I did not speak out—Because I was not a Socialist. Then they came for the Trade Unionists, and I did not speak out—Because I was not a Trade Unionist. Then they came for the Jews, and I did not speak out—Because I was not a Jew. Then they came for me—and there was no one left to speak for me" (United States Holocaust Memorial Museum 2016). Niemöller's conviction, held deeply within many everyday Euro-American understandings of morally acceptable social practice, is that voices must be both recognized and checked by other voices. Singularity can be fatal.

And yet, Pastor Niemöller did speak out, loudly and often (Bentley 1984). At a church meeting held in 1936, for example, the voices of Niemöller and other dissenting clergy were drowned out in volume by their opponents in the pro-Hitler German Christian movement. He held himself responsible for not creating the kind of dialogue that could stop the rise of a murderous regime. But could anyone have successfully initiated such a dialogue in 1930s Germany? We want to think so, not only because the cherished fantasy of stopping the Holocaust needs to be entertained continually so that new Holocausts do not happen but also because as modern democratic subjects we maintain firm faith in the benign effectiveness of dialogism. But as we have argued throughout this volume, understanding dialogism requires understanding monologism, and monologism deserves to be recognized as something more profound than dialogism's impoverished other.

References

Bentley, James. 1984. *Martin Niemöller.* Oxford: Oxford University Press.

Clifford, James, and George E. Marcus, eds. 1986. *Writing Culture: The Poetics and Politics of Ethnography.* Berkeley: University of California Press.

Cornille, Catherine. 2008. *The Im-Possibility of Interreligious Dialogue.* New York: Crossroad Publishing Company.

Demick, Barbara. 2009. *Nothing to Envy: Ordinary Lives in North Korea.* New York: Spiegel and Grau.

Handman, Courtney. 2015. *Critical Christianity: Translation and Denominational Conflict in Papua New Guinea.* Berkeley: University of California Press.

Jin-Sung, Jang. 2014. *Dear Leader: From Trusted Insider to Enemy of the State, My Escape from North Korea.* Trans. Shirley Lee. London: Rider.

Kang, Chol-hwan, and Pierre Rigoulot. 2001. *The Aquariums of Pyongyang: Ten Years in a North Korean Gulag.* Trans. Yair Reiner. New York: Basic Books.

Keane, Webb. 2002. "Sincerity, 'Modernity,' and the Protestants." *Cultural Anthropology* 17(1): 65–92.

Keane, Webb. 2007. *Christian Moderns: Freedom and Fetish in the Mission Encounter.* Berkeley: University of California Press.

Kirsch, Thomas G. 2010. "From the Spirit's Point of View: Ethnography, Total Truth and Speakership." In *Beyond Writing Culture: Current Intersections of Epistemologies and Representational Practices*, ed. O. Zenker and K. Kumoll, 89–112. New York: Berghahn.

Mannheim, Bruce, and Dennis Tedlock. 1995. "Introduction." In *The Dialogic Emergence of Culture*, ed. D. Tedlock and B. Mannheim, 1–32. Urbana: University of Illinois Press.

Nicholson, Larissa, Mex Cooper, and Lucy Carroll. 2014. "Pope Not Likely to Change Stance on Gay Unions." *Canberra Times*, March 7, 4.

Outler, Albert C., ed. 1964. *John Wesley.* New York: Oxford University Press.

Robbins, Joel. 2001. "God Is Nothing but Talk: Modernity, Language, and Prayer in a Papua New Guinea Society." *American Anthropologist* 103(4): 901–912.

Sang-Hun, Choe. 2015. "North and South Korea on Alert Over Loudspeakers Blaring Propaganda." *New York Times* online, August 21. http://www.nytimes.com/2015/08/22/world/asia/north-korea-attack-on-south-triggered-by-propaganda-loudspeakers.html?_r=0.

United States Holocaust Memorial Museum. 2016. "Martin Niemöller: 'First They Came for the Socialists . . .'" https://www.ushmm.org/wlc/en/article.php?ModuleId= 0007392.

Urban, Greg, and Kristin Smith. 1998. "The Sunny Tropics of 'Dialogue?.'" *Semiotica* 121(3–4): 263–281.

INDEX